Istria
Croatian peninsula
Rijeka • Slovenian Adriatic

the Bradt Travel Guide

Thammy Evans
Rudolf Abraham

edition
I

www.bradtguides.com

Bradt Travel Guides Ltd, UK
The Globe Pequot Press Inc, USA

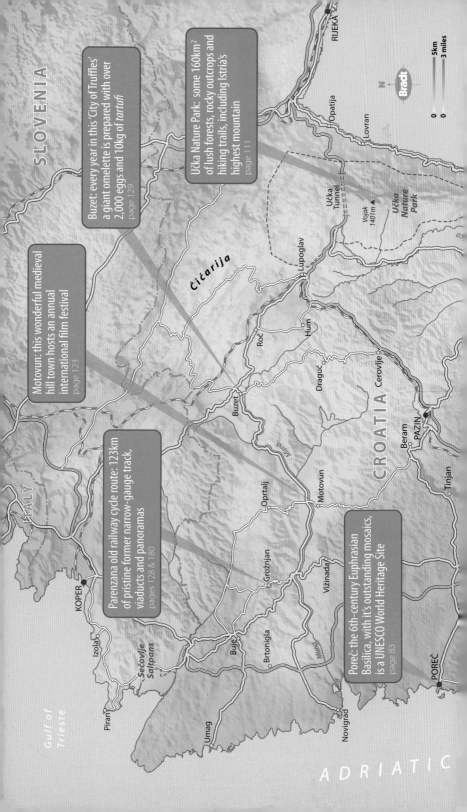

SLOVENIA

ITALY

Gulf of
Trieste

Piran

Izola

KOPER

Sečovlje
Saltpans

Umag

Novigrad

POREČ

ADRIATIC

CROATIA

Čičarija

Lupoglav

Roč

Hum

Draguč

Buzet

Cerovlje

Beram PAZIN

Opatija

Lovran

Učka
Tunnel

Vojak
1401m ▲

Učka
Nature
Park

RIJEKA

Motovun

Tinjan

Oprtalj

Vižinada

Grožnjan

Buje

Brtonigla

Mirna

Dragonja

Mirna

0   5km
0   3 miles

N

Bradt

Motovun: this wonderful medieval
hill town hosts an annual
international film festival
page 123

Buzet: every year in this 'City of Truffles'
a giant omelette is prepared with over
2,000 eggs and 10kg of *tartufi*
page 129

Učka Nature Park: some 160km²
of lush forests, rocky outcrops and
hiking trails, including Istria's
highest mountain
page 111

Parenzana old railway cycle route: 123km
of pristine former narrow-gauge track,
viaducts and panoramas
pages 128 & 180

Poreč: the 6th-century Euphrasian
Basilica, with it's outstanding mosaics,
is a UNESCO World Heritage Site
page 83

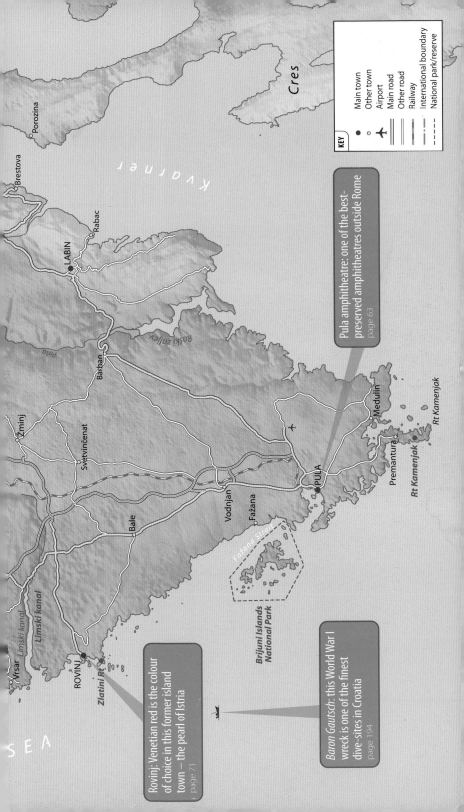

SEA

Vrsar

Limski kanal

Limski kanal

Poreč

Žminj

Svetvinčenat

Bale

ROVINJ

Zlatni Rt

Rovinj: Venetian red is the colour of choice in this former island town – the pearl of Istria
page 71

Fažana Strait

Brijuni Islands National Park

Vodnjan

Fažana

Baron Gautsch: this World War I wreck is one of the finest dive-sites in Croatia
page 194

Roški zdenec

Pašo

Barban

PULA

Premantura

Rt Kamenjak

Rt Kamenjak

Medulin

Pula amphitheatre: one of the best-preserved amphitheatres outside Rome
page 63

Porozina

Brestova

Rabac

LABIN

Kvarner

Cres

Istria
Don't
miss...

Roman architecture
Pula's amphitheatre, dating from the 1st century AD, is one of the largest and best-preserved Roman amphitheatres in the world (RA) page 63

Food and wine
Istria is renowned for its excellent *pršut*, a dry-cured ham similar to Italian prosciutto (RA) page 121

Inland Istria
The enchanting walled citadel of Motovun overlooks the Mirna Valley and is surrounded by vineyards
(D/VP/S) page 123

Festivals
At the Giostra festival in Poreč you can see jousting on orseback, colourful period dress, and sample the usual offering of great Istrian food
(ML/XP/C) page 91

Sun and sea
Whether you are a weathered sea dog or a novice swabbie, sailing along the Istrian peninsula is a delight
(TM/VP/S) page 44

Istria
in colour

left   Erected in 1956, the *Maiden with a Seagull* is an icon of Opatija (SS) page 101

below left   Built in 1882 and known as the 'Adria Palace', the Jadrolinija building's sheer grandeur is one of the finest reflections of Rijeka's pre-eminent maritime history (RA) page 145

below   With fewer than 100 residents, the village of Draguć is a popular film location and has appeared in Croatian as well as international productions (RA) page 134

above Most visitors miss the little town of Pazin, which is a shame as it has a cracking castle, a dramatic gorge and literary associations aplenty (SS) page 113

right Detail of one of the magnificent Byzantine mosaics in Poreč's Euphrasian Basilica (RA) page 85

below Once the capital of Istria, the coastal town of Poreč has a beautiful and quite typical Croatian old town (SS) page 83

top	Slovenia's Predjama Castle sits massive and impregnable-looking within a 123m-high cave in an overhanging cliff (RA) page 167
above left	Formed over a million years ago, the magnificent Postojna Cave in Slovenia is bristling with stalagmites and stalactites of all imaginable shapes and sizes (RA) page 166
above right	With its pale-pinkish skin and 'fingered' hands it is not difficult to see why Postojna's native olm came to be nicknamed the 'human fish' (DL/VP/S) page 168
below	Boasting some of the best-preserved medieval architecture in all of Istria, many consider Piran to be the jewel in the Slovenian Adriatic crown (PT) page 158

AUTHORS

Rudolf Abraham (*www.rudolfabraham.co.uk*) is an award-winning writer and photographer specialising in Croatia and eastern Europe. He first visited Croatia in 1998, lived in Zagreb from 1999 to 2001, and continues to spend several weeks a year in his favourite country in Europe. His other books include the first English-language hiking guides to Croatia and Montenegro, as well as guides to Northumberland and Patagonian Chile, and he updates the Bradt guides to Croatia and Transylvania. He lives in London with his wife and daughter, though is just as likely to be found in Zagreb, a small village near Zadar or the Istrian hinterland.

Thammy Evans, born in London of Welsh and Peranakan parents, has travelled and lived abroad for 25 years. Her first overseas trip was to Malaysia at the age of eight, and she has been dabbling in numerous foreign languages ever since. Amongst many other travels, her most memorable are the Trans-Mongolian Railway from Tianjin to Moscow in 1991, mountaineering in Bolivia in the summer of 1999, and doing the field research for her second Bradt travel guide *Great Wall of China* in 2005. She has also written the Bradt guide to Macedonia. She and her family now have a small stone house by the sea in Istria.

DEDICATION

Rudolf Abraham – To Ivana and Tamara
Thammy Evans – To Plamenka, Dalibor and Korvin

PUBLISHER'S FOREWORD   *Adrian Phillips, Publishing Director*

There's nothing more satisfying than a successful bit of matchmaking. For many years, Thammy and Rudolf have separately worked for Bradt on different guidebook projects. They'd never met or spoken, but they were united in a fondness for Istria. Thammy has a farmhouse on the peninsula, and Rudolf has always loved to explore the area with his Croatian wife. When we decided that Istria lacked proper room to breathe in our full-country guides to Croatia and Slovenia – that its Roman and Byzantine sites, medieval hill settlements, hiking trails and fabulous cuisine deserved a regional guidebook of their own – we knew the two people to write it. We put them in touch, and together they have forged the perfect guidebook-writing team.

First edition February 2013

Bradt Travel Guides Ltd
IDC House, The Vale, Chalfont St Peter, Bucks SL9 9RZ, England
www.bradtguides.com

Print edition published in the USA by The Globe Pequot Press Inc, PO Box 480, Guilford, Connecticut 06437-0480

Text copyright © 2013 Rudolf Abraham and Thammy Evans
Maps copyright © 2013 Bradt Travel Guides Ltd
Illustrations copyright © 2013 Carole Vincer
Project Manager: Greg Dickinson
Cover image research: Pepi Bluck

British Library Cataloguing in Publication Data
A catalogue record for this book is available from the British Library
ISBN: 978 1 84162 445 7
e-ISBN: 978 1 84162 751 9 (e-pub)
e-ISBN: 978 1 84162 653 6 (mobi)

Photographs Rudolf Abraham (RA); Alamy: Waterframe (W/A); Corbis: Miso Lisanin/Xinhua Press (ML/XP/C); Croatian National Tourist Board (CNTB); Dreamstime: Amidala76 (A/DT), Tinieder (TI/DT), Travelpeter (T/DT); FLPA: Imagebroker (I/FLPA); Kimmo Parhiala (KP); Shutterstock: Deymos/View Portfolio (D/VP/S), Domen Lombergar/View Portfolio (DL/VP/S), lero/View Portfolio (I/VP/S), Igor Karasi/View Portfolio (IK/VP/S), Sinisa Botas (SB/S), Titus Manea/View Portfolio (TM/VP/S), Tupungato (T/S), Vadim Po/View Portfolio (VP/VP/S); SuperStock (SS); Paul Turner (PT)

Front cover Rovinj old town (T/DT)
Back cover Motovun (SB/S), Musicians in Buzet (SS)
Title page Maiden with a Seagull, Opatija (SS), Plomin old town (T/S), Rijeka Carnival (RA)
Author photos Phil Lampron (Thammy Evans) and Ivana Jović Abraham (Rudolf Abraham)

Maps David McCutcheon FBCart.S; colour map relief base by Nick Rowland FGRS; includes map data © OpenStreetMap contributors (under Open Database Licence)

Typeset from the authors' disks by Wakewing
Production managed by Jellyfish Print Solutions; printed and bound in India
Digital conversion by The Firsty Group

Acknowledgements

RUDOLF ABRAHAM Firstly I must thank Thammy, for sharing her knowledge of and enthusiasm for this little wedge at the top of the Adriatic, and for making co-authorship such a straightforward and enjoyable process. I'd also like to thank Marko Marković, Marketing Manager at the Istrian Tourist Board; Radenko Sloković, Director of the Central Istria Tourist Board in Pazin; Meri Matešić, Director of the Croatian National Tourist Board in London; Tine Murn, Head of Communications at the Slovenian National Tourist Board in London; Erika Erik Legović and Ana Luch at Hotel Kaštel in Motovun; Hotel Vela Vrata in Buzet; Lisa Woodman of PPHE in London; Tomislav Korošec at Park Plaza Histria in Pula; Tina Ružić at Jadran Hoteli; Ratko Matijević at Apartments Arena in Pula; Ivana Malović and Marko Gregurić at Gral Putovanja in Buzet; Peter Štefin, Sales Manager at Postojnska jama; Klaudio Ipša of Ipša Olive Oil; Oliver Arman of Franc Arman Wines; Radmila Karlić of Karlić tartufi; Mladen Dujmović of Pršutana Dujmović; Antonio Giudici; Branko Maglica at Ranch Goli vrh; Rijeka Tourist Board; Jess Hilliard of JPR; and Milka Šćulac Sennett and family in Zamask and E17. Last but very much not least, I must thank my wife Ivana and daughter Tamara for their patience while yet another Croatian holiday was hijacked in the name of guidebook research.

THAMMY EVANS For my part, the secrets of Istria that have made it into this book would not have become known to me without the wonderful hospitality of my good neighbours Teta Ita, Plamenka, Dalibor and Korvin, and my good friends Deborah, Mauricio, Viktor and Petar. I thank the entire crew of Commodore Travel for a wonderful ferry trip from Rovinj (Aldino Vlašič Žiga, the captain Nikolas Korić, Danijela, Mareg, Miran, Mirna, PT, et al). For help with matters diving, I thank Miloš and Olwyn Trifunac, Lars, Stipe, and Damir of Poreč Diving Centre, and Filip Vušič of Puffer. Katie and Andy have helped with Rovinj; Paul and Anne with Piran; Bridget Jordan for lots of the east coast. I must also thank my mother again, not least for looking after our Dani, and for dropping everything at the last minute to assist. Finally, as ever, I thank my husband, Vic, for conducting last-minute primary and secondary research. And for her contribution to a second guidebook I must thank my daughter, Daniella (aged five), for doing the field research on travelling with children. *Hvala svima.*

Contents

Introduction

Long the seaside playground of the central, landlocked-Europeans, Istria's attractions are becoming increasingly well-known and popular with English-speakers. Whilst Croatia's Dalmatian coast has topped tourist destinations for a while now, it is little Istria's proximity and accessibility that attract those who want to stay and play a while and really appreciate what life on the Adriatic has to offer. Istria has some of Croatia's most famous sites, including Pula's Roman amphitheatre, UNESCO protected Byzantine mosaics in Poreč, picturesque Medieval hill towns and hidden frescoes, and Brijuni Islands national park, home to Tito's former summer residence. Renowned for its cuisine (and food-related festivals), in particular its truffles, game, first-rate pasta, seafood, wine and olive oil – and a whole host of earthy peasant stews – Istria also hosts Croatia's two most famous international film festivals (Pula and Motovun), while Rijeka, on the edge of the Istrian peninsula, boasts the second largest carnival in Europe after Venice.

And that's just a taste of the cultural stuff. Then there's the outdoors – both above and below the water. A mix of Mediterranean and continental fauna adorn the peninsula, as well as some rare indigenous species. Istria's cuisine is a further testament to the wealth of the soil here, and its geographic diversity for such a small area is matched only by the region's diversity in outdoor sports which includes well-marked and well-trodden hiking trails, the Parenzana long-distance cycle route, one of Croatia's best spots for windsurfing at Rt Kamenjak, paragliding from the slopes of Ćićarije and Učka, and diving among WW1 wrecks.

This very first guidebook to Istria is not bound by national boundaries, but looks at the whole of geographic Istria, including the Slovenian Capodistria region, which offers hot spring spas, glorious castles and beautifully-lit caves. All these are within a day-trip from anywhere in Istria, meaning you can happily stay in one location if you wish, making it ideal for families and for making the most of the beach. And for those wishing to stay a little longer, we've included a section on buying and maintaining your very own Istrian homestead. Distances in Istria are small, and within half an hour's drive you can move from the labyrinthine streets and Venetian splendour that is Rovinj, to rolling olive groves punctuated by traditional stone shepherd huts.

Both of these authors are happiest in Istria, sipping a glass of Malvazija wine with local meat and truffle starters and a seafood dinner whilst looking out over the sea, be that from up high in an Istrian hill town, down on the shore, or from a gently-bobbing yacht. We hope you'll enjoy it too.

LIST OF MAPS

NOTE ABOUT MAPS

Several maps use grid lines to allow easy location of sites. Map grid references are listed in square brackets after listings in the text, with page number followed by grid number, eg: [54 C3].

Part One

GENERAL INFORMATION

ISTRIA AT A GLANCE

Country name The Republic of Croatia (Republika Hrvatska)

Region name Istria (Istra)

Location A peninsula at the head of the Adriatic. Bordered by Slovenia to the north and the Kvarner region of Croatia in the northeast

Official language Croatian

Other languages and dialects Italian, Istriot, Istro-Romanian, Venetian

Population of Istria County: 208,440 (2001 census)

Religion Roman Catholic

Župan (equivalent of mayor) Ivan Jakovčić

Main political parties Istarska Demokratska Stranka (IDS)

Regional capital Pazin (population 9,227)

Economic centre Pula (population 58,594)

Other major towns Poreč, Rovinj, Labin, Buzet, Umag

Local government units 41 (ten towns, 31 municipalities)

Area 2,820km²

National parks Brijuni Islands

Nature parks Učka

Nature reserves and other protected areas Rt Kamenjak, Zlatni rt, Limski kanal, Palud

UNESCO World Heritage Sites Euphrasian Basilica, Poreč

Total length of coast 441km

Airports Two (international airport, Pula; local airfield, Vrsar)

Highest point Vojak (Mount Učka) 1,401m

Time GMT+1

Currency Kuna (HRK); usually written as kn

Exchange rate £1 = 9.2kn; US$1 = 5.7kn; €1 = 7.5kn (December 2012)

Average annual income US$8,520 (World Bank, 2010)

International telephone code +385 for Croatia, +386 for Slovenia

Electricity 220 volts AC. Sockets are round two-pin.

Local symbols Goat and *boškarin* ox

National holidays 1 January (New Year's Day); 6 January (Epiphany); Easter Sunday & Easter Monday (31 March & 1 April 2013, 20 & 21 April 2014, 5 & 6 April 2015); 1 May (Labour Day); Corpus Christi (60 days after Easter Sunday); 22 June (Day of Antifascist Struggle); 25 June (Statehood Day); 5 August (Victory and Homeland Thanksgiving Day and the Day of Croatian Defenders); 15 August (Assumption of the Virgin Mary); 8 October (Independence Day); 1 November (All Saints' Day); 25 and 26 December (Christmas)

1

Background Information

GEOGRAPHY

A wedge-shaped – some might say, heart-shaped – peninsula at the head of the Adriatic, Istria covers an area of around 2,820km², and is bordered by Slovenia in the north and the Kvarner region of Croatia in the northeast. The Istrian coast, like that of the rest of Croatia, is highly indented and riddled with small, rocky coves, and runs to a total length of some 441km – roughly double its length as the crow flies. Most beaches are pebble or rocky, though there are some notable exceptions such as the broad, sandy beach called Bijeca, near Medulin. The Limski kanal, often incorrectly described as a fjord (it's actually a drowned river valley), cuts deep into the west coast, while the Raški zaljev makes a prominent break in the southeast coast. Just off the west coast near Pula are the Brijuni Islands, now a national park, and further north towards Rovinj another scattering of islands lies just off the coast.

The hilly Istrian interior is divided from the east coast by the Učka and Ćićarija mountains, which rise steeply from the Opatija Riviera to an altitude of 1,401m and 1,272m respectively. These form part of the Dinaric Alps, an extended chain of mountains which stretches southeast through Croatia parallel to the coast, down through Montenegro and Albania and into northern Greece. In the west the transition between the interior and the coast is more gentle. Inland Istria is bisected by three main rivers: the Mirna and the Dragonja in the north, both running from east to west, and the Raša in the east, running more or less north to south. A large lake in the northeast, Butoniga jezero, is actually a manmade reservoir.

The Istrian landscape is remarkably green when compared with some of the islands of the nearby Kvarner and northern Dalmatia, with well-cultivated soils supporting grape vines, olives, corn and other crops, and around 35% of Istria is covered by forest.

Despite Istria's predominantly rural character, around 70% of the population live in towns.

See box on pages 188–9 for underwater geography.

FOREST FIRES

Like much of the rest of Croatia, Istria's hot, dry climate makes it particularly prone to forest fires. High temperatures in the summer frequently combine with a lack of rain and the presence of dry winds, leaving forests and grasslands tinder-dry, and easily ignited by a carelessly discarded cigarette. Owing to the risk of forest fires you should *never* light an open fire in the wild.

KARST

Istria – like much of Croatia – is predominantly a karst landscape. Karst is formed through the gradual action of rainwater on limestone (rainwater contains carbon dioxide, making it mildly acidic, and able to slowly dissolve a soluble rock such as limestone). Cracks in the rock and surface drainage holes are enlarged as the acidic water seeps downwards, leading over millennia to the creation of a distinctive surface texture, pockmarked and scored by vertical fissures, and a profusion of caves and sinkholes. An elaborate subterranean drainage system develops, as a consequence of which most surface water rapidly disappears underground, to flow as subterranean streams, which may later re-emerge as karst springs, only to vanish into the rock once more further along their course.

Istria's deepest cave is found at Rašpor in the Ćićarija Mountains – though at 365m it's still relatively small by Croatian standards (a cave in northern Velebit plunges over 1,400m into the depths of the mountain, making it one of the 15 deepest caves in the world). It has been estimated that there are at least 1,000 caves and sinkholes in Istria, perhaps double this number.

Among the most prominent karst features in Istria accessible to visitors are Baredine jama near Poreč (see *Chapter 5*, page 93), and Pazinska jama or 'Pazin abyss' (see *Chapter 7*, page 119), a cave and sinkhole at one end of a gorge below Pazin Castle, into which the River Pazinčica disappears. Near the inland entrance to the Učka tunnel is a small canyon called Vranjska draga, with some spectacularly slender rock pinnacles.

The term 'karst' is derived from the limestone Kras region in neighbouring Slovenia – an area which formed the basis of early studies into karst from the late 17th century onwards, in particular Cerkniško jezero, a huge intermittent lake which fills over the winter, only to drain away gradually through a labyrinth of sinkholes during the summer. This part of Slovenia is also home to one of the world's most-visited caves, Postojnska jama (see *Chapter 9*, page 166).

CLIMATE

As along the rest of the Croatian coast, Istria is characterised by warm dry summers and mild winters. In comparison with the Dalmatian coast, Istrian summers tend to be a couple of degrees cooler, reaching 30–34°C from mid-June to the end of August, when it's very unlikely to rain. August tends to be slightly cooler than July, in part due to the slightly shorter days, and so the evenings are likely to be quite cool such that you might even need a light jacket. Correspondingly, winters are usually a few degrees warmer than on the Dalmatian coast, with the Opatija pocket in particular being especially sheltered. With the exception of the Učka and Ćićarija mountains, Istria rarely sees snow, or frost, and if it does it dissipates quickly in the morning sun. It is almost always sunny.

The peninsula is characterised further by three winds in particular. The *maestral* is the summer breeze blowing from east to west; the *jugo* brings warm air and rain from the south; and the *bura* reigns from the northeast bringing cold winds, which can whip up the sea. Although the *bura* can appear at any time of year, when it arrives characteristically around October-time, it signals the end of summer.

FLORA AND FAUNA With over 38,000 taxa of wildlife in Croatia, the count continues and final numbers are estimated by the State Institute for Nature Protection (*www. dzzp.hr*) to possibly lie somewhere between a minimum of 50,000 to over 100,000. Istria used to be densely wooded until much of it was used during Venetian rule for shipbuilding. Nonetheless, a lot of Istria remains wooded and is still favoured for picking wild asparagus, chestnuts and other local delicacies, as well as for seasonal hunting. Outside the towns you will often see various species of deer in the fields, especially at dawn and dusk, and it is not uncommon to see buzzards, owls, bats, woodpeckers, hedgehogs, squirrels, lizards, frogs and toads.

Native to Istria is the **boškarin** cow, allegedly one of the oldest species in Europe. It used to be a work animal until the tractor arrived, and almost became extinct. It is now protected and whilst it is no longer used to plough fields or pull carts, it is farmed for meat, which is considered a delicacy.

The only potentially fatally venomous animal in Istria is *Vipera ammodytes*, known in English as the **nose-horned viper** or **sand viper**, and in Croatian as *poskok*, meaning 'something that jumps', because it is known occasionally to lurch from the ground to catch its prey. It is mostly found on rocky or stony ground,

WHAT TO DO IF YOU SEE A DOLPHIN

Nine species of cetaceans (dolphins and whales) are known to visit the Adriatic, all of which are strictly protected in Croatia. Only the bottlenose dolphin lives in Adriatic waters, and they are often seen around Istria, especially in deeper waters. With increasingly frequent sightings, the State Institute for Nature Protection issued the following guidelines for conduct when encountering a dolphin or whale:

* Do not chase the dolphins or drive your boat directly towards them.
* If you wish to approach the dolphins, do it very slowly, keeping parallel to their course and avoid sudden changes of direction or speed, which could confuse or disorientate them.
* It is better to give them the choice of approaching you. The motor should be maintained in neutral or switched off.
* Do not make sudden noises, especially with the engine as these could alarm the animals.
* Ensure that no more than one boat is within 100m of the dolphins, or three boats within 200m.
* Do not stay with the dolphins for more than 30 minutes.
* For your safety and theirs avoid diving or swimming with them, never offer them food or try to touch them.
* Leave the area, accelerating gradually, when the boat is more than 100m from the animals.
* Do not throw litter overboard or leave it on the beach; plastic bags can accidentally be swallowed by the dolphins, causing their death.
* Any deliberate disturbance of dolphins or whales must be reported to the Directorate for Inspection of Nature Protection and the local police.
* Findings of injured, sick and dead animals must be reported on the emergency number (℡ *112*).

but can also be encountered in drystone walls or grass, and only becomes a threat if trodden on while basking in the sun or when it is protecting its eggs or young during the summer. For the most part, *poskok* are lethargic (hence you might tread on one) and unaggressive. Most will slither away if disturbed, some might hiss and expect you to slither away, and every now and again one will bite, especially if you step on it. If you are unlucky enough to get bitten by one, try to remain calm, keep the affected part below the level of your head and heart and phone emergency services (☏ *112*) immediately. Do not attempt to suck out the venom. The **common viper** or **adder** (*Vipera berus*) is also found in Istria but is much less venomous. Make sure you wear sturdy boots and long trousers if hiking in the summer. Wide tracks can become remarkably narrow in Istria.

Another venomous creature in Istria that people tend to fear is the **scorpion** (*Euscorpius italicus*). No species of *Euscorpius* is considered dangerous and its effects are usually localised (mainly pain at the sting site). At only 4–5cm in length, what little venom they have can stun a fly or a small grasshopper, but can't kill it.

ENDANGERED FISH OF THE MEDITERRANEAN

Fish stocks have been on the decline globally since industrialisation brought about the freezer and a rise in the human population has outstripped the rate at which fish can reproduce to meet human consumption demands. In trying to reverse this trend, and stop the extinction of now vulnerable fish species, the International Union for the Conservation of Nature (IUCN) has produced Red Lists of all animals and where they rate on the continuum of Extinct to Least Concern[ed]. Croatia has also produced local lists (see *www.dzzp.hr*).

Owing to differences in local tastes, fishing trends and national laws, some fish might be threatened in some areas of the world but not in others. Fish farming has started to make up for stocks in some breeds, but there is a vast difference between farming from spawn, and farming from wild catch – the latter being very inefficient due to the high death rate among trapped fish. Fish quotas and international fishing rights are big politics and affect the lives of many local fisherpeople as well as big businesses. Enforcement of the law is difficult, especially once the (by then dead) fish make it to market or the restaurant table. Below is an overview of some of the most commonly found endangered fish along the Adriatic, and suggested alternatives for consumption. See also *Chapter 12, Diving*, on page 189.

SHARK The common Croatian name for all shark species – which are, among other things, defined by the cartilaginous skeleton to their classic fish shape – is *morski pas*. Almost all shark species in Adriatic waters are at least near threatened with being endangered, and some are critically endangered. The only shark species which is of least concern is *Scyliorhinus canicula*, the **small-spotted catshark**, known locally as *mačka bljedica*. Whilst there is a high chance that this is the *morski pas* that is served up at the local market and the many fish festivals, you might prefer not to take the risk. An alternative to the large flaked, sweet white flesh of the shark is swordfish *Xiphias gladius*, or *sabljan* in Croatian. Data is, however, deficient on the vulnerability of swordfish in the Adriatic, although some sources say that it is overfished generally in the Mediterranean. So far, we have not seen swordfish served in Istria.

SKATE OR RAY *Raža* in Croatian, skate is mostly near threatened or data deficient. The only ray of least concern in the Adriatic is *Raja miraletus*, or *raža modropjega*

Some people might be allergic, but still unlikely to die from the venom of *E. italicus*. These scorpions do tend to like rocks and crevices, and in the dry summer season can be found in houses. They are not at all aggressive unless you provoke them seriously. I usually just brush them into a dustpan when I find one, and it sits there waiting for me to throw it out.

On a friendlier note, protected swallow-tail **butterflies** are common sightings here, as are the slow worm, pheasant and weasel. In the Učka and Ćićarija mountains wild boar are common, and eagles, chamois, deer, foxes and rabbits are also to be seen, as well as pine marten and dormouse, although you are highly unlikely to come across the protected brown bear. The native **Učka zvončić** with its lilac-blue bell-shaped flowers can only be seen in the Učka Mountains, and is protected, as are all the varieties of **native orchid**, which can be found more commonly nearer the sea. Rt Kamenjak (*rt* means 'cape' or 'point' in Croation) alone is home to at least 28 species of orchid, many classified as facing extinction and two of them endemic to southern Istria. One of the last recorded sightings of the endangered **Mediterranean monk**

in Croatian. Again it's hard to find an alternative to skate in Croatia, as even flounder *Bothus podas* (*razok* in Croatian) is near threatened. *Microchirus ocellatus*, **sole** or *list* in Croatian, is a smaller flatfish alternative with very fine sweet flesh.

JOHN DORY *Zeus faber* in Latin and German, *kovač* in Croatian, the John Dory is a near threatened species. This big disc-shaped fish with large spiky fins and a characteristic black circle on its side can be found served occasionally in restaurants. It's expensive precisely because it is rare. **Dentex** (*zubatac*) or sole (*list*) are good alternatives.

SCORPIONFISH *Scorpaena scrofa* in Latin, *škrpina* in Croatian, the scorpionfish is also near threatened. It is not commonly eaten in the UK, but is very popular along the Mediterranean. In Istria it is a key ingredient for *brodet* fish soup, because it is a firm-fleshed fish, which does not fall apart in a soup. Monkfish or angler *Lophius piscatorius*, or *grdobina* in Croatian, would be a good alternative if it wasn't also near threatened. The **black-bellied angler** *Lophius budegassa*, or *grdobina žutka* in Croatian, is of least concern and can be safely used as an alternative.

Other **fish to avoid** are turbot *Psetta maxima* NT (*oblič*); brill *Scophathalmus rhombus* NT (*romb*); black seabream *Spondyliosoma cantharus* NT (*kantar*); sturgeon *Acipenser* VU (*jesetra*); northern bluefin tuna *Thunnus thynnus* DD (*tunj*); and **all forms of whitebait** – a generic term used for the juvenile fry of fish – because eating fish fry before maturity is detrimental to the sustainability of their species.

Fish to eat, you'll be glad to know, include the ubiquitous sea bass (*brancin*) and gilthead seabream (*orada*), as well as mackerel (*škomber* or *skuša*) and fresh sardines (*sardele*).

IUCN key: EX = extinct; EW = extinct in the wild; RE = regionally extinct; CR = critically endangered; EN = endangered; VU = vulnerable; LR = lower risk; CD = conservation dependent; NT = near threatened; LC = least concern; DD = data deficient; NE = not evaluated.

seal, of which only some 600 individuals survive in the wild, was off the coast of Istria. It's also worth noting that within easy striking distance of Istria is the last Croatian stronghold of the griffon vulture, at Beli on the island of Cres.

The karst caves and subterranean rivers of Istria are home to a fascinating cave fauna, including the **olm** or cave salamander, the distribution of which is limited to the karst landscapes of Slovenia, Croatia, northeast Italy and Bosnia (see page 168).

ENVIRONMENTAL EFFORTS In line with the International Union for Conservation of Nature, Croatia has protected all the species currently known to be under threat in Croatia, and is in the process of creating Red Books specific to Croatia. These are not yet all published, online or in English, but some can be found at www.dzzp.hr. There are over 2,300 highly protected species in Croatia, meaning that they must not be deliberately disturbed, never mind killed. A further 817 are simply protected and may not be hunted or harvested without licence.

Istria has its fair share of nature reserves, which include the Učka Nature Park (see page 111); Limski kanal (see page 99), between Vrsar and Rovinj; Palud bird sanctuary (see page 81), south of Rovinj; Brijuni Islands National Park (see page 68), off the west coast; Rt Kamenjak (see page 66), on the southern tip of Istria; and Sečovlje saltpans (see page 164) and Škocjan Bay nature reserve (see page 154), both of which lie in Slovenia.

For more on protected fish species, see box, pages 6–7.

Environmental contacts in Istria

DZZP (State Institute for Nature Protection) Trg Mažuranića 5, Zagreb; ☏01 550 2900; e info@dzzp.hr; www.dzzp.hr. The central institute dealing with nature conservation in Croatia, established in 2002. Projects include protection of the Mediterranean monk seal & the Croatian large carnivore initiative. **Natura Histrica** Riva 8, Pula; ☏052 830 350; e info@natura-histrica.hr; www.natura-histrica.

hr. Founded in 1996 with the aim of protecting, maintaining & promoting protected areas in Istria. **Zelena Istra** Gajeva 3, Pula; ☏052 506 065; www.zelena-istra.hr. Zelena Istra (Green Istria) is a non-governmental, non-political & non-profit environmental organisation founded in 1995, with the aim of protecting the environment & natural resources.

HISTORY

FROM PREHISTORY TO THE ILLYRIANS Some 4,000 to 8,000 years ago, **Neolithic** man wandered through the wooded landscape of what is now the Istrian Peninsula. These early farmers and hunters tended flocks, and later began cultivating cereal crops. They left traces of their passing at several sites across Istria, in the form of pottery, stone flakes and polished stone tools – including Vižula near Medulin, and caves such as Pupićina and Vela in Vela draga, a steep-sided valley in the Učka Mountains, near the inland entrance to the Učka tunnel. Evidence of much earlier human habitation has been found in the Sandalj Cave near Pula, dating back to the lower Paleolithic, perhaps as early as one million years BC.

Istria takes its name from the **Histri**, an **Illyrian** tribe which inhabited the region in the centuries before the Roman conquest, from around 1000BC. Another Illyrian tribe, the Liburni, also inhabited parts of the coast, while the Japodes inhabited the area inland to the northeast, including Trsat, above modern Rijeka.

ROMAN ISTRIA The **Romans** conquered Istria in 177BC – it took them two military campaigns – when they took the Illyrian settlement of **Vizače** (Roman Nesactium) at Valtura, near Pula's airport, defeating the Histrian king Epulon (who, according to the Roman writer Tito Livio, stabbed himself and threw himself from the town walls rather than being captured alive). Following the Roman conquest, Roman settlements were established at Polentium (Pula), Parentium (Poreč), Tarsatica (Rijeka) and elsewhere (it took the Romans a further 150 years to defeat the Illyrian tribes further south in Dalmatia, which then became part of Roman Illyricum, with its capital at the old Illyrian stronghold of Salona, near Split). Istria became an important source of olive oil and wine for the Romans, as well as limestone and other resources; you can still see the remains of olive oil production and storage on Brijuni (see page 68), and there's a permanent exhibition in the passages below Pula's 1st-century amphitheatre, the single most impressive Roman monument in Istria and one of the largest and best preserved in the world (see page 63).

BYZANTINE AND MEDIEVAL Following the collapse of the Roman Empire in AD476, the Istrian Peninsula was successively overrun by the Visigoths, Huns and Ostrogoths, before **Byzantium** established control over the Istrian and Dalmatian coast in the 6th century, under the emperor Justinian. It was during this period of reasonably extended peace that Bishop Euphrasius built the large basilica in Poreč named after him, the exquisite mosaics of which are listed as a UNESCO World Heritage Site. This peace was interrupted towards the end of the 6th century when the **Avars** swept into the region, causing widespread destruction (including, further south, sacking the former Roman capital of Dalmatia at Salona in AD612), before Byzantium once again regained control. Also during the 6th and 7th centuries the **Slavs**, a people originally from an area north of the Black Sea, began migrating into the valleys of the Danube and the Sava, reaching the Adriatic by the early 7th century. Istria was taken by the **Lombards** in 751, before falling back into the hands of the Avars only some 25 years later, and was annexed by the Frankish ruler **Charlemagne** in 789, becoming (along with almost all of Dalmatia by 812) part of the **Carolingian Empire**.

The Franks initially attached Istria to the **Duchy of Friuli**, but from the end of the 8th century it became one of several marches or **margraviates**, established – along with Carniola (in what is now Slovenia) and Verona – as a frontier defence against attack or invasion of Frankish Italy from the northeast. Following the division of the Carolingian Empire Istria became part of the Middle Frankish Kingdom ruled by Lothair I, after which it was passed backwards and forwards between various Bavarian and Carinthian dukes and the Patriarchs of Aquileia.

Meanwhile, further south in Croatia during the 9th and 10th centuries, a series of increasingly powerful **Croatian dukes**, and then kings, succeeded in wresting control of a large part of what is now modern Croatia from Byzantine and Hungarian control, with Zvonimir (1075–89) having the title King of Croatia and Dalmatia conferred upon him by Pope Gregory VII. It was during this period of increasing autonomy that **Glagolitic** (the written form of Old Church Slavonic) was adopted instead of Latin (which much of the local population was unable to understand) by local priests. Croatia's brief 'golden age' was cut short in 1091, when **Hungary** invaded northern Croatia and installed a Hungarian *ban* or governor.

VENETIAN RULE In 1267 the increasingly powerful **Republic of Venice**, which had anyway already been in control of much of the peninsula's west coast since the 9th century, annexed Istria. Only a small area around **Pazin** remained part of the Duchy of Carniola, which in turn belonged to the Austrian House of Habsburg, and Austria also gained **Rijeka** in the 15th century.

A legal document has survived from 1275 (with some additions from the 14th century, which show that it was still used at that time), known as the *Istrian Book of Boundaries* (*Istarski razvod*). Originally written in Latin, German and Glagolitic (though only later transcripts of the Glagolitic version have survived), the document defines the borders between the different spheres of rulership in Istria at that time – the Patriarchate of Aquileia, the Principality of Pazin and the Republic of Venice.

Sometime between the 10th and the 14th centuries, **Vlachs** (mercenaries and their families from what is now Transylvania and elsewhere) were settled in the northeastern part of Istria to defend the borders of Austria, and in the 17th century the **Uskoks** of Senj – famed pirates who had been the bane of both Ottoman and Venetian shipping in the Adriatic, in the pay of Austria – were settled here after being forcibly disbanded. During the 17th century outbreaks of **plague** decimated the population of Istria, with the town of Dvigrad being abandoned, and Pula reduced to a mere 300 inhabitants.

NAPOLEON AND AUSTRIA The Venetian Republic was extinguished with the arrival of **Napoleon** at the end of the 18th century, and in 1797 the Treaty of Campo Formio awarded Venice's Istrian territories to Austria – until in 1805 Napoleon's victory over Austria at Austerlitz resulted in Istria and Dalmatia becoming part of his Illyrian Provinces. In 1815 Istria, along with the rest of Croatia, became part of Austria's Küstenland or Austrian Littoral, which included Trieste and the Kvarner Islands, and then Austria-Hungary, with the Istrian capital established at Poreč from 1861.

This period saw the Istrian coast, in particular the northeast around **Opatija**, develop into an extremely fashionable resort for the well-heeled Austrian elite – visitors included Gustav Mahler, and the emperor Franz Joseph himself, who purchased a villa in nearby Voloska for his mistress. Rijeka became the site of the Austro-Hungarian Naval Academy, and rail connections between Rijeka and Budapest and Trieste and Vienna opened in the 1880s. On the west coast the formerly malarial swamps of the **Brijuni Islands** were transformed into a luxury health resort by wealthy businessman Paul Kupelweiser in the 1890s.

THE 20TH CENTURY After **World War I**, the Treaty of Rapallo (1920) gave Istria to the Kingdom of Italy, while Rijeka was annexed by the Italian poet Gabriele D'Annunzio, who set up his own, short-lived regency there, from 1919 to 1921. On 1 December 1918, partly in response to fears that Croatian territory would be bartered as part of the post-war settlement, the first communal Yugoslav state, the Kingdom of Serbs, Croats and Slovenes, was founded, later called the Kingdom of Yugoslavia. It was to last until 1941, although never recognised by the Treaty of Versailles. Rijeka was formally handed to Italy with the Treaty of Rome (1924). During this period the border between Italy and the Kingdom of Serbs, Croats and Slovenes ran down the River Rječina in Rijeka (Italian Fiume).

The 1920s and 1930s and the rise of Italian **fascism** witnessed a policy of forced Italianisation in Istria, with the closure of a number of Croatian and Slovenian schools, a suppression of local language and culture, and the torching of the Narodni dom in Pula and Trieste. In response, the militantly anti-fascist group TIGR, considered one of the earliest anti-fascist movements in Europe, was established in Slovenia, and was active in Istria.

Following the outbreak of **World War II** Italy annexed further parts of Croatia, establishing concentration camps (including on the island of Rab), while the rest of Croatia and the Kingdom of Yugoslavia was occupied by Nazi Germany.

Armed resistance was organised by the Partisans under Josip Broz Tito. The Italian surrender in 1943 and the defeat of Germany in 1945 were accompanied in Istria by reprisal killings and massacres, most notoriously the 'foibe massacres', in which the bodies of Italians were disposed of in karst sinkholes (*foiba* means 'sinkhole' in Italian) – a practice in fact perpetrated throughout the war to some degree or another by all sides, German, Partisan and Italian. In any case, between 1943 and 1954 a significant proportion of Istria's Italian population moved to Italy in several waves – through fear of persecution, economic uncertainty and with encouragement from both Italy and Yugoslavia. This **Istrian exodus** is estimated to have amounted to between some 230,000 and 350,000 people, a figure which includes Italians from both Istria (Croatia) and Slovenia, and a significant number of anti-communist Croats and Slovenes.

From 1945 Istria, along with the rest of Croatia, became part of Tito's **Federal Republic of Yugoslavia**, which endured for several years after Tito's death in 1980, until its bloody collapse in the early 1990s.

In May 1991 Croatia held a referendum, in which over 90% voted in favour of **Croatian independence**, which was formally declared on 25 June. In response, Serbs in the Krajina region of Croatia held their own referendum and voted to remain part of Yugoslavia. In June 1991 heavy fighting broke out in the Krajina and eastern Slavonia, after which the Serb-dominated JNA (Yugoslav People's Army) increasingly intervened on its own authority in support of Serbian irregulars. In the three months following 25 June a quarter of Croatian territory fell to Serb militias and the JNA, and by December 1991 thousands of people had died in the fighting in Croatia, and more than half a million fled their homes. Unlike many other parts of Croatia, Istria emerged largely unscathed from the 1991–95 Homeland War (Croatian War of Independence).

Over the past two decades Croatia has seen tourism soar, a new network of motorways has been built and foreign property buying has boomed. Croatia achieved candidate status in its bid for EU membership back in 2004, and in June 2013 is finally scheduled to join the EU.

GOVERNMENT AND POLITICS

Istria is one of Croatia's 20 counties or prefects. Known locally as *županija*, counties emerged as administrative districts only after the war ended in 1995. The county is headed by a *župan*, akin to a mayor, but there is also a local assembly, which in Istria's case comprises 41 representatives. The latter represent 41 local government units, consisting of ten towns (Buje, Buzet, Labin, Novigrad, Pazin, Poreč, Pula, Rovinj, Umag and Vodnjan) and 31 municipalities. The Istrian Democratic Party (IDS) has been the strongest party by far for many years as the region has never been particularly nationalistic. They currently hold 20 seats while the next closest rivals, the Social Democrats, who currently head the government at the national level, boast a mere five seats. The Croatian Democratic Union (HDZ), which is the party of the late Franjo Tuđman, the first president of Croatia, also has only five seats.

ECONOMY

If you think the Istrian economy is primarily about tourism, you wouldn't be entirely wrong. It gathers about one third of all the tourists in Croatia each year. In 2011 that was roughly three million people passing through Istria. But other industries are present, although struggling in the current financial environment. Unsurprisingly among them is fishing – both commercial fishing in the open Mediterranean and also fish and mollusc farming close to shore. Istria also has a solid agricultural sector – as the legions of vineyards and olive groves around the region attest. Around 10% of Istria is covered with vineyards. Also unsurprising, shipbuilding leads Istria's production sector with Pula's Uljanik shipyard building five ocean-going vessels per year. Rijeka's two yards, 3 Maj and Viktor Lenac, are also a major employer in the region and build a further ten vessels a year.

The entire Croatian economy suffered during the break-up of Yugoslavia, but overall Istria wasn't hit as hard as other regions that suffered both material damage and loss of economic activity. Unemployment in Istria currently hovers around 13%, up from 8% in 2003, and even those who are employed don't always receive their pay cheques on time. It is not uncommon for a construction worker to be owed several months of back pay. Road construction has been a key source of economic activity in Istria and elsewhere in Croatia as the government has built hundreds of miles of new highway in the past 20 years.

PEOPLE

Vo se veživa za roge, a čovik za besidu (An ox is tied to his horns, man to his word)

Istrian proverb

The 2011 census shows the population of Istria to be 71.9% Croatian, 6.9% Italian, 3.2% Serbian, 1.5% Bosnian, 1% Slovene, 1% Albanian, plus several other nationalities listed below 1%. The percentage of the population who did not state their nationality was 11.1%. It's worth pointing out that just because someone lists their nationality or ethnicity as Italian, for example, doesn't necessarily mean they consider themselves any less 'Istrian'. Before the end of World War II, the number of Italians living in Istria was much higher (see *History* on page 11).

Istrians – whether of Croatian, Italian or other ethnicity, and whatever their mother tongue – are in the experience of both authors an incredibly warm, friendly and open people, justifiably proud of their peninsula's rich cultural heritage and delicious cuisine. A testament to this is how often different ethnicities live side-by-side, and despite having gone through a period of fascism and an exodus in the first half of the last century, Istrians remain open-minded and forward-looking.

LANGUAGE

The official language in Istria is Croatian, though much of the population (particularly on the west coast) is bilingual, with Italian as a second language, attesting to centuries-long historical and cultural ties. The area with by far the highest proportion of people describing Italian as their first language is the municipality of Grožnjan – some 66% of the population in 2001 – followed by Brtonigla (41%), Buje (39%) and Oprtalj (32%). In contrast, the equivalent figure for the town of Rovinj – despite the fact that it's frequently seen as the most 'Italianate' place in Istria – is only around 10%.

Most Croatians in Istria – at least, those within the areas more frequented by tourists – speak excellent or at least reasonable English, so getting by without speaking any Croatian isn't usually a problem unless heading well off the beaten track, though you will undoubtedly get most out of your visit if you can learn a few words of Croatian. In addition, there is a small scattering of places where Istriot and

Istriot, which has been variously classified as a sub-dialect of the Venetian language (see below) or an entirely separate Romance language, is spoken by fewer than 1,000 people (400 who speak it as a first language, plus another 400 who claim only to speak it as a second language) in just six towns in Istria: Vodnjan, Rovinj, Šišan, Bale, Fažana and Galižana. **Istro-Romanian** is an eastern Romance language, related to Romanian, which most probably owes its presence in the region to mercenaries and their families from what is now Transylvania (a people now more generally referred to as Vlachs, not only in Istria but also in several areas of southeast Europe), who were settled in the northeastern part of Istria sometime between the 10th and the 14th centuries to defend the borders of the Austrian Empire. It is now estimated to be understood or spoken by between only 300 and 400 people, in two small areas of Ćićarija and Učka, in particular the villages of Žejane and Sušnjevica (for more information, see http://istro-romanian.com and www.istro-romanian.net). **Venetian** is spoken by around two million people in and around the Veneto region of northern Italy, as well as in Istria and Slovenia. It is related to Vulgar Latin but was influenced by several other languages in the region, and attained the status of a lingua franca under the Republic of Venice. Both Istriot and Istro-Romanian are classified as severely endangered on the UNESCO list of endangered languages, Venetian as vulnerable.

Istro-Romanian are still spoken – both of them distinct local languages (sometimes referred to as languages, sometimes as dialects), now spoken by only a handful of people and in danger of becoming extinct – see box, above. Croatian belongs to the south Slavonic branch of the Indo-European family of languages, and is similar to, though not entirely the same as, Serbian and Bosnian. The relationship between Croatian and Serbian since the break-up of the former Yugoslavia, following almost 50 years of the two being amalgamated as Serbo-Croatian, is variously seen as similar to that between British and American English, or as that between two wholly separate and distinct languages, depending very much upon on one's particular point of view.

For more information on language, pronunciation and vocabulary, see *Appendix* 1 on page 199.

RELIGION

With close ties to Italy and the Austro-Hungarian Empire, Istria is of course Roman Catholic. In 1900 Istria had a population of 344,000, 99.6% of whom were Catholic, under the ecclesiastical jurisdiction of three bishops. Under communism and socialism, religion did die down to a degree across the country, and the Catholic population of Istria is now 78%. Church services are regular and welcome tourists. The service in the Euphrasian Basilica (see page 85) is particularly popular. Only 3% of Istria is Orthodox Christian.

There are around 5,000 practising Muslims in Istria according to the Medzlisa Islamic community in Pula, headed by Imam Esad Jukan, and a further 3,500 non-practising Muslims according to the census of 2001, making a total of just over 4% of the peninsula. They run prayer services in the Islamic community building (*Medžlis islamske zajednice Pula; L da Vinci 11;* \ *052 211 175;* e *medzlis_pula@*

yahoo.com) not far from the Roman amphitheatre. The building, originally built in 1895, began renovation in 2012 and will be upgraded to a mosque, including the addition of a small minaret in the courtyard.

EDUCATION

Literacy in Istria is slightly higher than the average for Croatia, which is 98.1%. Compulsory education starts at age six or seven, and continues to the age of 18. Many schools teach Italian as a second language, and certainly on the coast most Istrians are bilingual Croatian/Italian, with many also speaking German.

Pula University (*www.unipu.hr*) specialises in humanities, economics and tourism, music, educational science, Italian and marine science. The University of Rijeka (*www.uniri.hr*) was founded in 1973 from the amalgamation of a number of other tertiary education facilities in the area. It traces its earliest educational roots, however, to the 17th century when there was a Jesuit high school in Rijeka. The university specialises in science and technology. There are also polytechnics in Pula and Rijeka. The Ruđer Bošković Science Institute in Zagreb also has a branch in Rovinj, which manages among other things the Rovinj aquarium.

CULTURE

Istria's rich, multi-layered culture is everywhere apparent – critical tools required to appreciate it are simply eyes and ears.

LITERATURE Among the most prominent figures in Istrian literature are the poet and novelist **Mate Balote** (1898–1963), who was born near Pula, and the poet and playwright **Drago Gervais** (1904–57), who was born in Opatija. You'll find busts of both men in Žminj (see page 122), beside the *kula*. The most popular literary association in Istria however is *Veli Jože*, the story of a kind-hearted giant living near Motovun, written by the great Croatian poet and politician **Vladimir Nazor** in 1908.

Some parts of Istria, along with the nearby island of Krk, were centres of **Glagolitic** learning during the medieval period, and one of the most important Glagolitic inscriptions in Croatia was discovered at **Plomin**. Churches in Roč, Hum and elsewhere in the Istrian interior still bear traces of Glagolitic graffiti among their frescoes, and a series of sculptures inspired by letters of the Glagolitic alphabet can be found along the road between Roč and Hum (see *Chapter 7*, page 133).

Istria is also linked to the names of several foreign novelists, including the likes of **Jules Verne** (who set part of his novel *Mathius Sandorf* in Pazin Castle, Pazinska jama and the Limski kanal), **James Joyce** (who taught English in Pula for a short period, at which time he worked on some of the material which would later become his novel *Portrait of the Artist as a Young Man*) and **Dante** (who visited Pazin and possibly based the entrance to Hell in his *Inferno* on Pazinska jama).

ART There are some beautiful and little-known medieval **frescoes** hidden away in the Istrian interior, many dating from the 15th century. You'll find them in churches in Roč, Hum, Draguć, Oprtalj and elsewhere (including over the Slovenian border at Hrastovlje) – though it is undoubtedly the *Dance of Death* scene at **Beram** that is the most striking (see page 120), painted in 1474 by Vincent of Kastav. The churches are usually locked, but a local keyholder will be happy to come and let you look inside – see details of individual churches in *Chapter 7*.

Istria has some superb Roman and Byzantine **mosaics**, including a large and mostly intact Roman floor mosaic in Pula illustrating the *Punishment of Dirce* (see page 61), and of course the magnificent Byzantine mosaics at Poreč (see page 85), the latter on a par with the Byzantine mosaics at Ravenna and in the Hagia Sofia in Istanbul.

The work of **Dušan Džamonja** (1928–2009), one of the best-known sculptors of the former Yugoslavia, can be seen in a sculpture park at **Vrsar** (see page 99), where Džamonja had a house. Vrsar had a strong influence on another contemporary Croatian artist, **Edo Murtić** (1921–2005), who spent much of his time there and included its landscapes in a number of his paintings. In **Brtonigla**, there's a gallery dedicated to the work of Zagreb-born sculptor and painter **Aleksandar Rukavina** (1934–85), who lived in Istria from the 1970s. The sculptures of the so-called **Glagolitic Alley** between Roč and Hum are the work of Croatian sculptor **Želimir Janeš** (1916–96).

If you're in Rovinj on the second weekend of August there's a big outdoor art fair on Grisia Street, when local artists exhibit and sell their work, and in September Grožnjan holds an art festival, Extempore (see page 127).

MUSEUMS AND GALLERIES Istria does not contain the phenomenal concentration of museums and galleries you'll find in the Croatian capital, Zagreb, but it does have several important collections.

To see the most extensive collection of Istria's prehistoric and Roman past, you should visit the **Istria Archaeological Museum** in Pula (*www.ami-pula.hr*; see page 63). The **Pazin Museum** (*www.tzpazin.hr*) and the **Ethnographic Museum of Istria** (*www.emi.hr*), both housed in Pazin Castle (see page 119), are also well worth visiting. Other museums and galleries include the **Maritime and Historical Museum** (*www.ppmhp.hr*) and **Rijeka City Museum** (*www.muzej-rijeka.hr*), both in Rijeka (see page 144), **the Istrian Museum of Contemporary Art in Pula**, the **Aleksandar Rukavina Memorial Gallery** in Brtonigla, the **Naval Museum** in Novigrad (see page 96) and the **Batana Boat Museum** in Rovinj (see *Chapter 4*, page 79).

ARCHITECTURE Istria's architectural heritage belies its historical ties with Venice, while at the same time evoking its periods of Roman, Byzantine and Austro-Hungarian rule – together with some distinctively Istrian elements.

Rovinj is perhaps the most familiar symbol of the area's **Venetian** past, with its Renaissance and Baroque palaces and narrow, cobbled streets. Less well known but equally evocative are the small towns of Sv Lovreč and Svetvinčenat, with their clear medieval street patterns and Venetian loggias.

Roman remains in Istria (or anywhere else in Croatia for that matter) don't get much more impressive than the 1st-century **amphitheatre** in **Pula** (see page 63), one of the six largest Roman amphitheatres in the world. Many of the region's Roman remains are now held in the Archaeological Museum in Pula. Istria's – and Croatia's – finest **Byzantine** remains are in Poreč, where the dazzling 6th-century mosaics of the **Euphrasian Basilica** (see page 85) are a UNESCO World Heritage Site. Smaller Byzantine monuments include the 6th-century Chapel of St Mary Formosa in Pula. In **Opatija** (see page 101) and **Rijeka** (see page 137) you'll find some wonderfully opulent **Secessionist** architecture, which hints at this part of Istria's former Austro-Hungarian grandeur.

Istria has some impressive **castles**, in particular **Pazin Castle** (which sits perched on the edge of a dramatic gorge; see page 119), **Trsat Castle** in Rijeka (see page

ISTRIA'S LIGHTHOUSES

Istria has nine lighthouses. Eight of them were built during the 19th century and are still active. Three of them have accommodation available (*www. lighthouses-croatia.com* and see page 98 for more information about the accommodation at Savudrija).

The very first was built by the Venetians in 1403 on the island of St Nicholas just off Poreč. At 15m high, it originally just burned a fire at the top to warn passing ships of the rocks below. Later, in the 17th century, the fire was replaced by a lantern which required less tending and was not so susceptible to the wind. Now the lighthouse is no longer active.

The first of the currently active lighthouses is at Rt Savudrija. At 29m high, it was officially opened by Emperor Francis I of Austria in 1818. It was also the first lighthouse in the world to be powered from coal and was financed by the Trieste Stock Exchange.

The next to be built was the lighthouse at Porer, a small islet south of Rt Kamenjak. It is the southernmost of all Istria's lighthouses, and at 35m high it is also the tallest.

St John's lighthouse, built in 1853, is on the outermost of Rovinj's archipelago of 13 islands. It is 23m high, with an octagonal tower, and is permanently staffed because it has no electricity supply from the mainland grid.

Next, the lighthouse at Rt Zub (Cape Tooth) on the mouth of the River Mirna was built in 1872. It is more like a traditional stone house than a lighthouse, but on one corner facing the sea is the light. The following year, Istria's shortest lighthouse, at 5m tall, was built at Rt Crna south of the village of Skitača near Labin.

In 1877, the southernmost tip of Veliki Brijuni Island gained its own lighthouse atop a two-storey building; another was built in the same year south of Pula at Rt Verudica opposite the island of Veruda. Both these lighthouses are now run on electricity and are automated, so do not need to be permanently manned.

Istria's last lighthouse was completed in 1880. Named Marlera lighthouse, it is on Punta Grkova on the eastern side of Medulin.

145), and the surprisingly large **Grimaldi Castle** at Svetvinčenat (see page 122), while just over the border in Slovenia the iconic **Predjama Castle** (see page 167) is built into an overhanging cliff. On a smaller scale but no less impregnable in appearance are the stout towers or *kula* which can still be found in some towns, sometimes remnants or more extensive fortifications – there is a good example in **Žminj** (see page 122).

Although the slender bell towers of Rovinj's St Euphemia Cathedral and Vodnjan's St Blaise Church might seem transplanted from the Piazza San Marco (St Mark's Square) in Venice, there are many smaller **churches** in the region which remain distinctively Istrian. The square, simple porch and single bell of these churches will soon become familiar to anyone who goes in search of frescoes in the Istrian interior.

Out in the countryside of central Istria, along with plenty of stone farmhouses, you might see *kažuni* – small, circular stone huts with a conical roof, which are built, like the drystone walls (*suhozid*) in the fields around them, without any mortar. These humble but beautifully constructed *kažuni* – just as much as 'Venetian' Rovinj or 'Roman' Pula – have become more or less emblematic of Istria.

MUSIC AND DANCE Istrian **folk music** is based on a distinctive six-tone musical scale (the so-called Istrian scale), and the peninsula's two-part, slightly nasal **singing** – sometimes with words replaced by emphatic syllables such as ta-na-na (a widespread variation known as *tarankanje*) – is inscribed on the UNESCO List of Intangible Cultural Heritage. Traditional **instruments** include the *roženice* (a woodwind instrument, similar to an oboe) and the *mih* (a type of large bagpipe made from a goat's skin). There are a number of traditional Istrian **folk dances**, the best known being the ***balun***, in which several couples dance in a circle while executing different steps and twirls.

The Istrian scale was first recognised and studied by the Lovran-born composer **Ivan Matetić Ronjgov** (1880–1960), who went on to write music in the style of local folk music. One of the biggest names in Istrian music these days is musician and ethno-musicologist **Dario Marušić** (*www.dariomarusic.com*), whose clean, sometimes jazz-infused musings on Istrian folk music have earned him great critical acclaim.

A good opportunity to catch performances of local folk music is Pazin's **TradInEtno** festival in June (see page 117). Istria also hosts several international **music festivals**, ranging from the outstanding jazz festivals in Grožnjan (see page 127) and Opatija (see page 40) to Europe's largest bass music festival at Pula (see page 60).

2

Practical Information

WHEN TO VISIT

The best times to visit Istria are undoubtedly spring and autumn: it's warm during the day, cool in the evening and the madding crowds of summer are absent. It's sunny almost all year round, and even the winter sun brings warmth. Cafés in winter will often still have outside terraces open for customers to benefit from the sun's rays (and of course for smokers since smoking inside was banned). T-shirt weather – at least during the main part of the day – can start as early as March and go into October. Cyclists wanting to take advantage of the lack of people on the roads combined with beautiful sunny days often come as early as February and as late as November. July and August are hot – usually over 30°C – and very busy with tourists (at least along the coast), but for those with families, this is of course the only time they can take their summer holidays.

If you're looking for certain festivals, see *Festivals,* page 39.

HIGHLIGHTS

FOOD AND WINE Oh, where to start? From superb **seafood** on the coast to the famed **truffle** dishes of inland Istria (especially around Buzet and Motovun), excellent local *pršut* (dry-cured ham) and delicious homemade pasta – it's worth coming to Istria just to eat. Istria also produces some of the best **wine** in Croatia – in particular its signature white, **Malvazija**, though the red **Teran** is also pretty good – and its superb **olive oil** is winning an increasing number of international accolades. See *Eating and drinking*, page 35, for more on food and wine in Istria.

CULTURAL AND ARCHITECTURAL For many, **Rovinj** (see page 71) is the real pearl of Istria. Its medieval old town – once an island – shows off its Venetian heritage among steep, narrow cobbled streets and the largest replica of Venice's St Mark's campanile. **Koper** (see page 150) and **Piran** (see page 158) in Slovenia, however in fact, display a grander Venetian style, which are well worth a day trip. Equally impressive is Istria's UNESCO World Heritage Site, the 6th-century Euphrasian Basilica and mosaics in **Poreč** (see page 15). **Pula** (see page 53) is home to a magnificent and very well-preserved amphitheatre, and unlike some other towns on the coast remains a vibrant, busy city throughout the year – while the medieval hill towns of the Istrian interior (see *Chapter 7*, page 113) offer a completely different picture of Istria, dotted with churches and little-known frescoes.

COASTLINE Whilst Istria has few sandy beaches, it has a lot of coastline for a small place, and almost everyone goes there for its crystal-clear waters. Sometimes wrecks at 20m can be seen from the surface. Some of the best beaches and coastline to enjoy are along the 12km **coastal walk** from the spa town Opatija beneath the mass of the Učka Mountains to Lovran (see *Lungomare to Lovran*, page 105), and the beaches in **Rt Kamenjak** coastal reserve (see page 66).

INLAND The **hill towns** and villages of the Istrian interior – Motovun, Buzet, Draguć, Hum and others – should not be missed, and remain beautifully unspoilt. There are hidden frescoes at Beram, Roč and Hum, and the area around Buzet and the Mirna Valley is renowned for its **truffles**. In Slovenia don't miss the opportunity to see the phenomenal underground world of stalagmites and stalactites at the **Postojna Cave** (see page 164).

OUTDOOR Istria is the **cycling** capital of the region, with extremely little traffic in spring and autumn for those wanting to roadbike. Off-road tracks, including old Roman roads and the Parenzana (see page 180) are simply delightful, and a good introduction for younger members of the family. See *Chapter 11*. There are some great **hiking** trails on the Učka and Ćićarija mountains (see *Chapter 10*) as well as elsewhere, and several exceptional **climbing** areas including Vranjska draga (see page 42), and paragliding and balloon flights.

WILDLIFE The **Brijuni Islands** (see page 68) are a national park, and the former summer residence of Yugoslavia's former president Tito (complete with safari park), while the **Učka Mountains** (see page 171) are a natural park. **Rt Kamenjak** (see *South from Pula*, page 66) has an astonishing flora including several rare or endemic orchids, as well as numerous butterfly species, and you can often see **dolphins** off the Istrian coast or even in the Limski kanal. Both **Učka** and the **Ćićarija** mountains offer a good chance of seeing wildlife, from deer to raptors. **Sečovlje saltpans** (see page 164) in Slovenia is a haven for birds (and for ornithologists) and holds the region's only Salt Museum.

DIVE Wreck diving is a real highlight of Istria with some wrecks as low as 28m, well within recreational diving for advanced open-water divers, and some of the larger wrecks at technical diving depths. Marine life is also varied, and it is a great place for expanding your diving experience. See *Chapter 12*.

SUGGESTED ITINERARIES

ONE OR TWO DAYS Rovinj (see *Chapter 4*, page 71) to see this old Venetian-era town, which was once an island, with its replica of Venice's St Mark's campanile and/or Pula (see *Chapter 3*, page 53) with its extremely well-preserved Roman amphitheatre. If you have your own transport you could even take a quick spin into the Istrian interior for half a day to visit the medieval hill town of Motovun (see *Inland Istria*, page 123).

ONE WEEK Rovinj, Pula, Poreč (see *Chapter 5*, page 83), Motovun and Buzet (see *Chapter 7*, page 129), plus a visit to one of the nature reserves or national parks, such as the Brijuni Islands (Tito's former summer residence, see page 68) or Rt Kamenjak (see page 66), and finally maybe a hike up to Vojak on Mount Učka (see page 171) if you're not too busy sunbathing and swimming on the local beach. Take a boat trip to one of the islands, or to the Limski kanal (see box, pages 96–7), or to see Rovinj by night.

TWO WEEKS As above, plus a trip to the Slovenian coast, especially Piran, and/or Postojna Cave (see page 164) and Predjama Castle (see *Chapter 9*, page 167); more time can be spent in central Istria to discover the best of Istria's vineyards (see box, *Istrian wine*, on pages 36–7), and hike or bike the Parenzana old railway line (see page 180). Discover scuba diving at one of the many dive centres (see *Chapter 12*, page 186) if you're not already a diver but have Istria's wrecks high on your list of things to do; or indulge in some of the best spas in Europe – eg: the spas at the Lone Hotel in Rovinj (see *Where to stay*, page 75) or at the Kempinski Palace in Portorož (see *Where to stay*, page 163), or Hotel Kaštel in Motovun (see *Where to stay and spa*, page 124). Take a hot-air balloon ride along the Mirna Valley (see *Gral Putovanja*, below), and make sure you take in some of the concerts and festivals of which there will be many over the summer: check on page 39, at www.istra.hr/en/attractions-and-activities/events, and at the local tourist office as soon as you arrive.

THREE WEEKS TO A MONTH If you've got this much time to spend in Istria, then you're bound to want to make the most of the sea, and probably to travel a little further afield along the Dalmatian coast and into the rest of Croatia, and perhaps to take a day trip to Venice. The Bradt guide to Croatia offers more for further afield, and for hikers there's *Walking in Croatia* by Rudolf Abraham. All the main towns on the west coast have ferries to Venice during the summer (see individual towns for more information) and every ferry company provides plenty of information about Venice on the 2½-hour sailing there.

TOUR OPERATORS

ISTRIAN TRAVEL AGENTS AND TOUR GUIDES In addition to the following selection of local travel agents, most **hotels** will be able to offer a variety of excursions.

Danijela Sankovič m 098 170 7765; e danijela. sankovic@gmail.com. Danijela is a local guide who specialises in providing a sensitive & personalised tour of Istria & surrounding regions. She has lived in Istria most of her life, & now spends the winters in Rijeka. Fluent in Croatian, English & Italian, she also speaks German & some Hebrew. She tends to be very busy in the summer, so book well in advance.

Gral Putovanja Trg Fontana 7/1, Buzet; 052 662 959; e ivana@gral-putovanja.eu; www.gral-putovanja.eu. Gral Putovanja is an excellent new agency based in Buzet, offering tailor-made as well as a variety of fixed tours throughout Istria. They specialise in outdoor activities, from road & mountain biking (including the Parenzana) to hiking in the wilds of Ćićarija & Učka, & canoeing in the Limski kanal, & can also arrange cultural, gastro, wine & other tours. Their balloon flights in the Mirna Valley (€110 pp) have been listed among the top 10 balloon flights in the world. Good English spoken. Highly recommended.

Istra Line Partizanska 4, Poreč; 052 427 063; e info@istraline.hr; www.istraline.hr. Poreč-based agency offering accommodation bookings.
Istriana Travel Vrh 28, Buzet; 052 667 022; e istriana.travel@ri.t-com.hr; www.toursistria. com. Agency based in the village of Vrh, offering truffle hunts, fresco workshops & various excursions.
Marco Polo Tours Ivana Mažuranića 21, Rovinj; 052 830 978; e info@marcopolo. hr; www.marcopolo.hr. Rovinj-based agency offering excursions, transfers & accommodation booking in Istria (& the rest of Croatia), Slovenia & elsewhere.
Montona Tours Kanal 10, Motovun; 052 681 970; e info@montonatours.com; www. montonatours.com. Motovun-based agency offering a range of private accommodation.
Paragliding Tandem Istria m 098 922 8081; e info@istraparagliding.com; www. istraparagliding.com. Company offering paragliding tandem flights for 550kn pp.

Tour Istra Tržni centar Katoro bb, Umag; ☎052 741 806; e touristra@inet.hr; www. touristra.hr. Umag-based agency specialising in accommodation throughout Istria.

CROATIAN TOUR OPERATORS AND TOUR GUIDES

Atlas ☎020 442 222; www.atlas-croatia.com. Croatia's largest tour operator, with offices in most towns.

Croatian Culinary Tours ☎01 488 1807; e info@croatiaculinarytours.com; www. croatiaculinarytours.com. Zagreb-based agency offering culinary tours throughout Croatia, including Istria & the Kvarner.

Sail and Bicycle Adventure Tours m 091 574 9022; www.sailandbicycle.com. Lošinj-based agency offering an Istrian sail-&-bike tour.

Zagreb Tours ☎01 482 5035; e info@ zagrebtours.com; www.zagrebtours.com. Zagreb-based operator offering a 1-week Istria tour, & several others which include Istria in the itinerary.

UK TOUR OPERATORS

Balkan Holidays Sofia Hse, 19 Conduit St, London W1S 2BH; ☎0845 130 1114; www.balkanholidays. co.uk. Long-standing southeast Europe specialist offering a number of itineraries in Istria.

Bosmere Travel Argosy Hse, 54 Springfield Rd, Lower Somersham, Ipswich IP8 4PQ; ☎01473 834094; e info@bosmeretravel.co.uk; www. bosmeretravel.co.uk

Completely Croatia 4 The Old Forge, Gardner St, Herstmonceux, East Sussex BN27 4LG; ☎0800 970 9149; www.completelycroatia.co.uk. Offering 2 1-week breaks in Istria.

Croatia Gems 11 Windsor Terr, Clifton, Bristol BS8 4LW; ☎0117 973 2643; e info@croatiagems. com; www.croatiagems.co.uk. Hand-picked villas rooms & apartments, including Istria.

Croatian Villas Wood Green Business Centre, 5 Clarendon Rd, Wood Green, London N22 6XJ; ☎020 8888 6655; e sales@croatianvillas.com; www.croatianvillas.com. Apartments & villas in Istria & elsewhere in Croatia.

Discovery Travel York Hub, Pope's Head Court Offices, Peter Lane, York YO1 8SU; ☎01904 632226; e info@discoverytravel.co.uk; www. discoverytravel.co.uk. Outdoor specialist offering 1-week self-guided cycling holidays in Istria.

Freedom Treks Alpha Hse, St John's Rd, Hove, East Sussex BN3 2FT; ☎01273 224066; e info@ freedomtreks.co.uk; www.freedomtreks.co.uk. Hiking, cycling & sailing tours in Croatia including an Istrian Trail bike tour & a sail-&-bike tour on Istria's west coast.

Headwater The Old School Hse, Chester Rd, Northwich, Cheshire CW8 1LE; ☎0845 527 6233; e sales@headwater.com; www.headwater.com. Offers a 1-week cycling tour in Istria.

Leger Holidays Sunway Hse, Canklow Meadows, Rotherham, South Yorkshire S60 2XR; ☎0844 504 6251; www.leger.co.uk. Offering tours of Poreč & the Istrian Riviera & Rovinj for singles.

Responsible Travel Pavilion Hse, 6 Old Steine, Brighton, East Sussex BN1 1EJ; ☎01273 600030; e rosy@responsibletravel.com; www. responsibletravel.com. Offering 2 cycling holidays in Istria (5 days & 8 days).

Thomson Lakes and Mountains DST Hse, St Mark's Hill, Surbiton, Surrey KT6 4QD; ☎0871 230 8181; e reservations@thomsonlakes.co.uk; www. thomsonlakes.co.uk. Offers holidays based in Lovran & Opatija.

USA TOUR OPERATORS

Adriatic Tours ☎+1 800 262 1718; http:// adriatictours.com. Offering escorted tours, pilgrimages & cruises.

Friendly Planet Travel ☎+1 800 555 5765; e questions@friendlyplanet.com; www. friendlyplanet.com. Philadelphia-based operator offering a 10-day Croatia package including Istria.

TOURIST INFORMATION

The **Istrian Tourist Board** (*www.istra.hr*) has made an enormous and highly successful effort to promote the region, particularly over the past few years, with a wealth of information available online as well in local tourist information offices. In fact it would be pretty safe to say that no other region in Croatia has so much practical, accessible and *useful* information available online to the potential visitor – from detailed cycling routes with maps (*www.istria-bike.com*) to food and wine (*www.istria-gourmet.com*). Further information is available online from local tourist board websites (see individual chapters and *Appendix 2*) and the **Croatian National Tourist Board** (*www.croatia.hr*), as well as from offices in Istria's main towns and tourist centres, where you will be able to pick up local or town maps, find out more on what the town or region has to offer, and (usually) book accommodation. Excellent English is spoken in every local tourist office we have visited. For other useful websites, see *Appendix 2*, page 211

Town **maps** are available free at local tourist information centres (and most hotels and other accommodation will have them available as well), usually along with regional maps, sometimes with hiking and cycling routes marked, and the excellent Istria Bike (*www.istria-bike.com*) maps. There's also a useful foldout map of Croatia, which is also free. Larger Istria maps can be bought in bookshops, or before you travel through the excellent The Map Shop (*www.themapshop.co.uk*), or Stanfords (*www.stanfords.co.uk*). These include *Kompass: Istria* (1:75,000) and *Freytag & Berndt: Istrian Peninsula & Pula* (1:100,000).

For information on hiking maps, see *Maps*, page 170.

RED TAPE

PASSPORTS/VISAS Nationals of EU countries no longer need a visa to stay in Croatia, and will merely need to show a valid form of identification such as a passport or an ID card. Most nationals of other countries may visit Croatia for up to three months within a six-month period starting from the first day of entry. You can easily essentially extend this to six months by popping over the border into a non-EU neighbouring country for a day or two, then return to Croatia, where you will be entitled to stay for another three months. If you want to stay for longer, you'll need to apply for a temporary residence permit (*privremeni borovak*) at the Croatian embassy in your home country. This is supposed to take up to 12 weeks, but don't be surprised if it takes almost as many months. Full details of who does and doesn't need a visa for Croatia, as well as up-to-date addresses and phone numbers of all the Croatia diplomatic missions worldwide – and foreign diplomatic missions in Croatia – can be found on the Ministry of Foreign Affairs' website (*www.mvp.hr*).

Make sure you keep your passport with you at all times, as the failure to produce an identity document to a police officer can incur a fine or imprisonment.

REGISTRATION The Law on Aliens governs the stay of foreigners in the country. It is essentially based on the old Yugoslav law and is similar in all the former Yugoslav republics. Under Article 150 a foreigner must be registered with the police at the latest within 48 hours of arriving in Croatia. If you are staying in a hotel or other licensed accommodation, then the hotelier will do this for you and must register you within 24 hours of your arrival at the hotel. The hotel will fill out the necessary *potvrda* (certificate) for you and you need do nothing except provide your passport for your identification details. You are entitled to keep your section of the *potvrda* (normally returned with your passport at the end of your stay) and it is advisable to make sure you keep your copy, because if you can't prove your official registration for any part of your stay in Croatia then you could be subject to deportation and a restriction on your return to Croatia.

If you are staying in private accommodation, with friends or in your own home bought in Croatia, then you or your host must register you within 24 hours of arrival at the accommodation. Your host should register your details at the nearest tourist office if there is one in the local town, or at the nearest police station. Registration costs 10kn per stay throughout the year, and in addition there is a sliding scale of tourism tax per day ranging from 4kn to 8kn depending on the time of year. This is included in your accommodation costs if you are renting.

Foreign homeowners in Croatia staying in their own home (*korisčenje nekretnine*) are exempt from the tourist tax outside the peak tourism season (15 June–15 September) and pay a reduced tourist tax during the peak tourism season. If as a homeowner you will be using your property a lot during the summer season, you can pay a reduced lump sum for the entire period, saving you the hassle of going in and out of the tourist office. This will register you in the country for 90 days, however, and you will then not be able to return for a further three months. You will need to bring proof of your ownership of the property in order to qualify for home ownership exemptions/reductions to the tourist tax.

In case you first read this section whilst waiting for a delayed bus after you've already been in Croatia a while and, therefore, have not yet registered, you'll find that most unregistered tourists will probably get away with just a discretionary warning. Application of the law is, however, much stricter. The Law on Aliens and a summary of useful information is available at the Ministry of Interior's website (*www.mup.hr/1266*).

EMBASSIES

CROATIAN DIPLOMATIC MISSIONS ABROAD
UK and Ireland
❺ UK Embassy of the Republic of Croatia in the United Kingdom of Great Britain & Northern Ireland, 21 Conway St, London W1T 6BN; ☏+44 207 387 2022; e croemb.london@mvp. hr; http://uk.mfa.hr; ⏰ 11.00–14.00 Mon–Thu, 10.00–12.00 Fri
❺ Ireland Embassy of the Republic of Croatia, Adelaide Chambers, Peter St, Dublin 8; ☏+353 1 476 7181; e dublin@mvpei.hr; http://ie.mfa.hr

USA and Canada
❺ Chicago Consulate General of the Republic of Croatia, 737 North Michigan Av, Suite 1030, Chicago, IL 60611; ☏+1 312 482 9902; e crocons.chicago@ mvep.hr
❺ Los Angeles Consulate General of the Republic of Croatia, 11766 Wilshire Bd, Suite 1250, Los Angeles, CA 90025; ☏+1 310 477 1009; e crocons.los-angeles@mvpei.hr
❺ Mississauga Embassy of the Republic of Croatia in Canada, 918 Dundas St E, Suite 302, Mississauga, Ontario L4Y 2B8; ☏+1 905 277 9051; e croconsulate.miss@mvep.hr

❺ New York Consulate General of the Republic of Croatia, 369 Lexington Av, New York, NY 10017; ☏+1 212 599 3066; e crocons.newyork@mvep.hr
❺ Ottawa Embassy of the Republic of Croatia, 229 Chapel St, Ottawa, Ontario K1N 7Y6; ☏+1 613 562 7820; e croemb.ottawa@mvpei.hr; http:// ca.mvp.hr
❺ Washington, DC Embassy of the Republic of Croatia, 2343 Massachusetts Av, NW, Washington, DC 20008; ☏+1 202 588 5899; e washington@mvep.hr or consular@croatiaemb.org; http://us.mvp.hr

Australia and New Zealand
❺ Canberra Embassy of the Republic of Croatia (also covers New Zealand), 14 Jindalee Crescent, O'Malley, ACT, 2606, Canberra; ☏+61 2 6286 6988; e croemb.canberra@mvep.hr
❺ Melbourne Consulate General of the Republic of Croatia, 9/24 Albert Rd, South Melbourne, 3205, Victoria; ☏+61 3 9699 2633; e croconmel@ mvpei.hr
❺ Perth Consulate General of the Republic of Croatia in Australia, 9/68 St George's Terrace, Perth, 6831, Western Australia; PO Box Z5366; ☏+61 8 9321 6044; e croconpe@mvpei.hr

S **Sydney** Consulate General of the Republic of Croatia, 4/379 Kent St, Sydney, 2001, New South Wales 1230; ✆ +61 2 9299 8899; e crocons. sydney@mvpei.hr

S **New Zealand** Consulate General of the Republic of Croatia, 291 Lincoln Rd, Henderson/ PO Box 83200, Edmonton, Auckland; ✆ +64 9 836 5581; e cro-consulate@xtra.co.nz

FOREIGN DIPLOMATIC MISSIONS IN CROATIA

UK and Ireland

E **UK** (Zagreb) Ivana Lučića 4, 10000 Zagreb; ✆ 01 600 9100; e Zagreb.consular@fco.gov. uk; http://ukincroatia.fco.gov.uk/en/. Note that all UK passport applications in Croatia are now handled by the British Passport Processing Centre in Düsseldorf.

E **Ireland** (Zagreb) Miramarska 23, 10000 Zagreb; ✆ 01 631 0025; e irish.consulate.zg@ inet.hr

Australia and New Zealand

E **Australia** (Zagreb) NovaVes 11/III (Kaptol Centar); 10000 Zagreb; ✆ 01 489 1200; visa section

✆ 01 489 1209; e australian.embassy@zg.t-com. hr; www.croatia.embassy.gov.au

E **New Zealand** (Zagreb) Vlaška 50a, 10000 Zagreb; ✆ 01 461 2060; e nzealandconsulate@ email.t-com.hr

USA and Canada

E **USA** (Zagreb) Thomasa Jeffersona 2, 10010 Zagreb; ✆ 01 661 2200; e irczagreb@state.gov; www.usembassy.hr. Located out of town, near the airport.

E **Canada** (Zagreb) Prilaz Đure Deželića 4, 10000 Zagreb; ✆ 01 488 1200; e zagrb@international. gc.ca

GETTING THERE AND AWAY

BY AIR Istria has one international airport, at Pula, or, more accurately, 7km northeast of Pula near the village of Valtura (*Valtursko polje 210;* ✆ *052 530 105; www. airport-pula.hr*). The following airlines operate flights to and from Pula airport.

✈ **Croatia Airlines** www.croatiaairlines. com. Operates daily flights from Pula via Zagreb to London Heathrow & Gatwick, as well as to Amsterdam, Barcelona, Brussels, Frankfurt, Munich, Paris, & other European cities.

✈ **Germanwings** www.germanwings.com. Twice-weekly flights from Pula to London Heathrow via Cologne–Bonn, as well as operating routes to Vienna, Bologna, Lisbon & elsewhere.

✈ **Norwegian** www.norwegian.no. Flies from Pula to Oslo Gardermoen on Sat.

✈ **Ryanair** www.ryanair.com. Runs direct flights from London Stansted to Pula, on Sat & Tue.

✈ **Thomsonfly** www.thomsonfly.com. Routes from Pula to London Gatwick, Birmingham & Manchester, on Tue & Sat between May & Sep.

Getting to and from Pula airport A **shuttle bus** departs Pula's bus station for the airport, daily except Thursday, at 09.10 and 13.50 on Monday, 11.50 on Tuesday, 09.10 on Wednesday, 09.10 on Friday, 09.10 and 18.20 on Saturday, and 09.10 on Sunday. Tickets cost 15kn. **Taxi** drivers usually mill around the exit of the arrivals area, and there is a **Cammeo Taxi desk** (✆ *060 700 700; www.taxi-cammeo.net*). Cammeo will charge 45kn per car into the centre of Pula, slightly more to Verudela; any of the other companies are likely to charge around double that amount, or more. There are also car-hire offices in the arrivals area.

Other airports Rijeka also has an international airport (*www.rijeka-airport.hr*), though it's actually on the island of Krk so is less convenient for Istria. Croatia Airlines, Ryanair and Germanwings all operate routes from Rijeka. A shuttle bus operated by Autotrolej connects the airport with Rijeka and Opatija (for timetables, see www.tz-rijeka.hr).

Croatia's other main airports include Zagreb, Zadar, Split and Dubrovnik, the most convenient of which as a staging post for Istria is **Zagreb** (*www.zagreb-airport.hr*), from which Croatia Airlines has flights to destinations throughout Europe including London, Paris, Frankfurt, Munich and Amsterdam, and both British Airways (*www.ba.com*) and Easyjet (*www.easyjet.com*) operate flights to London. From Zagreb's main bus station (*www.akz.hr*) there are fast bus services to Rijeka, Pula, Poreč, Rovinj, Pazin, Buzet and elsewhere in Istria, and trains to Rijeka. Over the border in Slovenia, Easyjet, Wizz Air (*www.wizzair.com*) and Adria (*www.adria.si*) operate flights from **Ljubljana** (*www.lju-airport.si*) to the UK and elsewhere in Europe. From Ljubljana there are bus services to Istria and during the summer a fast train from Maribor to Pula.

BY TRAIN Over Easter and from the last week in June until around 25 August, there is a fast daily train service between Pula and Maribor (Austria), via Ljubljana (Slovenia). It's not particularly convenient for connecting up with flights in Ljubljana, but the Easter and summer timetable connects well with overnight trains from Munich at Ljubljana. The MV 1472 train leaves Ljubljana at 06.33 and stops at Postojna (07.31), Hrpelje-Kožina (08.25), Podgorje (08.54), Rakitovec border crossing with Croatia (09.15), Buzet (09.22), Lupoglav (09.53), Pazin (10.18), Kanfanar (10.46) and Pula (11.13). In reverse the MV 1473 train leaves Pula at 18.15, via Kanfanar (18.42), Pazin (19.06), Lupoglav (19.35), Buzet (20.03), Rakitovec (20.11), Podgorje (20.32), Hrpelje-Kožina (20.47), Postojna (21.45), Ljubljana (22.41), arriving in Maribor at 01.33. The train has ample cargo space for bicycles and its most up-to-date timetable can be found at www.slo-zeleznice.si/en/passengers/abroad/destinations/croatia/pula.

More international trains come into Rijeka and Zagreb, and connect with the line to Pula at Lupoglav. At the time of writing the Croatian railway website was still not very user-friendly, but at least available in English (*www.hznet.hr/timetable*). It includes services to some international destinations such as Ljubljana, Belgrade and Sarajevo. For other, less 'local' services check at Deutsche Bahn (see the link on the website above).

If you're travelling across Europe by train and including a visit to Istria or elsewhere in Croatia, an **InterRail pass** could be the way to go. InterRail **multi-country passes** are valid in up to 30 countries in Europe (including Croatia) and are available for five days' travel within a ten-day period (£225), ten days' travel within a period of 22 days (£321), 15 days' continuous travel (£355), 22 days (£416) or one month (£537). InterRail passes, once a privilege of those under the age of 26, are now available for all ages. The prices quoted above are for adult tickets (26+); those aged 25 and under go for considerably less, as do over 60s. You'll also need to pay for seat reservations on most international trains. A **one-country pass** for Croatia is also available, valid for three, four, six or eight days' travel within one month – though this won't save you any money if you're only visiting Istria, and train tickets are cheap within Croatia anyway.

BY BUS The Istrian coast is well connected to the rest of Croatia and several international destinations by bus. Pula has five buses a day to Trieste, one or two to Ljubljana, three to Belgrade, and three a week to Frankfurt, while Rovinj and Poreč have daily services to Trieste, Ljubljana and Belgrade. Rijeka has international services to Trieste, Ljubljana and Munich, and is well connected to most places in Istria by bus. Pazin is the only place in inland Istria with international bus connections, with one service a day to Trieste, Venice and Belgrade. If you're travelling from Zagreb by bus try to get one of the direct services, which will have only a couple of scheduled stops and will be quite a bit faster – for example Zagreb–Pazin or Zagreb–Rovinj.

BY BOAT International ferry routes operate between both Trieste and Venice in Italy and Poreč, Rovinj and Pula in Istria during the summer.

Trieste Lines (*www.triestelines.it*) sails from Trieste to Rovinj (€22.50) and Pula (€27.50) between the last weekend in June and the first weekend in September, daily except Wednesday. The service departs from Trieste at 09.00, arriving in Rovinj at 10.45 and Pula at 11.50, returning from Pula at 17.05 and Rovinj at 18.05, and arriving in Trieste at 19.55.

Venezia Lines (*www.venezialines.com*) sails every day from Venice to Rovinj via Poreč during July and August, departing Venice at 17.00 and arriving in Poreč at 19.30 and Rovinj around 20.30 (later on some sailings). The service returns from Rovinj at 07.00 and Poreč at 08.00, arriving in Venice at 10.30. In June and September the service is reduced to two sailings per week, departing on Wednesday and Saturday.

Venezia Lines also sails from Venice to Pula on Tuesdays (June–September), Wednesdays and Fridays (July/August) at 17.00, arriving in Pula at 20.00; and on Saturdays (July–August) at 14.30, arriving at 17.30. Sailings from Pula are at 08.00, arriving in Venice at 11.00.

In July and August Venezia Lines also operates ferries to Rabac (Sundays, departing Venice at 17.30, arriving Rabac at 21.30) and Umag (Fridays, departing Venice at 17.00, and arriving in Umag at 19.45).

Commodore Cruises (*www.commodore-cruises.hr*) has ferries between Venice and Pula (Wednesdays, departs Venice 16.30, arrives Pula 20.00; departs Pula 07.45, arrives Venice 10.45), Venice and Rovinj (Sundays, departs Venice 16.30, arrives Rovinj 19.30; departs Rovinj 08.00, arrives Venice 11.00), Venice and Poreč (Tuesdays and Fridays, departs Venice 16.30, arrives Poreč 19.30; departs Poreč 07.30, arrives Venice 10.30) and Venice and Umag (Thursdays, departs Venice 17.00, arrives Umag 19.30; departs Umag 08.00, arrives Venice 10.30).

Jadrolinija (*www.jadrolinija.hr*) operates a twice-weekly ferry service from Rijeka to Split, Stari Grad (Hvar), Korčula and Dubrovnik (from where you can continue to Bari in Italy), and also has sailings from Rijeka to the islands of Cres and Rab, and from Brestova to Porozina (Cres).

BY CAR Istria is easy to get to by car. For those flying in, or arriving by boat, major car-rental companies such as Europcar, Budget and Sixt are all available at the main airports serving onward travel to Istria. These will all also allow you to pick up in one country and drop off in another if you wish (at a cost). See *Driving and road safety*, page 28, for the specifics of driving in Istria.

The border crossings from Slovenia which can gather very long queues in the high season will go once Croatia is in the EU, which will ease car access to this part of Croatia considerably. The Učka tunnel near Rijeka can sometimes see tailbacks, but rarely. What is more common is the closure of certain high bridges, especially when the *bura* blows. These closures are announced in several languages including English on the radio stations HRT1 and HRT2.

HITCHHIKING The Croatian online forum for finding a ride in Croatia and the wider region is www.gorivo.com. For more on hitchhiking in Istria, see page 33.

Istria has reasonable health services and some good private doctors. There is a hyperbaric chamber for diving-related accidents at Pula (see *Chapter 12*). All the major towns have some hospital services, with Pula being the main hospital for Istria (see *Other practicalities*, page 60). Larger facilities are available in Rijeka (see *Other practicalities*, page 143) with the country's best services of course in Zagreb. From Slovenia, the best services are in Ljublana. Croatia already has very good public health services for tourists, which are available at most hospitals. It is not part of the European Economic Area (EEA) but visitors may still be entitled to reduced-cost, sometimes free, medical treatment. The agreements do not cover the cost of repatriation or routine monitoring of pre-existing conditions, therefore additional health insurance is still strongly recommended.

MOSQUITOES These are prevalent in Istria from April through to November, and in the height of summer they'll get busy as early as midday. However, there is no risk of malaria. Istria has particularly vicious tiger mosquitoes, which are black-and-white striped, so ensure any repellent you buy is good for repelling this kind of mosquito. Mosquito-repellent creams, sprays, smoke coils and electric plug-in repellents are ubiquitous, and usually state if they are good for tiger mosquitoes, sometimes by showing a drawing of a black-and-white striped mosquito. If you prefer the wristbands or solar sonic repellents, you'll need to bring these from home (but they might not be so effective against the tiger mosquito). Natural repellents such as Citronella are not as easy to find in Istria and are best brought from home (though they may be less effective against tiger mosquitoes).

FIRST-AID KIT As with any travels away from your medicine cabinet at home, it's good to have a small first-aid pack with you. You can buy these ready made from any good pharmacy at home, such as Boots in the UK, or Walgreens in the US, or you can just make up a small kit yourself from the following items:

- plasters/Band-Aids
- painkillers such as aspirin, paracetamol or Tylenol
- lipsalve
- sunscreen
- antiseptic cream (or diluted tea-tree oil)
- mosquito-bite cream
- spare contact lenses if you are a contact lens wearer
- small sewing kit

VACCINATIONS There are no compulsory vaccinations for Croatia. You should be up to date with tetanus, diphtheria and polio which comes as the all-in-one vaccine Revaxis and lasts for ten years. Hepatitis A vaccine may be recommended for travellers with underlying medical conditions such as chronic liver disease or haemophilia.

While Croatia is classed as a high-risk country for rabies, Istria is likely to have a similar low risk as northeast Italy. Nonetheless, a rabies vaccination may be recommended for all travellers, particularly for longer trips. Rabies is spread through the saliva of an infected animal, usually through a bite or scratch. It can be carried by any warm-blooded mammal though dogs and related species and bats are the most likely carriers. Having the vaccine before travel removes the need for

Practical Information HEALTH

2

rabies immunoglobulin (RIG) and reduces the number of post-exposure doses of rabies vaccine. Washing the wound with soap and water for a good ten minutes will help to stop the virus entering the nervous system and is the first thing that should be done. RIG is not always available which is why pre-exposure vaccine is a sensible precaution to take: if you contract rabies then it is almost 100% fatal.

SECURITY AND SAFETY

Emergency number ☏112
Roadside safety ☏987

PERSONAL SAFETY The security situation in Istria is completely safe – even theft and pickpocketing seem to be largely unheard of. As with any travel abroad, ensure you register or update your details with your national foreign office for the period of your travel abroad. Brits can do this at **LOCATE** (*https://www.locate.fco.gov.uk/locateportal*). Americans can do this at the **Smart Traveler Enrollment Program (STEP)** (*https://step.state.gov/step*).

DRIVING AND ROAD SAFETY Istrians are generally very good drivers and courteous. Istrian roads are also well kept, with new highways and little traffic outside the peak summer season. Speed restrictions are enforced with limits being 50km/h in built-up areas, 90km/h outside built-up areas, 110km/h on dual carriageways, and 130km/h on motorways. Drivers under the age of 24 must drive at no more than 10km/h less than these speeds.

Seat belts must be worn in the front and back seats of a car if fitted. Children under the age of 12 are not allowed in the front of cars, and suitable child seats are required for children under the age of six. The blood alcohol limit is 0.05%. Visibly drunk people may not travel in the front of a vehicle. Dipped headlights during the day are compulsory. As with the rest of Europe, certain minimum equipment must be held in your car in case of emergency, and specific winter equipment (such as chains and a shovel) once there is risk of ice and snow. Crash helmets are compulsory for motorcyclists. For more on Croatian driving regulations, see www.theaa.com/motoring_advice/touring_tips/croatia.pdf.

TICK REMOVAL

Ticks should ideally be removed as soon as possible, as leaving them on the body increases the chance of infection. They should be removed with special tick tweezers that can be bought in good travel shops. Failing that you can use your fingernails by grasping the tick as close to your body as possible and pulling steadily and firmly away at right angles to your skin. The tick will come away completely as long as you do not jerk or twist it. If possible, douse the wound with alcohol (any spirit will do) or iodine. Irritants (such as Olbas oil) or lit cigarettes are to be discouraged as they can cause the ticks to regurgitate and therefore increase the risk of disease. It is best to get a travelling companion to check you for ticks and if you are travelling with small children remember to check their heads, and particularly behind the ears. An area of spreading redness around the bite site, or a rash or fever coming on a few days or more after the bite, would require a trip to the doctor.

If you get into an accident or breakdown, the **Croatian Automobile Club (HAK)** (✆ *1 987; www.hak.hr/en*) can assist. Their website also has links to webcams and gives regular updates on the traffic states of border crossings.

WOMEN TRAVELLERS Sexual harassment is not usually a problem in Istria and it is not considered strange to be a woman traveller on your own. Dress for women here is as in the rest of western Europe, but take care not to be in swimwear or skimpy attire in churches.

As with anywhere in the rest of the world, if you are a single female driver and an unmarked police car indicates that you should pull over, you should turn on your hazard lights and drive slowly to a public area such as a petrol station before stopping. You could also phone the police on 192 to check whether the police car is genuine.

GAY TRAVELLERS The gay and lesbian scene is very limited in Istria although it is more accepted throughout Croatia and Slovenia than in other parts of former Yugoslavia. This said, the most popular gay resort this side of Zagreb is Rovinj. Whilst the town itself may not offer much overtly to the gay and lesbian visitor, Punta Križa Beach north of Rovinj town, between Amarin and Valalta campsites, is the renowned gay mecca. As an extension of the Valalta nudist camp, it is full of bronzed males perfecting every last inch of their tan.

DISABLED TRAVELLERS Istria is not so easy to get around for the disabled, in part because of a lack of public transport in small towns and because of the steep cobbled streets in most of the former island seaside towns, and the hill towns of the Istrian interior. Poreč, being at least more flat, is easier to get around. Disabled car-parking spaces are common, however. Pula airport has ramps until you get to enter the plane itself where there is no gangway, so disabled people must at least be able to walk up the plane steps. For the blind or partially sighted, there is equally little assistance. Modern newer hotels, and those of the large conglomerates are more disabled-friendly and do have some specially fitted rooms.

TRAVELLING WITH CHILDREN Istria, being Mediterranean in nature, is very tolerant of children, who will be welcome in all restaurants, and are expected to be out in the late evenings when it is cool. Croatian children, who are in nursery till they are six or seven years old, have a two-hour siesta at nursery; hence they are all still awake at 22.00. Finding washrooms with baby-changing facilities or restaurants with high chairs is more difficult, so do bring travel change mats with you and portable booster seats. Big hotel restaurants are better equipped.

Every medium to large town and resort along the coast will have a burgeoning funfair, known as a *luna park* in Croatian (from the name of the first amusement park to be opened at Coney Island in the USA in 1903), with lots of amusement rides and games to fritter your money away. Most rides are 5, 10 or 15kn, with the suspended tree gyms being 80–100kn for up to one hour. Every town and village will also have a free play park with the usual slides and swings and a climbing frame. The major seaside towns also have small aquariums and glass-bottom boats, and most resorts will also have an aquapark of inflatables out in the cordoned areas of the sea. Go-karting and paintballing are also popular across Istria. Funtana (see *South to Limski kanal*, page 99) has a dinopark, and there are numerous caves, including one to abseil down (Baredine; see *What to see and do*, page 93), which children find fascinating.

Should your child need paracetamol in suspension, the local brand is called Lupocet. This is a quarter of the price of what international brands such as Calpol are sold for in Croatia.

WHAT TO TAKE

You don't need to bring a great deal with you when visiting Istria, or Croatia in general, at least during the summer – and it's easy enough to buy anything you might have forgotten when you're there. Light summer clothes, and a light sweater or similar for the occasional cool evening (or if visiting caves, which tend to be quite cool), should suffice. Suncream and a sunhat will be indispensible sitting around on the beach during the summer, and if you're travelling with small children or a baby, bring some sort of collapsible sunshade for the beach. Sandals are definitely worth bringing, not least for wandering around rocky beaches. Something with longer sleeves, long trousers or long skirt are more appropriate for visiting churches (swimwear and skimpy attire will not usually be acceptable in a church). Reading material in English is a good idea, this being available only from bookshops in larger towns and cities. Mosquito repellent of some sort or another (see *Mosquitoes*, page 27) may also prove useful. If you're hiking, make sure you have adequate footwear, a waterproof jacket (Gore-tex or similar material) and a warm fleece in case the weather changes, as well as a small first-aid kit, whistle (for attracting attention in an emergency) and reflective 'space blanket'. The best fabric strip plasters for protecting your feet against blisters are those made by Hansaplast, available in pharmacies such as DM. Don't forget to bring an adaptor for phone chargers, etc. The electricity supply in Istria is the same as in the rest of mainland Europe, at 220V and 50Hz. Croatian plugs are the familiar round two-pin type, also the same as the rest of Europe.

MONEY

The Croatian currency is the **kuna**, usually officially abbreviated HRK but usually written as kn. Notes come in denominations of 10, 20, 50, 100, 200, 500 and (less commonly) 1,000 kuna, and there are 1, 2 and 5 kuna coins. Each kuna consists in turn of 100 lipa, though the smaller denominations of lipa went out of circulation several years ago, and these days you'll only see them in denominations of 5, 10, 20 and 50. However, prices *are* often given to a smaller lipa value, for example 4.99 (ie: 4 kuna 99 lipa), but this will just be rounded up to the nearest value, ie: 5kn.

ATMs (*bankomat* in Croatian) are easily found in larger towns and cities, though don't necessarily expect to find them in small towns and villages, especially in inland Istria. **Credit cards** are widely accepted in hotels, restaurants and larger shops, but not for private accommodation, or in smaller shops and cafés. Accommodation prices are often given in **euros**, with this being converted according to the daily exchange rate. Smaller shops tend not to carry a lot of change, so don't expect to be able to pay with a 500kn note every time – try to always carry some notes in small denominations.

CHANGING MONEY Foreign currency is best exchanged in **exchange offices** (*mjenjačnica* in Croatian) – banks almost always involve a lot of queuing. These can be found throughout larger towns and cities, and should have daily exchange rates posted at the counter. If you're carrying travellers' cheques you'll need to exchange them in banks. The most widely accepted are American Express.

BUDGETING

Istria and Croatia are fast catching up with the rest of western Europe in terms of prices. Once you've got to Istria, you can expect to pay around 300kn (€30) per day per person on food and lodging (in private accommodation), more if you add bus fares. At the other end of the scale, you can easily pay €200 per person per day to stay at the five-stars, eat at the best restaurants and drink the best wine. Most accommodation is almost double the price in the high season compared with the low season, so you can make considerable savings on the figures quoted above if you can visit outside July and August. You can also make good savings if you book for a week or more in the same accommodation – and as Istria is small, it is possible to visit most places in a day, even by public transport.

If you're hiring a car in Croatia, then expect to pay 350–700kn per day for a five-seater car. Petrol and diesel are quite a bit cheaper than in Italy, but it's still not cheap.

At the time of writing these are the shop prices for:

1½ litres water	5kn
½ litre local beer	7kn
Loaf of bread	6kn
Street snack	15kn
Postcard	3–6kn
T-shirt	15–50kn
Litre of petrol	10kn
Local city bus ticket	12kn
Intercity bus ticket (Rovinj–Pula)	40kn
Train ticket (Pula–Pazin)	37kn
Cup of coffee (espresso) in café	5kn–8kn
Pizza in pizzeria	40kn
Museum/gallery entrance ticket	15–25kn

TIPPING It is normal in Istria to round your bill up to the nearest 10kn on a reasonably large bill, or to leave a 1kn piece for smaller drinks. More upmarket restaurants increasingly charge *kuvert*, usually around 15kn (€2) per person, which includes the ubiquitous bread, often a small starter to put on the bread, and possibly a *rakija* (local brandy) at the end. If you know you're definitely not going to want all of that (eg: if you're allergic to wheat) then let the waiter know as soon as (s)he takes your drinks order, so that it can be omitted from the bill.

GETTING AROUND

BY TRAIN Train travel within Istria is limited to the Pula–Pazin line, which continues to Lupoglav and then north to Slovenia. From Pula there are eight daily trains to Pazin (1 hour 10 minutes) via Vodnjan and Sv Petar u Šumi, continuing to Lupoglav (1 hour 40 minutes) and Buzet (2 hours 10 minutes) – the station for which, by the way, is nowhere near the town. Rijeka is well connected to Zagreb by rail.

Rail fares are very reasonable in Croatia, eg: Pula–Pazin 37kn, Rijeka–Zagreb 102kn. There are four categories of train in Croatia: ICN (high speed, currently only Zagreb–Split); IC (fast intercity); *brzi* (fast); and *punički* (slow – stops at every station), though (with the exception of the service running to Ljubljana and Maribor during the summer) you'll only encounter the last two when travelling in Istria.

You need to buy train tickets (*karta*) before you travel (ticket office is *prodaja karta* in Croatian), but you don't need to validate them by stamping them in a machine before travelling as in Italy or France. Buying a train ticket doesn't give you a seat reservation, which costs a few kuna extra, but is very unlikely to be required on most trains except the faster intercity or international services, where it is sometimes mandatory. A return ticket (*povratna karta*) will be cheaper than two singles, and two people travelling together can sometimes get a joint ticket, which is slightly cheaper but means you must travel together. For timetables, see www.hznet.hr.

BY BUS Bus is the most convenient means of public transport in Istria, with frequent, fast services between all main centres on the coast. Pazin also has a good, fairly regular bus timetable, but most other places in inland Istria do not (most notably Motovun, despite being by far the most visited town in the Istrian interior).

You can buy tickets at the bus station (advisable, since it will guarantee you a seat) or on the bus itself. Return tickets include a seat reservation for the outward journey, but not the return – if you want a seat reservation on the way back (and you probably do, to make sure get a place on the bus if it's busy), you need to buy one at the ticket office once you get to your destination (they only cost a few kuna). Return tickets also mean coming back with the same bus company. Bear in mind however that once you've reserved a seat for your return journey it will tie your otherwise 'open' return ticket (albeit limited to the same bus company) to that specific time; if you change your mind you may be allowed on an earlier or later bus operated by the same company, but it's very much at the driver's discretion.

You need to pay for luggage (except small bags etc, which you can carry on the bus) when you put it in the hold; usually 8kn per bag. You'll be given a small receipt to match the tag on your bag.

For timetables, see www.autobusni-kolodvor.com (though it's worth noting that this is not an entirely comprehensive coverage of services) or contact the bus station you intend to travel from (see individual chapters).

Sample (one-way) bus fares: Pula–Rovinj 40kn, Pula–Poreč 72kn, Pula–Rijeka 100kn, Rijeka–Buzet 49kn, Buzet–Zagreb 147kn.

BY BOAT Travelling by ferry is a lovely way to get around the Croatian coast, and tickets for foot passengers are a bargain (if you're taking a car on the ferry it's another matter). The state ferry company Jadrolinija (*www.jadrolinija.hr*) operates services from Rijeka to the islands of Cres and Rab, and from Brestova to Porozina on the island of Cres, as well as a twice-weekly ferry service from Rijeka down the coast to Split, Stari Grad (Hvar), Korčula and Dubrovnik. During the summer several companies operate services from Italy to Poreč, Rovinj and Pula, and these can be used to travel between these cities (for more details, see *Getting there and away*, page 26). Small boats run a regular service between Fažana and the Brijuni Islands. Boat tours are offered from major centres such as Pula, Rovinj and Poreč to numerous places around the coast, including the Limski kanal (see *South to Limski kanal*, page 98) and the islands around Rovinj (see *Activities*, page 81).

See box on pages 44–5 for information on sailing off the Istrian coast.

BY CAR Istria is very easy to get around by car, and the peninsula has been on a tarmacking spree in recent years with many roads in the interior also being upgraded from the old dirt tracks (though some of the smaller minor roads still are dirt tracks, called *makadamska cesta* or *bijela cesta*). Istria's only motorway, known locally as the *ipsilon* because of its 'y' shape, is a toll road like all motorways in

Croatia. The maximum fee from the Učka or Dragonia to Pula is less than 40kn and can be paid in cash or by credit card. In 2012, the Učka tunnel crossing cost 28kn. The old road over the Učka Mountains is, of course, much more scenic, and longer.

Cars are easy to hire once in Istria, although in the summer you will need to book several days or preferably even weeks in advance to be sure of getting the type of car you want, especially if you're looking for a seven-seater for the family. Car-hire companies are listed in individual chapters. In addition to the major car-rental companies such as Europcar, Budget and Sixt, the local company **Vetura** (*www. vetura-rentacar.com*; see pages 75 and 88) is also very good. For an eco-friendly car-hire company, see box on page 49. For more on driving safety, see page 28.

TAXIS Taxis are plentiful in the main towns on the coast (Rovinj, Poreč, Pula, etc), with several taxi companies operating in each, and a smaller number of operators in towns in inland Istria (Buzet, Pazin, etc). Taxi prices here, and elsewhere in Croatia, used to be somewhat extortionate – but the arrival of **Cammeo Taxis** a couple of years ago saw the introduction of much, much lower fares, initially causing outrage among other taxi companies and leading to strikes and protests, but finally forcing them to lower their fares as well (though Cammeo fares are still significantly lower). Cammeo (*www.taxi-cammeo.net*) now operate in several towns and cities across Croatia, including **Pula** (✆ *060 700 700 from Croatian mobiles & landlines, or* ✆ *052 885 885 from foreign mobiles & overseas lines*) and **Rijeka** (✆ *051 313 313*). There's an office at Pula airport. Fares start from 15kn (which includes the first 3km) in Pula plus 6kn per kilometre after that, and from 20kn in Rijeka (which includes the first 5km) and 5kn per kilometre after that. Their intercity fares are extremely reasonable, especially if there are two or more of you travelling together (for example Pula airport to Rovinj costs 300kn per car). Cammeo don't use taxi stands, so you'll need to call or flag them.

BY BIKE Cycling can be a great way to travel in Istria, particularly some of the inland areas where public transport is minimal. See *Chapter 11* for more information on cycling and a selection of sample routes.

HITCHHIKING Hitchhiking is not a particularly good way to get around Croatia, particularly on the main coast roads where few people are likely to stop. You may have more luck inland, but don't hold your breath. The Croatian online forum for finding a ride in Croatia and the wider region is www.gorivo.com.

ACCOMMODATION

Not surprisingly for a region which hosts around three million tourists per year and a third of all overseas visitors to Croatia, there is certainly no shortage of places to stay in Istria. These range from humble bed and breakfasts to luxurious five-star hotels, and from small boutique establishments to earthy farmhouse accommodation, and campsites beside the clear blue waters of the Adriatic.

Stays of fewer than three nights, especially in private rooms and apartments, will usually incur a surcharge of 30%, and many rooms and apartments are only available on a weekly basis during high season.

Accommodation in Croatia carries a small (around €1, that's per stay, not per night) **tourist tax**, which is usually not included in the price of a room but is added onto your bill at the end. It may sound obvious but if you're travelling in the peak months of July and August, many places will be fully booked, so make sure you book in advance at this time of year. **Registration** with the Croatian police (see *Visas and red tape*, page 22) – a compulsory and frankly annoying legacy of the former Yugoslavia which is very much at odds with Croatia's bid to attract more visitors – will be carried out automatically by your hotel, private accommodation or campsite.

HOTELS Istria offers a range of hotels to suit most tastes and budgets, including new headliners such as the exceptionally swish Hotel Lone near Rovinj, as well as older though still charming Secessionist buildings in Opatija and Rijeka, oozing Austro-Hungarian opulence. If it's something more along the lines of a resort you're after, the large complexes at Rabac, Medulin and elsewhere will more than suffice. Many (though still not all) of the large and less inspiring hotel complexes built during the 1970s are now receiving a much-needed facelift, while an increasing number of small, boutique hotels such as Hotel Kaštel in Motovun and the newly opened Vela Vrata in Buzet can be counted among the nicest places you could hope to stay anywhere in Croatia.

Hotel **prices** tend to be comparatively high by Croatian standards, particularly in the high season (August), though dropping slightly in the mid (July) and shoulder (June and September) seasons. Prices drop considerably during the low season and winter, with many places offering large **discounts**, sometimes up to 50%. Online booking, where available, will frequently net you special deals well below the standard rates, especially off-season. Hotels usually include **breakfast** (*doručak*) in the cost of a room (*noćenje i doručak*), and **half board** (*polupansion*) is often available for very little additional cost (as little as €6). Some have exceptionally nice **spa** and wellness centres (eg: the Hotel Kaštel in Motovun). Many hotels close over the winter (November to March), in particular some of the large resorts.

PRIVATE ACCOMMODATION Private accommodation – either rooms (*sobe*) or apartments (*apartman*) – is the most common forms of accommodation (*smještaj*) in Croatia. It is popular with Croatians (who typically book an apartment *na more* – by the sea – for one or two weeks during the summer) as well as foreign visitors, and is usually quite a bit cheaper than hotels. Expect to pay around €40–60 per night for a double room on the coast in high season, €60–70 for an apartment, around €10 less in shoulder seasons. Weekly bookings usually run from Saturday to Friday (which adds a corresponding increase in traffic to, and from, the coast on those days respectively).

Rooms and apartments can be booked through local tourist offices and travel agencies, as well as websites such as www.apartmanija.hr. People offering rooms (both licensed and unlicensed) often congregate at bus and train stations. If you haven't already booked something and you're offered a room on the spot, it's better

ACCOMMODATION PRICE CODES

Based on a double room per night.

Exclusive	$$$$$	€150+	1,120kn+
Upmarket	$$$$	€90–150	670–1,120kn
Mid range	$$$	€60–90	450–670kn
Budget	$$	€40–60	300–450kn
Shoestring	$	up to €40	up to 300kn

to establish the price, and exactly where it is (some places might be located quite a way from the old town, beach or tourist attractions that you've come here to see), before you go trudging off with the owner and your bags.

AGRITOURISM Recent years have witnessed a notable and very welcome increase in agritourism or village tourism (*seoski turizam*) in Istria, and in Croatia as a whole. Staying in a traditional old stone home, you will often get to see a much more genuine slice of Istrian life than in a hotel or resort on the coast, and enjoy home-cooked food (often including homemade wine and cheese, and home-cured *pršut*). Some farms offer horseriding (eg: Ranch Goli Vrh, near Umag; see page 97) or other activities.

CAMPING Camping is enormously popular in Croatia, and Istria is no exception. Campsites are usually large and very well serviced, with electricity, showers, kitchens, barbecue areas and all manner of other conveniences, and cater either to motorhomes and caravans or tents, or both. Many of those by the coast have their own beaches. Wild camping, on the beach or elsewhere, is prohibited in Croatia.

Istria is also well known for its **naturist** (nudist) campsites, including the largest in Croatia (and purportedly the largest in Europe) near Vrsar on the northwest coast. Naturist campsites generally have their own beach, though sometimes a naturist campsite is combined with a non-naturist beach, or vice versa. To avoid confusion, non-naturist campsites are often described as 'textile'.

For more information on camping in Croatia, see www.camping.hr.

EATING AND DRINKING

FOOD Breakfast for many people in Istria is a fairly light affair and might just include fruit and yoghurt, and perhaps bread, cheese and ham – though hotels usually offer a more substantial buffet-style continental or cooked breakfast. Otherwise, buying a pastry from a bakery and sitting outside a café to eat it while you drink your coffee is quite acceptable (providing the café doesn't serve food). For most people, **lunch** is the main meal of the day, often starting with soup of some kind or another (most traditionally, *maneštra*; see below), followed by meat or fish, with homemade pasta possibly being served in between this and the soup, or replacing the main course. **Dinner** is again lighter, at least when eating at home.

The words *restoran* and *konoba* are both used to describe places you can eat out in Istria. A *konoba* is usually the slightly more homely of the two – though that in no way implies the food is inferior (in fact, many of the best restaurants I know in Istria are in fact *konobas*).

A quintessential Istrian recipe is **maneštra**, a thick, delicious **soup**. There are several versions; one of the best known is made with potatoes, fresh or ground

RESTAURANT PRICE CODES

Based on the average price of a main course.

Expensive	$$$$$	€20+	150kn+
Above average	$$$$	€14–20	90–150kn
Mid range	$$$	€7–14	50–90kn
Cheap and cheerful	$$	€4–7	30–50kn
Rock bottom	$	up to €4	up to 30kn

corn, beans, chickpeas, fennel and cabbage, and sometimes *špek* (bacon) – simple, filling and delicious.

Seafood is very popular, especially along the coast, with freshly caught gilthead bream and monkfish jostling for position on the menu with shellfish from the Limski kanal, lobster, baked octopus and risotto with king prawns.

Meat is as popular in Istria as it is elsewhere in Croatia, from the proverbial *roštilj* (mixed grill) to tender beef carpaccio. The ***boškarin*** or native Istrian ox is considered a great delicacy. **Game** (*divljač*) is often found on the menu in Istria, either venison (*crnetina*) or wild boar (*vepar*), the latter being fairly widespread on the Ćićarija Mountains, where it is hunted. *Fuži* (a traditional type of Istrian pasta) with a sauce of wild game (*fuži sa šugom od divljači*) is fantastically rich and highly recommended. Istria is also renowned for its excellent *pršut* (dry-cured ham, similar to Italian prosciutto), especially that produced around the viallge of Tinjan (see box page 121).

Vegetarians may find Istria slightly easier to travel in than some other parts of Croatia, with plenty of pasta and truffle dishes to choose from – although here, as elsewhere in Croatia, fish, sausages or even turkey might not be considered 'meat' by some. Say *Ja sam vegetarijanac* (*Ja sam vegetarijanka* if you're a woman) – 'I'm a vegetarian' – or *Imate li nešto bez mesa?* ('Do you have something without meat?'). **Fruit** and **vegetables** are plentiful, from wild asparagus (in season during spring) to corn, figs, chestnuts and cherries.

Pasta is an important part of Istrian cuisine, with several distinct local homemade varieties, the best-known of which is *fuži*. **Pizza** is another favourite, thin-based and delicious, and extremely good value. **Polenta** (*palenta*) is a traditional Istrian staple – and then there are the truffles (*tartufi*) for which Istria is justifiably famous (see box, *Tartufi*, page 38).

Traditional Istrian **cakes** and deserts include *fritule* (small, doughnut-like pastry balls), *kroštule* (fried sweet pastry ribbons, dusted with icing sugar) and *pinca* (a traditional sweet Easter roll). **Ice cream** (*sladoled*) is available in myriad different flavours and is almost always excellent.

Snacks include various sandwiches and sliced pizza ('*pizza cut*', vastly inferior to the real thing), and **burek**, a very tasty cheese-filled pastry, available from some bakeries (usually in the morning) and particularly around markets. Also around markets, bus and train stations you are likely to find places serving *ćevapčići*, small grilled meatballs, although they may be less easy to come across than elsewhere in Croatia.

DRINKS Istria produces some exceptionally good **wine** (see box below), some of which might be counted among the best in Croatia.

A traditional Istrian drink is ***supa***, red wine (usually Teran) heated with olive oil, sugar and pepper, and served in a *bukaleta* (traditional pottery jug) with slices of toasted bread on top.

Istria's local brand of **beer** (*pivo*) is Favorit, which is brewed on the outskirts of Buzet. Other Croatian beers include Ožujsko and Karlovačko. Local beers are cheap, whether on tap (*točeno*) or bottled, though imported beers cost more.

Rakija, a potent local spirit, comes in several guises including *loza* (made with grapes, and similar to grappa), *šlivovica* (made with plums) and the deceptively easy-to-drink *medovača* (*rakija* with a smidgen of honey to take the edge off).

Homemade **lemonade** (*limunada*) is available in many cafés, and traditionally comes in a tall glass with a spoon and a sachet of sugar to add to your own taste. **Fruit juices** are widely available – unless you have a particularly sweet tooth, try

Malvazija Classic (oak-aged for 9 months), & a robust Teran (barrique-aged for 12 months), the 2006 vintage of which won best *zreli* (aged) Teran at Vinistra 2010. Tastings available.
Benvenuti Kaldir 7, Motovun; 052 691 322; e info@benvenutivina.com; www.benvenutivina. com. Livio, Albert & Nikola Benvenuti's Malvazija has been awarded a string of gold medals in the 'young Malvazija' category at Vinistra. They also produce a Malvazija aged in oak for 2 years, & an award-winning Teran & Muscat.
Dešković Kostanjica 58, Grožnjan; 052 776 315; m 098 1977 985; e info@vina-deskovic.hr; www.vina-deskovic.hr. The 2009 Teran took the Vinistra award for the best aged Teran in 2012. Tastings available.
Kozlović Vale 78, Momjan; 052 779 177; m 099 2779 177; e info@kozlovic.hr; www.kozlovic. hr. Their 2009 Santa Lucia Malvazija, oak-aged for 18 months, took the award for best *zrela* (aged) Malvazija at the 2012 Vinistra.
Roxanich Kosinožići, Nova Vas; m 091 617 0700; e info@roxanich.hr; www.roxanich.hr. Mladen Roxianich produces some superb wines using natural & ecological methods of viticulture, & has won a whole slew of awards for his wines. His Merlot is exceptionally good, & his Teran Ré (2006) is one of the best reds you are likely to find anywhere in Istria – & frankly knocks the socks of any Croatian red I've ever had the pleasure of tasting.
Tomaz Kanal 36, Motovun; 052 681 717; m 098 335 769; www.vina-tomaz.hr. Wines include a Malvazija Avangarde (the 2011 vintage took the award for best young Malvazija at Vinistra 2011), & a Teran Barbarosa, aged in oak for 12 months. Tastings available.
Trapan Veruda 10, Pula; m 098 244 457; e info@trapan.hr; http://trapan.hr. Bruno Trapan's wines include a Malvazija Potente & Malvazija Uroborus, the latter (which in an innovative twist is aged in acacia barrels) taking best aged Malvazija at Vinistra 2010.

No visit to Istria would be complete without sampling the truffles, or *tartufi*, for which the deciduous woodlands of the Istrian interior (and in particular, the area between Buzet, Motovun and Oprtalj) are famed. You'll find *tartufi* on the menu in most parts of Istria – in pasta sauces, infusing local cheeses, shaved over the top of steaks, even in ice cream (which is actually much tastier than it might sound) – and they are generally cheaper here than their counterparts in Italy and France (indeed, plenty of Italians come to Istria to eat, or buy, truffles).

Truffles are tubers which grow among, and in symbiosis with, the roots of oak, hazel and beech trees, about 10–15cm beneath the surface. They are invisible from above ground, but when ripe can be sniffed out by specially trained dogs. The largest, most intensely flavoured (and also the most highly priced) variety are white truffles (*Tuber magnatum*), the 'white gold' of Istrian woodlands which sell, depending on size and quality, for around €800 per kilo for small ones or, for larger ones over 120g, over €2,000 per kilo. Black or 'summer' truffles (*Tuber aestivium*) are smaller, but still sell for around €600 per kilo. The white truffle season lasts from September to January, while black truffles can be gathered throughout the year.

In November 1999, **Giancarlo Zigante** and his dog Diana discovered what was at that time the largest white truffle ever recorded, near Buje. Weighing 1.31kg and measuring nearly 20cm in diameter, it gained a place in the *Guinness Book of Records* (though since then an even larger one has been discovered in Italy, weighing 1.5kg). Instead of selling his 'Millennium' truffle, as it came to be known, Zigante used it to prepare an elaborate banquet for 100 carefully selected guests. He now sits at the centre of what might be described as a small empire as far as truffles are concerned, with shops all over Istria and beyond (www.zigantetartufi.com), and a highly regarded restaurant in Livade (www.restaurantzigante.com; see *Where to eat on* page 126).

Karlić tartufi in the village of Paladini, near Buzet (*Paladini 4;* 052 667 304; m *091 575 9196; www.karlictartufi.hr*), can take visitors out on truffle hunts in their local woods, after which they'll make an omelette with fresh truffles. They also sell some excellent cheese and sausages infused with truffles. See page 40 for truffle festivals.

to get one without added sugar (*bez dodanog šećera*). The **coffee** in Istria is almost always excellent, and you'll never be far away from a café with tables spilling out onto the street, or a pleasant terrace, perhaps overlooking the sea or in the shade of ancient chestnut trees.

There are plenty of **wine roads** in Istria, usually well signposted as *vinska cesta* (though in Istria a wine road doesn't necessarily imply that there are numerous wineries on that particular route, perhaps only one or two). For more information on some of the wine roads in Istria see www.istra.com/vino.

PUBLIC HOLIDAYS AND FESTIVALS

PUBLIC HOLIDAYS On these days, expect banks and most shops to be closed. Public transport will operate to a reduced Sunday timetable, or not at all.

National holidays

1 January	New Year's Day
6 January	Epiphany
Easter Sunday & Easter Monday	31 March & 1 April 2013, 20 & 21 April 2014, 5 & 6 April 2015
1 May	Labour Day
Corpus Christi	60 days after Easter Sunday
22 June	Day of Antifascist Struggle
25 June	Statehood Day
5 August	Victory and Homeland Thanksgiving Day and the Day of Croatian Defenders
15 August	Assumption of the Virgin Mary
8 October	Independence Day
1 November	All Saints' Day
25 and 26 December	Christmas

FESTIVALS

February The **Rijeka Carnival** (*www.ri-karneval.com.hr*) is the second-largest carnival in Europe, and should be considered unmissable if you're here in February (see *Rijeka Carnival*, page 142).

April Lovran's two-week **Asparagus Festival**, held in mid-April during the wild asparagus season, sees all manner of asparagus dishes on the menu at local restaurants, and culminates in the preparation of a giant omelette in the town's main square, made with 30kg of wild asparagus (see *Lovran*, page 105).

May The village of Roč holds an **Accordion Festival** in mid-May (Z armoniku v Roč, International Meeting of Diatonic Accordion Players) (see *Chapter 7*, page 133).

June Pazin's lively **TradInEtno Festival** sees traditional and folk musicians from Croatia and across Europe arriving to perform in the castle and on the street (see *Pazin*, page 117).

Lovran's **Cherry Festival**, which takes place in the second week of June, celebrates (as you might have guessed) the delicious cherries which grow in the area (they were probably introduced around 100 years ago), and culminates in the preparation of a giant cherry strudel (see *Lovran*, page 105).

In mid–June, Pazin's **Jules Verne Days** (*www.julesvernedays.com*), which has been running since 1998 to celebrate the connection between the town and Jules Verne's 1888 novel *Mathius Sandorf*, sees balloon and helicopter flights, theatre performances and even a treasure hunt for kids (see *Pazin*, page 117).

For more on Rovinj's **Bijelilav Underwater Film Festival** (*www.bijelilav.org*), see *Chapter 12*, page 190

Istra Inspirit (*www.istrainspirit.hr*) sees a series of events taking place across Istria from late June to early September, celebrating the history, myths and legends (and of course, cuisine) of the region.

July The **Pula International Film Festival** (*www.pulafilmfestival.hr*) is Croatia's largest film festival and runs for two weeks, with screenings of Croatian and international films in the amphitheatre and elsewhere in town. The festival has been running since 1953, making it one of the world's oldest (see page 60).

The **Motovun Film Festival** (*www.motovunfilmfestival.com*) only kicked off in 1999, but is now enormously popular. The festival runs for five days, and showcases mainly small budget films and World Cinema (see page 125).

The **Istra Open** (*www.buzet.tici.hr*) is Croatia's top paragliding championship, and takes place at Raspadalica, a cliff just east of Buzet (see *Festivals*, page 131).

The **International Jazz Festival** (*www.jazzisbackbp.com*) in Grožnjan has been voted among the world's best boutique jazz festivals (see page 127).

The **Svetvinčenat Festival** (*www.svetvincenatfestival.com*) sees open-air performances of dance and theatre within the impressive castle of this beautiful little town (see page 122).

Seasplash (*www.seasplash-festival.com*) is a huge drum'n'bass, dub, reggae and electronic music festival, and kicks off in Pula's Fort Punta Christo (see *Festivals*, page 59) in July.

August The annual **Tilting at the Ring** (Trka na prstenac) in Barban, first held back in 1696, sees horsemen charging about and competing to spear a large ring (see *Barban*, page 110).

Velika Gospa or **Assumption Day** (15 August) is one of the most important feast days in Croatia's religious calendar. Expect celebrations of some kind or another wherever you are.

Opatija's excellent **Liburnia Jazz Festival** (*www.liburniajazz.hr*) takes place on the first weekend of August, with concerts all over town (see *Opatija*, page 101).

Pula's **Outlook Festival** (*www.outlookfestival.com*) at Fort Punta Christo is now Europe's largest bass music and sound-system culture event, and takes place over the last weekend of August/first weekend of September.

Labin's **Art Republika** (*www.labin-art-republika.com*) runs through July and August, with theatre, music and dance performances taking place all over town (see *Labin*, page 108).

September One of Istria's most colourful festivals is the **Subotina**, held in Buzet on the second weekend of September. Expect traditional and period costumes, music, and stalls selling local handicrafts and produce. On the previous night, to celebrate the opening of the truffle season, a giant omelette is prepared in the lower town from over 2,000 eggs and 10kg of truffles. And of course, you get to eat it, too (see box, *Tartufi*, on page 38).

Giostra, the medieval re-enactment festival held in Poreč, is also gaining in popularity. Here you can see jousting on horseback along the seafront, colourful period dress, and the usual offer of great Istrian food (see *Festivals*, page 91).

Grožnjan's festival of the arts, **Extempore**, also takes place in September (see *National holidays*, page 39).

October Pršut Festival, Tinjan. Istria produces some of the finest *pršut* (air-cured ham) anywhere in Croatia, and the best of it comes from the area around Tinjan, which celebrates its pre-eminence with a festival on the first weekend in October (see box, *Pršut*, page 121).

The **Chestnut Festival** (Marunada) is Lovran's biggest festival, and has been running since 1973. Expect limitless cakes, pastries and other dishes, all prominently featuring chestnuts of course, to be available throughout the town. There's also local folk music and other entertainment (see *Lovran*, page 101).

The tiny settlement (technically a town, and loudly proclaimed to be the smallest town in the world) of Hum holds a **Rakija Festival** in October (see on page 134).

November Buzet's **Truffle Festival** or 'Weekend of Truffles' takes place on the first weekend in November, and is the biggest truffle-related event in the region (see box, *Tartufi*, on page 38).

Sv Martinje Festival celebrates the patron saint of Vrsar (see page 99) on 11 November – it's when locals taste the first of their wine harvest, and you'll find up on their big square one of the biggest fish festivals of winter.

Sv Mauro Festival in Poreč (see *Festivals*, page 91) complete with brass bands and chamber music starts on 21 November, and is definitely worth a visit if you're in the region.

December Mid-December is the time to see, or take part in, the **Parenzana** bike tour (*www.parenzana.com*; see *Biking*, page 180). There are also many Christmas markets throughout Istria's towns, one of the best being in Sv Lovreč, near Poreč, where the whole of the old town turns into a Bethlehem scene. Drinks and snacks are free!

SHOPPING

There are plenty of large supermarkets (Konzum, Diona, etc) and chemists (DM etc) in Istria where you can buy whatever you need for a self-catering holiday, or things you may have forgotten to bring from home. You'll also find no shortage of clothes (and shoe) shops, including plenty of designer labels – though don't expect prices to be any cheaper than at home.

OPENING HOURS Shops are generally open 08.00–20.00 Monday–Friday, with supermarkets (especially larger ones) often open longer hours (07.00–21.00), and a number of shops including bakeries as well as cafés open from 06.00 or 06.30. On Saturday supermarkets keep the same hours as during the week, but other shops may close earlier. On Sunday supermarkets open 08.00–15.00 or similar; a few shops may be open on Sundays in larger towns, but most will be closed. The exception to this rule is large shopping malls (Tower Centre in Rijeka etc), which open late on Sundays as well. During the week and on Saturday smaller shops and those in smaller towns and villages may also close for an hour or two at lunchtime. Markets are usually open from early (07.00) and are at their busiest before lunchtime, with some closing (or at least partly closing) by 14.00.

See *Public holidays and festivals*, page 38 for a list of public and bank holidays in Croatia, when you can expect to find most shops closed.

SOUVENIRS OF ISTRIA When it comes to buying typical Istrian products to take home, you won't be short of choice. Istrian wine, olive oil, *pršut*, spirits, truffle paste, honey, lavender and other products can be bought in various boutique shops in most major towns in Istria – **Aura** is one example, with several branches including Buzet and Hum, and **Zigante** has branches of its truffle shops seemingly around every corner. **Hafne** wine bar in Pula is a great place to try Istrian wine before buying a bottle or two.

You can also buy wine and olive oil direct from many producers, although this may not be possible during harvest (*berba* – September for grapes, mid-October for olives). These include **Franc Arman wines** (*Narduči 5, Vižinada;* ✎ *052 446 226;* m *091 446 2266;* e *info@francarman.hr; www.francarman.hr*), where the Malvazija and Teran are very good, and the Malvazija Classic (oak-aged for two years) heavenly; and **Ipša olive oil** (*Ipši 10, Livade;* ✎ *052 664 010;* m *098 219 538;*

e *klaudio.ipsa@pu.t-com.hr; www.ipsa-maslinovaulja.hr*), where you can buy four types of homemade olive oil including an outstanding blend from several olive varieties.

There are many small shops selling local handmade **jewellery**, including Venetian (murano) glass, and local art. A *bukaleta*, the distinctive painted pottery jug which wine is often served in, makes a good souvenir. Traditional handmade baskets can be bought on markets and at festivals such as the Subotina in Buzet.

ARTS AND ENTERTAINMENT

It can be hard on first arriving in Istria to see beyond the tourist kitsch and the budding modern art, which is popular in the region. However, Istria's primary cultural claim has to be its musical heritage. The Istrian scale is a unique musical scale, made up of six non-equal tempered tones and half-tones, and is inscribed in the UNESCO list of intangible cultural heritage (for more, see www.unesco.org/culture/ich/index.php?RL=00231). It is most prevalent in Istrian and Kvarner folk music, and may have been experimented with by Tartini (see page 158), and Haydn in his *String Quartet in F minor, Op 20 No 5*. The scale was first noted by the Istrian composer Ivan Matetić Ronjgov at the beginning of the 20th century, and as a result of fathoming the scale he was able to document local folk songs and compose new works based on the scale.

The townsfolk of Rovinj are also known for their *bitinada* and *aria da nuoto* (night aria). The *bitinada* is a choral vocal accompaniment to a soloist, whereby the choir or *bitinaduri* imitate string instruments by repeating onomatopoeic phrases in a waltz-like manner. You can learn more at www.bitinade.eu and hear a *bitinada* live during the many summer performances in Rovinj. The *aria da nuoto* were song phrases echoed from boat to boat at night. Both forms use improvisation and are now very much a part of Croatia's cultural heritage.

Music schools are many in Istria, and the town of Grožnjan itself (see *Chapter 7*, page 127) becomes a summer school every year. Musical concerts abound, often held outdoors in the summer, or in the many medieval churches or town squares. Attending a concert in Pula's Roman amphitheatre is not to be missed. Jazz festivals are also popular (see *Music and dance*, page 17).

OUTDOOR PURSUITS

HIKING Istria is a lovely area for hiking, from the high peaks of the Učka and Ćićarija mountains in the northeast, to easy walks around hill towns, and balmy coastal walks such as Rt Kamenjak and the Opatija Riviera. See *Chapter 10* for more details of hiking in Istria and a selection of hiking routes.

CLIMBING Istria has some fine areas for climbing, in particular **Vranjska draga** (also known as Vela draga), a small canyon near the inland entrance to the Učka tunnel, with sheer walls and slender rock pinnacles offering some fiendishly difficult routes graded up to 7b+. Spring and autumn are the best times of year to climb here – August may be a little too hot – and winter routes are also possible (though you'll want to avoid climbing when the *bura* is blowing). Other good climbing spots include the cliffs at Raspadalica near Buzet, and a crag near the ruins of Dvigrad. Routes on sea cliffs include the walls of the Limski kanal, and Zlatni rt near Rovinj.

CYCLING Istria is the best area for cycling in Croatia, with comparatively little traffic in inland areas, a wealth of information (including detailed route maps and descriptions) available online at www.bike-istria.com, and at least one route, the excellent Parenzana (*www.parenzana.net*), which now has an international reputation. See *Chapter 11* for more details of cycling in Istria and a selection of routes.

PARAGLIDING Istria's best area for paragliding is in the northeast, on the inland slopes of the Ćićarija Mountains, especially the area above Gornja Nugla just east of Buzet. Gornja Nugla is home to a large paragliding festival in July. See www.istra. hr for a list of take-off sites in northeast Istria.

CANOEING AND KAYAKING There is little scope for canoeing in Istria itself (the largest lake in Istria, Butoniga jezero, is a drinking-water reservoir so is off-limits). However the Limski kanal is a good spot for canoeing and sea kayaking (for canoe tours contact the Buzet-based agency Gral Putovanje; see *What to see and do*, page 132).

WINDSURFING The best spot for windsurfing in Istria is Premantura in the south which, given its position at the tip of the Istrian Peninsula, is more or less guaranteed good winds. For further information, see www.windsurfing.hr.

PHOTOGRAPHY

Istria is a highly photogenic part of the world and abounds in subjects to point a camera at, from gorgeous architecture to bustling markets, stunning coastline and colourful festivals.

Nevertheless, however beautiful a scene might be, lighting conditions will make a huge difference to whether a photo captures something of that beauty. You can't control the weather of course, but you can choose to return at a better time of day for photography if necessary. In general, the harsh sun in the middle of the day and early afternoon will produce flat, rather lifeless images – the best times of day to shoot are early in the morning and in the late afternoon/early evening – the golden hour, as it's sometimes called. Using a circular polarizer can be helpful in bright sunshine, particularly on the coast, to reduce reflections on water and other surfaces, and darken and add contrast to skies (but take it off in less bright conditions since it reduces the 'speed' of your lens by a couple of stops).

Some people, particularly in rural areas (and including market stalls in major towns), may be reluctant to have their photo taken, and in general when photographing people – unless it's a candid shot from across the road or similar – it's always preferable to seek permission first. Ask *Mogu li slikati?* ('Can I take a photo?') or *Smeta li vam ako slikam?* ('Does it bother you if I take a photo?'). Of course they might decline, but if you can engage someone a little in conversation the chances are you'll end up with a much more intimate and compelling portrait than you would snapping something quickly halfway behind their back. Having said that, I've generally found people in Istria to be much less bothered about having their photo taken than in some other parts of Croatia.

The freedom of the open sea beckons. Whether you are a weathered sea dog or a novice swabbie, there is an unmatched serenity in wind-powered motion – gliding over the blue mirror that is the Adriatic. Coasting along the Istrian Peninsula seaside, one can explore inlets and the Limski kanal (complete with pirate's cave; see *Limski kanal*, page 96), as well as the incomparable towns – peninsulas in their own right – of Pula, Rovinj, Poreč and Novigrad. Or simply enjoy some sunshine, lounging on deck with a *gemišt*. Sailing brings out some of the best Istria has to offer.

WHEN TO GO Sailing is year-round in Istria, but the best times are spring and autumn (early May and mid-October). April, May and October have the best wind conditions for the real yachtsman, while the remaining months, with gentler breezes, are better for learning or for a relaxing family cruise.

WHO CAN SAIL As in the rest of Croatia, sailing in Istria offers something for everyone. From sailing lessons at all levels, to boat rentals for licensed captains (known as 'bareboat'), and chartered boats that include a captain (particularly helpful if you're not good at manoeuvring large floating objects into small spaces). For those who like being driven and served, a captain with crew are available. Most charters offer a diving option.

FOR BEGINNERS The larger coastal cities in Istria have sailing clubs where would-be captains can learn the ropes, literally. A list of sailing clubs in Istria is at *Appendix 3*. Special courses are offered on a weekly basis for kids aged seven to 14, and are very reasonably priced. Adults should check at the marina for courses. In Poreč the marina (e *marina-porec@pu.tel.hr*) offers a weekly course which, after six days on a boat and four hours of theory, offers students the opportunity to sit the *A Category* test (€460 for the course, plus another €50–70 for expenses). Ask for the *Škola Jedrenja*.

CHARTERING Hiring a boat (chartering) comes in many forms. You can hire a boat and a crew, the boat only (bareboat) or just get a cabin. Then there are the myriad types of boat: sailing yachts, catamarans, motorised yachts, and *gulets* (largish, crewed wooden boats with several cabins – usually taking groups). After the type, boats are usually classified by their length in metres. A four-berth motor-yacht (eg: a Bavaria 27 – 27, referring to the length of the boat in feet) can cost up to €3,500 per week (bareboat) in the high season. In addition, a skipper can cost €1,050 per week, or €130 per day, and a crew €100 per person per day, for whom you will need to provide food and drink and a berth on the boat or onshore. Similarly, a four-berth sailing yacht (eg: a Bavaria 33; 10.5m) costs about €1,800 for a week during the high season, and about €1,400 the rest of the year. A luxurious catamaran runs to about €4,500 per week. For each of these you will have to leave a deposit of €1,000–1,500.

Istria Yachting S Rajka 38, 52440 Poreč; 023 25 877; m 098 771 718; e info@istra-yachting.com; www.istra-yachting.com. Istria Yachting offers a full range of boat rentals & associated services. Most of their Istria-based boats are moored at Tehnomont Marina near Pula.
Pinizel Tours Ščavonija 42a, 52470 Umag; 052 732 265; m 091 250 3329; e pinizel-tours@vip.hr; www.yachtfinsa.com/engl-index.html. Based in Umag, Pinizel operates a 21m Finsa motorised yacht with captain & crew/chef. It sleeps 8 guests in 4 cabins with a separate space for the crew. The high-season price of €7,400 gets you the fully equipped boat & crew for a week, necessary

insurance, fuel for 4hrs of sailing per day, taxes & mooring fees, a dinghy, water skis, a kayak, fishing equipment, linen & final cleaning. Although food is not included, you can add a half-board option for another €190 per week (kids under 6 eat free, while older ones get 30–50% off, depending on their age). Pinizel will also arrange day trips & onshore excursions.

Croatian Yachting Lindengasse 24/18; 1070 Vienna, Austria; ☏ +43 1 956 17 08; e see website contact form; www.croatianyachting.com

Sail Croatia 2 The Carriages, Barley Mow Rd, Englefield Green, TW20 0NX, UK; ☏ +44 845 257 8289; www.sail-croatia.com/index.php/traditional-cruises. Offers larger group cruises on larger boats, including one that leaves from Opatija.

MOORING For those with their own boat sailing into Istria, you can rent a berth in any of the peninsula's public marinas – and there are dozens of them, at least one in each city. Fees are set annually and vary from marina to marina. They also relate to the size of your boat's beam and its length (size matters) – or at least the space along the pier your boat occupies. For example, in Vrsar Marina in 2012, a 10m boat that's under 4m wide cost about €45 per day to moor in the port – add 10% during the high season. Monthly berths cost roughly €500 during the high season, about €400 the rest of the year. The same boat can be stored on land throughout the year for about €200 per month. During July and August it's a good idea to phone ahead and reserve a berth. If you get caught out, dropping anchor for the night out in a bay is usually free, but some harbours might charge you a fee for an extended stay, although the fee should include some service such as rubbish collection (get a receipt). Marinas in Croatia are open year-round, but the fuel depots might only work mornings in the winter. Water and electricity are available in all marinas. They all also have at least basic repair services and most have a crane and offer winter drydocking. The larger marinas also offer cleaning and maintenance services year-round. The contact details of Istria's marinas and details of their facilities are listed in *Appendix 3*.

REGULATIONS Croatian sailing regulations are not unlike those elsewhere. The law requires at least one person on the boat to be a licensed skipper – which means both a navigational and a VHF licence. There must also be an accurate 'crew list' on board, and any changes must be recorded and a new list issued. Speciality activities like diving or fishing require their own licences.

WHAT TO BRING For those unfamiliar with sailing, if you do decide on a sailing holiday, bear in mind that the cabins are not large. You will want to bring the minimum, but there are a few essentials: don't bring hard suitcases, but rather cloth or canvas (foldable) bags which can be more easily stored in tight spaces. Clothing should include waterproof outerwear, with long sleeves a must. You'll also want a jumper or other warm outerwear for the evenings – as the breeze off the water at night can be chilly even after the hottest of days. Otherwise, light cotton items are good, some short- and long-sleeved shirts, shorts or trousers. Think carefully about your footwear. You want waterproof, protective sandals or deckshoes – especially good is footwear that can be used on board, in the water and on the rocky shores. Don't forget a good hat (with a strap!), your sunscreen and lip balm. You may also want to bring beach towels and/or a mat, your snorkelling gear and extra batteries for all your electronics. A small torch and a deck of cards are also helpful.

MEDIA Istria has its own television station, TV Istra (*www.tvistra.hr*), several local radio stations (which also broadcast partly in Italian), and its own newspaper *Glas Istre* (*www.glasistre.hr*), which gives all the local ins and outs of what's going on among the few big players who control the region's business.

A fascinating website called Istarske novine online (*www.ino.com.hr*) is putting all of the newspapers ever published in Istria online for all to read. Starting from as early as 1850 and going to as late as 1938, the range of newspapers published in Istria cover Croatian, Italian, German and Slovenian.

THINKING OF BUYING A HOUSE IN ISTRIA?

Many who come to Istria think of one day owning their own *hiža* (old stone farmhouse), or a seaside apartment, or a new villa with a pool. Hundreds, if not thousands, of foreigners have already taken the plunge. And with Croatia set to join the EU in 2013, the process will be getting easier. Foreigners have only been able to buy private property in Croatia since about 2000 and not all of the kinks in the system have been worked out. Still, finding and buying the right property can be incredibly gratifying, and perhaps even lucrative.

FINDING THE RIGHT PROPERTY Property agents are plentiful around Istria – easily recognisable by their faded photos and computer-generated images of soon-to-be-built villas in the glass case outside. *Nekretnine* signs (literally 'immovables') are also a giveaway. Most agents will have at least one member of staff who speaks English, so don't hesitate to go in and have a chat about what you're looking for. And don't dream of buying without an agent, as the process is filled with obstacles for the unsuspecting (ie: foreign) purchaser. Typically an agent will charge 3–4% of the purchase price.

THE PURCHASE Appraisals are not obligatory in Croatia, but are still a good idea. Expect to pay in the region of €250. On the other hand, a lawyer or solicitor is obligatory. (You will be able to find an English-speaking one at *http://ukincroatia.fco.gov.uk/en/help-for-british-nationals*.) They charge around €1,000 for the full process. Their job is to ensure your property has clear title – meaning there are no encumbrances or faulty deeds in its history that have not been properly rectified. Also, be aware that at least until Croatia joins the EU, UK and most other foreigners need permission from the Ministry of Foreign Affairs in order to buy. That permission can take years, but it won't stop you from taking possession of your new home in the meantime, and getting your money back if for any reason you are rejected (almost unheard of, but language to this effect should be in the contract).

The contract is usually done in two stages, a pre-contract and a final contract. The pre-contract is often 10% of the value of the property, and upon payment serves to hold the property for the buyer exclusively. A failure to complete the purchase normally results in losing that deposit. After all the paperwork is in order, the purchaser and seller both sign a final contract in front of a notary. The transaction is recorded at the cadastre office. Once you've transferred the money, you should get the keys. Oh, and you'll have to pay about 5% in sales tax. You'll also need a Croatian *kuna* currency bank account, homeowner's insurance

German and Italian newspapers are still very easy to get in Istria, but English ones are more difficult. If anything in English is on offer, it's usually the *Daily Mail*, and very occasionally you might get the *International Herald Tribune*. *The Economist* is a little easier to get hold of. You best bets for finding English-language newspapers and magazines in Istria are Algoritam (*www.algoritam.hr*), which has a branch in Pula, and Profil (*www.profil-mozaik.hr*), which has branches in Pula and Rijeka.

POST The postal system is improving in Croatia, and whilst not superfast, mail between Istria and the rest of Europe usually takes one week (postcards take longer). Allow two to three weeks for the rest of the world. Stamps can be bought at

(*www.devondirect.net* or *www.allianz.hr*), an OIB number (personal ID number, takes a week or so to be issued, and can be done by the bank), and phone and utility hook-ups, but your property agent will likely assist with all that (make sure to ask upfront). Alternatively, property management companies can take on these tasks for a fee, for example Solis (*www.solis-porec.com*) or Istria Property Management (*www.istriapropertymanagement.com*).

AFTER SALE Homes need looking after. Landscape, painting and general upkeep are costly; providing it from abroad is even more so. Wood and stone houses look lovely, but need more maintenance than a modern build – walls need treating to reduce debris, wooden shutters need constant varnishing, and beams need regular treating against woodworm of the house longhorn beetle. Arranging repairs can be prone to misunderstandings – whether caused by translation or by cultural differences. Be prepared to not get exactly what you wanted, and for it to take longer than promised.

If your house is in need of repair or refurbishment, make sure you get a licensed/bonded contractor. Major alterations to the house will require planning through a professional architect, and may also require planning permission (the architect will sort this out for you). Try Mauricio Matukina (*mauricio.matukina@pu.t-com.hr*) for complete house renovation – he specialises in old stone houses and fireplaces. Ensure you ask any contractor if VAT (22%) is included in the estimate. Property management companies can be helpful here to set you up with contractors and architects.

OTHER CONSIDERATIONS If you're thinking of renting your house to generate some extra income, then you should consider buying through a company rather than as a private individual. The process takes a bit longer, and while you'll have to file a company tax return (via a licensed bookkeeper – at least €1,200 per annum) and pay income tax on the rent, you'll be able to deduct many of expenses for refurbishment, repairs and maintenance. Until Croatia is in the EU, you cannot rent out your property as a private individual. One knowledgeable English-speaking company that can take care of all of this for you is Croatia Holiday and Home (*www.croatia-holidayandhome.co.uk*).

Buying your own special place under the Istrian sun can be tremendously rewarding. Who knows, in a few months you could be picking your own figs off the tree outside your bedroom window or enjoying a glass of wine lounging on the terrace looking out over the Adriatic.

Practical Information   MEDIA AND COMMUNICATIONS

2

local kiosks as well as at the post office. A postcard to Europe costs 4kn, and a letter 6kn; to Australia, New Zealand or the USA a postcard costs 8kn. A town's main post office opens 07.00–19.00 Monday–Friday and 07.00–13.00 Saturday. Sub-post offices only open until 17.00 Monday–Friday. To have post sent to you at the post office, have it addressed to you at Poste Restante, Pošta, postcode of the town and the town name, Croatia.

PHONE The international telephone code for Croatia is +385. The dial-out code from Croatia is 00 and then your country code (eg: +1 for Canada and the USA, +44 for the UK, +61 for Australia, +64 for New Zealand). Despite the dominance of mobile phones, public phones are still generally available in Istria, both outdoors and in the post office, taking coins, telephone cards and, increasingly, credit cards. Calls are cheaper in the evenings (19.00–07.00) and on Sundays than during the day on weekdays and Saturdays. Several mobile-phone operators are available in Istria, including T-Mobile, VIP and Tele 2. Tele 2 has a very good tourist package, whereby phone calls are comparatively priced with their competitors; text messages to anywhere in the world are free. It's still cheaper to use a Croatian SIM to call within Croatia than it is to use your home phone but, depending on your home phone package, it might be cheaper to use your home mobile phone to phone home. Check with your home mobile phone provider before making a call. Within Europe at least, roaming charges are fast becoming a thing of the past. Croatian SIM cards and top-up cards come in 50kn (valid for three months), 100kn (valid for six months) and 200kn (valid for one year).

Useful telephone numbers for telecommunications in Croatia are:

General information	☏981	**International operator**	☏901
Local operator	☏988	**International directory enquiries**	☏902
Long-distance operator	☏989		

TIME Croatia and Slovenia are one hour ahead of Greenwich Mean Time, six hours ahead of New York, and eight hours behind Sydney. Croatian Summer Time falls at the same time as British Summer Time.

INTERNET Istria has extensive internet coverage. You can even buy internet access anywhere with a credit card for around 40–60kn per hour. Most hotels and many restaurants offer free Wi-Fi to their guests, but many cafés still don't have Wi-Fi. With mobile Wi-Fi becoming standard, internet cafés are dying out. The few we've found are listed in each chapter.

BUSINESS

Business hours in Istria vary a lot between winter and summer, with summer hours for shops extending often until 22.00, but perhaps taking a siesta from 12.00 to 16.00. In the winter most businesses open 08.30–16.30. Government offices and utilities will be open 07.00–10.30 and 11.30–14.00.

Work culture in Istria is very much shaped by the sea. Within the tourist industry it's perfectly normal to go to a meeting in just board shorts and flip-flops. For more formal meetings, a short-sleeved shirt is acceptable and long trousers. Istrians are not particularly timely, but that's no reason to keep them waiting, of course.

With only a few exceptions (such as antique markets), bargaining is no more acceptable than in Western Europe – prices are posted and un-negotiable.

CULTURAL ETIQUETTE

Istrians are proud of their peninsula and like to see it kept clean and tidy. They are also very courteous to visitors and, for instance, will generally stop at a zebra crossing for pedestrians (not something that can be said for the whole of Croatia!), and expect the same from foreigners.

If invited to an Istrian house, you should never turn up empty-handed, but bring a small gift of food, even if it's only local biscuits or chocolates. You'll be more than reciprocated during your visit, and usually offered homemade *rakija* or coffee, which would be considered rude to turn down. If you're ever handed a plate of food or cakes to take back to your apartment, never return the plate empty, but make sure that you return it with cake or chocolates.

On the Istrian coast, skimpy dresses and bare chests are completely the norm. Some beaches are nudist (naturist, often called FKK for *Frei Körper Kultur* after the German saying), and even on the non-nudist beaches, it is not uncommon for women to be bare-bosomed. Most restaurants, except those right on the beach, will expect people to wear some sort of top when eating. Wearing swimming costumes or excessively revealing clothing will be considered unacceptable for visiting churches.

Drugs, on the other hand, are not acceptable. Whilst, of course, they can be found, the penalties for drug possession, sale or smuggling are harsh.

INTERACTING WITH LOCAL PEOPLE Istrians are very well versed in interacting with foreigners, and so you'll find them friendly and helpful, not least because tourism is the main employer in the region. In the height of the season, most Istrians will be too busy working to spend too much time with you, never mind invite you to their house.

The cosmopolitan heritage of Istria means that, compared with the rest of Croatia, you will be on much safer and more neutral ground if you want to enquire into the break-up of Yugoslavia. Otherwise, even Istrians can be quite conservative, and homosexuality, for instance, will still strike most of them as odd, although at least you won't usually get an allergic reaction.

TRAVELLING POSITIVELY

As with anywhere in the world, you should try to buy local and think global. Even within Istria, there are four or five big businesses that run almost everything,

---

EGOZERO

Egozero (*www.egozero.si*) is a new, eco-friendly Slovenian company providing battery-powered car rental and an easy to use, flexible online booking system – simply plot your route and choose accommodation, activities (such as hiking or cycling) based on possible mileage per battery charge (with the time of year, and likely battery life in corresponding temperatures, taken into account), and then book the lot in a single transaction. This all ties in neatly with a network of charging facilities, so when you wake up in the morning at your chosen hotel or pension your car is charged and ready to go. You'll even find your planned route stored on the GPS of your hire car when you collect it. Launching in parts of Slovenia (including Ljubljana and Postojna) in 2013, it is expected to extend to the coast by 2014. Brilliant idea.

making it very difficult for small businesses to thrive, provide variety and provide true competition. So the more you can do to support small family-run hotels, apartments and businesses or local guides the better, especially outside the main tourist season. Agritourism (see *Accommodation*, page 35) is one good way to ensure you are doing this.

To help or support the environment in Istria, check out **Zelena Istra (Green Istria)** (*www.zelena-istra.hr*), who run lots of campaigns and activities to educate the public, raise awareness and change behaviour for the better.

If the sea is your true love, then you might be interested in contributing towards Pula's **turtle rescue centre** (*www.aquarium.hr/eng/marine-turtle-rescue-centre*). There you can adopt a rescued turtle until it is released back into the wild, by donating to its care and rehabilitation at the centre.

Part Two

THE GUIDE

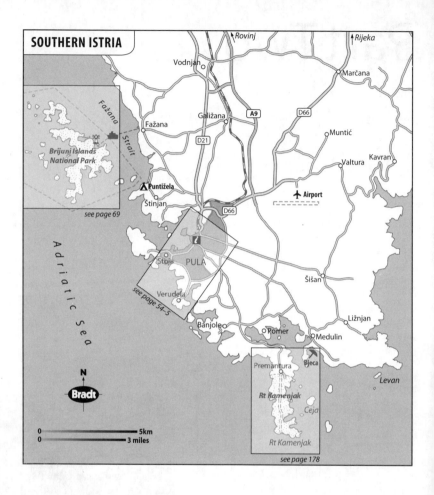

Rovinj

Rijeka

Vodnjan

Marčana

Fažana Strait

Galižana   A9   D66

Fažana

D21

Muntić

Brijuni Islands
National Park

Valtura   Kavran

Puntižela

see page 69

Štinjan

Airport   D66

A d r i a t i c   S e a

Stoja   PULA

see page 54-5   Verudela

Šišan

Banjole   Pomer

Ližnjan

Medulin

N

Bradt

Premantura   Bijeca

Levan

Rt Kamenjak

Ceja

0   5km
0   3 miles

Rt Kamenjak

see page 178

3

Pula and Southern Istria

PULA

Located towards the southern tip of the Istrian Peninsula, Pula often (quite undeservedly) receives less attention than neighbouring Rovinj and Poreč. Yet it is a thriving city, as becomes the largest urban area and economic centre of Istria, with some of the finest Roman ruins anywhere in Croatia – most spectacular among these is its huge amphitheatre, one of the six largest Roman amphitheatres to have survived anywhere in the world. There are popular beaches south of the centre at Medulin, Premantura and Stoja, cosy bars in town where you can acquaint yourself with a variety of local wines or listen to live jazz, a terrific open market, and Istria's main archaeological museum. Croatia's largest film festival is held in Pula in July.

HISTORY Legend tells that Pula was founded by Jason (he of the Golden Fleece) and the Argonauts, following their pursuit by the enraged Colchians. There was certainly an Illyrian settlement here from at least 500BC, and Roman Pula – or to give it its full title, Colonia Julia Pollentia Herculanea – was probably founded by the emperor Augustus around the middle of the 1st century BC. It rapidly grew into a flourishing commercial city, with an estimated population in its heyday of some 25,000 to 30,000 inhabitants. After being plundered by the Ostrogoths in the 5th century and sacked repeatedly during the struggle between Venice and Genoa in the 13th and 14th centuries, the population was further decimated by plague in the 17th century, when only some 300 inhabitants were left. It was converted into a major port by Austria in the 19th century, but lost its importance under Italy following World War I, and was later bombed by both the Germans and the Allies in World War II. These days Pula is Istria's main economic centre.

GETTING THERE AND AWAY

By air Pula's international airport (*Valtursko polje 210, Ližnjan;* \ *052 530 105; www.airport-pula.hr*) is around 7km northeast of the city at Valtura. Croatia Airways (*www.croatiaairlines.com*) has daily flights from Pula to London Heathrow and Gatwick via Zagreb; Ryanair (*www.ryanair.com*) has direct flights between Pula and London Stansted. Thomsonfly, German Wings, Austrian Airlines and Norwegian also all operate out of Pula. See *Getting there and away*, page 24 for more information.

Getting to and from the airport A **shuttle bus** runs between the airport and Pula's bus station, daily except Thursday, though its timetable does not always coincide particularly well with arrivals, in particular the Ryanair flight from London (unless you're extremely fast through passport control and baggage).

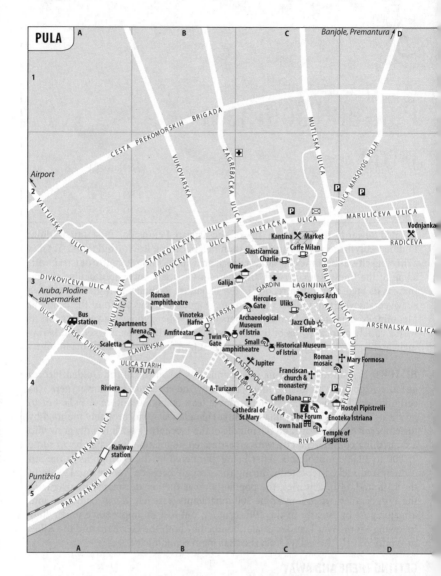

PULA

Airport

Banjole, Premantura

Aruba, Plodine supermarket

Bus station

Apartments

Arena

Scaletta

Roman amphitheatre

Vinoteka Hafne

Amfiteatar

Twin Gate

Riviera

A-Turizam

Cathedral of St Mary

Railway station

Puntižela

Galija

Omir

Slastičarnica Charlie

Kantina ✗ Market

Caffe Milan

Vodnjanka ✗

RADIĆEVA

GIARDINI

Hercules Gate

Uliks

Sergius Arch

Archaeological Museum of Istria

Jazz Club Florin

Small amphitheatre

Historical Museum of Istria

Jupiter

Franciscan church & monastery

Caffe Diana

The Forum

Town hall

Enoteka Istriana

Temple of Augustus

Roman mosaic

Mary Formosa

Hostel Pipistrelli

Buses leave from outside the arrivals area at 08.30, 09.45, 10.35, 12.15, 13.35, 14.35, 16.20, 19.30, 20.20 and 20.45 daily; and depart from Pula's bus station for the airport at 09.10 (Monday, Wednesday, Friday–Sunday), as well as 13.50 (Monday), 11.50 (Tuesday) and 18.20 (Saturday). Tickets cost 15kn. **Taxi** drivers congregate around the exit of the arrivals area, where there is also a Cammeo Taxi desk (✆ *060 700 700; www.taxi-cammeo.net*); see *Taxis*, page 33. Cammeo charge 45kn per car into the centre of Pula, slightly more to Verudela; any of the other companies are likely to charge around double that amount, or more – so it's worth booking with Cammeo in advance. **Car-rental** offices at the airport include Budget (✆ *052 218 252 or 062 300 331; www.budget.hr*) and Sixt (✆ *052 530 218; www.sixt.hr*). You can expect to queue for a while at the offices after a flight has arrived.

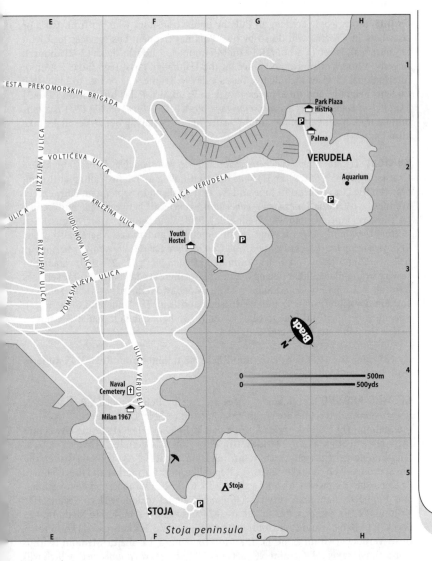

By train Pula is connected by rail to Pazin (1 hour) and other stations inland, including Vodnjan and Sv Petar u Šumi (departures from Pula at 05.05, 06.55, 09.15, 13.20, 14.27, 15.30, 17.20 and 19.40 Monday–Friday, 05.05, 09.15, 14.27 and 19.40 Saturday, and 09.15, 14.27 and 19.40 Sunday), with some services continuing to Lupoglav (from where there are connecting bus services to Rijeka) and Buzet. During the summer there's also a fast train to Maribor via Ljubljana (5 hours; departs Pula at 18.00, departs Ljubljana for Pula at 06.33). Pula's **railway station** [54 A5] (*Željeznički kolodvor; Kolodvarska 5;* ☎ *052 541 982*) is a ten-minute walk north of the amphitheatre: from the amphitheatre continue along Flavijevska towards the bus station, then turn left at the roundabout and head downhill past the Hotel Riviera. The last stretch is apt to be a bit dark, so you may not want to walk late at night.

By bus Most people arriving in Pula by public transport, whether from Istria or elsewhere in Croatia, will do so by bus. Pula has frequent bus services to Rovinj (45 minutes), Poreč (1½ hours), Pazin (45 minutes–1 hour), Rijeka (2–2½ hours), Zagreb (4 hours or more) and cities on the Dalmatian coast (eg: Zadar 7 hours). International services include five buses a day to Trieste, one or two to Ljubljana, three to Belgrade, and three buses a week to Frankfurt. Pula's **bus station** [54 A3] (*Autobusni kolodvor, Trg I Istarske brigade bb;* ✆ *060 304 090 or 304 091*) is a ten-minute walk northeast of the amphitheatre (if you're staying out at Verudela, take local bus #2a).

By boat Trieste Lines (*www.triestelines.it; tickets available from Commodore Cruises, Riva 14;* ✆ *052 211 631*) sails between Pula and Trieste, calling at Rovinj, between the last weekend in June and the first weekend in September, daily except Wednesday; Venezia Lines (*www.venezialines.com*) sails between Pula and Venice on Tuesday (June–September), Wednesday, Friday and Saturday (July/August). See *Getting there and away* on page 26 for timetables and prices. There's also a fast LNP (*www.lnp.hr; tickets available from Commodore Cruises, see above; you can buy tickets in Zadar from Mia Tours, Vrata Sv Krševana bb;* ✆ *023 254 400*) catamaran service from Pula to Zadar during the summer, calling at Mali Lošinj (some services also call at Unije, Ilovik and Silba), sailing Monday, Wednesday, Friday, Saturday and Sunday (July/August), and Wednesday and Saturday (June and September). The journey time from Pula to Mali Lošinj is two hours, Pula to Zadar five hours; tickets from Pula to Zadar cost 100kn.

By car Pula is a 1½-hour drive from Rijeka, 45 minutes from Rovinj, 45 minutes from Pazin, and four hours from Zagreb.

GETTING AROUND Local **bus** services are run by PulaPromet (✆ *052 501 973; www.pulapromet.hr*) and are cheap, frequent and reliable. Useful services from the bus station (*Trg I Istarske brigade bb;* ✆ *060 304 090 or 304 091*) or the city centre include #1 to Stoja, #2a to Verudela (travelling towards Verudela, #2a also stops at Giardini, near the Sergius Arch; returning from Verudela, #3a will take you to the bus station, or you can take #2a to Trg Republike, near the market and the old town, or Koparska from where it's only a short walk to the bus station), and #5 for Štinjan and Puntižela. Suburban services (*Prigradske linije*) include #21 to Fažana (for Brijuni), #22 to Vodnjan, #23 to Valtura, #24 and #25 to Šišan, #25 to Medulin, #26 and #28 to Banjole and Premantura (for Rt Kamenjak). Tickets cost 11kn in town or to Verudela (within Zone 1), 15kn to Premantura, Fažana or Medulin (within Zone 2). For **taxis** call **Cammeo** (✆ *060 700 700; www.taxi-cammeo.net*), which will definitely be the cheapest, or **Taxi Pula** (✆ *052 223 228; www.taxipula.com*).

TOURIST INFORMATION Pula's **tourist information office** [54 C4] (*Forum 3;* ✆ *052 219 197;* e *tz-pula@pu.t-com.hr; www.pulainfo.hr;* ☉ *Jun–Aug 08.00–22.00 Mon–Fri, 09.00–22.00 Sat/Sun; Sep–May 08.00–21.00 Mon–Fri, 09.00–21.00 Sat/Sun*) is conveniently located on the forum, and has maps and plenty of local information.

WHERE TO STAY Pula has no shortage of places to stay, from larger and boutique hotels to hostels and campsites. As well as a good number of long-established hotels out of town at Verudela (including the excellent, recently renovated Park Plaza Histria), there is an increasing choice of places to stay in the city centre itself.

Hotels

🏠 **Hotel Milan 1967** [55 F4] (12 dbls) Stoja 4; 📞052 300 200; e hotel@milanpula.com; www.milan1967.hr; ⊕ all year. Family-run for 3 generations, the Milan lies on the southern edge of town near the Naval Cemetery, at the base of the Stoja Peninsula, & is well known for its standout seafood restaurant (see *Where to eat and drink*, page 58). **$$$$**

🏠 **Hotel Palma** [55 G2] (132 dbls) Verudela 15; 📞052 590 760; e palma@arenaturist.hr; www.arenaturist.com; ⊕ all year. Positioned next to the Park Plaza Histria, the Palma is not in the same league as its neighbour, with modest rooms (not all of which have AC) – though the staff are friendly, & guests can use the swimming pools, restaurants & other facilities at the Histria. **$$$$**

🏠 **Park Plaza Histria** [55 G1] (241 dbls) Verudela 17; 📞052 590 000; e pphpres@pphe.com; www.arenaturist.com; ⊕ all year. The newly spruced-up Histria, now associated with the Park Plaza brand, is easily the nicest option on Verudela, & one of the best places to stay in or around Pula. The rooms have small balconies & swish new bathrooms, & there is a large terrace area with comfortable lounge chairs, as well as indoor & outdoor swimming pools at the hotel & another (as well as a kids' pool) 5 mins' walk away, & a nice pebble beach a few minutes beyond that. The rate for half board is only around €6 above that of a room with breakfast, & the buffet-style restaurant is excellent – so unless you plan to spend all your evenings in Pula itself, this is well worth considering. There is also a good à la carte restaurant, Istrian Taverna. **$$$$**

🏠 **Hotel Amfiteatar** [54 B3] (16 dbls, 2 sgls) Amfiteatarska 6; 📞052 375 600; e info@hotelamfiteatar.com; www.hotelamfiteatar.com; ⊕ all year. Newly opened boutique hotel positioned squarely between the arena & the old town, with a decent restaurant. Note that the prices on the website are for longer than 2 nights; for 1-night stays, add 20% (these are the prices indicated here). **$$$–$$$$**

🏠 **Hotel Galija** [54 G3] (10 dbls) Epulonova 3; 📞052 383 802; e info@hotelgalija.hr; www.hotelgalija.hr; ⊕ all year. Small 3-star just around the corner from the Omir. **$$$**

🏠 **Hotel Omir** [54 C3] (19 dbls) Serđa Dobrića 6; 📞052 213 944 or 218 186; e info@hotel-omir.com; www.hotel-omir.com; ⊕ all year. Long-standing, good-value 2-star just a short distance from the Hercules Gate & the amphitheatre, with its own pizzeria. The street name is sometimes written as Dobricheva (including on the map given out by the tourist office). **$$$**

🏠 **Hotel Riviera Guesthouse** [54 A4] (67 dbls) Splitska 1; 📞052 211 166; e riviera@arenaturist.hr; www.arenaturist.com; ⊕ all year. In a grand old Secessionist building just a few mins' walk from the bus & train stations, the Riviera is now long overdue for an overhaul. At present it is somewhat overpriced for what it actually is – a 1-star establishment, offering 5 floors of faded grandeur, & no AC. **$$$**

🏠 **Scaletta** [54 A4] (12 dbls) Flavijevska 26; 📞052 541 599; e krtalic@pu.t-com.hr; www.hotel-scaletta.com; ⊕ all year. Stylish (& very popular) German-owned boutique hotel close to the amphitheatre, with its own, highly rated restaurant (see page 58). **$$$**

Hostels

🏠 **Hostel Pipistrelli** [54 C4] (30 beds, inc 2 dbls) Flaciusova 6; 📞052 214 725; e info@pipistrelo.com; www.hostel-pipistrelo.com; ⊕ all year. Excellent new hostel just around the corner from the forum, with stylish, themed rooms, shared kitchen, Wi-Fi, friendly, helpful staff, several dorms as well as 2 doubles with en suite. **$$**

🏠 **Pula Youth Hostel** [55 F3] (152 dorm beds) Zaljev Valsaline 4; 📞052 391 133; e pula@hfhs.hr; www.hfhs.hr; ⊕ all year. Simple, well-priced dorm beds at Valsaline, a bay at the base of the Verudela Peninsula (bus #2 or #3, or take the #2a to the crossroads before Verudela). There are a further 64 beds in mobile homes with private bathrooms, each sleeping 4; & a campsite in the pine trees. **$–$$**

Private rooms Private rooms and apartments can be booked through a number of agencies including **A-Turizam** (*Kandlerova 24;* 📞*052 212 212;* e *istra@a-turizam.hr; www.a-turizam.hr*), and many are listed on www.pulainfo.hr.

☛ **Apartments Arena** [54 B3] Flavijevska 2; ☎ 052 506 217; m 098 486 109; e booking@ pula-apartments.com; http://pula-apartments. com. This consists of 4 large – no, huge – renovated apartments, with AC & right next to the amphitheatre (some of the apartments have windows overlooking it), within easy walking distance of the old town & the bus station. 2 of the apartments sleep 3, 1 sleeps 4 & the other sleeps 5. Excellent value. **$$–$$$**

Camping
The most popular camping area for Pula is the **Stoja Peninsula**, around 3km west of the city centre. **Camp Stoja** (*Stoja 37;* ☎ *052 387 144;* e *acstoja@ arenaturist.hr; www.arenacamps.com;* ⊕ *Mar–Sep*) caters mainly for 'campers' with caravans or motorhomes, and has 713 lots priced from around €30 for two adults with a tent and car in summer. Around 7km northwest of the city centre at **Puntižela**, overlooking the Brijuni Islands, **Camping Brioni ex Puntižela** (*Puntižela;* ☎ *052 517 490; www.puntizela.hr;* ⊕ *Mar–Nov*), has 480 pitches from €20 for two adults with a tent in the summer (expect to pay more for a 'premium' site near the sea, or for a pitch with electricity). They also have a hostel. One of the cheapest places to camp is Pula's **youth hostel** at Valsaline (see *Hotels*, page 57), with 50 simple pitches for €20 for two adults with a tent in summer; you can also hire a tent for €2. Alternatively there is camping at **Medulin** (see page 65) and **Premantura** (see page 66).

✗ WHERE TO EAT AND DRINK
Pula has plenty of choice when it comes to eating out, both in the old town itself and along the coast at Verudela – though the better tables in the town centre tend to be fairly well hidden off the main drag, whereas the obvious concentration of restaurants around the forum and towards the west end of Sergijevaca cater mainly to tourists and have been uniformly unmemorable, in our experience. Among the nicest places to eat in town are the family-run Vodnjanka; Jupiter, on the road up to the fort; and Kantina, behind the main market. Milan 1967, out at Stoja, has been winning accolades for years, while further out of town at Banjole, you'll find one of the most pleasant dining experiences anywhere in Croatia, at Konoba Batelina.

✗ **Milan1967** [55 F4] Stoja 4; ☎ 052 300 200; www.milan1967.hr; ⊕ 11.00–midnight daily, closed Sun during winter. Top-rated seafood restaurant at the base of the Stoja Peninsula, with a wide range of freshly caught fish & shellfish & an extensive wine cellar. **$$$$**

✗ **Scaletta** [54 A4] Flavijevska 26; ☎ 052 541 599; www.hotel-scaletta.com; ⊕ summer 10.30–23.00 daily, winter 10.30–23.00 Mon–Sat. Refined dining just along the road from the arena, at the hotel of the same name. **$$$$**

✗ **Konoba Batelina** Čimulje 25, Banjole; ☎ 052 573 767; ⊕ 17.00–23.00 Mon–Sat. This superb seafood restaurant in the village of Banjole, a few kilometres southeast of Pula, is run by the friendly Skoko family, with a menu featuring whatever was brought ashore in that day's catch. Dishes include a range of imaginatively prepared & classic entrées, from lightly dressed crab meat served in its shell, to succulent scallops or a light mousse made from conger eel, & homemade pasta, while for mains there could be brodetto with polenta, or perfectly grilled monkfish or sea bass. The outstanding food is complemented by excellent wines & a range of local spirits, & the setting is relaxed & unpretentious. Highly recommended. Since it was recently included in a list of Europe's top 101 places to eat, reservations are definitely advised. Buses #26 & #28 will take you out to Banjole from Pula, otherwise a taxi shouldn't set you back much more than getting to the airport. **$$$–$$$$**

✗ **Kantina** [54 C2] Flanatička 16; ☎ 052 214 054; www.kantina-pula.com; ⊕ 08.00–23.00 daily. A great place next to Pula's large open market, with a wide range of dishes served in a lovely vaulted stone interior. **$$$**

✗ **Vodnjanka** [54 D2] D Vitezića 4; ☎ 052 210 655; ⊕ summer 09.00–23.00 Mon–Sat, winter 09.00–17.00 Mon–Sat. Lovely family-run restaurant with an emphasis on traditional Istrian dishes, such

as *fuži* with game, as well as plenty of seafood dishes – & seasonal dishes such as steamed dandelion leaves with hard-boiled egg. About as close as you're likely to get to genuine home cooking without being invited to somebody's house. $$$
✗ **Jupiter** [54 C4] Castropola 42; ☎ 051 214 333; ⏰ 10.00–23.00 Mon–Fri, 12.00–23.00 Sat,

13.00–23.00 Sun. Excellent place hidden away from the main drag on the road leading up to the fort, with a range of dishes, from legendary pizzas to great portions of succulent grilled squid served with lashings of *blitva*. Friendly & unpretentious & deservedly popular with locals. $$

Bars and cafés
You'll rarely be short of a place to stop for a coffee or a drink in Pula, but here are a few favourites:

⏛ **Caffe Diana** [54 C4] Forum 4; ⏰ 07.00–22.00 daily. There's no shortage of cafés on & around the forum, but this has always proved a reliable choice.
⏛ **Caffe Milan** [54 C3] Narodni trg bb; ⏰ 10.00–23.00 Mon–Fri, 07.00–21.00 Sat, 07.00–14.00 Sun. Nice café right beside the covered market, packed with locals, with a large covered terrace, impeccable coffee & plenty of shade.
⏛ **Caffe Uliks** [54 C3] Trg Portarata 1; ⏰ 07.00–22.00 daily. Small café tucked on a corner behind the Sergius Arch, where you can combine a stop for a coffee with the requisite look at the James Joyce sculpture seated outside (see box on page 61).
⏛ **Jazz Club Florin** [54 C3] Sergijevaca 24; ⏰ 06.00–midnight daily. Small café/bar

on Sergijevaca with live jazz from 21.00 on Fri evenings (free).
⏛ **Slastičarnica Charlie** [54 C3] Flanatička 17; ⏰ 07.00–22.00 daily. A popular choice for ice cream near the market, with plenty of tables outside.
⏛ **Vinoteka Hafne** [54 B3] Istarska 11; ⏰ 07.00–23.00 daily. Newly opened wine bar just up the road from the amphitheatre, with an excellent range of Istrian wines, including at least 5 reds & 5 whites by the glass, as well as 1 or 2 dessert wines, all very reasonably priced & changing weekly. Wine is also sold by the bottle, making it the perfect place to try a few local wines before buying some to take home. Cosy, relaxed & intimate with a small terrace planned for 2013.

ENTERTAINMENT AND NIGHTLIFE
☆ **Aruba** [54 A3] Šijanska cesta 1; www. arubaclub-pula.com. Popular club with summer terrace & dance floor inside, northeast of the town centre, beyond the bus station.

☆ **Jazz Club Florin** [54 C3] Live jazz from 21.00 on Fri evenings.

Arena As well as constituting Pula's star attraction and providing a venue for the Pula Film Festival (see box on page 60), the city's 1st-century amphitheatre is also used as a venue for large, high-profile concerts, from Croatian singers such as Oliver Dragojević to international acts such as Seal, Elton John and Sting.

FESTIVALS
Fort Punta Christo Situated on the Štinjan Peninsula just north of Pula, this is now home to three large international music festivals. **Seasplash** (*www.seasplash-festival. com*) kicks off in the middle of July, with four days of reggae, dub, drum'n'bass, hip-hop, electronic and dance music, featuring international and Croatian DJs. **Outlook Festival** (*www.outlookfestival.com*) is Europe's largest bass music and sound-system culture event, running for four days at the end of August and the beginning of September. Outlook is followed a few days later by **Dimension Festival** (*www. dimensionsfestival.com*), which features four days of underground electronic music.

Pula International Film Festival
See box on page 60.

Pula Superiorum (*www.pulasuperiorum.com*) Pula's 'days of antiquity' take place in June, in the forum, the arena and in front of the Golden Gate, and include staged gladiator combat, music and theatre, an antique crafts fair and plenty of entertainment for kids.

SHOPPING

Enoteka Istriana [54 C4] (*Forum 11;* ⊕ *10.00–22.00 daily*) This is a good place to shop for Istrian wine on the forum itself.

Market (Tržnica) [54 C2] (*Narodni trg; www.trznica-pula.hr;* ⊕ *07.00–13.30 Mon–Sat, 07.00–12.00 Sun*) Pula's large, busy main market (sometimes referred to as the *placa*) is only a five-minute walk from the Sergius Arch, and has stalls selling all manner of fresh fruit and vegetables as well as local honey and other produce, and a covered area selling seafood and fresh and cured meat.

Supermarkets There's a large Plodine supermarket [54 A3] northeast of the bus station, near the junction of 43 Istraske divisije and Prekomorskih brigada (*Jurja Žakna 12, Šijana;* ⊕ *08.00–21.00 Mon–Sat, 08.00–13.00 Sun*), and several other large supermarkets nearby; smaller, local supermarkets (Konzum, Plodina, Diona, etc) are dotted around town. If you're staying at Verudela, the nearest supermarkets are a long hike away in Nova Veruda.

Vinoteka Hafne [54 B3] (*Istarska 11;* ⊕ *07.00–23.00 daily*) As well as being the best wine bar in town (see *Bars and cafés*, page 59), Hafne is an excellent place to shop for Istrian wine.

OTHER PRACTICALITIES

✚ **General Hospital** [54 C2] (Opća bolnica) Zagrebačka 30; ☎ 052 376 000 or 376 500; www.obpula.hr

✚ **Pharmacy** [54 C3/4] Istarske ljekarne (*www.istarske-ljekarne.hr*) has branches on Giardini (*Giardini 14;* ☎ *052 222 544;* ⊕ *07.00–20.00 daily* *plus a night shift) & near the forum (Sergijevaca 2;* ⊕ *07.00–20.00 Mon–Fri, 07.30–15.00 Sat). For* other branches & opening times, see their website.

✉ **Post office** Trg Republike 1; ⊕ 08.30–17.00 Mon–Fri

WHAT TO SEE AND DO All of the main sights in Pula are concentrated within a relatively small area and can easily be explored on foot.

For a walking tour of Pula's old town centre, start at the Sergius Arch on Trg Portarata. The **Sergius Arch** [54 C3] (Slavoluk Sergijevaca) probably dates from the years 29–27BC, and was commissioned by Salvia Postumia Sergi, a member of the prominent Sergi family, as a tribute to her husband Lucius Sergius Lepidus and two other family members. It is a triumphal arch rather than a city gate, though it was built against what would once have been one of the 12 original city gates, the Porta Aurea or Golden Gate, which disappeared in the early 19th century when the old city walls were pulled down (two of the original city gates survive, but more on them later). It is richly decorated on its western (town-facing) side and flanked by Corinthian columns, with winged victories in the spandrels (the other side, of course, would have been hidden against the city gate). Over the centuries the Sergius Arch was studied and drawn by a succession of artists and architects including Michelangelo, Palladio, Piranesi and Robert Adam.

On the far side of the arch is **Sergijevaca**, which runs down to the old Roman Forum – but before you leave the arch, have a look at the nearby statue of **James Joyce** outside Café Uliks, commemorating the Irish novelist's brief sojourn here as an English teacher at the beginning of the 20th century (see box, below).

About halfway along Sergijevaca a small and easily missed sign on your left leads to an unlikely looking courtyard next to a hairdressing salon, where you'll find one of the most complete and best-preserved **Roman floor mosaics** [54 C4] in Croatia. The scene depicted is one from Greek mythology, the brutal punishment of Dirce – she was tied to the horns of an enraged bull – by the sons of Antiope, for the cruel treatment of their mother at the hands of Dirce (Dirce was Antiope's aunt). The story forms the subject of Euripedes' play *Antiope*, and has been widely illustrated – including the walls of a villa at Pompeii, and the famous *Farnese Bull* in Naples. The mosaics probably date from the 3rd century AD, and would originally have been part of a Roman villa (note the dramatic change in floor level over the past two millennia: around 2m). They were only discovered comparatively recently – under the ruins of a block of houses, following a bombing raid in World War II.

3

JAMES JOYCE

The Irish novelist James Joyce, author of *Ulysses*, lived and worked in Pula for around six months between 1904 and 1905, after eloping to mainland Europe with Nora Barnacle, his future wife. The young Joyce taught English to Austro-Hungarian naval officers at the Berlitz school in Pula, and though the school itself is long gone, there is a café named after his novel *Ulysses* just behind the Sergius Arch (Café Uliks – Uliks being the title of Ulysses in Croatian – see page 59). A bronze sculpture of Joyce sits outside the café, cane in hand and watching passers-by from under his broad-brimmed hat. During his stay Joyce worked on some of the material which would later become his novel *Portrait of the Artist as a Young Man* – though he had little if anything positive to say about Istria in his letters home, and moved to Trieste in Italy as soon as he could get a position teaching there.

Before returning to Sergijevaca, continue from the mosaics towards Flaciusova ulica, where you'll find the small 6th-century **Chapel of Mary Formosa** [54 D4] (Kapela Sv Marije Formoze), which once formed part of an enormous Byzantine basilica (much of which was apparently used as building material by the Venetians, and according to some, finding its way into St Mark's). The chapel is usually locked, but some of the surviving floor and wall mosaics from inside can be seen in the Archaeological Museum (see opposite).

A little further along Sergijevaca, a street on the right leads up to the 14th-century **Franciscan church and monastery** [54 C4] (*Sv Franje;* ⊕ *10.00–19.00 Mon–Sat; entry 7kn*), built in Romanesque style with some Gothic elements and an attractive cloister.

At the far (western) end of Sergijevaca you'll find a large square which was once the **Roman forum** [54 C4], now surrounded by cafés with tables spilling out onto the square. Two temples once stood here, one of which, the Temple of Augustus, is still standing. Built in the years 2BC–AD14 (there's an inscription with the date on the architrave), and dedicated to the goddess Roma and the emperor Augustus, the **Temple of Augustus** [54 C4] (*Forum;* \ *052 351 300; www.ami-pula. hr;* ⊕ *15 May–15 Oct 09.00–21.00 Mon–Fri (Jul/Aug until 22.00, Sep until 20.00), 09.00–15.00 Sat/Sun; outside these months open by appointment; entry 10kn*) is an exceptionally beautiful building, with refined, slender proportions, and tall columns with Corinthian capitals. It was converted into a church under Byzantine rule, and later the Venetians used it as a theatre, before its fortunes waned and it came to be used as a granary, and – not that you'd guess looking at the building now – was completely blown to bits in a bombing raid during World War II. Painstakingly restored to its former glory between 1945 and 1947, it now houses a small though interesting collection of Roman stonework and sculpture, including statues of several emperors and a fragment of a rather wild-eyed medusa. The **Temple of Diana** [54 C4], which once stood next to the Temple of Augustus, was incorporated into the back of the **town hall** [54 C4] during the 13th century – walk around the back of the latter building and you'll find its outline still clearly visible in the wall. An inscription on the town hall (Gradska palača) gives the date of its construction as 1296, though it probably existed in an earlier form before that, and the façade dates from the 16th century. It was the seat of the local duke during the Venetian period, and is still used by the mayor.

Walking northeast from the forum along Kandlerova ulica leads you to the **Cathedral of the Assumption of the Blessed Virgin Mary** [54 C4] (Katedrala uznesenja Blažene Djevice Marije). The cathedral was built during the 5th century, on the foundations of an even earlier building, but following a fire in 1242 and other damage during the conflict between Venice and Genoa for control of the city, several parts of it were rebuilt over the next four centuries. The Renaissance façade dates from the 16th century, but traces of the earlier 4th-century building can be seen in the back wall. Inside you'll find re-used Roman and Byzantine columns and fragmentary 5th- or 6th-century floor mosaics, and a 3rd-century sarcophagus masquerading as an altar – which, some say, contains the relics of the 11th-century Hungarian king Solomon (who officially died on the battlefield near Edirne in modern Turkey, but according to legend escaped and ended his life as a monk in Pula). Note the lintel dated 857 embedded in the south wall. The bell tower dates from the late 17th century, and includes a large amount of building material pillaged from the arena, including a number of seats in its foundations.

Turning right onto Carrarina ulica you'll find the first of the two surviving city gates, the Porta Gemina or **Twin Gate** [54 B3] (Dvojna vrata), which dates from the 2nd or 3rd century and leads to the **Archaeological Museum of Istria** [54 C3] (*Carrarina 3;* \ *052 351 300; www.ami-pula.hr;* ⊕ *May–Sep 09.00–20.00 Mon–Fri, 09.00–15.00 Sat/Sun; Oct–Apr 09.00–14.00 Mon–Fri; entry 20kn, or 50kn including entry to the amphitheatre & the Temple of Augustus*). Istria's most important museum has extensive Roman and prehistoric collections, with objects from Pula as well as sites all over Istria (including the former Histrian capital Nesactium, Buzet, Dvigrad, and Parentium, better known these days as Poreč), ranging from early floor mosaics to classical sculpture and Roman funerary monuments, pottery, glass and jewellery. There's also a medieval collection with stonework including fragments from the lost Byzantine complex of Mary Formosa. The displays can seem a little chaotic at times, but the objects themselves are certainly worth seeing. You can also walk up to the fort and the Historical Museum of Istria from the twin gate, but it's not really the most impressive part of Pula and our advice is to leave that until last. Continue up Carrarina, passing fragments of the old **city walls**, to the **Hercules Gate** [54 C3] (Herkulova vrata), built in 47–44BC and now flanked by two medieval bastions. At the top of the arch is a worn relief of Hercules with his club, and an inscription which includes the names of the two Roman officials, Lucius Calpurnius Piso and Gaius Cassius Longinus, entrusted by the Roman Senate with the duty of founding a colony at Pula.

PULA AMPHITHEATRE

Pula's exceptionally well-preserved Roman amphitheatre was probably built during the first few years of the 1st century AD, during the reign of the emperor Augustus, and was completed in its present form under Vespasian (AD69–79), making it roughly contemporary with Rome's Colosseum. It is one of the six largest surviving Roman amphitheatres in the world, slightly elliptical in plan and measuring some 132m x 105m, with an estimated capacity of around 20,000 spectators. Its remarkably intact outer walls reach a height of some 32m, with two tiers of arches surmounted by a third tier of rectangular apertures, and on the landward side (where the ground level is higher), only two levels. The walls also incorporate four towers, each with a spiral staircase which gave access to the seating areas, and with a water storage tank (supplied by an aqueduct), from which water was then distributed around the arena by channels. The underground passages, through which unfortunate gladiators once made their way into the arena and mortal, bloody combat, now hold an exhibition of wine and olive oil production in Roman Istria. The arena itself now holds major concerts and operas, and some screenings of the Pula Film Festival (see box on page 60), with seating for between 5,000 and 8,000. It stands just outside the city walls on Flavijevska or Via Flavia, formerly the Roman road leading to Poreč and Trieste.

Over the centuries it has been pillaged for its fine, locally quarried stone (the cathedral's 17th-century bell tower being just one example of its re-use in other buildings). In fact the arena came close to disappearing altogether in the 15th century, when the Venetian Senate decided that the whole thing should be dismantled and reassembled in Venice – an idea fortunately thwarted by a Venetian senator, Gabriele Emo, whose name is commemorated on a plaque on the northwest tower of the arena. As a friend from the nearby town of Šišan once commented in horror at the idea, 'Just imagine – what would we do without our arena?!'

3

Finally, turn left onto Istarska and follow this down to Pula's number-one star attraction, its 1st-century Roman **amphitheatre** [54 B3] (see box on page 63) – if, that is, you haven't abandoned this itinerary and headed there first.

On top of the hill at the centre of the old town is the 17th-century Venetian fort, restored by Napoleon and then under Austro-Hungary, with a star-shaped plan and four bastions. The fort now houses the **Historical Museum of Istria** [54 C4] (*Gradinski uspon 6;* \ *052 211 566; www.pmi.hr;* ⊕ *Apr–Sep 08.00–21.00 daily; Oct–Mar 09.00–17.00 daily; entry 10kn*), interesting mainly for the views of the city below from its ramparts. The hill was probably the site of an earlier, pre-Roman settlement, and there's also a **small Roman amphitheatre** up here, one of three which originally provided the city's entertainment (one of the others is probably the reason you've come to Pula; the third disappeared long ago, but once stood on the slopes of Montezaro, southeast of the city walls).

Out towards Stoja near the Hotel Milan 1967 is the **Naval Cemetery** [55 F5], dating from 1866, a leafy green oasis which is the final resting place of some 150,000 soldiers from the Austro-Hungarian navy. There are also several little-known Austrian **forts**, in various stages of decay, scattered around the headlands which surround Pula.

BEACHES Pula's best beaches for **swimming** are a short distance north and south of the town centre, at **Štinjan** (in particular the pebbly Vile Beach, which might sound like an unfortunate choice of name until you know that it means 'fairy'; bus #5) and **Stoja** (pebbly, quite busy as it's also the main camping area; bus #1) respectively, and at **Verudela** (pebble beaches such as Ambrela and 'Hawaii'; bus #2a). A little further south are the sandy (and very popular) Bijeca Beach at **Medulin** (bus #25) and the rocky coves of **Rt Kamenjak** (beautiful and remote feeling, but the currents can be quite strong so it's not advisable for kids; buses #26 or #28 to Premantura, then hire a bike or walk down the cape; see the short hike on page 177). If it's a **windsurfing** beach you're after, then head

MARINE TURTLE RESCUE CENTRE

Though they are an endangered species, it is estimated that each year around 6,000 marine turtles get accidentally caught in fishing nets in the Adriatic, around 2,500 of those in the eastern part of the Adriatic. Many of these animals drown, since once in the net they are unable to come to the surface to breathe. Turtles also accidentally swallow plastic bags and other waste, not to mention fishing hooks, and since they spend a comparatively long time at the surface while breathing they are prone to being struck by powerboats and other motorised craft.

The Marine Turtle Rescue Centre at Pula Aquarium was founded in 2006, following the establishment of the Pula Marine Educational Centre at the aquarium the previous year, and is the first centre of its kind in Croatia. Apart from the care and treatment of injured sea turtles, its activities include tagging turtles in the wild, and working to increase awareness among locals and fishermen of the dangers posed to turtles.

If you find an injured sea turtle in the wild, contact the aquarium staff who will send someone to collect it, and in the meantime try to cover it with wet rags or a wet towel to prevent it drying out. You can also **adopt a marine turtle**, for 200kn, which goes directly towards the work of the rescue centre – see the aquarium website, opposite, for details.

south to Premantura and Medulin for some of the best windsurfing conditions anywhere in Croatia – Stupice has a windsurfing school and hire facilities (*www. windsurfing.hr*), Pomer or Bjeca beaches have slightly more sheltered conditions, so are particularly suitable for beginners, and for experienced windsurfers who want to catch the full force of the *bura* wind, there's Kuj Beach at Ližnjan. There's a **naturist** beach at the large Camp Kažela near Medulin.

STOJA AND VERUDELA Just beyond the southern edge of Pula are the **Stoja** and **Verudela** (often written Verudella) peninsulas, the former Pula's main camping area and the latter home to several of its larger hotels. Both have pleasantly indented coastlines, with plenty of coves and rocky or pebble beaches and wooded areas, and are easily accessible by local bus (see *Getting around* on page 56).

Verudela is also where you'll find the excellent **Pula Aquarium** (*Fort Verudela;* ✆ *052 381 402;* e *infos@aquarium.hr; www.aquarium.hr;* ⊕ *daily Jul/Aug 09.00– 22.00; Apr/May & Sep 10.00–18.00; Oct–Mar 10.00–16.00; entry adults 60kn, children 7–18 years 50kn, 3–7 years 30kn, under 3s free*), which is a must for those travelling with children, partly as recompense for having dragged them around Pula's Roman monuments. The aquarium is housed in a late 19th-century Austro-Hungarian fort, and was transformed into its present use in 2002. There are currently about 60 tanks, with a wide range of species and several interactive displays for kids, and on the first floor the **Marine Turtle Rescue Centre** (see opposite). There are plans to transform the central area of the fort into a large tank for sharks.

SOUTH FROM PULA

MEDULIN The small town of Medulin is these days a large, busy holiday resort, with one of those coveted and fairly rare things in Croatia – a big, sandy beach. **Bjeca Beach** is popular with families as well as with windsurfers, and you can expect it to be packed in the summer. **Bus #25** runs between Pula's bus station and Medulin. The **tourist information office** (*Centar 223;* ✆ *052 577 145;* e *info@tzom. hr; www.medulinriviera.info*) is open June–September 08.00–21.00 daily.

You can also get out to some of the ten uninhabited islands of the **Medulin archipelago**, including Ceja and Levan, both of which have restaurants, and Levan has a small sandy beach. Taxi-boats run between Medulin and several of the islands as well as Rt Kamenjak, including Taxi Boat Dijana, which departs for Ceja from near the Hotel Holiday at 09.30, 10.30, 11.30, 13.30 and 14.30 and returns at 12.00, 14.00, 17.00, 18.00 and 19.00 daily (return ticket adults 50kn, children 20kn).

There's no shortage of accommodation, including:

 Where to stay

🏠 **Park Plaza Medulin** [55 G1] (190 dbls) Osipovica 31; ✆ 052 572 601; e ppmres@pphe. com; www.parkplaza.com. Newly renovated 4-star with pools & a fitness centre; all rooms have balconies. Close to Bjelica Beach. **$$$$**

🏠 **Hotel Belvedere** (450 dbls) Osipovica 33; ✆ 052 572 001; e belvedere@arenaturist.hr; www. arenaturist.hr. Huge resort-style hotel with 450 rooms on 4 floors spread over 2 wings, 3 pools (2 outdoor, 1 indoor), some rooms with balconies & sea views. Close to the beach. **$$$**

Camping options include the large **Camp Kažela** (*Kapovica 350;* ✆ *052 577 277;* e *ackazela@arenaturist.hr; www.arenacamps.com;* ⊕ *31 Mar–21 Oct*), which has 965 lots and 2km of beach including a separate naturist beach (lot with small tent from €10.20, plus €7.40 per adult).

RT KAMENJAK AND PREMANTURA Rt Kamenjak (Cape Kamenjak) meanders out into the waters of the Adriatic between Medulin and Banjole, a slender, highly indented peninsula which constitutes the southernmost tip of Istria. **Premantura**, the small town at the base of the peninsula, can be reached by **bus** #26 and #28 from Pula's bus station. There's a **tourist information office** in Medulin (see page 65), and another small kiosk at Banjole, not that either of these will be of much help to you if you've just arrived from Pula on the bus.

There are several **campsites** around Premantura, including the large **Camp Stupice** (*Selo 250;* ✆ *052 575 111;* e *acstupice@arenaturist.hr; www.arenacamps.com;* ⏲ *30 Mar–4 Nov*) with around 1,000 lots (lot with small tent from €10.20, plus €7.40 per adult); **Camp Runke** (*Runke 60;* ✆ *052 575 022;* e *acrunke@arenaturist. hr; www.arenacamps.com;* ⏲ *20 Apr–16 Sep*) is much smaller, with 'only' 247 lots, set amid pine trees (lot with small tent from €9.10, plus €6.50 per adult). There are no hotels or campsites in the southern half of the peninsula – fortunately, since it's a nature reserve (see below) – though it's possible to book a stay in a lighthouse on the tiny island of Porer (see *Istria's lighthouses,* page 16).

The southern half of **Rt Kamenjak** is one of the most beautifully unspoilt stretches of coastline anywhere in Croatia, and is a nature reserve. Some 530 plant species have been recorded on Kamenjak, including at least 28 species of orchid, many of them classified as rare or endangered and two of them endemic to the southern part of Istria; there are numerous butterfly species; and the only spotting of the endangered Mediterranean monk seal in Croatia in the past ten years was in these waters – an animal now reduced to only 600 individuals in the wild. The nature reserve is administered from a small office in Premantura (*Javna ustanova Kamenjak, Selo 120;* ✆ *052 576 513;* e *ju.kamenjak@pu.t-com.hr; www.kamenjak.hr*), and is the place to go if you want to find out more about the flora and wildlife and marine life on and around Rt Kamenjak. The best time of year to visit Kamenjak for wildflowers is June. There are also **dinosaur footprints** on the rocky northwest coast of Kamenjak, with an educational trail and dinosaur models – great fun for kids.

There are seemingly endless rocky coves and bays along the length of Kamenjak, so there's no shortage of places for a **swim**, but be aware that the currents are quite strong here – don't swim too far out to sea, and don't let kids swim alone. A couple of the bays have small bars, including the Safari Bar at Mala Kolombarica. The best way to explore Kamenjak is by bike or on foot (see page 177); those determined to bring a car will need to pay a fee to drive on Kamenjak.

The east coast of Rt Kamenjak is also one of the best **windsurfing** spots in Croatia, since it is exposed to all the different winds experienced in the northern Adriatic – the *bura, burin, maestral* and *jugo.* There's a **windsurfing centre** at Premantura (*contact Boris Ivančić;* m *091 512 3646; www.windsurfing.hr*), at Camp Stupice, where you can rent or buy equipment, or join classes (in several languages, including English) from beginners to advanced level. The best seasons are spring and autumn since they have the highest percentage of days with winds, though for beginners summer is preferable, since the water is warmer, and the more moderate *maestral* will be blowing.

NORTH FROM PULA

FAŽANA The small fishing village of Fažana lies around 8km north of Pula (bus #21), and its lively little harbour is the departure point for boats to the Brijuni Islands (see page 70 for sailing times). Fažana lay on Via Flavia between Pula and Trieste and was an important pottery centre during the Roman period, producing large **amphorae** which were used to transport Istrian wine and olive oil to various parts of the Roman Empire including the Danube region and northern Italy, and a Roman kiln was excavated in the town centre. The **Parish Church of SS Cosmas and Damian** (Fažana's patron saints) dates from the 15th century and has a *Last Supper* by Zorzi Ventura of Zadar (1598), as well as traces of 16th-century frescoes; the 14th-century **Church of Our Lady of Mount Carmel** contains fragmentary remains of 15th-century frescoes and a 14th-century wooden statue of the Virgin Mary. Fažana holds several foodie **festivals**. In July local women prepare *maneštra* and a variety of other traditional Istrian stews, and in early August there's a festival celebrating the humble **sardine** or pilchard, which is fished in the straits between here and the Brijuni Islands, and can be eaten freshly grilled on the waterfront. The Brijuni National Park Office is on Brioska, near the jetty from where the boats to Brijuni depart (*Brionska 10;* ☏ *052 525 888;* e *brijuni@brijuni.hr; www.brijuni.hr*).

🏠 **Where to stay** Most people pass through Fažana on the way to and from Brijuni, but if you want to stay there's plenty of accommodation, and great views of the islands from the waterfront. The **tourist information office** (*43 Istarske divizije 8;* ☏ *052 383 727;* e *tz-fazana@pu.t-com.hr; www.infofazana.hr;* ⊕ *Jul–Aug 08.00–22.00 daily; Jun/Sep 08.00–20.00 daily, Oct–May 08.00–15.30 Mon–Fri*) can give details of private accommodation, otherwise there are a couple of hotels and a new hostel.

🏠 **Hotel Marina** (9 dbls) Trg stare škole 2; ☏ 052 521 071; e info@marina-fazana.com; www. marina-fazana.com. Smart little boutique hotel, recently renovated & right on the waterfront, with its own terrace restaurant. **$$$**

🏠 **Hostel Amfora** (2 sgls, 7 dbls, 4 quad dorms) Vladimira Gortana 10; m 098 163 4605; e hostelamfora@hotmail.com; www.infofazana. hr. Newly opened hostel offering double & single rooms as well as quad dorms, with plain, simple décor & a shared kitchen. **$–$$**

VODNJAN Around 10km northeast from Pula on the old road to Pazin, or just off the 'ipsilon' (the main road between Pula and Rijeka), Vodnjan (Dignano) is a quiet little town with narrow, cobbled streets and some grand Venetian and Baroque architecture – not to mention a rather macabre collection of mummified saints.

The neo-Baroque **Parish Church of St Blaise** (Sv Blaž) was built between 1761 and 1808 on the site of an earlier Romanesque church destroyed in 1760, and is the largest parish church in Istria, with a 25m-high dome. The 62m-high bell tower, which is clearly modelled on the one in Venice's Piazza San Marco, is the tallest in Istria and was built between 1815 and 1882 after designs by Antonio Porta of Trieste. The most interesting thing about the church, however, is its **mummies**. Hidden in a curtained, dimly lit room behind the main altar are six glass cases, containing the intact bodies of three saints – St Leon Bembo (a chaplain in the Doge's Palace in Venice, who died in 1188), St Giovanni Olini (died 1300) and St Nicolosa Bursa (a Benedictine nun who died in Venice in 1512) – as well as various body parts of three other saints (St Barbara, St Sebastian and St Mary of Egypt). The bodies are clothed, and the skin and fingernails have darkened, giving them a strange, almost wooden appearance. Exactly how or why the bodies – which were not embalmed – have failed to decompose remains a mystery (the body of St Nicolosa is particularly well preserved, and is often described as the best-preserved mummy in Europe). They were brought to Vodnjan from Venice in 1818 by the artist Gaetano Gresler. In total the church holds some 370 relics, belonging to 250 different saints.

Vodnjan makes an easy day trip from Pula, either on **bus** #22 (runs every 90 minutes or so on weekdays, less frequently at weekends; journey time 30 minutes)

3

or on the **train** heading towards Pazin (see *Getting there and away*, page 55, for departure times). The **tourist information office** is on the main square (*Narodni trg 3;* ☎ *052 511 700; www.vodnjandignano.com;* ⊕ *Jun–mid Sept 08.00–15.00 & 19.00–21.00 daily; mid-Sept–May 08.00–15.00 Mon–Fri).*

� WHERE TO EAT

✕ **Vodnjanka** Istarska bb; ☎ 052 511 435; ⊕ 11.00–midnight Mon–Sat. If you're eating in Vodnjan you won't find much better than this – dishes include homemade pasta with truffles & beefsteak with porcini & truffles. $$

BRIJUNI ISLANDS

The Brijuni (Brioni) Islands lie around 3km offshore from the village of Fažana (see page 66), north of Pula. National park, state residence and modern safari park, they have both Roman and Byzantine remains (and a golf course), and are an extremely popular day trip from the Istrian coast.

Brijuni National Park (*Nacionalni park Brijuni; Brionska 10, Fažana;* ☎ *052 525 888;* e *brijuni@brijuni.hr; www.brijuni.hr*) is one of eight national parks in Croatia, and the only one in Istria (though there's a nature park, Učka, and several protected reserves). It covers all the islands and a larger area of the sea around them – a total area of just under 40km², 7.4km² of that being on land. There are a total of 14 islands, the largest of which by a long way is Veliki Brijun ('Big Brijun').

There was a Bronze Age hill fort on Veliki Brijun, above Verige Bay, and the island was settled both during the Roman period and under Byzantium. The largest Roman site on the island is the settlement of **Kastrum**, on the west coast. A villa was built here in the 2nd–1st century BC, which later developed into a small walled settlement where olive oil and wine were produced and stored – the storage areas and channels through which the olive oil flowed can still be seen clearly. The site continued to be inhabited through the Byzantine and Carolingian periods, and was still in use under Venice. There are remains of an early (5th–6th century) basilica nearby. There are also remains of a Roman villa at Verige Bay.

In 1893 – by which time they were largely overgrown and rife with malaria – the islands were purchased by Austrian businessman **Paul Kupelwieser**, who within a relatively short time had eradicated the malaria and converted Veliki Brijun into a luxury health resort, complete with fine hotels, heated pools, a zoo and even an ostrich farm. Kupelweiser's resort became immensely fashionable, with everyone from George Bernard Shaw and Thomas Mann to the Austrian archduke Franz Ferdinand coming to stay on the island (on just one day in 1911 no fewer than 16 princes and princesses as well as 15 counts and countesses were in residence). From 1949 onwards, **Tito** made the islands his summer home, importing tropical plants and animals (with more of the latter arriving as gifts from visiting dignitaries) – the basis of the **safari park** you'll find on Veliki Brijun today, including blue and marsh antelope, mountain zebra and Somalian sheep. Tito entertained a vast array of heads of state, dignitaries and celebrities on the island – from Winston Churchill and Queen Elizabeth II to Elizabeth Taylor, Richard Burton and Sophia Loren.

There is an **ornithological reserve** at Saline, where three large, shallow, marshy lakes (the remnants of antique and medieval saltpans) attract a wide range of bird species from waders to songbirds and raptors, including some rare species such as great white egrets and black storks.

Plantlife on the islands includes several rare species such as the marine poppy, while imported species of exotic plants include Himalayan and Lebanese cedars,

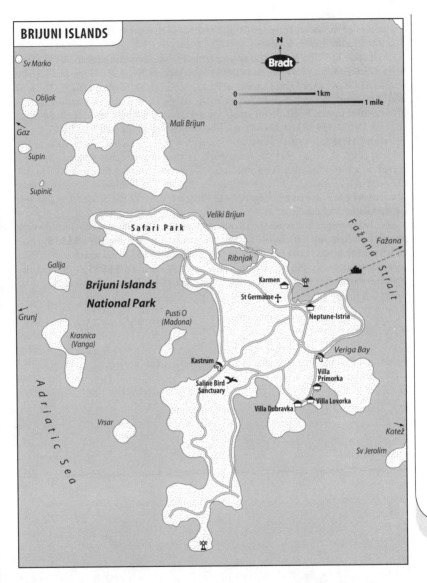

Greek and Spanish firs and sequoia. There's also a giant, twisted, **ancient olive tree** on Veliki Brijun which radiocarbon dating has shown to be about 1,600 years old. It was damaged by a storm in the 1970s, but still produces fruit.

Dinosaur footprints have been found at several locations on Veliki Brijun (Rt Pogledalo in the north, Rt Ploče, Rt Kamnik and Rt Trstike in the south, as well as on the smaller islands of Vanga and Galija), formed when these large reptiles walked across tidal and mud flats – now sedimentary rock – some 100 to 115 million years ago. An informative little booklet in Croatian and English, *Šetalište dinosaura – Promenade of Dinosaurs*, is available from the national park office and can also be downloaded free from their website (see www.brijuni.hr).

Before you leave Brijuni, step inside the small **chapel** by the museum, where the copies of medieval **frescoes** from Beram and elsewhere may persuade you to venture into the Istrian interior.

Boat trips to Veliki Brijun run all year from Fažana, departing Fažana daily May–September at 06.45, 07.45, 08.45, 10.15, 11.30, 13.00, 14.20, 15.45, 17.00, 18.30, 20.00 and 21.45, March/April and October at 06.45, 08.45, 11.30, 13.00, 14.20, 17.00, 18.30 and 21.45, and November–February at 06.45, 08.45, 11.30 and 14.20. Sailing time is around 20 minutes. Boats do fill up so you are advised to call a few days in advance to book (↝ *052 525 883 or 525 882;* e *izleti@brijuni.hr*). Boats sailing at 08.45, 11.30, 13.00 and 15.45 form part of an excursion with a guide, which includes visits to the Roman ruins at Verige and the safari park, as well as the archaeological museum, travelling around the island in a small train. Tickets cost 210kn for adults, 105kn for children in July/August, less in other months, and must be booked in advance. Plenty of excursions are offered from agencies in Pula, but some of these don't actually stop on the islands – check first.

It's also possible to stay on the islands, in one of a small number of (frankly very pricey for what you get) hotels (either the three-star Neptune-Istra **$$$$$**, close to where the boats arrive, or the two-star Karmen **$$$$$**) and apartments (Villa Lovorka is probably the nicest, renovated in 2010, sleeps 6 **$$$$$**) – contact the national park office in Fažana to book (↝ *052 525 888;* e *brijuni@brijuni.hr*).

4

Rovinj

Rovinj is without doubt the pearl and the envy of Istria. Favoured by the Venetians when it was ruled by the Republic of Venice, it was also a favourite of the touristing classes of the Austro-Hungarian Empire. The colourful hues of Rovinj's houses hail from these influences, especially the dominant Venetian red. Often overwhelmed with visitors in the height of summer – when it's popular with tours from Poreč and Pula where it is easier to get accommodation – in the winter it is almost deserted. The tightly packed houses of Rovinj's old town form some of the narrowest of cobbled streets, which pop out atop the hill of the once-upon-a-time island to a magnificent vista from the generously wide courtyard of the equally generously endowed St Euphemia Church. Being so popular, the town of course has a couple of Istria's best restaurants, festivals and enviable bars.

HISTORY

As an island Rovinj was inhabited by man in the Bronze and Iron ages. It was known later to the Romans as Mons Rupineum, which was one of four islands of the Rovinj archipelago to be inhabited at the time, along with the islands of St Catherine, St Andrew and Cissa. Cissa, mentioned by Pliny the Elder in his writings in AD1, no longer exists, having sunk in an earthquake in the late 8th century.

By the 4th century, a fortification named Castrum Rubini was built on Mons Rupineum, and this grew gradually into the town known today as Rovinj. Mons Rupineum maintained a large level of autonomy until 966 when, under the Patriarch of Aquileia, it was annexed to the Bishopric of Poreč. From 1188 Rovinj threw its allegiance in with Dubrovnik in today's southern Croatia, signing the Renovatia pacis, which brought it into conflict on several occasions with cities further to the north in today's Slovenian Adriatic.

By 1283, however, Rovinj followed the lead of Poreč and other Istrian towns in joining the Most Serene Republic of Venice (known as the Serenissima). This in turn brought Rovinj into conflict with inland Istria, which was ruled by the Counts of Gorizia and then by the Habsburgs from 1374. Rovinj was fortunate to survive the plague of 1312 which decimated the populations of other towns and cities in Istria, but Rovinj continued to see destruction in Venice's war with Genoa in 1379, and then later from marauding pirates.

By the end of the 16th century, immigrants fleeing Ottoman rule further south started to settle in big numbers in Rovinj, and its population almost doubled over a period of 60 years to 5,000 by 1650. By 1775, Rovinj's population grew to over 13,000, slightly larger than its population today, and it was during this period of expansion that the town came to look as it does today. It was also during this period that Rovinj grew as an important shipping base and producer of stone for building

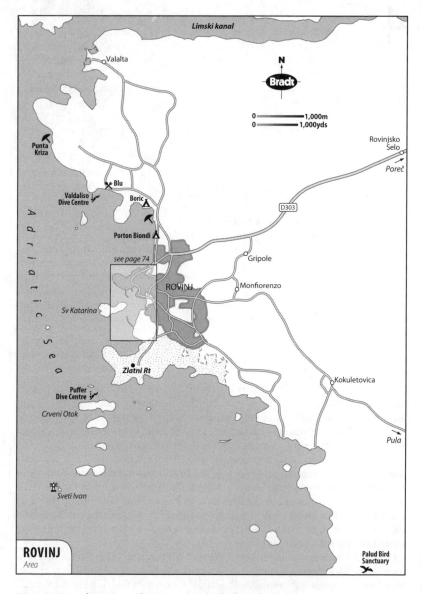

Map titled "ROVINJ Area" showing the coastline along the Adriatic Sea with labelled locations including Limski kanal, Valalta, Punta Kriza, Blu, Valdaliso Dive Centre, Boric, Porton Biondi, Sv Katarina, ROVINJ, Zlatni Rt, Puffer Dive Centre, Crveni Otok, Sveti Ivan, Gripole, Monfiorenzo, Rovinjsko Selo, Poreč, Kokuletovica, Pula, Palud Bird Sanctuary, and D303 road. Includes a compass rose, Bradt logo, and scale bars. "see page 74" noted within a boxed area near Rovinj.

Venice. Venice's taxes on the town were high though, and Rovinj's competitiveness began to wane, especially after the Habsburg Empire proclaimed Rijeka and Trieste to be free ports with considerably relaxed taxes. Thereafter the Serenissima had to quell several town uprisings.

In 1763, the isthmus between the island and the mainland was filled in as the town grew to well beyond the town walls. With the abdication of the Grand Council of Venice in 1797, Rovinj joined the rest of Istria, ruled first by Austria, then briefly by Napoleon from 1809. Under Austrian rule again from 1813, industrialisation brought numerous factories to Rovinj, including today's still dominant tobacco factory Adria, and the railway arrived in 1876.

GETTING THERE AND AWAY

BY BUS Rovinj **bus station** [74 D3] (*Trg na Lokva bb;* ☎ *052 811 453;* ⏲ *06.30–22.00 daily*) is very centrally located on the edge of the pedestrian zone, with a taxi stand, Non-Stop car hire (see *Car hire,* below), and Bike Planet all within a stone's throw. There are daily buses to Ljubljana, Belgrade and Trieste, and several buses a day to Zagreb, Pula, Poreč, and Rijeka.

BY BOAT Rovinj runs two summer services to Italian ports, all arriving and leaving from Grande Molo pier next to the harbour master's office.

Venice Two lines serve Venice: the slightly smaller and more popular **Commadore Travel** (*www.commadore-cruises.hr*) sails on Sundays. It leaves at 08.00, arrives at Venice St Basilio pier at 11.00 and returns at 16.30, arriving at 19.30 in Rovinj. It has an upper and lower deck and some outdoor seating. If you book through Topline (see *Tourist information,* page 150) you will also get a free hotel transfer. **Venezia Lines** (*www.venezialines.com*) sails at 07.30 every day via Poreč, arriving at 10.30 at St Basilio port. This boat has no outdoor seating.

Both lines offer tickets at €55 for singles, €65 for returns.

Trieste A **Trieste Lines** ferry (*www.triestelines.it*) sails from Trieste at 09.00, arriving at 10.45 in Rovinj, returning at 18.05 and arriving in Trieste at 19.55. The line operates from the last weekend in June to the first weekend in September, daily except Wednesday. The same ferry also stops at Piran and Pula (see *By boat,* page 26 for times).

GETTING AROUND

The old town of Rovinj has no public transport and is perched on a steep hill, with the flagstones on the main street of Grisia up to St Euphemia Church being quite polished.

BY BOAT Taxi-boats are available from Mali Mol pier. Regular passenger boats ply between the main resorts:

Sv Katerina and Crveni Otok Leaves from the main pier every hour on the half=hour 06.30–00.30. Return boat leaves Crveni Otok on the hour and Sv Katerina at a quarter past the hour. Guests of hotels on the island travel on the boats for free. Return tickets are purchased at the kiosk on the island near the pier or at the reception of Hotel Istra: adults 40kn, half price for children.

Valdaliso Boats leave the pier behind Rovinj market at a quarter past the hour 10.15–00.15, and return from Valdaliso on the half-hour 09.30–00.30. Buy tickets on the boat for 20kn (children up to seven years of age travel free).

CAR HIRE Services are available through most travel agencies, or you can go direct to:

🚗 **Non-Stop** [74 D3] Trg na Lokva 6; ☎ 052 812 054; m 099 810 4000; e rentacar@stop-rentacar.com; www.stop-rentacar.com. Excellent friendly service at good prices, Non-Stop will try their hardest to find you something, even if it is a last-minute request.
🚗 **Uniline** Istarska 19; ☎ 052 815 199 or 390 039; e info@uniline.hr; www.uniline.hr.

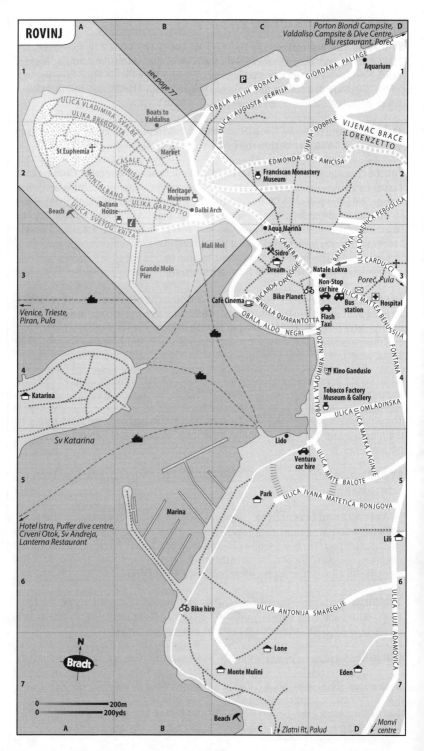

ROVINJ

A B C D

Porton Biondi Campsite,
Valdaliso Campsite & Dive Centre,
Blu restaurant, Poreč

Aquarium

see page 77

ULICA VLADIMIRA SVALBE

ULIKA BREGOVITA

OBALA PALIH BORACA

ULICA AUGUSTA FERRIJA

GIORDANA PALIAGE

VIJENAC BRAĆE LORENZETTO

JURJA DOBRILE

Boats to
Valdaliso

CASALE CA GRISA

St Euphemia †

Market

EDMONDA DE AMICISA

Franciscan Monastery Museum

MONTALBANO

Heritage
Museum

 ULIKA GARZOTTO

Balbi Arch

CARRA

ULICA DOMENICA PERGOLISA

Batana
House

Beach

ULICA SVETOG KRIŽA

Aqua Marina

Sidro

RATARSKA

ULICA CARDUCCI

Poreč, Pula

Mali Mol

Dream

RICARDA DAVEGGIE

Natale Lokva

Non-Stop
car hire

ULICA MATE BENUSSIJA

Grande Molo
Pier

Café Cinema

NELLA QUARANTOTTA

Bike Planet

Bus
station

Hospital

Flash
Taxi

OBALA ALDO NEGRI

FONTANA

Venice, Trieste,
Piran, Pula

OBALA VLADIMIRA NAZORA

Kino Gandusio

Katarina

Tobacco Factory
Museum & Gallery

ULICA OMLADINSKA

ULICA MATKA LAGINJE

Sv Katarina

Lido

Ventura
car hire

ULICA MATE BALOTE

Park

ULICA IVANA MATETIĆA RONJGOVA

Marina

Lili

Hotel Istra, Puffer dive centre,
Crveni Otok, Sv Andreja,
Lanterna Restaurant

ULICA LUJE ADAMOVIĆA

Bike hire

ULICA ANTONIJA SMAREGLIE

N

Bradt

Lone

Monte Mulini

Eden

0 ———— 200m
0 ———— 200yds

A B C D

Beach

Zlatni Rt, Palud

Monvi
centre

74

A franchise of Europcar, & a representative of Alamo and National, so whilst in theory they should be well connected, they are also often fully booked. Booked well in advance, they can pick up & drop off in other cities in Croatia or Europe.

🚗 **Vetura-rentacar** [74 C5] Vladimira Nazora bb; ☎ 052 815 208; m 091 730 4408; www.vetura-rentacar.com; ⏱ all year round. Can provide you with cars equipped with winter tyres (a legal requirement in the winter in Croatia), child seats & Garmin GPS.

BY TAXI Taxis wait round the corner from the bus station at Trg na Lokva. **Flash Taxi** [74 D3] (m 098 224 905; e info@taxi-rovinj.com; www.taxi-rovinj.com) also does airport transfers.

BY BIKE Most of the travel agencies provide bike hire, and many hotels too, and they can be picked up at the entrance to the coastal path south just after the marina. For bike servicing and rental see:

🚲 **Bike Planet** [74 C3] Trg na Lokva 3; ☎ 052 830 531; m 091 723 2094. Run by 2 friendly brothers. Rental available at 70kn/day.

TOURIST INFORMATION

Rovinj's **tourist information bureau** [77 C2] (*Obala Pina Budicina 12;* ☎ *052 811 566;* e *tzgrovinj@tzgrovinj.hr; www.tzgrovinj.hr;* ⏱ *15 Jun–15 Sep 08.00–21.00 daily, with gradually lesser times towards the winter; closed Sun in winter*) is located almost opposite the harbour master's office and the police station at Grande Molo (the large pier). Here, online and in person, you can find accommodation of all types and some fairly useful information. This is where to register if you are staying in private accommodation or on your own boat.

Another useful website for information and accommodation on Rovinj is www.rovinj.info.

WHERE TO STAY

As elsewhere in Istria, most of Rovinj's hotels are dominated by a local monopoly: in Rovinj's case this is Maistra, which is part of the local Adris tobacco group. The joy of Rovinj is best appreciated, however, from one of the many high-grade private apartments in the old town, and so it is worth going through one of the tourism agencies below.

HOTELS

🏠 **Angelo D'Oro** [77 A1] (24 rooms) Vladimira Svalbe 38–42; ☎ 052 840 502; e hotelangelo@rovinj.at; www.rovinj.at. This might only be a 4-star because it lacks a pool & fitness room, but the service & the setting in this 17th-century former bishop's palace are my favourites by far. Bijou & exquisite, it has the tiniest of spas & a miniature library corner & terrace on the top floor. Here you're transported back to how travel could be for the Venetian classes complete with antique furniture pieces (OK, minus the Wi-Fi, TV

& AC now available here). Painted in Venetian red at the back of the old town, it has a cavernous dining room, which is always cool in the summer. **$$$$$**

🏠 **Lone Hotel** [74 C7] (248 rooms) Luje Adamovica 31; ☎ 052 632 000; e lone@maistra.hr; www.lonehotel.com. The local monopoly Maistra's 5-star designer hotel that looks like a cruise ship. Newly opened with all the trimmings, from rooms with their own private terrace pools to staff uniforms by Croatian designer I-GLE. **$$$$$**

⌂ **Monte Mulini** [74 C7] (113 rooms) A Smareglia bb; ☎ 052 636 000; e montemulini@maistra.hr; www.montemulinihotel.com. Another Maistra high-end hotel & only 300m from the Lone. Has a full spa service open to non-hotel guests. Standard chic. **$$$$$**

⌂ **Casa Garzotto** [77 C2] (4 rooms) Garzotto 8; ☎ 052 811 884; e casagarzotto@gmail.com; www.casa-garzotto.com. This lovely little boutique hotel is in the centre of town, & offers 4 studio apartments in a renovated house with polished wooden floors & beams, & exposed stonework. **$$$$**

⌂ **Istra** (326 rooms) Otok Sv Andreja, Crveni Otok; ☎ 052 802 500; e istra@maistra.hr; www.maistra.com/Accommodation/Hotels/Istra_Rovinj. The island's only accommodation, which offers the complete package, including spa centre & entertainment. **$$$$**

⌂ **Katarina** (120 rooms) Otok Sv Katarina; ☎ 052 804 100; e katarina@maistra.com; www.maistra.com/Accommodation/Hotels/Katarina_

Rovinj. On the island visible from the old town, this hotel is another Maistra island-takeover. Good for families wanting everything nearby. **$$$**

⌂ **Residence Dream** [74 C3] (4 rooms) Joakima Rakovca 18; ☎ 052 830 613; m 091 579 9239; e dream@dream.hr; www.dream.hr. Right in the middle of this popular alley between Carrera & the marina, this tiny hotel has an excellent restaurant serving breakfast through to dinner. Decorated with old-time paraphernalia, & with free Wi-Fi, their linguine dishes are extremely tasty. **$$$**

⌂ **Villa Lili** [74 D5] (20 rooms) A Mohorovičića 16; ☎ 052 840 940; e vila-lili@pu.t-com.hr; www.hotel-vilalili.hr. Not far from the harbour & access to the old town, this friendly family-run boutique hotel shows lots of attention to detail & a breakfast to match – you might want to have a good swim before breakfast to make sure you make the most of it. Pets welcome. Telescope available for star-gazing. **$$$**

APARTMENTS There are lots of gorgeous little apartments to be rented in the old town. A couple are listed here and many more can be found through the property management agencies listed; www.rovinj.info (see *Tourist information*, page 75) is a good source, as are many other tourist agencies around Rovinj.

⌂ **Art Decolab Apartments** [77 B2] (3 apts) Montalbano 17; ☎ 052 813 184; e labfoudc@box455.bluehost.com; www.artdecolab.com. Leo Tosic, an Art Deco restorer with a gallery in the old town & a workshop outside town, offers 3 apartments in the old town. **$$$**

⌂ **Villa Cissa** [77 C1] (3 apts) Zdenac 14; ☎ 052 813 080; e info@villacissa.com; www.villacissa.com. Beautifully renovated & furnished apartments. **$$$**

Dik & Co [77 C1] Petra Ive bb; ☎ 052 818 181; e info@dik-rovinj.com; www.dik-rovinj.com;

⊕ Jul/Aug 09.00–20.00 daily, rest of the year 09.00–16.00 Mon–Sat. The property management company is conveniently located not far from the main car park if you're arriving by car. Offers a wide range of apartments all also bookable online.

Elim Property Agents [77 C2] Andronella 12a; ☎ 052 811 573; m 091 786 3219; e info@rovinjapartments.info; www.rovinjapartments.info; ⊕ Jul/Aug 09.00–20.00 daily, rest of the year 09.00–16.00 Mon–Sat. A wide variety of self-catering property is available through this agent, & their office is located right in the old town itself.

CAMPING

🅐 **Porton Biondi** Alija Porton Biondi; ☎ 052 813 557; e portonbiondi@web.de; www.portonbiondi.com; ⊕ mid-Mar–Oct. The closest campsite to the town, being only 700m north of the Balbi Arch. It can accommodate 1,200 people on 11ha of pine-wooded grounds & affords some nice beaches & views of the town. Pets allowed. Pitches start at €10 for the first day for 1 person.

🅐 **Valdaliso** Monsena bb; ☎ 052 805 505; e ac-valdaliso@maistra.hr; www.campingrovinjvrsar.

com; ⊕ Apr–mid-Oct. Almost at the mouth of the Limski kanal & still only 4km from the old town, this campsite, part of the bigger Maistra hotel & camping conglomerate, is very well equipped, with shuttle buses & taxi-boats to Rovinj, Wi-Fi, & water & electricity at all pitches. Valdaliso Diving Centre (see *Diving centres*, page 192) is co-located, & Blu restaurant (see *Where to eat and drink,* opposite) is 500m away. No pets. Pitches start at €10 for the first day for 1 person.

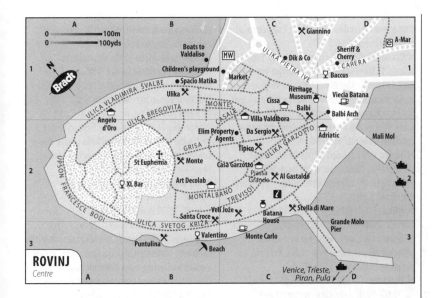

✕ WHERE TO EAT AND DRINK

✕ Al Gastaldo [77 C2] Iza Kasarne 14; ☎052 814 109; ⏰ 11.00–15.00 & 18.00–23.00 daily. This little restaurant, tucked away behind Balbi's Arch, is open year-round, & being almost underground is welcomingly cool in the summer & hearteningly warm by the fire in the winter. Surrounded by wine bottles & bare stone walls, the food is equally sublime. Try their *Sv Jakov školkje* scallops, which are the best I've tasted anywhere. **$$$$**

✕ Lanterna [74 A5] Sv Andreja, Crveni Otok; ☎052 802 580; ⏰ mid-Apr–mid-Oct 12.00–23.00 daily. For those not staying on the island, the 40kn return boat ride to Crveni Otok does add to your bill, but if you want somewhere exclusive & quiet to eat lunch, I can't think of a better place midweek. Set in the courtyard of the 19th-century country manor of the former owner, the stone pillars, bright red sofas & massive standing silver candelabras provide a sublime setting against the view of the sea & the main shore. Sea-bass carpaccio, warm octopus salad, & risotto with Kvarner prawns are among the fare on offer here. Reserve for the front tables on the terrace. The Captain's Club on the corner of the manor is a popular high-end bar with exceptional views. **$$$$**

✕ Monte [77 B2] Montalbano 75; ☎052 830 203; ✉ restaurant@monte.hr; www.monte.hr; ⏰ mid-Apr–mid-Oct 18.30–23.30 daily. This is the best of fine dining & fusion cuisine in Rovinj, & earns itself a place in the *Gault Millau*. Not just the fish but the lamb & suckling pig are exquisite. Although the highest restaurant in Rovinj, it does not afford views of the sea, but it is a stone's throw from the cathedral. **$$$$**

✕ Puntulina [77 B3] Sv Križa 38; ☎052 813 186; ✉ puntulina@gmail.com; ⏰ Easter–Oct 12.00–15.00 & 18.00–22.00 Thu–Tue (& Jul/Aug Wed). Without doubt the restaurant with the best view in the whole of Rovinj. With balconies perched high on the side of the building overlooking the sea, the sunset here rivals anywhere in the world. Small & cosy, it's the place for a romantic dinner, & the food's good too. Try their local speciality squid with polenta, or their house special St Jacob's scallops with brandy. Book in advance to be sure of a table. **$$$$**

✕ Santa Croce [77 B2] Sv Križa 11; ☎052 842 240; ⏰ 18.00–midnight daily. Set in a little square called Poljana Sv Barnabe. Very popular restaurant serving fabulous seafood with interesting twists. The monkfish with truffles is superb. **$$$$**

✕ Blu [74 D1] Val de Lesso 9; ☎052 811 265; ⏰ 12.00–23.00 daily. Located on the Rovinj side of Camp Valdaliso, the tarmac runs out just behind this restaurant. With an enviable view onto the sea & Rovinj old town, its tables also spill out onto a small veranda on the beach. Excellent food reasonably priced. $$$

✗ **Giannino** [77 C1] Augusta Ferrija 38; ☎052 813 402; ⏰ 11.00–14.00 & 18.00–midnight Tue–Sun, closed 10 Nov–1 Mar. About 100m up Augusto Ferri St, Giannino's serves excellent, no-nonsense seafood dishes such as plaice with truffles, & linguine with clams. Well established & a locals' favourite with a cosy bare-stone interior. $$$

✗ **Tipico** [77 C2] Grisia 32; m 091 724 0621; ⏰ 12.00–23.00 daily. Excellent local dishes, including lamb, cold cuts & the usual array of fresh fish. Small & friendly. $$$

✗ **Ulika** [77 B1] Vladimira Svalbe 34; ☎052 818 089; ⏰ 12.00–14.00 & 18.00–midnight Tue–Sun. An atmospheric little bistro, run by a former ballerina, serving tapas-type dishes. Portions are not large, but are very tasty. $$$

✗ **Veli Jože** [77 C2] Sv Križa 1; ☎052 816 337; ⏰ 10.00–02.00 daily. Easily recognisable by the old diving suit & complete head mask standing outside the front door, & its abundance of seafaring paraphernalia on the inside, this restaurant is a must-visit, even if the service is brusque & the seafood merely average. Serves better meat dishes, including a good spit-roast lamb. $$$

✗ **Balbi** [77 D1] Veli trg 2; ☎052 817 200; ⏰ Apr–Oct 11.00–23.00 daily. Beyond Balbi's Arch is the ambitiously named little square 'Piassa Grande'. Here Balbi restaurant serves a good range of seafood, meat & pasta dishes. $$

✗ **Da Sergio Pizzeria** [77 C2] Grisia 11; ☎052 816 949; www.rovigno.it; ⏰ 11.00–15.00 & 18.00–23.00 Mon–Fri, 11.00–23.00 Sat/Sun. Da Sergio has won awards for a reason. As the newspaper articles pasted in the windows attest, the chefs here – using a traditional wood-burning oven – make some of the most authentic Italian thin-crust pizzas you'll experience outside Italy today. More than 30 different pizzas to choose from. $$

CAFÉS AND BARS

♀ **Baccus Wine Bar** [77 D1] Trg Giovanni Pignatona (cornered with Carrera); ⏰ 10.00–01.00 daily. Baccus has an excellent selection of Istrian wines, & is also a good place to buy bottles of wine to enjoy later.

▱ **Café Cinema** [74 C3] Trg brodogradilišta bb; ⏰ summer 07.00–02.00 daily, winter 07.00–midnight Sun–Fri, 07.30–02.00 Sat. Playing cool rock among black-&-white old movie décor on its wide exclusive corner at the edge of the pedestrian zone, this is a great place to relax. Away from the hubbub of the centre yet still in view of the sea & islands, it's very popular with locals for large coffees, *spremutan* (freshly squeezed orange juice) & *brioches* (filled croissants) or *tost* sandwiches in the morning. Serves a very wide range of hot drinks, including a decent tea (although you'd still need 2 teabags for builder's strength) with milk or soy in large Dammann Frères cups.

▱ **Monte Carlo** [77 C3] Sv Križa 2. A relaxing café bar overlooking the sea & a great place to have a coffee after a morning swim off the rocks.

♀ **Valentino** [77 B3] Sv Križa 28; ☎052 830 683; e info@valentino-rovinj.com; www.valentino-rovinj.com; ⏰ Apr/May 12.00–midnight daily; Jun–Sep 18.00–02.00 daily; closed Oct–Mar. No credit cards. This is by far the classiest & coolest cocktail bar in Istria, & ranks high I'm sure worldwide. Your drinks are served 'on the rocks' (with ice) literally, also, on the rocks of the seashore, with pillows & candles strewn for comfort & decoration. Whilst the cocktails might not be expensive by world standards, they're certainly so by Croatian standards.

▱ **Viecia Batana** [77 C1] Trg maršala Tita bb. *The* place to drink as a local. Serves great coffee & is prefect for sitting & watching the world go by. **Al Ponto & Caffeteria Piazza,** also on the square, are equally good for taking in the atmosphere.

♀ **XL Bar** [77 C2] Josipa Tankovica bb; m 098 814 445; ⏰ 11.00–22.00 daily. The ideal place for sundowners after you've visited St Euphemia Church. It's a bit hidden, sitting between the front of the church & the sea. Head a bit to your right after coming down the main stairs at the front of the church. Cross the open area & go down 1 set of stairs. Angle left through the stone doorway. It's tough to find a more idyllic view.

ENTERTAINMENT AND NIGHTLIFE

The place for **clubbing and partying** in Rovinj is the **Monvi Centre** (*Luja Adamovića bb;* ☎ *052 545 117;* m *091 654 5117;* e *brid@pu-t-com.hr; www.monvicenter.com*), where you'll find restaurants, bars, and clubs open till 06.00, showcasing a variety of different events and sounds for most tastes.

SHOPPING

Aqua Maritime [74 C2] Carrera 55; www. aquamaritime.hr; ☼ summer 10.30–22.00; winter 10.00–16.00, closed Sun. This store capitalises on the navy blue & cream stripe-effect & their brand logo of a cartoon ship & a fat whale. More than just T-shirts in every size, this is a great place for souvenirs as well as something for yourself – summer dresses, hoodies, babygros, towels, thick-soled flip-flops, bags, fish soaps & much more.
Rovinj Tržnica [77 C1] A small compact market, half of which is occupied by the fish hall.

In addition to fruit & veg, the outdoor area also has a lot of souvenir products, including Istrian liqueurs, lavender, olive oil, strings of brightly coloured peppers & garlic, honey & other local produce.
Sheriff and Cherry [77 D1] Carrera 6; www. sheriffandcherry.com; ☼ summer 10.30–22.00; winter 10.00–16.00, closed Sun. An eclectic choice of urban clothing designs. This is the original store of Rovinj-born Mauro Massarotti, a Barcelona-based fashion consultant. Branches also available in Dubrovnik & Zagreb.

OTHER PRACTICALITIES

✚ **Hospital** [74 D3] Istarska bb (entrance on Mateo Benussi); ☏ 052 813 004. This is the local accident & emergency ward.
🖳 **Internet** A-Mar internet café [77 D1] (*Carrera 26,* ☼ *09.00–22.00 daily*) provides over 20 terminals & has printing facilities. Few cafés offer Wi-Fi, but several restaurants do, including Dream

& Marina (*Obala Adla Rismonda 2;* ☼ *summer 12.00–midnight daily*)
✚ **Pharmacy** Mateo Benussi 5; ☏ 052 813 589; ☼ 07.00–20.00 Mon–Fri, 09.00–15.00 Sat, 09.00–12.00 Sun
✉ **Post office** [74 D3] Mateo Benussi 4; ☏ 052 811 262; ☼ 07.00–19.00 Mon–Fri

WHAT TO SEE AND DO

Rovinj has its fair share of events, festivals and concerts. In June don't miss the Bijeli Lav Underwater Film and Photo Festival (see *Chapter 12*). For a full list of events pick up the events brochure in the tourist information office.

Built in 1678, when Rovinj was still an island, the **Balbi Arch** [77 D1] (*Trg maršala Tita*) was the main entrance to the town. A Turk's head adorns the top of the outside of the arch as a symbol to ward off Ottoman invaders, while on the inside of the arch a Venetian's head adorns the apex as a symbol to safeguard the Venetian population on the inside of the town walls.

Almost next door to the Balbi Arch is the **Heritage Museum** [77 C1] (*Trg Maršala Tita 11;* ☏ *052 816 720;* e *muzej-rovinj@ pu.htnet.hr; www.muzej-rovinj. com;* ☼ *10.00–14.00 & 18.00–22.00 Tue–Fri, 19.00–22.00 Sat/Sun, closed Mon; entry 30kn*), which has a permanent exhibition of modern art that almost does justice to Rovinj's resident artists. Sadly, most of the 'modern' art dates from the '70s and there isn't a nameplate or explanation anywhere in sight. For 200kn you can buy a book that catalogues all the museum's pieces and where you'll find the artist, title and date. Otherwise the museum houses temporary exhibitions and hosts concerts.

The **Batana House** [77 C2] (*Obala P Budicina 2;* ☏ *052 812 593;* e *batana@rv-batana. htnet.hr; www.batana.org;* ☼ *10.00–14.00 & 19.00–23.00 daily; entry 10kn*) is an eco-museum devoted to the old wooden fishing boats you can still find in Rovinj's harbour, as well as to the fishing culture associated with them. There are recordings of Rovinj dialect, explanations of how the various nets were used for

4

different varieties of fish, and samples of all the tools, sails and accoutrements of these old vessels. A fast-motion movie of the making of a *batana* shows in ten minutes how the boats are built from scratch in just one week. Apparently there's only one *batana*-maker left in Istria and the guide will give you his details if you're interested in owning your own. A new one sells for about €3,500. Watch for the live *batana*-making exhibition across from the entrance to the museum on Tuesdays throughout the summer. Good souvenirs.

Rovinj's **St Euphemia Church** [77 B2] (*Petro Stankovica;* ⊕ *visitors 10.00–14.00 & 15.00–18.00; mass 08.00, 09.00 (Italian), 10.30, 12.00, 18.00, 19.00 Sun; 07.30, 18.00, 19.00 Mon–Sat*) sits at the top of the hill on which the old town was built, and is one of the most iconic buildings in Istria. A church of St George was first on this site, and his statue remains on the central altar, but when the remains of St Euphemia came in a stone sarcophagus from Constantinople, the numbers of pilgrims quickly outgrew the small chapel. A new church bearing St Euphemia's name was built during the 10th century. Then in 1725, the townspeople rebuilt the structure into what is today – save for the façade, which was built in the 1900s. One of its most notable features is the bell tower, modelled after that of St Mark's in Venice. For €2/15kn you can climb the 170 steps for an unparalleled view of Rovinj and environs. On top of that St Euphemia reigns as a weathervane. Make sure to see the exquisitely restored *Last Supper* by Giovanni Contarini, originally painted in 1574.

Built in the style of the old taverns where fishermen ate and drank after their return from the sea, the **Spàcio Matika** [77 B1] (*35 Vladimira Švalbe;* ↘ *052 812 593;* e *batana@rv- batana.htnet.hr; www.batana.org;* ⊕ *Jul/Aug 20.00–23.00 Tue, Thu & Fri*) offers a unique way to experience old Rovinj fishing culture, including traditional singing and traditional recipes for cooking up the day's catch. Guests can opt for a *batana* boat ride at 20.00, taking them around Rovinj's old town to their dinner destination. Off season, Spàcio is available for groups of 25 or more and must be booked three days in advance.

ST EUPHEMIA

Born in the village of Chalcedon near Constantinople in the 3rd century AD (Diocletian's reign), Euphemia was the daughter of a Roman senator. But her belief in the Christian God soon put her at odds with the Governor of Chalcedon, Priscus, who was demanding sacrifices to the pagan gods. Euphemia and her friends were discovered in hiding and for their failure to convert were subjected to various grisly forms of torture including 'the wheel'. It seems she survived the ordeal only to be fed to the lions (or a bear, depending on who you ask) in the arena.

As a martyr, St Euphemia's relics were later placed in a golden sarcophagus and the church built in Chalcedon to house them soon became a popular pilgrimage. So popular in fact that her relics eventually had to be moved to Constantinople to avoid their destruction by Persian invaders. Unfortunately, in the early 7th century Iconoclasts dumped St Euphemia's remains into the sea. They were allegedly rescued by two boat-owning brothers, who secreted them away on the island of Lemnos. Some 200 years later they were returned to Constantinople. However, a portion of her reliquary miraculously turned up in a large stone sarcophagus in Rovinj where they have been ever since. The rest of her can be found in the Church of St George in Istanbul.

Just east of the old town is the **Franciscan Monastery Museum** [74 C2] (*De Amicis 36;* m *095 871 6773;* ⊕ *10.00–12.00 Mon–Sat; entry 10kn*). The monastery itself was completed in 1710 and is dedicated to St Francis of Assisi. The museum holds a fascinating mix of articles from old habits and reliquaries to large wall maps charting the lineage of man from 4004bc to 1799, or more in-depth from ad0 to 1800. Only a minuscule number of the monastery's library of 12,000 books are on show. Sadly the exhibits could do with a lot of care, but are worth the visit nonetheless. Outside museum times, the church itself is open for services and sometimes holds concerts.

Just south of the old town heading towards the marina is **Kino Gandusio** [74 D4] (*Trg Valdibora 17;* ✆ *052 811 588;* e *pou-grada-rovinja@ pu.t-com.hr; www.rovinj. hr/rovinj/rovinj/kultura/kazaliste-gandusio;* ⊕ *20.00 when films are showing; entry 20kn*). Current movies in a classic old theatre house. There is also local theatre, burlesque, operas and operettas, political, comedy and other cultural events. Movies start at 21.00 and are normally subtitled, rather than dubbed.

Just beyond Kino Gandusio is the **Tobacco Factory Museum and Gallery** [74 D4] (*Obala Vladimira Nazora 1;* ✆ *052 844 000;* e *tdr@tdr.hr; www.tdr.hr/svijet_ duhana/price_duhan/duhan_muzej.html;* ⊕ *by prior engagement only; entry free*). Tvornica Duhana Rovinj (TDR) is the maker of the ubiquitous Ronhill, Walter Wolf, York and Benston cigarettes, among others. Established in 1872, the tobacco factory built its place in smoking history by supplying officers of the Austro-Hungarian military with cigarettes. It is now Croatia's top-selling tobacco company. In 1998 it opened the country's first tobacco museum and for smoking enthusiasts it is a must-see.

In a grand building opposite the main town car park, Rovinj's small **aquarium** [74 D1] (*G Paliaga 5;* ✆ *052 804 700;* e *cmrr@more.cim.irb.hr; www.cim.irb.hr;* ⊕ *09.00–20.00 daily; entry 10kn*) has only 20 tanks in all, but the fish, molluscs and plantlife are a fine selection from the nearby Adriatic. Overall it's well presented, and works nicely for a quick escape from the heat. Look out for the enormous sunfish on the wall – apparently caught in the 1700s and well ... it looks it... (the years have not been kind).

ACTIVITIES

Hiking and **biking** along the coast are very popular activities, and large overview maps for these can be picked up at the tourist information office. Heading south of the old town takes you around **Zlatni rt** nature reserve (locally also called by its Italian name Punta Corrente, both meaning 'golden cape') towards Palud bird sanctuary (see below). Less than 1km south of the town is a large bolted **rock climbing face** along the top section of the sea cliff, with a very wide access area. **Horseriding** is also available at Farm Haber (*Val de Lesso 1;* m *098 368 454;* e *mirjam.haber@pu.t-com.hr*), and at the Horse Ranch at kilometre marker 4 just outside Rovinjsko Selo.

Palud bird sanctuary, 8km southwest of Rovinj, is a former freshwater marsh, which was flooded with seawater when the Austro-Hungarian army based in Barbariga dug a 200m canal connecting it to the sea in 1906 in order to stop mosquitoes thriving there. Now it is Istria's only bird sanctuary, and has become an important stop for migratory birds. A cycle ride there along the coastline is some 13km, and take care to follow the signs for the bicycle path in case you end up in the maze of nudist campers at Camping Oaza Polaris. Entrance to Palud is free, two-hour guided tours are available for 30kn, and longer birdwatching trips from

50kn, including binoculars. Contact the tourist information bureau (see *Tourist information,* page 75) to arrange tours.

The **19 islands** of Rovinj's archipelago are best seen by boat. Many trips are available from Mali Mol, but if you want to charter your own boat, then see the charter companies listed on *Sailing the shores of Istria,* page 44. On my last trip through the islands, I saw a solitary plastic beach lounger on a spit of rock in the middle of the sea, circled only by a pair of dolphins.

BEACHES You don't have to go far to jump in the water or lounge around in swimwear. Around the south side of the old town there are stretches of rock that are popular with sunbathers and swimmers, and where there are ladders especially for entering and exiting the water. To bathe and tan in your birthday suit, you'll need to go a little further, and Istria's most famous gay beach is a few kilometres north of the town. North of Rovinj from closest to furthest are the rock and pebble beaches of **Porton Biondi**, **Borik**, **Valdaliso** and **Amarin**. After Amarin is **Punta Kriza** nudist and gay beach.

Fine gravel and/or sand beaches
Kuvi Bay Small pebble beach, which stretches 1km along the coast and is 2km south of the old town.

Lone Bay Near the five-star Lone Hotel complex 1km south of the old town, but accessible to the public.

Valalta North of Rovinj at the Limski kanal entrance – for naturists.

Villas Rubin Some 3km from the town centre by road & 7km by the coast after Kuvi Bay sport & recreation zone.

Other public beaches
Baluota Rocky beach at the end of the old town, down from St Euphemia Church.

Cape Rusi Not so much a beach as a series of large boulders, but has some spots for jumping at height into the water. Be careful!

Katarina Otok Rock, pebble and play areas for children. Take the regular passenger boat across from Mali Mol (see *Getting around,* page 73).

Škaraba Bay Nice beach with flat stones, but also very rocky and thus a bit less frequented by tourists.

Zlatni rt A really beautiful rock and pebble beach located within the Zlatni rt nature reserve.

5

Poreč and the Northwest Coast

Poreč and the northwest coast is where the grand majority of visitors to Istria stay, play and beach. Although there are more popular sites to visit, such as Rovinj, Pula and the hill-town retreats of Motovun and Buzet, Poreč has the copious accommodation to deal with the many summer visitors who arrive by car from nearby countries. Poreč itself has a beautiful and quite typical Croatian coastal old town, jutting like a small island into the sea, and is home to renowned 6th-century BC mosaics in its UNESCO World Heritage Site basilica.

POREČ

Back in Roman times Poreč was the capital of Istria. Today it retains a life of its own year-round, unlike the more highly praised Rovinj, which burgeons in the summer and is deserted in the winter. Poreč life picks up as early as the end of February, when the first of the cycling enthusiasts come to take advantage of the mild weather and light traffic on Istrian roads. And while beach facilities might close in mid-October, outdoor-sports types, especially divers, will stay into early November, when the water can retain a wonderful 18°C temperature, often warmer than the outside air.

HISTORY The Histri tribe settled in and around the area of Poreč some 6,000 years ago. By as early as 4,000 years ago, an observatory, settlement and ritual site was located at Picugi (halfway between today's Dračevac and Garbina east-southeast of Poreč), which may give an indication of the importance of the area at the time. When the Romans defeated the Histri in 177BC, they fortified the miniature peninsula that is now Poreč as a defensive encampment, or *castrum*. Easily accessible by ship, the encampment grew, and by AD14, Emperor Augustus had officially upgraded it to a city, known as Parentium.

By the 3rd century, Christianity was taking hold of Parentium. Mavar (later known as Maurus) of Parentium became the first bishop of the city and also its patron saint when he was martyred by Emperor Diocletian in AD304. His remains were transferred to the first basilica built in Parentium in the second half of the 4th century and remain in the current Euphrasian Basilica rebuilt there in the 6th century. The mosaics from the first basilica can still be seen today in the church gardens.

After the demise of the Roman Empire in 476, Poreč fell to the Huns and then in 493 to Theodoric the Ostrogoth. By 539 the Byzantine emperor Justinian had extended his empire to include Istria, and it was during this time of extended peace that Bishop Euphrasius built the current cathedral complex named after him. Euphrasius set a trend in building this church, by adding an additional apse (the

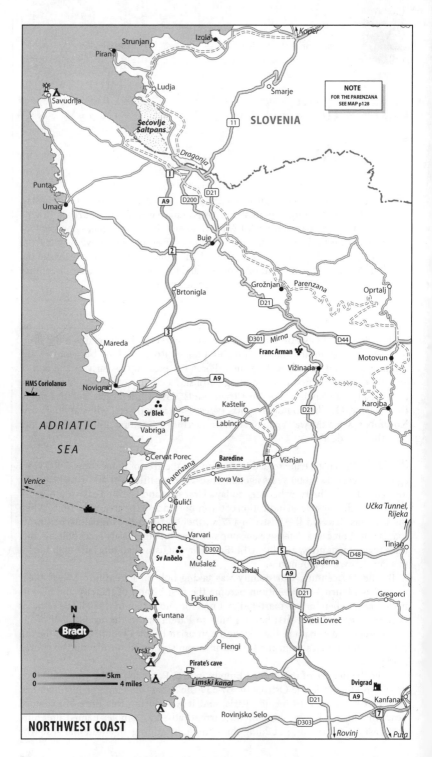

NOTE
FOR THE PARENZANA
SEE MAP p128

SLOVENIA

Koper

Izola

Strunjan

Piran

Ludja

Šmarje

Savudrija

Sečovlje
Saltpans

Dragonja

11

Punta

Umag

A9

D200

D21

Buje

2

Brtonigla

Grožnjan

Parenzana

Oprtalj

D21

3

D301

Mirna

D44

Franc Arman

Vižinada

Motovun

Mareda

A9

HMS Coriolanus

Novigrad

Karojba

Kaštelir

Sv Blek

Tar

Labinci

D21

Vabriga

ADRIATIC

SEA

Cervat Poreč

Baredine

4

Višnjan

Parenzana

Nova Vas

Venice

Gulići

Učka Tunnel,
Rijeka

POREČ

Varvari

Tinjan

Sv Anđelo

D302

5

Baderna

D48

Mušalež

Žbandaj

A9

Gregorci

Fuškulin

D21

Funtana

Sveti Lovreč

Flengi

6

Vrsar

Pirate's cave

Dvigrad

Limski kanal

N

Bradt

0   5km

0   4 miles

Kanfanar

7

Rovinjsko Selo

D21

A9

D303

Rovinj

Puta

NORTHWEST COAST

84

semicircular hollow usually found at the head of the central nave of the church) at the end of the aisles on either side of the main nave. It is thus the very first triple-apse church to be built in western Europe. For more on the UNESCO status and history of the basilica, see box below.

Byzantine rule ended for Poreč in 751, and by 788 was part of Germanic Middle Frankia, and then fought over by western and eastern Frankia until in 1267, Poreč became the first Istrian city to join the Republic of Venice. Venetian rule lasted for 530 years, and was marred only briefly when the Republic of Genoa invaded and destroyed large swathes of the town.

In 1797 Venice retreated from Istria and Poreč was ruled by the Habsburg monarchy. An interlude of ten years from 1805 to 1814 saw Napoleon's Kingdom of Italy and then the First French Empire rule Poreč, after which it returned to Austria-Hungary. The Austrian Empire brought with it a century of modernity and the flavour of things to come. The year 1844 saw the first steamship leave Poreč bound for Trieste, and then in 1845 Poreč's first guidebook went into print, written by Petro Kandler. In 1895 Poreč opened its first public beach and by 1902

EUPHRASIAN BASILICA

Today's Euphrasian Basilica in Poreč was built at the behest of Bishop Euphrasius in AD553. It was built to replace the smaller 5th-century basilica that originally stood there, which in itself was built on an earlier basilica dedicated to Sv Maurus dating from AD313. The current 6th-century structure is one of the finest examples of early Byzantine architecture and, along with the 5th-century floor mosaics still to be seen there, and some of the 4th-century mosaics unearthed there, it was inscribed into the UNESCO World Heritage List in 1997. Elements of the 4th-century mosaics, including a mosaic of the fish symbol of Christ, are to be found in the garden at the far end of the basilica courtyard (entry 15kn), along with the bishop's palace. The 5th-century mosaics can be seen under glass on either side of the main entrance into the church (entry free).

The shape of the 6th-century basilica is particularly noteworthy. At first, it looks completely normal, and that is because it is. In fact, it is the first example in western Europe of a triple-naved and triple-apsed church. Equally noteworthy are the mosaics of the basilica. In the vault above the main apse, you'll find the only early Christian depiction of Mary to be found in a western European church. To one side is the depiction of Euphrasius himself, holding a model of the church. The triumphal arch edging the top of the apse shows Christ and the 12 Apostles, and below them the Lamb of God and 12 medallion portraits of female martyrs.

While the shape of the 6th-century basilica remains intact, a number of alterations were made over the years. A bell tower was added opposite the entrance to the church in the 16th century. You can climb this for 20kn, but entry to the baptistery at the bottom of the tower is free, and usually contains a small art exhibition. Between the bell tower and the church a colonnaded atrium courtyard with several stone sculptures was later added, and then in the 17th century a clover-shaped memorial chapel.

The church is free to visit 07.00–17.30 daily, after which is mass Monday–Saturday. Mass is held at 10.00 on Sunday. Photography inside the church is allowed.

5

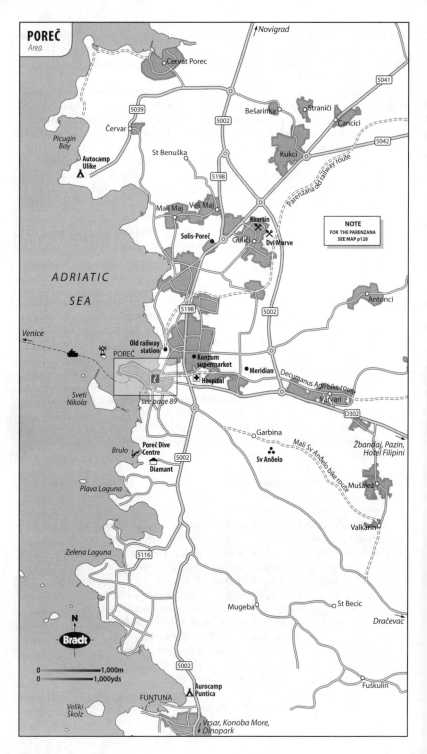

Europeans were flocking to Poreč on the Parenzana narrow-gauge railway (see page 128) that ran from Trieste.

Poreč became the capital of Istria in 1861 and thus home to the regional parliament. Following its Roman history it also became a centre for shipbuilding. Prized by Italy, it was annexed in 1918 and remained a part of the Kingdom of Italy until 1945. The Allies air-raided Poreč 34 times in 1944 (an American Consolidated B-24 Liberator heavy bomber, shot down from outside Poreč in 1944, lies southwest of Vrsar), leaving 75% of the city in ruins. Many Italian-speakers from Poreč left with the Istrian exodus after World War II. Although many Slav-speakers from the rest of Croatia took their place, most people in Poreč, along with the entire west coast of Istria, remain bilingual.

GETTING THERE AND AWAY

By train The nearest train station is Sveti Petar u Šumi (local stop), or Pazin, which is served once a day on the Pula–Ljubljana line (see *Getting around*, page 31). Details of other local trains to Rijeka and Ljupoglav can be found at www.tzpazin. hr/index_eng.php?stranica=22.

By bus Poreč is poorly served by buses from the rest of Croatia or Trieste or neighbouring Slovenia. Timetables for Croatian buses serving Poreč can be found at www.buscroatia.com or www.akz.hr. There are more frequent services to the rest of Croatia via Rijeka (see *Getting there and away*, page 138). Italian buses from Trieste leave daily at 09.00, 11.00 (not Sunday), 14.00, and 18.00 (not Sunday), taking up to two hours and ten minutes. There are more frequent buses to Buje, where you can change for a local bus, but do check connections. The Trieste bus station timetable is at www.autostazionetrieste.it. Buses to Trieste leave daily at 07.00 (not Sunday), 11.30 (not Sunday) and 17.30. In the summer months there are also minibuses to and from Koper in Slovenia (see www.ap-ljubljana.si).

Poreč **bus station** [89 E4] (*Karla Huguesa 2;* ↘ 052 432 153; ⊕ 05.20–22.00 daily) is on the outskirts of town, with the taxi stand on the road right outside. It does have a small café and an ATM.

By boat Reminiscent of its seafaring heritage, a great way to arrive in Istria is to take the ferry from St Basilio international ferry terminus in Venice (leaving at 17.00) to Poreč (arriving at 19.30). This runs from mid-April to mid-October on Wednesday and Saturday, and runs daily in the peak season. Two operators ply this route: **Venezia Lines** (*www.venezialines.com*) and **Adriatic Lines** (*www.adriatic-lines.com*). The return to Venice (supposedly arriving at 10.30, but it will be 11.00 by the time you've disembarked and gone through border control and customs) leaves Poreč at 08.00. You need to be at the ferry at least 40 minutes prior to boarding and outside the peak season it's possible to buy tickets at the ferry. Tickets cost €65 return for an adult (€55 single), with discounts for children, and infants go free. The *Prince of Venice* (Adriatic Lines) is the (slightly) most luxurious of all the boats and has an outdoor deck. Venezia Lines' boats have a first-class upper deck (indoor), access to which can be purchased for an extra €7.50 once on board. Both lines include a free tour guide speech on the boat in one of several languages and sell maps and guidebooks of Venice. Both ferry boat tour guides also arrange tours around Venice (for a fee).

Poreč ferry terminal (*Obala Maršala Tita, opposite Hotel Neptune*) is just a border hut on a pier, with no waiting lounge or shelter. Located in the old town, several waterside cafés and benches nearby are available to watch the boats come in.

Being also in the pedestrian area, taxis can only approach to within 150m of the terminal, and usually wait by the pedestrian area barrier when the ferry arrives.

By car Poreč is a 40-minute drive from Trieste, two hours from Ljubljana, 2½ hours from Zagreb, six hours from Munich, eight hours from Geneva and Vienna, and ten hours from Skopje. Cammeo taxis (see *Taxis*, page 33) cost 400kn per trip from Pula airport to Poreč.

GETTING AROUND Poreč is small enough to walk around, and there is no town bus service. **Taxis** (*Dotto Taxi & Bus;* m *098 255 245 or 095 553 7300; www.porec-taxi. com*) are available and can usually be found outside the bus station. **Bicycles** are readily available for rent at many accommodation bureaux and car-hire services, and you can pick up details for these at the tourist information bureau (see next). Vetura-rentacar (see below) also rent out bicycles.

Car-hire services are few in Poreč. **Europcar** (\ *052 433 413; www2.europcar. co.uk*) operates from Hotel Poreč (see page 90) in the summer only. A local operator, open all year round, who can also provide you with cars equipped with winter tyres (a legal requirement in the winter in Croatia) is **Vetura-rentacar** [89 E2] (*Trg J Rakovca 2;* \ *052 434 700;* m *091 206 3070; www.vetura-rentacar.com*). Child seats and Garmin GPS are also available.

TOURIST INFORMATION Poreč **Tourist Information Office** [89 E2] (*Zargrebačka 9;* \ *052 451 293 or 451 458;* e *info@to-porec.com; www.to-porec.com;* ☉ *15 Jun–15 Sep 08.00–21.00 daily, with gradually lesser times towards the winter, except over the Christmas period when there are extended opening hours, closed Sun in winter*) is a fantastic resource for information on Poreč including listings of accommodation and a calendar of events. This is where you must go to register if you are staying in personal accommodation (see *Registration*, page 22)

A number of small free **maps** are available at the tourist office, including basic cycling maps. For 1:30,000 topographic hiking and biking maps you'll need to go to any number of kiosks, newsagents or supermarkets around town.

 WHERE TO STAY Poreč is awash with accommodation until the high season when it's booked out, and then you'll have to look a little further inland or up and down the coast (not ideal if you don't have wheels). Most of Poreč's tourism infrastructure is divided between two giant companies: Valamar and Plava Laguna. This is not great for competition, not least because smaller boutique hotels can't survive the winter when the summer season is controlled by a duopoly. Private accommodation is best found through one of the property agents listed below.

Hotels

⌂ **Riviera & Neptun** [89 B2] (105 rooms, 8 suites) Obala Maršala Tita 15; \052 400 800; e reservations@valamar.com; www.valamar. com/porec-hotel-valamar-riviera; ☉ Apr–Nov. Rivalling the Palazzo (below) & even stealing its old name, the Riviera has all the advantages of a conglomerate hotel (see Hotel Diamant below). **$$$$$**

⌂ **Grand Hotel Palazzo** [89 A2] (70 rooms, 4 apts) Obala Maršala Tita 24; \052 858 800;

e info@hotel-palazzo.hr; www.hotel-palazzo. hr; ☉ Feb–Dec. Built in 1910 in the heyday of early 20th-century tourism, the originally Hotel Riviera fell into disuse with the disintegration of Yugoslavia. At the turn of the 21st century it found new owners, but didn't get a complete renovation, new name & the Modernist grey additions to the ground floor until 2009. Sadly it has not profited off its heritage & has a fairly cookie-cutter, if very nice, 4-star style on the inside. A small spa

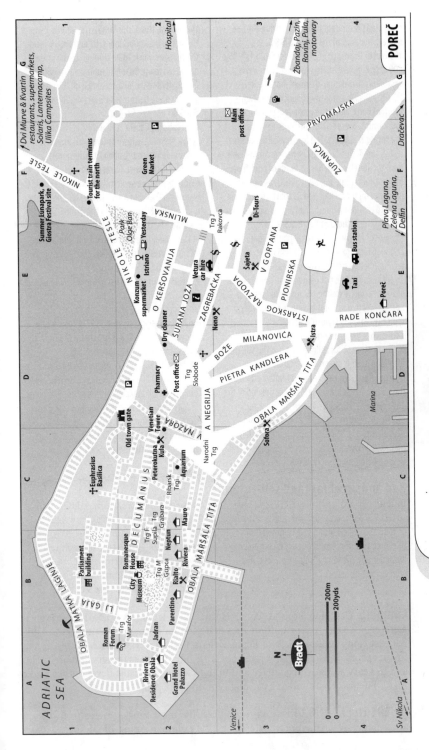

89

downstairs & outdoor pool overlooking the sea make it the envy of the town. **$$$$**

🏠 **Hotel Diamant** (244 rooms) Brulo 1; ✆ 052 400 000; e reservations@valamar.com; www. valamar.com/valamar-diamant-hotel-porec; ⊕ Feb–Dec. A 4-star tower-block hotel 1km south of Poreč along the coast. It is popular with tour groups, & especially with cycling tours in the spring & autumn. Full beach facilities, with a restaurant & Poreč Diving Centre, are 5mins' walk from the hotel, which has an outdoor pool & pool fitness programme for hotel guests, as well as an indoor pool, sports hall, tennis courts, gym & spa open to non-hotel guests. Has a children's activity programme in the summer. **$$$$**

🏠 **Hotel Filipini** (4 rooms, 4 apts) Near Žbandaj, 6km from Poreč; ✆ 052 463 200; e hotelfilipini@net.hr; www.istra.com/filipini; ⊕ all year. Despite not being in walking distance of the sea, this acclaimed & beautiful boutique hotel is worth going out of your way for. Not quite typically Istrian in style, it is nonetheless rustic with an open fire, outdoor seating, tennis courts & plenty of space for children to play. The village of Filipini itself is quaint & hails after Captain George Filipin, whose extended family settled in the village & neighbouring Vrvari at the end of the 16th century. **$$$$**

🏠 **Hotel Mauro** [89 C2] (21 rooms) Obala Maršala Tita 15; ✆ 052 219 500; e info@hotel-mauro.hr; www.hotelmauro.com; ⊕ year-round. Despite being supposedly of the same address as

the Riviera, this 4-star family-run hotel is by far the better value for money. Its entrance is inside the passageway leading through to the interior of the old town. Beautiful rooms, some with the possibility to take your breakfast on the ornate 19th-century balconies overlooking the sea. **$$$$**

🏠 **Isabella Castle** (10 suites) St Nikola Island; ✆ 052 406 600; e reservations@valamar.com; www.valamar.com/isabella-castle-porec; ⊕ May–Oct. More a former fancy villa than a true castle, & you'd never know you were in a castle (or even a villa) in your 3-star suite. Still, the location is unrivalled & has access to the giant 187-room Fortuna Island Hotel complex on the front side of the island. Take the regular boat service (free for hotel guests) from St Nikola boat pier on the mainland. **$$$$**

🏠 **Hotel Poreč** [89 E4] (54 rooms) Rade Končar 1; ✆ 052 451 811; e info@hotelporec.com; www. hotelporec.com; ⊕ all year. This former state-run hotel was privatised in 1997 & completely renovated in 2004. It has the charm of simplicity & is very close to the bus station. **$$$**

🏠 **Jadran** [89 A2] (22 rooms) Obala Maršala Tita 24; ✆ 052 400 800; e reservations@valamar. com; www.valamar.com/jadran-residence-porec; ⊕ May–Sep. Opposite the swanky Grand Hotel Palazzo, this 2-star hotel is simple & pleasant & has access to all the facilities on St Nikola Island for free (see Isabella Castle above). **$$$**

Bed and breakfast and self-catering

Di-Tours [89 F3] Prvomajska 2; ✆ 052 432 100; m 091 939 8395; e di-tours@di-tourss.hr; www. di-tours.com. Specialising in accommodation in the Poreč area, this tourist agency is conveniently located inside the town if you are on foot. Also offers excursion services.

Solis-Poreč Bračka 47; ✆ 052 433 624; m 099 221 1886; e info@solis-porec.com; www.solis-porec.com; ⊕ Jul/Aug 09.00–20.00 daily; rest of the year 09.00–16.00 Mon–Sat. A wide variety of self-catering property is available here, & is conveniently located outside of town if you're arriving by car. Also offers bike & car rental.

Camping Camping around Poreč is run by Laguna (✆ *052 410 102; www. lagunaporec.com*). They run three sites that cater for both caravans and tents. Ulika naturist camp is 4km north of Poreč. Zelena Laguna is 5km south. Puntica, 3km further south down the coast on the outskirts of Funtana, is the smallest of the sites and has easy access to the village and to the fisherman's festival every other Friday night. Pitches are around €12 per night for up to six people.

✖ **WHERE TO EAT AND DRINK** Poreč suffers like most tourist towns from having an abundance of mediocre eateries in the summer. Some of the best *konoba* and fine dining are a drive away outside the town. For spit-roast pork and lamb, there are any number of roadside restaurants on the drive through Funtana, with suckling pig a speciality in Flengi. Here are some of the best restaurants in town and around.

✗ **Dvi Murve** Grožjanska 17; ☎052 434 115; www.dvimurve.hr; ⊕ 12.00–23.00 daily, closed 10 Jan–3 Feb. Despite being 4km outside of town, in the suburb of Vranići northeast of the centre, this *konoba* is well worth the visit, & is much acclaimed by locals. It serves a wide range of Istrian wines &, of course, excellent fish, octopus carpaccio, as well as local game & pasta. **$$$**

✗ **Istra** [89 D3] Bože Milanovića 30; ☎052 434 636; ⊕ 12.00–midnight daily, closed 15 Jan–15 Mar. Genuinely good food in a traditional atmosphere at the edge of the old town. Excellent seafood & local wines. **$$$**

✗ **Konoba Kvartin** Humska 14; ☎052 438 364; ⊕ 17.00–23.00, closed Mon. In the same part of town as Dvi Murve (above), but this place offers more traditional surroundings with an open fire & thick wooden tables. Excellent local food. **$$$**

✗ **Konoba More** A Gašparini 3, Funtana; ☎052 445 202; ⊕ 12.00–midnight daily. A kilometre or so beyond Funtana on the main road, this restaurant serves fantastic food by a beautiful fireplace, & offers freshly made fritole for dessert. Try also their dried figs from the bowl on the counter on the way out (or in). **$$$**

✗ **Peterokutna Kula** [89 C2] Decumanus 1; ☎052 451 378; www.kula-porec.hr; ⊕ 11.00–23.00 daily. As the address suggests, this restaurant is housed in one of the towers of the old Roman town wall. Unrivalled views from the rooftop terrace, & not bad food & prices either. **$$$**

✗ **Bistro Nono** [89 E3] Zagrebačka 4; ☎052 453 088; ⊕ 11.00–23.00 daily. Many a tourist is very happy with a pizza at Nono's. Wide variety of pizzas, pastas & other dishes. **$$**

✗ **Šajeta Pizzeria** V Gortana 13; ☎052 452 897; ⊕ 11.00–23.00 daily. A favourite with the locals, this pizzeria also delivers within a 10km radius for free! **$$**

Cafés and bars

🖵 **Bacchus** Eufrazijeva 10; ☎052 433 539; e porec.bacchus@gmail.com; ⊕ daily 11.00–02.00 summer only. A popular vinoteka & bar offering Istrian wines & souvenirs. Conveniently located next to Fishfood fast food restaurant, where you can also grab a bite to eat to soak up your wine.

🖵 **Torre Rotonda** Narodni trg 3a; m 098 255 731; www.torrerotonda.com. A Venetian tower built in 1474, this café is beautifully cool in the summer & offers sea views from the top of the tower.

🖵 **Yesterday** [89 E2] Park Olge Ban 2; m 098 323 954; ⊕ 07.30–23.00 daily. Owned by a Beatles fan from the UK & her Croatian husband, Yesterday is a must for those wanting something a little different. Beatles photos adorn the interior. Conveniently next to a small park if you need to occupy the kids. Coffee to go & ice creams available.

♀ **Istriano** [89 E2] Park Olge Ban 3; m 099 433 8888; ⊕ 11.00–midnight daily, closed Sun in the winter. A tiny little wine bar serving a fantastic choice of Istrian wines as well as some from further afield. All their wines are available to drink on the premises or buy by the bottle to take away. They also stock medica (honey rakija) with truffles, boškorin salami with truffles, & serve great bruscetta & toasted sandwiches.

FESTIVALS There's so much going on in Poreč from May to October that it's hard to keep up. Check the Poreč Tourist Information Office calendar of events (*www. to-porec.com/en/calendar-of-events-porec*) to see what's in store. Here are a few highlights:

Giostra On the first weekend of September every year, Poreč winds the clocks back to 1745. There's jousting on horseback on the beach, costumed events, music and dancing and, of course, food. For more information, go to http://giostra.info.

Malvasia Wine Festival Usually the first weekend of June, this is a great opportunity to sample from the top-rate wineries of Istria and bag some bargains to boot.

Ribarski fešt Every Friday along the quay in either Vrsar or Funtana is the weekly fisherman's festival, when you can truly gorge yourself on more fish than you can shake a stick at. Fresh – it's almost jumping out of the pan. For an idea of what you're eating, and what is or is not becoming endangered, see the fish chart in the *Endangered fish* box, page 6.

Sv Maurus As a means of celebrating a final fling before winter sets in, Poreč celebrates its patron saint's day on 21 November. Depending on when the weekend falls, there is usually several days of festivities surrounding the day itself, including cello concerts, polenta competitions and tastings, and a spectacular church service in the patron saint's Euphrasian Basilica. One of the nicest things about the festival is that it is so late in the season that it is predominantly a festival for locals, and thus a real treat as a visitor to be there.

SHOPPING Supermarkets abound in Poreč. Konzum [89 E2] has a small branch near Olge Ban Park and a huge store at Nikole Tesle is the closest to the centre, with Lidl, Plodine and Kaufland all on the same road but further east.

Green Market [89 F2] This is the place to get fresh locally grown produce and fish caught that morning. **Terzolo wines and olive oil** also has a shop there. Bring your own plastic or glass bottles and they can sell you Malvasia, Teran, Plavac (and early in the wine season also a fantastic Muscat) direct from their metal vats in the shop for as little as 15kn per litre. In the same quadrant of the market, **Pisinium** has a small store for their local dried and cured meats, sausages and salami, including their magnificent truffle salami. Local liqueurs, *medenica* made with honey, and *bistra* made with mistletoe, are also available. A **health food store** can also be found in the corner of the indoor market should you need one.

Meridian (*Servisna zona Čimižin, Mate Vlašića 24a;* \ 052 453 096; e *shop@meridian.hr; www.meridian.hr*) A nautical and camping shop conveniently located by the big superstores if you're in a campervan – not so convenient for sailors. The usual assortment of camping, fishing and sailing gear, and much more reasonably priced than those usually found in a Croatian marina.

OTHER PRACTICALITIES

✚ **Accident and emergency** Dom zdravlja, Ul Dr Mauro Gioseffi 2; \ 052 451 611. The hospital reception for tourists is clearly marked at the driveway into the Poreč hospital. A pharmacy is also located here.

🚲 **Bikepoint** B Parentina 19; m 098 908 3255. Situated across the road from Konzum supermarket, Aldo & his son here will provide you with excellent service for all your bike needs. Bikes for hire at 75kn/hour, daily prices available.

Laundry and dry cleaning Kemiskija, Nikole Tesle 4; \ 052 432 910; ⊕ 07.00–19.00 Mon–Fri,

07.00–14.00 Sat. A tiny little place with not the friendliest of staff, but excellent rates.

✚ **Pharmacy** [89 D2] Trg Slobode 12; \ 052 432 362; ⊕ 07.00–22.00 Mon–Fri, 07.00–18.00 Sat, 08.00–13.00 Sun. This pharmacy is the easiest to find being right on the main square, but there are many others around. The staff here all speak excellent English, German & Italian & can advise you on what to take for minor illnesses.

✉ **Post office** [89 D2] Trg Slobode bb; ⊕ 07.00–17.00 Mon–Fri, 08.00–12.00 Sat.

This branch sells philatelic covers as well as stationery & games & videos. A wider selection of stationery including printer ink if you live near Poreč is available in the newsagent across the square.

WHAT TO SEE AND DO Poreč's **old town** is a testament to Roman military planning, and is characteristically bisected by the Decumanus, a Roman street running west to east through the main encampment and the Cardo Maximus running north to south. Awash with souvenirs and ice cream, the side streets hide crafts and art exhibitions, sales of local *rakija* from house doorways, and the odd hidden café. Unlike Rovinj, it's possible to walk all the way around the edge of the peninsula old town, and there is a small pebble beach and swimming area around the back of the town near the Hotel Palazzo.

The main attraction in the town is the **Euphrasian Basilica** [89 C1] (see box, page 85). Further along the back of the town is the **Istrian Parliament** [89 B1] (*Matka Laginje 6;* \ *052 432 263;* ⊕ *daily in the summer until late in the evening if hosting concerts*), which started out as a Gothic Franciscan church in the 13th century, and was renovated in the Baroque style during the 18th century, after which it housed the parliament of Istria. In the parliament, the lapidarium of the basilica and at various other venues throughout the town, there are concerts and exhibitions throughout the summer. See www.poup.hr for an up-to-date agenda. **Trg Marafor** is the location of the old **Roman forum** [89 A2], although that may not be so obvious now, for it appears as a large open space with some raised stonework on the floor. Nonetheless the locations of two Roman temples – the Temple of Mars (later thought to have been one of the largest in Istria) and the Temple of Neptune – have been marked out there. Near the old forum is also a well-preserved **Romanesque House** [89 B2], although it is very rarely open. At this end of Decumanus, look up at the house façades as you walk along, and you will notice some amazing architectural works from over the centuries showcasing a number of different styles from Gothic to Venetian. If you get a chance you might also want to visit the **Heritage Museum of Poreč** (*Zavičajni muzej; Dekumanska 9;* \ *052 431 585;* e *info@musejporec.hr; www.muzejporec.hr; currently closed for renovation*), which is the oldest museum in Istria, opening to the public for the first time in 1884.

It's also worth taking the regular boat (every 20 minutes in the high season) over to **Sv Nikola Island**, which can be walked around in a leisurely hour or so (but beware of veering off to the nudist beach if that's not your thing). The town **aquarium** [89 C2] (*Franje Glavinića 4;* \ *052 428 720; www.aquarium-travel.com;* ⊕ *summer 15 Apr–15 Oct 09.00–23.00 daily, rest of the year 10.00–15.00 w/ends only; entry 40kn, half price for children, under 3 years free*) tucked away in the eastern end of the old town is really quite good. Small, it is easy to get around in an hour, and holds some fascinating little exhibitions, including local endangered sea horses (*Hippocampus hippocampus*). If you can't get to go diving, this is a good way to see what's in the local sea.

There's lots of **hiking, biking and diving** to be done in the area (see the dedicated chapters), and there are two small electric coastal **sightseeing trains** which run from Valamar Pinia to the northern edge of the old town, and from the marina to Zelena Laguna. Southeast of Poreč less than 1km beyond the village of Gradina is the **megalithic hill-fort site and observatory** Mordele, Picugi and Mali Sv Anđelo.

Baredine Caves (*Nova Vas, 9km northeast of Poreč;* \ *052 421 333;* m *098 224 350;* e *info@baredine.com; www.baredine.com;* ⊕ *1 Apr–31 Oct 10.00–16.00; Jul/ Aug until 18.00, individual & group tours available rest of the year with prior notice;*

entry 60kn) At a cool 14°C, this is a great trip in the heat of summer. Tours take 40 minutes and depart every half an hour. With some additional on-site instruction, it's also possible to abseil to a further section of the cave. Whilst this might not rival the best cave exhibits in the world, the exhibition in the adjoining museum and the tractor exhibition outside are added attractions.

BEACHES Rocky outcrops and pebble beaches abound north and south of Poreč, most with cafés, entertainment and children's play areas lining the coast. At the back of the old town is a promenade allowing entry to the sea, popular with the townspeople. Brulo, 1.5km south of Poreč, has the Poreč Diving Centre, and a small enclosed bathing area especially for infants, as well as big land trampolines, huge water trampolines, bumper cars and other entertainments to draw on your money. For those who prefer a less commercial feel, the bay of Červar offers wonderful shallow sandy access, which is ideal for young children and for playing *picugin*, the popular Dalmatian handball game played in knee-high waters.

NOVIGRAD

This mini walled town, at less than 500m² is a gem of a feature on the Istrian coast. Known as Cittanova in Italian, it holds three of the top-rated restaurants in Croatia (yes, not just in Istria) as well as some unique hotels, and some particularly rich naval attractions. Follow it all up with a drink at Vitriol (*Ribarnička 6*) or one of the popular bars on Mandrač quay around the harbour, where you'll also find the tourist information office (*Mandrač 29a;* ☎ *052 757 075*).

GETTING THERE AND AROUND The most scenic way to get to Novigrad from Poreč is to take the coastal road past the pretty estuary of the River Mirna and the gateway of Antenal quarry. The bus station (*Epulanova bb;* ☎ *052 757 660*), which is a ten-minute walk from the centre, serves frequent buses to and from Poreč and many to further afield. The town itself is very small and easy to walk around.

 WHERE TO STAY AND EAT

⌂ **Hotel Nautica** (38 rooms, 4 apts) Sv Antona 15; ☎ 052 600 400; e info@nauticahotels. com; www.nauticahotels.com. On the marina just north of the town, this hotel gives direct access to your boat mooring. The hotel décor follows a distinctly naval theme & can seem a bit like a large ferry at times. Beautiful spa facilities & indoor pool. **$$$$**

⌂ **Hotel Cittar** (14 rooms) Prolaz Venecija 1; ☎ 052 757 737; e info@cittar.hr; www.cittar.hr. This hotel has an impressive exterior & entrance built into the old town wall. The inside, however, is your standard hotel. **$$$**

⌂ **Old Stone Guest House Santa Maria** (13 rooms) Gradska Vrata 37; ☎ 052 757 444; online reservations through booking.com. Conveniently near the old town, the exterior looks modern, but the indoor reception shows off its old stone look. Popular & pet-friendly. **$$**

✗ **Damir i Ornela** Zidine 5; ☎ 052 758 134; ⊕ 12.00–23.00, closed Mon. Listed in *Gault Millau*, this tiny restaurant is the best fine dining this side of the Istrian coast. Excellent local fish carpaccios, fresh pastas & sinful desserts. **$$$**

✗ **Pepenero** Poporela bb; ☎ 052 757 542; ⊕ 18.30–23.30 daily. Another *Gault Millau* listing, this restaurant has recently moved out of the Hotel Cittar into a larger & more luxurious location. The cuisine specialises in being locally harvested & exquisitely served. Signature dishes include plaice carpaccio on a bed of mandarin & carrot juice with black pepper. Fusion in Istria. **$$$**

✗ **Konoba Čok** Sv Antona 2; ☎ 052 757 643; ⊕ 12.00–23.30, closed Wed. Another *Gault Millau* listing, this *konoba* is worth it alone to come to Novigrad. The food is simply good, well presented & accompanied by a very wide variety of local wines. **$$**

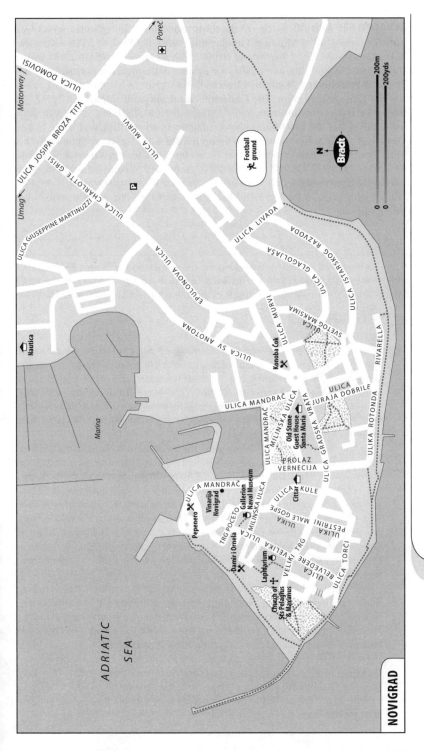

NOVIGRAD

WHAT TO SEE AND DO A tour of the town takes only a few minutes, so it's well worth stopping off at **Museum Lapidarium** (*Veliki Trg 8a;* ☏ *052 726 582; www. muzej-lapidarium.hr;* ⊕ *year-round 10.00–13.00, plus summer 18.00–22.00, winter 17.00–19.00, closed Mon; entry 20kn*) for a glance at the local Roman artefacts, and in the **Sv Pelagius and Maximus Church** (*Veliki Trg*) for its Baroque artwork inside and its 12th-century crypt. The **Gallerion Naval Museum** (*Mlinska 1;* ☏ *052 720 866; www.kuk-marine-museum.com;* ⊕ *May–Nov 10.00–12.00 & 17.00–23.00 daily; entry 20kn*) has the best model-ship exhibition in all of Istria, and has a prized display of artefacts from Georg von Trapp (of *The Sound of Music* fame) from his time as a U-boat commander in Pula. Finish up with a visit to **Vinarija Novigrad** (*Mandrać 18;* ☏ *052 726 060;* ⊕ *08.00–22.00 daily, until 14.00 only Sun*) to stock up on locally grown wine at only 16kn or 17kn per litre if you bring your own empties. Their highly popular homegrown Muscat is quick to sell out, so be sure to buy it while you can.

UMAG

Umag is most well known for **tennis**, where the Association of Tennis Professionals holds one of its World Tour events each July (*www.croatiaopen.hr*) at the Stella Maris Tennis Centre on the north side of the town. More than just tennis, the event

---

LIMSKI KANAL

No trip to the Poreč area would be complete without a trip to the **Limski kanal**. The karst area here, mostly made of limestone (*lim* in Istrian comes from the Latin *limes*, plural *limites*, meaning 'channel/path/boundary', and is not related to the word limestone) sank some 10,000 years ago forming the current sea gorge. Protected from the wind and currents it is the home of several shellfish-farming beds and is a protected natural monument, as a result of which it is illegal to swim in the eastern half of the channel.

At the eastern end of the gorge on the south bank is **Romuald's Cave**, so called because St Romuald of Ravenna lived there as a hermit from 1002 to 1004. The cave, which is 105m long and several metres high, but with an entrance only 1m in height, shows evidence of Stone Age rock art on its western side (but, strangely none on its eastern side), and the fossils of 41 different animals from Stone Age times have been found there. The cave is open to the public every day during the high season and at weekends in spring and autumn. At other times a visit can be arranged through Natura Histrica (*www.natura-histrica.hr*) or Kanfanar tourist offices (*www.istria-kanfanar.com*). Entry is 30kn, children under seven free.

Romuald left the cave, deciding that those wanting to dedicate themselves to God should in fact live in a community as monks, so he returned to his monastery, now no longer in existence, which he had built earlier on the north bank at Kloštar. There are legends that Sir Francis Drake left treasure there, and it has been the backdrop for a number of films, including *The Vikings* staring Kirk Douglas (1958). There is ample parking at the road entrance to the Limski kanal on the old road between Poreč and Rovinj, where you can find information boards on the cave and local flora. It's a 15–30-minute hike up to the cave entrance, which becomes a Grade 3 scramble at the top with very little railing support. Dress shoes and flip-flops are not advised.

has a daily gourmet, wine, jazz and a kids' festival. The **Umag Adrenalin Park** (*http://umag-adrenalin-park.com*) just up from the tennis courts provides tree-to-tree rope bridges at 1.5m, 7m and 11m heights for the adventurous (on a harness) for less than 110kn. **Aquarium Umag** (*1 Svibnja bb;* ☏ *052 721 041; www.aquarium-travel.com*), run by Aquarium Poreč (see *What to see and do*, page 93), is also open every day in the summer till late in the evening.

If you're in the area, stop to eat at **Mare e Monti** (☏ *052 710 984;* ⏲ *12.00–23.00 daily*) on the west side of the Stella Maris Tennis Centre, for better than the standard tourist fare. Also outstanding, just to the southeast of Umag on the road to Buje, is **Konoba Nono** (*Umaška 35, Petrovija;* ☏ *052 740 160;* e *konoba.nono@pu.t-com.hr; http://konoba-nono.com;* ⏲ *11.00–23.00 daily*). The food is superb, from delicious homemade ravioli stuffed with spinach to sea bass baked in salt, and a heavenly signature dessert (torta 'Nona'); many of the ingredients are from their own farm. It's enormously popular, so it's well worth calling to reserve a table. **Ranch Goli vrh** (*Goli vrh 31;* ☏ *052 730 207 or 721 820;* e *maglica.babsy@gmail.com*) is a lovely, peaceful place to stay in the area, with a rustic wooden bungalow (sleeps five) set on around 60ha of land, with horseriding available as well as homemade *pršut* and delicious homemade cheese. A place worth going out of your way for between Umag and the border is **Konoba Buščina** (*Buščina 18;* ☏ *052 732 088;* e *info@konoba-buscina.hr; www.konoba-buscina.hr;* ⏲ *12.00–midnight, closed Tue*).

A third of the way into the channel is the **Pirate Cave** – a watering hole and souvenir stall for the tourist boats visiting the gorge. Entry to the cave (which is more a very large hollow than a standard cave) is 5kn and includes a postcard. A bar there serves drinks and sells pirate paraphernalia. A signposted trail also leads down from the cliffs above, which can be reached from the end of the road going to Vrsar airport (private jets only).

Boat trips run from Poreč, Rovinj and Vrsar several times a day in the high season for around 120kn per person for a two-hour round trip, including a stop at the Pirate Cave. One of the best to take is the *Sveta Ana* small galleon replica from Vrsar leaving only once a day at 10.00. For 200kn a six-hour trip including lunch, two hours in Rovinj and a swimming stop at the Limski kanal leaves regularly at 10.00 and 12.30. Diving trips are available from Poreč Diving Centre and from Starfish Dive Centre (in Vrsar).

It's possible to drive a short way into the fjord from the eastern end, where there are a few standard restaurants and lots of souvenir and local produce stalls. A couple of viewing towers adorn the north shoulder of the eastern entrance to the gorge, from where you can get the best views of the gorge. The steep winding road on either side of the valley down to the water is very narrow, so be on the lookout for cyclists. Tour groups do arrive in their busloads to the eastern end of the gorge, so if you prefer a more secluded visit to the channel, then hike down from the cliff trail behind the airport.

Further inland up the Lim River is the now-ruined fortress town of **Dvigrad** (meaning 'two towns'), which was decimated by the plague in 1631, and finally abandoned by the last remaining inhabitants in 1714. Its tall towers and the remains of Sv Sofia Church are visible from the highway over the Limski kanal, but it's best reached from Kanfanar. Now it's slowly undergoing restoration, and you are currently free to wander the few half-cobbled little streets and open-air halls.

This delightful traditional stone *konoba*, with huge garden and fireplaces, offers a great mix of coastal and inland local recipes. A small self-catering Istrian house is also available for guests.

SAVUDRIJA

Tiny little Savudrija on the northwesternmost tip of Istria used to belong to the county of Piran. Its rocky outcrop has the oldest working lighthouse in the Adriatic (see box, *Istria's lighthouses*, on page 16), built in 1818. It's only possible to visit the lighthouse if accommodated in the apartment next door or on a private tour. Savudrija also offers the only golf course in all of Istria.

 WHERE TO STAY

🏠 **Kempinski Hotel Adriatic** (135 rooms) Alberi 300a; ☎ 052 370 700; e; www.kempinski-adriatic.com. Sheer luxury with a price tag & golf to match, facing Portorož. **$$$$$**

🏠 **Svjetionik Savudrija** (sleeps 4) Savudrija; www.istria.info/en/lighthouse-savudrija-istria-4810. This little self-catering apartment to the side of Savudrija lighthouse is relatively basic, & although it's in a small plot of land on its own with private boat mooring, it is surrounded by a caravan/camping site & has thus lost the idyllic charm that is seen in many of its online photos. **$$$$$**

BUJE

From the northwest of Istria, Buje is the gateway to the interior, and the first of a series of hilltop towns in the north. At 222m above sea level this 'Sentry over Istria', as the town is known, has retained many of its former fortress features, including several fortified towers, the old cathedral and some of its stone paved interior. In the surrounding hills are several excellent vineyards, olive groves, the old Parenzana railway route (see *Chapter 10*) and some beautiful private accommodation. The **Buje Tourist Board** (*Istarska 2*; ☎ 052 773 353; e info@tzg-buje.hr; www.tzg-buje.hr) can help you with finding private accommodation, but a treat not worth missing, even if it is only for a meal, is the aptly named La Parenzana. Some other very good restaurants await the intrepid in the hills.

 WHERE TO STAY AND EAT

🏠 **San Rocco** (12 rooms) Srednja ulica 2, Brtonigla; ☎ 052 725 000; e info@san-rocco.hr; www.san-rocco.hr. Awarded best boutique hotel for the past 5 years in a row, the San Rocco has set a standard in Istria, which many can only hope to aspire to. It is spacious, with full spa facilities, & an excellent restaurant serving the likes of handmade *boškarin* tortellini with wild asparagus sauce. **$$$$$**

🏠 **La Parenzana** (10 rooms) Volpia 3; ☎ 052 777 460; e info@parenzana.com.hr; www.parenzana.com.hr. A mere 2km north of Buje & close to the old railway line, the beautifully restored Istrian farmhouse & *konoba* are dedicated to the memory of the Parenzana. Austrian Guido & his Croatian wife Maruška are true enthusiasts, which shows through in everything they do from the boutique nature of the rooms to the Istrian cooking classes they offer. Cuisine is hearty, welcoming & a nice change from a lot of the mediocrity on the touristy coast. **$$$**

✗ **Morgan** Bračanija 1; ☎ 052 774 520; e konoba.morgan@gmail.com; www.konoba-morgan.eu; ⊕ 12.00–22.00, closed Tue. 2km from Brtonigla off the road towards Buje, is a true *konoba* with not a fish in sight. For meat lovers you'll find here *boškarin* tagliata, fiorentina porterhouse steak, boar & a host of other finger-licking good grills, sausages, pastas & soups. **$$$**

VRSAR A few kilometres south of Poreč is the small coastal town of **Vrsar**. It has a charming (and steep) old town, which is not remarkable by Istrian standards (already high). Judging by the class of the boats in the marina, however, this town is certainly a favourite place to dock for the international jet set who own a luxury yacht or cruiseboat. The marina car park is equally filled with high-end motor cars. Yet you wouldn't guess that from the town itself, which draws its main crowd on those Fridays of the month when it holds its very popular and mouth-watering **Fisherman's Festival**. During this event (which is mirrored in Funtana on alternate Fridays), local fishermen line the harbour with grilling fish, shellfish, *brodet* (hearty fish stew) and quaffable local wine, obscuring the stone sculptures which otherwise visibly adorn the view, courtesy of an annual stonemasonry competition at the otherwise abandoned Montraker quarry. There's also a **sculpture park** featuring the work of **Dušan Džamonja** (1928–2009), one of Croatia's most famous sculptors (*www.dusan-dzamonja.com*).

Boat rides to the Limski kanal (see box, pages 96–7) leave regularly during the day, and in the evening there are boat trips to see Rovinj by night for 160kn. Glass-bottom boats, for those who want to view underwater but can't dive, cost 75kn per person.

To get away from fish for a change, head into **Flengi** for suckling pig at one of the many roadside restaurants, or explore further at Fuškulin to visit Damjanić **vineyard** (℡ *052 444 553;* m *091 202 0495; www.damjanic-vina.hr*) or end up at the Konoba Gradina for roast pork and an overgrown children's playground.

Located on the busy road to Vrsar, **Funtana** has lots of restaurants and a Dinopark (*www.dinopark.hr;* ⊕ *Apr–Sep, 10.00–18.00 daily; entry 80kn for children aged 5–17; 100kn adults*).

SV LOVREČ Just off the *ipsilon* motorway north of the Limski kanal as you drive south from Poreč, the village of **Sv Lovreč** (an important military base for Venice during the 14th century) has a well-preserved medieval centre. A short walk from the main gate (Vela vrata) with its Venetian lion (and strange head, said to represent Attila the Hun, who is connected in legends to several towns in Istria) takes you past an attractive loggia to the Parish Church of St Martin – note the triple apse from the original 11th-century construction, visible on the back exterior walls. Keep going past the church to arrive at one of the large ruined defence towers from the old town walls, which gives a good impression of how well fortified the town once was.

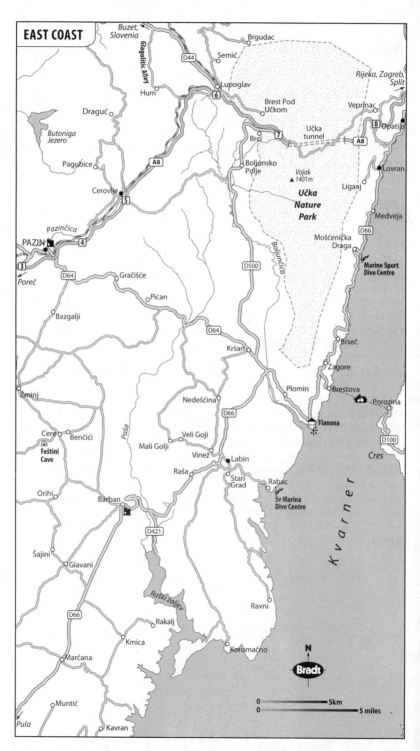

EAST COAST

Buzet, Slovenia
Glagolitic Alley
D44
Semić
Brgudac
Lupoglav
6
Hum
Draguć
Butoniga Jezero
Pagubice
A8
Cerovlje
5
Pazinčica
PAZIN
4
3
Poreč
D64
Gračišće
Pićan
Bazgalji
Zminj
Cere
Benčići
Feštini Cave
Orihi
Barban
Šajini
Glavani
D66
Kmica
Marčana
Muntić
Pula
Kavran

Rijeka, Zagreb, Split
Brest Pod Učkom
Veprinac
8
Opatija
Brci
7
Učka tunnel
A8
Boljunsko Polje
Vojak ▲1401m
Lovran
Liganj
Medveja
Učka Nature Park
D66
Mošćenička Draga
Marine Sport Dive Centre
D500
Boljunčica
D64
Kršan
Brseč
Zagore
Plomin
Brestova
Porozina
Nedešćina
D66
D100
Veli Goji
Mali Golji
Cres
Vinež
Labin
Raša
Stari Grad
Rabac
Sv Marina Dive Centre
Flanona
D421
Kvarner
Raški zaljev
Rakalj
Ravni
Koromačno
N
Bradt
0   5km
0   5 miles

100

6

Opatija and the East Coast

The east coast of the Istrian Peninsula is much less frequented than its western neighbour. This in itself makes much of it an attraction in the summer in particular, when the hordes have amassed on the western beaches. Rocky beaches here can still be found with hardly a soul in sight.

Historically, the east coast has had much less influence culturally from Italy, although it remained under Venetian, Aquilian or Italian rule for much the same period as the west coast. However, the population here had a higher percentage of Slavic speakers during those times. So whilst the fascist Italian dictator Mussolini did leave his mark culturally in the construction of the towns of Raša and Podlabin (see box, *Black gold*, on page 106), some might argue that these were an aberration rather than evidence of the symbiotic relationship which Italian culture has had with the west coast.

Two main centres stand out on the east coast: Labin and Opatija. Labin is an old **medieval hilltop fortified town**, once a centre of mining and now a centre of art. Opatija, being technically in the county of Primorje-Gorski Kotar (along with Rijeka), is the **riviera** of Kvarner Bay, and arguably more amenable than commercialised Rijeka. Other hilltop forts of note are Plomin and Barban, where the annual **ring tilting festival** takes place. From Opatija it's worth taking the coastal road into Istria, as the backdrop of the Učka Mountains against the vista of the Kvarner Bay islands is sublime.

OPATIJA

A mere fishing village 200 years ago, Opatija became the first spa resort on the entire Croatian coast. Largely only for the rich, privileged and noble 150 years ago, it still has as a result what must be the highest concentration of high-end spa hotels in Croatia, especially for its size. These hotels and villas alone are worth a stroll along the **12km promenade**, and many think there is only this to see and do in Opatija. Yet Opatija hides a few more gems around it in its **botanical gardens**, **Benedictine abbey** of Sv Jakob, and **medieval fort** at Veprinac.

HISTORY Opatija derives its name from the Slavic word for abbey, and hence it grew originally from the mid 15th century as a hamlet around the Benedictine abbey of Sv Jakob (St James), which still stands on the seafront south of the Hotel Kvarner. The abbey stood in contrast to the hill fort of Veprinac situated above the hamlet at 519m above sea level. Then in 1844, a fabulously wealthy industrialist from Rijeka, Iginio Scarpa, built the Villa Angiolina with its botanical gardens as a retreat for himself and his guests, naming it after his deceased wife. The rich, famous, influential and royal, all stopped to stay, and soon the mild winter climate and pleasant summer showers were heralded as a tonic for the stressed elite of the Austro-Hungarian Empire and beyond. Opatija's renown as a spa resort doubled after 1873, when the Rijeka to Pest railway was completed, and in 1884 the first hotel on the Croatian Adriatic, the Hotel Quarnero (today's Hotel Kvarner), was opened, followed by the Hotel Imperial and the Palace Bellevue. Opatija has never looked back.

GETTING THERE AND AROUND

By bus The **bus station** (*Trg Vladmira;* ☎051 271 617) is lively as the bus is the only public transport available in Opatija. As a result it is fairly well served by even long-distance buses to elsewhere in Croatia and to Trieste (four per day). Information on buses to and from Dubrovnik, Split, Zagreb, Rovinj, Poreč and Pula can be found at www.akz.hr or www.autobusni-kolodvor.com.

Local and city buses also run regularly, from as early as 04.30 to just gone midnight. **City bus #1** (Liburnija) runs from Slatina Beach north past Park Angiolina through Vološko inland to Pobri village. **City bus #3** (Veprinac) runs in the opposite direction during the school year only (September–June) from Slatina Beach via Ićići to the hill-fort village of Veprinac, and from 07.30 to 18.30 also runs a loop through town to Vološko and back. Timetables for city buses and bus transfer to the **airport** are accessed from the front page of the tourist board website (*www.opatija-tourism.hr*).

Local bus #32 runs between Rijeka bus and train stations all the way down the coast to Mošćenička Draga; **bus #35** plies the short route between Opatija and Ičići; while **bus #36** runs the entire length of the promenade between Opatija and Lovran, so if you run out of steam partway along the route, you can always just hop on the bus. Long-distance buses with local stops also ply these routes. Single tickets can be bought on board, although cheaper return tickets can be bought from local kiosks.

By car Parking is almost impossible during the peak season, although there are five public **car parks** between Opatija harbour next to Park Angiolina and Vološko. In summer you may be better off parking in Lovran and walking the Lungomare promenade or taking the bus into the centre and back.

By taxi Taxis can be found at the stand outside the Hotel Milenij, or call **Hallo Taxi** (*Matka Laginje 14;* ☎ 051 704 100; m 091 270 4100; e taxi@opatija.net; www. hallotaxi.opatija.net).

TOURIST INFORMATION Opatija, being in the county of Primorje-Gorski Kotar, comes under the regional tourism board of Kvarner, whose head office is also in Opatija (*Nikola Tesle 2;* ☎ 051 272 988; e kvarner@kvarner.hr; www.kvarner.hr; ⊕ 09.00–17.00 Mon–Sat). This is where you can find out about the whole county. Accommodation registrations take place in local branches.

Opatija Town Tourist Information Office (*Vladimira Nazora 3;* ☎051 271 710; e info@opatija-tourism.hr; www.opatija-tourism.hr; ⊕ 15 Jun–15 Sep 08.00–21.00 daily, out of season 09.00–16.00, closed Sun in winter) is located one street further north than the county office, and also covers Vološko. It has useful city maps and bus timetables.

WHERE TO STAY There's no end of ultra-expensive hotels in Opatija, such as the hotels Admiral, Ambassador, Opatija and Milenij. Here we list a couple of the earlier high-end hotels for historical value, as well as the less well-advertised mid-

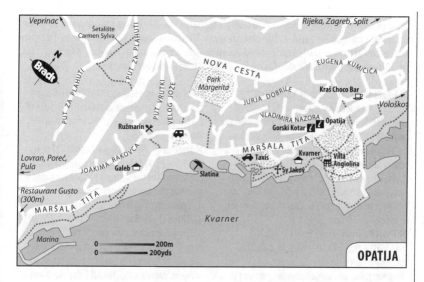

range hotels. Budget hotels simply don't exist here (we look forward to being proven wrong), not least because the Liburnia Group has bought up almost all the hotels in the Kvarner bay area and has stifled competition. **Private accommodation** can be found through the Opatija town tourist office (see opposite), and accommodation specifically in Vološko at www.opatija-apartments.com.hr.

⌂ **Kvarner** (87 rooms) Pave Tomašiča 1–4; ✆051 271 233; e reservations@liburnia.hr; www. liburnia.hr. The original spa-resort hotel opened in 1884, but has since been updated with a crystal ballroom which opened in 1913 – & all other mod cons since. You can't get more central than this, surrounded by parks Angiolina & Jakov, with the harbour close by. **$$$$**

⌂ **Mozart** (29 rooms) Maršal Tita 138; ✆051 718 260; e info@hotel-mozart.hr; www. hotel-mozart.hr. Opened in 1984, this beautiful family-run boutique hotel has had a tumultuous history, including as an army HQ & a children's home, & as many names to match. Attention to every detail best describes the service & furnishings of this completely renovated

establishment, which retains some beautiful examples of antique furniture & has its own small spa. **$$$$**

⌂ **Galeb** (25 rooms) Maršal Tita 160; ✆051 271 177; e info@hotel-galeb.hr; www.hotel-galeb. hr. Run by the Brko family, this neat hotel has a small wellness spa & swimming pool, & a lovely glasshouse restaurant. Spillover accommodation is also available at the nearby Hotel Savoy. **$$$**

⌂ **Ika** (23 rooms) Ika bb; ✆051 291 777; e info@hotel-ika.com; www.hotel-ika.com. Closer to Lovran than to Opatija, this family-run hotel & restaurant spills out onto the beach, & even boasts its own boat crane for those needing to launch their own boat or bring it back into dry dock. Free Wi-Fi. Children under 10 half-price. **$$$**

Motor Camp Opatija is in fact located closer to Lovran, between Ika and Ićiči (*Liburnijska 46;* ✆ *051 704 830;* e *info@rivijera-opatija.hr; www.rivijera-opatija. hr*). The usual complicated scheme of tariffs applies, depending on the number of people and type of pitch, starting at €10 for one person with a tent for the first night.

✖ **WHERE TO EAT AND DRINK** Opatija is filled with a mix of exclusive high-end restaurants and pizzeria-grills. Something in the middle is more difficult to find, unless you go out of town. The fishing village of Vološko, just north of Opatija, is the preferred place for many, where the tiny quay overlooking all the local fishing boats houses one of the best restaurants in all Croatia (Le Mandrać), and several others of excellent quality and value for money. Viennese-style coffee houses (despite the incongruence with landlocked Austria) are in abundance along Maršala Tita, including the popular cafés Camelia, Palma, Paris and Stephanie.

✗ **Le Mandrać** Frana Supila 10, Vološko; 051 701 357; www.lemandrac.com; ⏰ 12.00–23.00 daily. Fine dining fusion overlooking the working boats, this has to be one of my favourite locations for a restaurant in all of Istria, with a glass-fronted terrace allowing for an outdoor feel even in the (mild) winters. The bijou servings are worth every lipa, & you can't help but feel indulgent here. The gourmet who misses this restaurant out, does her or himself a disservice. $$$$

✗ **Plavi Podrum** Frana Supila 4; Vološko; 051 701 223; ⏰ 12.00–midnight daily. This restaurant, called the Blue Basement, is more for the gourmand, & as a result popular seats on the terrace are always packed, but it is possible to reserve. True to its name, it specialises in all things blue, using squid ink as a colouring, including for the bread & the coffee! Tasty & novel. $$$

✗ **Gusto** Maršala Tita 264; 051 670 426; ⏰ 11.00–23.00 daily. Although located a little

out of town, some 500m south of the bus station, this restaurant is very reasonably priced & is one of the few places on this part of the Istrian coast with outdoor seating. $$

✗ **Ružmarin** Veprinački put 2; 051 712 673; ⏰ 11.00–23.00 daily. This great little grill-house not far from the bus station is a little more caring & generous than the seafront restaurants tend to be, & its reputation is much more local than tourist. $$

🍵 **Kraš Choco Bar** Maršala Tita 94; 051 603 562; www.kraschocobar.com; ⏰ 08.00–midnight daily. One of only 5 cafés run by Croatia's number-one chocolate manufacturer Kraš (the others are in Rijeka, Zagreb, Banja Luka & Sarajevo). If you like very sweet chocolate this is without a doubt the place for you. Offers a mouth-watering array of truffles, including one covered in zingy bright-red dried strawberry pieces, as well as a variety of hot & cold chocolate drinks, coffees, cocktails & ice creams.

WHAT TO SEE AND DO The **coastal road** from Opatija down to Plomin is peppered with little fishing villages. The road is idyllic for most of the year, but can get jammed with day trippers and those wanting to take the ferry from Brestova to the island of Cres. Our advice to enjoy the road at its best once the boardwalk from Rijeka stops at Lovran, is to bike or drive the road very early in the morning: sunrise from the bay is spectacular, and usually the privilege of only fishermen in the summer. If you get the chance, stop at **Johnson** (*Sv Petar bb, 51417 Mošćenička Draga;* 051 737 578; *www.johnson.hr;* $$$) for truly excellent seafood in this restaurant named after US president Lyndon B Johnson. You'll find it on the upper road from Mošćenička Draga on the southwest edge of the village.

The impressive **Sv Jakov Church** dates back to 1420, when it is believed to have been built as part of a monastery for Benedictine monks. Little remains of the original church, which saw major renovation and expansion in 1506, over the course of the end of the 18th century and lastly in 1930. During the 19th century the church housed Opatija's first school. Today it remains a fully working church and occasionally holds chamber concerts.

Located in the centre of Opatija is the beautiful **Villa Angiolina** and **botanical garden** (*Park Angiolina 1;* 051 603 636; e *info@hrmt.hr; www.hrmt.hr;* ⏰ 09.00–13.00 & 17.00–22.00, closed Mon; entry free). The villa has become the Museum of Croatian Tourism and is filled with fantastic old photos. The garden itself is home to over 150 species of flora including Japanese camellia. The grounds were originally bought by the wealthy industrialist Iginio Scarpa for 700 florins, and later in 1910 were sold for the princely sum of 2.5 million crowns. Sadly, the original grounds have been divided between the Park Angiolina and Sv Jakov Park by the church and old abbey, and only a total of 3.6ha remain.

Carmen Sylva Forest Path This 5km path in the woods above Opatija was created with funding from King Carol of Romania after he got lost horseriding in the woods there on a visit in 1896. It was completed in 1901, but only named Carmen Sylva – after the pen name of his wife Elizabeth, a literary and musical artist – from 1998. To get onto the path, follow the narrow road straight uphill from the end of Nikola Tesle Street. Once up onto the well-signposted path, the gradient remains gently undulating and offers great shaded views of the bay. The path is popular in early spring (March, April) for gathering wild asparagus, and in autumn for sweet chestnuts.

Lungomare to Lovran The 12km promenade from Preluk Bay to Lovran is known as the Lungomare. It was started in 1888 and finished in 1911, and was designed (along with the Carmen Sylva, see previous section) to place Opatija as the leader in health tourism. It boasts 39 separate points of interest along its route, all of which are described at www.opatija.net/en/sights/lungomare-the-seaside-promenade. The path ends at the minute old town of Lovran (from the Roman Lauriana, meaning 'laurel'). For those who still have the energy a stairwayed path leads from the old town up to the Učka Mountains. In the hills between Lovran and Medeja is the **Draga di Lovrana restaurant** (*Lovranksa Draga 1;* \ *051 294 166;* e *info@dragadilovrana.hr; www.dragadilovrana.hr;* ☺ *12.00–midnight daily;* $$$$), which is well worth the hike or drive for its impressive views and excellent food. Originally opened in 1910, but then dormant from 1923 when it was consumed by fire, it was reopened in 2005, and in addition to its reputation as a restaurant, it offers four lovingly renovated double rooms and a large suite with jacuzzi and fireplace.

BEACHES There are three public beaches in Opatija. The main one with extensive facilities is Kupalište Slatina, which is the southernmost in town. The smaller central and original Lido is accessed from Park Angiolina. Northernmost is Kupalište Tomaševac next to the Hotel Ambassador.

Further down the coast, Kupalište Medveja, south of Lovran, is renowned as one of the best beaches in Istria. It has a modern funky feel, with trendy café bars and music, which you can enjoy on rented four-poster bed-loungers.

LOVRAN

Named after the bay leaf tree, or laurel, Lovran is the first main town on the western coast of Kvarner Bay. In Roman times it was called Lauriana. Lovran had been a main shipbuilding town until the late Middle Ages, when Venetian expansion of Trieste and Pula, and later Rijeka's rise on the shipbuilding scene, dwarfed the town's further development. The expansion of Opatija as a spa resort of the Austro-Hungarians in the 19th century brought renewed life to Lovran. As the end destination of Opatija's 12km *lungomare* its medieval architecture, surrounded by early 20th-century villas and parks, makes for a fitting rest to a healthy walk, or a scenic start to a hike up from sea level to the 1,401m Mount Vojak (see hike on page 171).

🔺 **WHERE TO STAY, EAT AND DRINK**

🏠 **Villa Astra** (6 suites) Viktora Cara Emina 11; \ 051 294 400; e sales@lovranske-vile.com; www. lovranske-vile.com. This is almost as exclusive as it gets. A neo-Gothic early 20th-century castle-like villa, offering its own bar, vitality restaurant, a heated outdoor pool in the winter, & a small exclusive beachfront. $$$$$

⌂ Hotel Flanona (10 rooms) Plomin bb;
☎ 052 864 426; e info@hotel-flanona.com.
hr; www.hotel-flanona.com.hr. Located at the
southern apex of the coastal road, known in
Roman times as Capo Pax Tecum ('the cape of
peace be with you'). Renovated in 2009 from the
former Motel Vidikovac (meaning 'lookout'), the
3-star hotel remains ostentatiously modern, &
has an enviable restaurant & terrace with a 180°
view of Kvarner Bay. The food is standard & a little
pricey, but worth the view. **$$$$**

⌂ Bristol (100 rooms) Maršala Tita 27;
☎ 051 291 866; e reservations@liburnia.hr; www.
hotelbristollovran.com. A standard 3-star, & not to
be confused with the much swankier 4-star Hotel
Bristol Opatija further up the *lungomare*. Has good
single room rates. **$$$**

⌂ Lovran (12 rooms) Maršala Tita 19; ☎ 051
291 222; e office@hotel-lovran.hr; www.hotel-
lovran.hr. This hotel, on the other hand, offers
excellent service, value for money, sea views & a
small wellness spa. **$$**

✕ Lovranska Vrata Stari grad 94; ☎ 051 291
050; www.restaurant-lovranska-vrata.com;
🕐 Apr–Oct 11.00–23.00 daily. In the quaint
stretch of the old town, this family-run restaurant
retreats to Konoba Bellavista at Stari grad 22 in the
winter. Great seafood, & a very good grill at the
konoba in the winter. **$$$**

♀ Loza Stari grad 5; ☎ 051 294 444. This tiny wine
bar, which spills out onto the street, is reminiscent
of a tapas bar, but offers hearty Istrian *pršut* & local
cheeses & olives to go with your wine, both local &
international.

WHAT TO SEE AND DO Lovran does not take long to get to know, and it is more
a base (quieter and cheaper than Opatija) for striking out to nearby activities. Trg
Sv Juraj, the town square, has a 12th-century Romanesque church dedicated to
St George. Opposite is the town hall, upon which is carved a relief of St George
himself, and one of the few in the region in which he is actually slaying a dragon.
One of the more famous reliefs in the square though is the *mustačon*, a blue curly
moustachioed face above the door of a Venetian red villa that is meant to ward off
evil. Built in 1722, back then we might have been more scared of what lay inside.

BLACK GOLD: THE FADS OF ECONOMIC DEMAND

Coal mining started in Istria in the 1600s, when coal resin used for the impregnation
of wooden boat hulls was ordered *en masse* by the Venetian governors of Istria.
This saw the rise of Labin as an important commercial centre. Although anthracite
(hard coal) was discovered in the Labin area in the 18th century, it was almost
another century before coal mining here was undertaken in earnest. Thus, shortly
after Venice was taken over by the French in 1805, Napoleon ordered further coal
mining in Istria. By 1881 a railway connected the mines of Raša to Raša Bay at
Bršica, and thus to the rest of the industrialised world.

THE REPUBLIC OF LABIN Ever the hazardous occupation, miners in the Labin area went
on strike in 1921 protesting against the working conditions imposed under Italian
rule. The strikes lasted for five weeks, during which time the strikers declared the
town's independence as the Republic of Labin. This prompted military intervention,
at which point the strike was quickly quelled.

COAL TOWNS In response to the coal miners' strikes of the previous decade and the
need for yet more coal, Mussolini ordered that a village be built for the miners of
Istria. Thus was born Istria's youngest village, **Raša** (named after a local river, even
though the village itself sits on a tributary), which was completed in 547 days and
opened on 4 November 1937. Designed to be the perfect village, Raša has a church,
and other public amenities built around a village square. The church, dedicated to

Ferry from Brestova to Cres Island For those wanting to visit the island of Cres (and Lošinj, which used to be connected to it at Osoj until the islands were divided by a seaway and reconnected by an opening road bridge) there is a regular car ferry, which operates from Brestova to the town of Porozina on Cres. The journey takes 20 minutes and ferries run in the high season every 90 minutes or less. Queues in the summer can be long. Timetables are at www.island-cres.com/etrajekt.htm. Cres is not as well visited as many of Croatia's other islands, which makes it attractive in its own right. The village of Porozina (whose name is derived from the Latin *pharum insulae*, meaning 'island light' from the lighthouse that used to be atop the hill there) is home to the well-preserved ruins of St Nicholas Franciscan Monastery and a 15th-century Gothic church with Glagolitic wall inscriptions.

PLOMIN Plomin signals the end of your view on the sea, but affords much to see of its own. Dating back to Roman times, this fortified village on a prominent hill has retained its Roman foundations, upon which current buildings were erected in medieval times. Originally the town was named Flanona after the bay plunging below it. Its narrow, cobbled steep streets hide two churches to the patron saint of the town, St George. The outside wall of the Church of St George the Elder (the second church is to St George the Younger) contains the Plomin tablet. Most historians agree that this is an 11th-century religious text dedicated to St George (before he was known as a dragon-slayer during the Crusades), but there is some dispute as to whether it might be an earlier carving of the Roman god Silvanus (god of flora and fauna) with the Glagolitic text graffitied on later which, incidentally, reads 'This is written S'.

Abandoned by its largely Italian population after World War II, the village now has a population of only 130. Catering facilities here are slight to say the least, but other places to dine and sup are not far away.

St Barbara, the patron saint of miners, is notable for being built in the shape of an upturned miner's barrow with a miner's lantern shape for the bell tower. More a strip than a village, the residential areas were divided firmly by class with lower Raša to the southwest housing ordinary miners, upper Raša to the northeast housing senior miners, and larger gated villas close to the village centre assigned to the mines' managers. A few years later **Podlabin** (or Pozzo Littorio as it was known then) was also further developed along functionalist lines for the miners.

DEATH KNELL At its heyday during World War II, the mining of black gold in Istria employed over 10,000 miners, mining 1.158 million tonnes of anthracite in the record year of 1942. Coal remained important in the post-World War II reconstruction period of Yugoslavia, but the advent of cheaper imports from Poland and the USSR, as well as the switch to oil as the fuel of choice, sounded the death knell for Istria's mines. By the mid 60s Istria's coal was largely exhausted under the mining practices of those days, and in 1989 the mines of Raša were closed down. Istria's last mine, with 300 miners at Tupljak at the start of the Raša River, was closed in 1999.

Today Raša is a mere ghost of its former functionalist fervour. It remains nonetheless a mesmerising spyglass on the past and the **Raša Kavana** (🕐 *year-round 07.00–11.00 daily*; $) on the main square provides a welcome coffee, *rakija* or simple grill.

LABIN

Perched on a hill 320m above the sea, Labin has a proud history, in which it has often asserted an independent spirit. Once a mining town, which is renowned for staging the first anti-fascist revolution, it's now better known within its medieval walls for its flourishing art.

Labin saw human settlement as early as 2,000 years ago, when a Bronze Age fort was founded under the name Kunci. Illyrian Celts later named the settlement Alvona, meaning 'town on a hill'. More recently it became the centre of Istrian coal mining (see box, *Black gold*, on pages 106–7) by the beginning of the 20th century.

GETTING THERE AND AROUND Labin bus station (*Trg 2 ožujka, Podlabin;* \ *052 333 888*) is well served by buses to Pula and Rijeka, and also has buses to Rovinj and Split. A local bus also runs regularly between Raša via Labin to Rabac. It's very easy to walk around the old town of Labin, and thus there is no public transport. **Taxis** can be called on m 098 916 1863.

TOURIST INFORMATION The main **tourist information office** (*Aldo Negri 20;* \ *052 855 560;* e *tzg.labin@pu.htnet.hr; www.rabac-labin.com;* ⊕ *15 Jun–15 Sep 08.00–21.00 daily; 09.00–16.00 out of season, closed Sun in winter*) lies on the main road between the old town and Podlabin. This is where to register for all accommodation on the east coast of the county of Istria from Brestova south. There is also a small information office in the old town (*Titov Trg 2/1;* \ *052 852 399; same opening hours as the main office*).

 WHERE TO STAY AND EAT Rabac on the coast is awash with huge hotels and self-catering apartments jammed against the hillside, all of which can be found on the Labin tourist information website (see above).

⌂ **Villa Calussovo** (10 dbls, 2 sgls) Kras 18, Ripena; \052 851 188; e villacalussovo@aol.de; www.villa-calussovo.com. Around 4km from Labin in the village of Ripenda, this old farmhouse has been lovingly restored & offers stone-exposed bedrooms, a fireplace for winter, & a restaurant that is worth visiting even if you don't stay. $$$$
✕ **Due Fratelli** Montozi 6; \052 853 577; www.due-fratelli.com; ⊕ 11.00–23.00, closed Mon in winter. As you might guess, this restaurant on the road down to Rabac is run by 2 brothers, who catch & then cook the fish themselves. A popular venue among shady trees, not least because of the memorable boat lurching out of the wall in the main dining hall. Reserve in the summer. $$$

✕ **Kvarner** Šetalište San Marco bb; \052 852 336; ⊕ 09.00–23.00 Mon–Sat, 12.00–23.00 Sun. On the south side of Labin town, on the edge of the town wall, the views from this restaurant over Kvarner Bay are magnificent. The food matches the view. Try their hot sampler plate of local pastas with meat & game, followed by *krafi* sweet ravioli, filled with different cheeses, raisins, sugar & a splash of pirate rum. $$$
⎁ **Velo Café** Titov trg 12; \052 852 336; ⊕ 11.00–23.00 daily. Popular café on the main square of the old town, with good tea & coffee for a very affordable price. Snacks available.

WHAT TO SEE AND DO **Porta Sanfior** are the main doors of the town wall, dating from 1589 with the Labin coat of arms and the Serenissima lion above. The cannon at the doors dates from Austrian times, and was reinstated there in 1995 after a long period in storage.

The **Labin Museum** (*I svbinja 6;* \ *052 852 477;* e *narodni.muzej.labin@put. t-com.hr; www.uciliste-labin.hr/sec_muzej.htm;* ⊕*summer 10.00–13.00 & 17,00–*

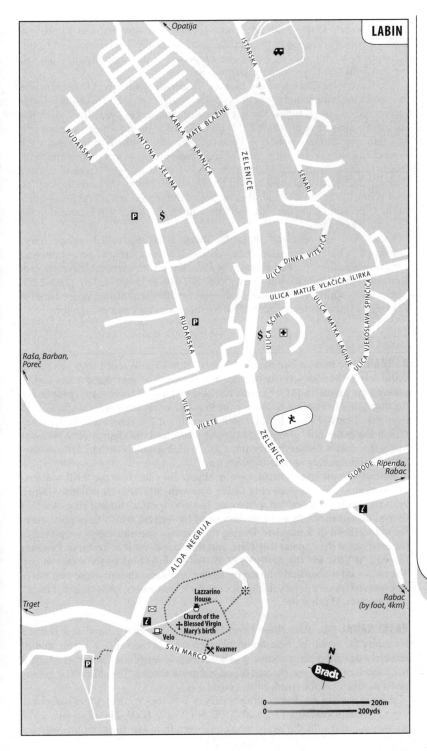

LABIN

Opatija

ISTARSKA

🚐

KARLA MATE BLAŽINE

ANTONA SELANA

KRANICA

RUDARSKA

ZELENICE

ŠENARI

🅿

$

ULICA DINKA VITEZIĆA

ULICA MATIJE VLAČIĆA ILIRKA

RUDARSKA

🅿

ULICA ŠĆIRI

$

➕

ULICA MATKA LAGINJE

ULICA VJEKOSLAVA SPINČIĆA

Raša, Barban, Poreč

VILETE

VILETE

ZELENICE

🧍

ALDA NEGRIJA

Trget

✉

i

🖥

Velo

Lazzarino House

✝ Church of the Blessed Virgin Mary's birth

✳

SAN MARCO

✕ Kvarner

🅿

SLOBODE

Ripenda, Rabac

i

Rabac (by foot, 4km)

N

Bradt

0 ——————— 200m
0 ——————— 200yds

19.00 Mon–Fri, 10.00–13.00 Sat; winter 07.00–15.00 Mon–Fri) was formerly a Baroque palace belonging to the Battiala-Lazzarini family. The last resident, Count Guiseppe Lazzarini, sold up his several properties in the Labin area and left just before World War II, portending what was to come.

The three-nave **Church of the Blessed Virgin Mary's Birth** in the centre was built in 1336 on the foundations of a smaller church from the 11th century. It was reconstructed several times. The last reconstruction was in 1993. The church has six marble altars, one of which holds the relics of St Justin, which were brought to Labin from Rome in 1664. A Venetian lion with a sphere in his mouth – a symbol of Labin recognising the Venetian government – was put on the front façade in 1604. By the end of that century, in 1688, a Baroque statue of Senator Antonio Bollani, a combatant against the Turks, was put on the same façade. The bust is one of the most beautiful examples of the secular sculptural art of Istria in the 17th century. On the right from the church is a palace that belonged to the Schampicchio family.

Some 3km east-southeast of Labin, **Rabac** is an unabashed seaside resort developed by the huge conglomerate Valamar. It offers a string of restaurants and entertainment along the bay, all much of a muchness with the notable exception of **Restoran Lino** (*Obala Maršal Tito 52;* ☎ *052 872 629;* ⊕ *15 Apr–15 Oct 12.00–23.00 daily; $$$$*), which serves all the usual suspects with additional signature dishes of Fra Davalo spicy lobster and Cres lamb for those who have had enough fish.

SOUTH TO PULA

BARBAN Barban, a well-preserved hill fort 12km southwest of Labin, has shown some sort of human settlement since the Bronze Age over 3,500 years ago. It suffered the plague in 1312, but was resettled by Finodol Dalmatians (people, not the dogs) shortly afterwards. During the Republic of Venice, it was bought in 1535 from the counts of Pazin by the Loredan family (of the Venetian nobility). They rebuilt the entire fort, giving it its current palace and the Church of St Nicholas inside the town walls, leaving the tiny Church of St Anthony with its 15th-century frescoes still standing outside the town gates.

Barban is most often visited now in August (in particular the third weekend in the month) for its annual **ring tilting tournament** – Trka na prstenac – when jousting knights compete on a charging horse to spear a hanging ring. Another festival of Barban worth a visit is the annual **fig festival**, which takes place every second weekend in September. During the festivals, live music gigs are played in the evenings at the popular **Roy Café**, and the place to eat is at **Restoran Prstenac** (*Barban 10;* ☎ *052 567 163;* ⊕ *07.00–22.00 Wed–Mon; $*), both on the village square. The restaurant is uber-lively during the festival and sleepy the rest of the year, but in all events offers very good value for money for its spit roasts, grills (fish and meat), game pastas and fish soup.

RAŠKI KANAL The Raša River (Arsa in Latin) has been a natural and political boundary for centuries, because of the steep sides of the valley it lies in, and its relatively straight if short course. It is only 23km in length, at the end of which is the Raški Kanal deep sea-channel of just ten nautical miles. The old mining railway and a footpath run the river's entire course.

A good place to eat down on this waterway is in the tiny deep-water harbour of Trget at **Martin Pescador** (*Trget 20;* ☎ *052 544 976;* ⊕ *12.00–23.00 Tue–Sun; $$$*). It's very popular with the locals, who come even from afar to eat on this working

Učka Nature Park (Park prirode Učka; *www.pp-ucka.hr*) stretches southwest from Opatija, parallel with and just inland from the coast, and covers an area of around 160km². It is one of 11 nature parks in Croatia – the only one in Istria – and includes the Učka massif as well as part of neighbouring Ćićarija. Fauna ranges from wild boar and roe deer to an endemic karst dormouse, endemic subterranean cave beetles and endemic land snails, and around 250 species of butterflies and moths.

The highest point on Učka, Vojak (also known as Vrh Učka), rises to just over 1400m above sea level, and is crowned by a stout stone tower (*kula*), as well as a paragliding ramp just below this – not to mention a gigantic telecommunications aerial, but don't let that put you off. The surrounding slopes are lushly forested, punctuated by the occasional meadow as well as some stark areas of limestone scenery, including the knobbly fingers of rock protruding from Vranjska draga, close to the inland entrance to the Učka Tunnel. The *kula* was built as an enhanced viewpoint in 1911 (and it is quite a view from up here), and was renovated in 2004 – you'll find a small information office here, and there are telescopes up on the viewing deck with which to survey the surrounding landscape.

A road leads up over a saddle below Vojak, passing a mountain hut (Poklon dom), and a bus comes up here from Rijeka and Opatija but only on Sundays (see page 171 for times). There are plenty of hiking trails on Učka, the best of which is the route from Lovran on the coast up to Vojak (see *Chapter 10*, page 171 for a description of this route).

quay overlooking the shipments of timber and marble. Decorated with fishing paraphernalia, it's hard not to want to eat the fresh fish here caught that morning, but offerings of the four-legged variety are also on offer. Entry to the restaurant goes past the timber and marble holds, and into the gated harbour, where the restaurant will suddenly appear, with ample parking.

Bradt Travel Guides

**Claim 20% discount on your next Bradt book when you order from
www.bradtguides.com quoting the code BRADT20**

Africa

Africa Overland	£16.99
Algeria	£15.99
Angola	£18.99
Botswana	£16.99
Burkina Faso	£17.99
Cameroon	£15.99
Cape Verde	£15.99
Congo	£16.99
Eritrea	£15.99
Ethiopia	£17.99
Ethiopia Highlights	£15.99
Ghana	£15.99
Kenya Highlights	£15.99
Madagascar	£16.99
Madagascar Highlights	£15.99
Malawi	£15.99
Mali	£14.99
Mauritius, Rodrigues & Réunion	£16.99
Mozambique	£15.99
Namibia	£15.99
Nigeria	£17.99
North Africa: Roman Coast	£15.99
Rwanda	£16.99
São Tomé & Príncipe	£14.99
Seychelles	£16.99
Sierra Leone	£16.99
Somaliland	£15.99
South Africa Highlights	£15.99
Sudan	£16.99
Swaziland	£15.99
Tanzania Safari Guide	£17.99
Tanzania, Northern	£14.99
Uganda	£16.99
Zambia	£18.99
Zanzibar	£15.99
Zimbabwe	£15.99

The Americas and the Caribbean

Alaska	£15.99
Amazon Highlights	£15.99
Argentina	£16.99
Bahia	£14.99
Cayman Islands	£14.99
Chile Highlights	£15.99
Colombia	£17.99
Dominica	£15.99
Grenada, Carriacou & Petite Martinique	£15.99
Guyana	£15.99
Haiti	£16.99
Nova Scotia	£15.99
Panama	£14.99
Paraguay	£15.99
Peru Highlights	£15.99
Turks & Caicos Islands	£14.99
Uruguay	£15.99
USA by Rail	£15.99
Venezuela	£16.99
Yukon	£14.99

British Isles

Britain from the Rails	£14.99
Bus-Pass Britain	£15.99
Eccentric Britain	£16.99
Eccentric Cambridge	£9.99
Eccentric London	£14.99
Eccentric Oxford	£9.99
Sacred Britain	£16.99
Slow: Cornwall	£14.99
Slow: Cotswolds	£14.99
Slow: Devon & Exmoor	£14.99
Slow: Dorset	£14.99
Slow: New Forest	£9.99
Slow: Norfolk & Suffolk	£14.99
Slow: North Yorkshire	£14.99
Slow: Northumberland	£14.99
Slow: Sussex & South Downs National Park	£14.99

Europe

Abruzzo	£16.99
Albania	£16.99
Armenia	£15.99
Azores	£14.99
Belarus	£15.99
Bosnia & Herzegovina	£15.99
Bratislava	£9.99
Budapest	£9.99
Croatia	£15.99
Cross-Channel France: Nord-Pas de Calais	£13.99
Cyprus see North Cyprus	
Estonia	£14.99
Faroe Islands	£16.99
Flanders	£15.99
Georgia	£15.99
Greece: The Peloponnese	£14.99
Hungary	£15.99
Iceland	£15.99
Istria	£13.99
Kosovo	£15.99
Lapland	£15.99
Liguria	£15.99
Lille	£9.99
Lithuania	£14.99
Luxembourg	£14.99
Macedonia	£16.99
Malta & Gozo	£14.99
Montenegro	£14.99
North Cyprus	£13.99
Serbia	£15.99
Slovakia	£14.99
Slovenia	£13.99
Svalbard: Spitsbergen, Jan Mayen, Franz Jozef Land	£17.99
Switzerland Without a Car	£15.99
Transylvania	£15.99
Ukraine	£16.99

Middle East, Asia and Australasia

Bangladesh	£17.99
Borneo	£17.99
Eastern Turkey	£16.99
Iran	£15.99
Israel	£15.99
Jordan	£16.99
Kazakhstan	£16.99
Kyrgyzstan	£16.99
Lake Baikal	£15.99
Lebanon	£15.99
Maldives	£15.99
Mongolia	£16.99
North Korea	£14.99
Oman	£15.99
Palestine	£15.99
Shangri-La: A Travel Guide to the Himalayan Dream	£14.99
Sri Lanka	£15.99
Syria	£15.99
Taiwan	£16.99
Tajikistan	£15.99
Tibet	£17.99
Yemen	£14.99

Wildlife

Antarctica: A Guide to the Wildlife	£15.99
Arctic: A Guide to Coastal Wildlife	£16.99
Australian Wildlife	£14.99
East African Wildlife	£19.99
Galápagos Wildlife	£16.99
Madagascar Wildlife	£16.99
Pantanal Wildlife	£16.99
Southern African Wildlife	£19.99
Sri Lankan Wildlife	£15.99

Pictorials and other guides

100 Alien Invaders	£16.99
100 Animals to See Before They Die	£16.99
100 Bizarre Animals	£16.99
Eccentric Australia	£12.99
Northern Lights	£6.99
Swimming with Dolphins, Tracking Gorillas	£15.99
The Northwest Passage	£14.99
Tips on Tipping	£6.99
Total Solar Eclipse 2012 & 2013	£6.99
Wildlife & Conservation Volunteering: The Complete Guide	£13.99

Travel literature

A Glimpse of Eternal Snows	£11.99
A Tourist in the Arab Spring	£9.99
Connemara Mollie	£9.99
Fakirs, Feluccas and Femmes Fatales	£9.99
Madagascar: The Eighth Continent	£11.99
The Marsh Lions	£9.99
The Two-Year Mountain	£9.99
The Urban Circus	£9.99
Up the Creek	£9.9

right The Rijeka Carnival is the second largest in Europe after Venice. Expect all manner of eccentric entertainments, including the Slovenian *kurenti (pictured)* (RA) page 142

below left A family from Zamask selling traditional handmade baskets at the Subotina festival (RA) page 42

below right Istria's humble but beautifully constructed *kažuni* houses have become emblematic of the region (CNTB) page 16

bottom A good chance to catch performances of local and international folk music is at Pazin's TradInEtno festival in early June (RA) page 117

left Built between 2BC and AD14, Pula's enchanting Temple of Augustus was used as a theatre by the Venetians and is now a lapidarium (RA) page 62

below The population of the now-ruined fortress town of Dvigrad was decimated by the plague in 1631 and the town was abandoned by the last remaining residents in 1714 (RA) page 97

bottom Brijuni's oldest Roman settlement, Kastrum, where both olive oil and wine were once produced (RA) page 68

right — One of the few surviving instances of a 'pillar of shame' in Istria, where those who had committed minor offences were bound and subjected to humiliation during the medieval period (RA) page 133

below — Detail of the *Dance of Death* fresco in the Church of St Mary of the Rocks, Beram (RA) page 120

bottom left — A dinosaur footprint on Brijuni, formed when these large reptiles walked across tidal and mud flats — now sedimentary rock — some 100 to 115 million years ago (IK/VP/S) page 69

bottom right — The 7km Glagolitic Alley is marked at various points by 11 sculptures or monuments relating to the Glagolitic alphabet (RA) page 133

above Lavender fields surround the well-preserved medieval town of **Sv Lovreč** (I/S) page 99

left Look out for wild deer roaming on **Veliki Brijun** (A/DT) page 68

below The **Limski kanal**, just north of Poreč, is a protected national monument rich with caves and excellent diving spots (I/FLPA) page 96

above   There are seemingly endless rocky coves and bays along the length of Rt Kamenjak, so there's no shortage of places for a swim (TI/DT) page 66

right   Once the summer home of President Tito, the beautiful Brijuni Islands comprise the only national park in Istria (CNTB) page 68

below   A prominent limestone outcrop near Dvigrad, typical of karst scenery in the region (RA) page 4

top left   *Fuži* (traditional Istrian pasta) with wild boar is a speciality at Stara Ostarija restaurant, Buzet (RA) page 36

above left   Boutique locally made spirits for sale in Hum (RA) page 134

above right   Around 10% of Istria is covered by vineyards, many of which offer tastings. Here, vineyards on the road to Motovun (I/VP/S) page 36

below   Truffle hunts and tastings can be arranged with Karlič tartufi in the village of Paladini, near Buzet (RA) page 132

above The night before Buzet's Subotina festival a giant omelette is prepared under the auspices of Zigante Tartufi, comprising over 2,000 eggs and 10kg of truffles (SS) page 131

below Award-winning beekeeper and honey producer Dario Vežnaver has a small shop just inside Oprtalj's main gate (RA) page 126

7

Inland Istria

Inland Istria is, without any doubt, the least-visited part of *terra magica* (as the Romans are said to have nicknamed Istria). While tourists throng to the coast to see the iconic Rovinj, the arena at Pula or the beaches of Medulin, the Istrian interior steps down a gear or two – enter a world of perfectly preserved medieval hill towns, hidden frescoes and heavenly food.

PAZIN

Pazin (Italian Pisino, German Mitterburg), despite being the capital of the Istrian *županija* or county, is one of those places most visitors miss – which is a shame because it's an interesting little town with a cracking castle, a dramatic gorge and literary associations aplenty, which for around 1,000 years followed an entirely different historical trajectory from the rest of Istria. You can even get here easily on public transport, which is saying something for inland Istria.

HISTORY Pazin is first mentioned (as Castrum Pisinum) in a document of AD983, when its castle was given to the Bishops of Poreč by Holy Roman Emperor Otto II. In the 12th century the bishops in turn gave it to Meinhard von Schwarzenburg, after whose death it was passed to the Counts of Gorizia through the marriage of his daughter to Count Engelbert of Gorizia. Under the Counts of Gorizia Pazin and its surroundings (including at times Tinjan, Vižinada, Žminj and other towns) were ruled as an independent estate, at a time when the rest of Istria belonged either to Venice or the Bishops of Aquileia. The complicated boundaries between these were recorded in a 13th-century document known as the *Istrian Book of Boundaries* (*Istarski razvod*; see *History*, on page 10). In 1374 the last Count of Gorizia died without an heir, and the county of Pazin (Pazinska knežija), as it was now called, went to the Habsburgs, who leased it to various nobles. This leasing and subleasing ultimately led to increased taxes on the local peasantry, who revolted on several occasions. In 1766, Pazin Castle was bought by Count Antonio Laderchi, Marquis of Montecuccoli. Pazin County endured until the early 19th century, when along with the rest of Istria it became part of Austria (and then Italy from the end of World War I), though the castle remained in the possession of the Montecuccoli family until 1945.

GETTING THERE AND AWAY

By train Pazin lies on the railway line between Pula and Ljubljana, and has departures for Pula at 05.13, 06.15, 08.05, 12.08, 13.52, 15.41, 16.48 and 20.49 Monday–Friday, 06.15, 08.05, 12.08, 16.48 and 20.49 Saturday, and 06.15, 12.08, 16.48 and 20.49 Sunday. Travelling north there are slightly less frequent trains to Lupoglav

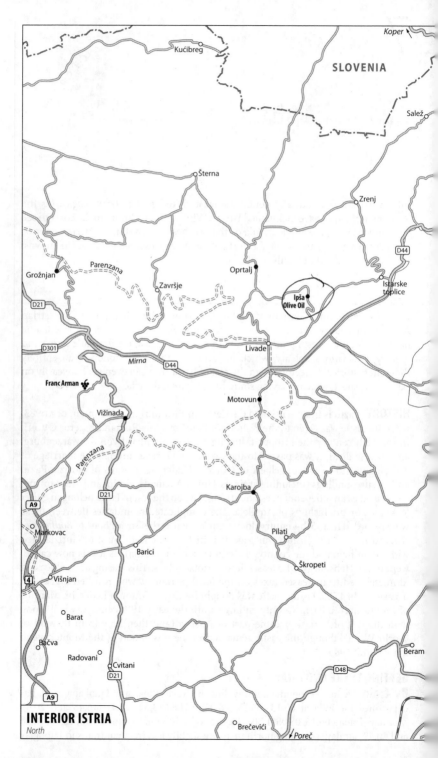

Koper

SLOVENIA

Salež

Kućibreg

Šterna

Zrenj

D44

Parenzana

Oprtalj

Grožnjan

Istarske toplice

D21

Završje

Ipša
Olive Oil

D301

Livade

Mirna

D44

Franc Arman

Motovun

Vižinada

Parenzana

D21

Karojba

A9

Markovac

Pilati

Barici

Škropeti

4

Višnjan

Barat

Bačva

Beram

Radovani

Cvitani

D21

D48

A9

INTERIOR ISTRIA
North

Brečevići

Poreč

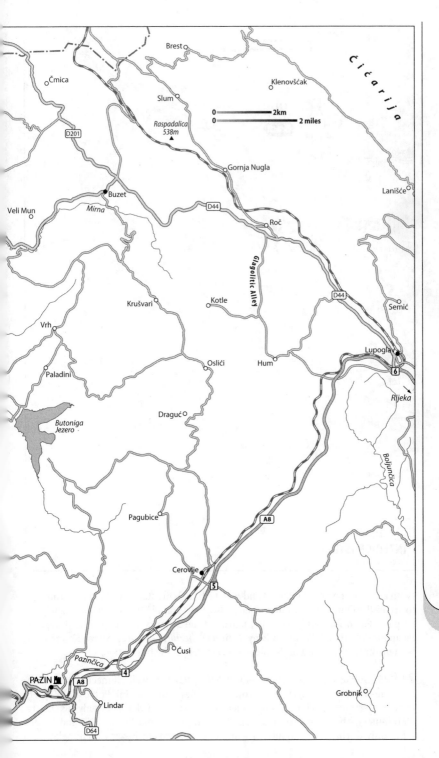

Čmica

Brest

Klenovšćak

Č i č a r i j a

D201

Slum

Raspadalica
538m

0 ——————— 2km
0 ——————— 2 miles

Gornja Nugla

Lanišće

Buzet

Veli Mun

Mirna

D44

Roč

D44

Semić

Glagolitic Alley

Krušvari

Kotle

Vrh

Osliċi

Hum

Lupoglav

Paladini

6

Rijeka

Draguċ

Butoniga
Jezero

Boljunčica

Pagubice

A8

Cerovlje

5

Ćusi

Pazinčica

4

PAZIN

A8

Grobnik

Lindar

D64

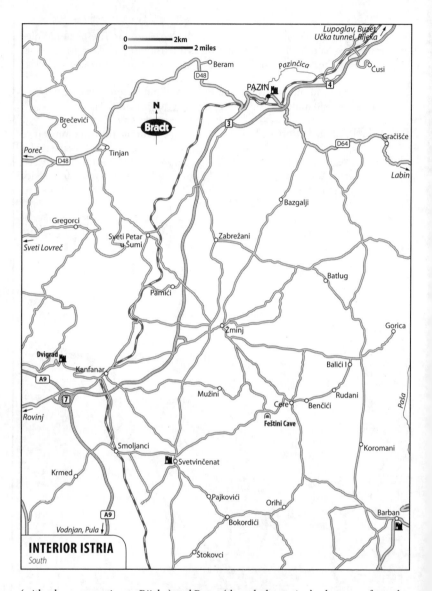

The map shows place names including:

Lupoglav, Buzet, Učka tunnel, Rijeka
Beram
Ćusi
Pazinčica
D48
PAZIN
3
Brečevići
Bradt
N
Gračišće
Poreč
D48
Tinjan
D64
Labin
Bazgalji
Gregorci
Sveti Petar u Šumi
Zabrežani
Sveti Lovreč
Batlug
Pamići
Zminj
Gorica
Dvigrad
Kanfanar
Balići I
A9
7
Mužini
Rudani
Cere
Benčići
Rovinj
Feštini Cave
Koromani
Smoljanci
Krmed
Svetvinčenat
Pajkovići
Orihi
Barban
Bokordići
A9
Vodnjan, Pula
INTERIOR ISTRIA
South
Stokovci

(with a bus connection to Rijeka) and Buzet (though the station's a long way from the town itself). During the summer there's also a fast train between Pula and Ljubljana (departs Pazin for Ljubljana 19.00, journey time 3 hours 40 minutes, and departs Pazin for Pula 10.23). Pazin's **railway station** (*Željeznički kolodvor; Stareh Kostanji bb*) is a ten-minute walk east of the old town centre, past the bus station.

By bus Unlike many places in central Istria, Pazin is well connected by bus to other destinations in Istria and beyond, including Pula, Rovinj, Poreč and Zagreb (a 'direct' service which only stops once and bypasses Rijeka takes only two hours 45 minutes). There are also three daily buses to Motovun (06.45, 13.15 and 15.20) – but only during the school term – and one daily bus to Buzet via Lupoglav and

Roč (06.15 Monday–Friday), and there's a daily departure for Trieste and Venice (06.15 Monday–Saturday). The **bus station** is a ten-minute walk east of the old town centre, on the corner of Šetalište pazinske gimnazije and Miroslava Bulečića.

By car Pazin is a 40-minute drive from Pula, 35 minutes from Rovinj, 2½ hours from Zagreb, and 40 minutes from Rijeka through the Učka tunnel.

TOURIST INFORMATION Pazin has an excellent **tourist information office** (*Franine i Jurine 14;* \ *052 622 460;* e *tz-pazin@pu.t-com.hr or info@tzpazin.hr; www.tzpazin.hr;* ⏰ *summer 10.00–18.00 Mon–Fri, 10.00–13.00 Sat; winter 09.00– 16.00 Mon–Fri, 10.00–13.00 Sat*), where you can find maps, brochures and advice on what to see and do in and around Pazin and further afield in central Istria.

WHERE TO STAY Pazin has one hotel, the two-star Lovac, and a decent number of places offering private accommodation, including the excellent Laura (for more private rooms and apartments, contact the tourist office).

🏠 **Hotel Lovac** (27 dbls) Šime Kurelića 4; \ 052 624 324; e tisadoo@inet.hr; www.tzpazin. hr. Small, fairly basic hotel which does however have a nice terrace café/restaurant overlooking the gorge. **$$**

🏠 **Laura** (2 dbls, 1 sgl, 4 apts) A Kalca 10/a; \ 052 621 312; m 099 593 9908; e elvis.milotic@ pu.t-com.hr; www.tzpazin.hr. Lovely place to stay, offering clean, quiet rooms & apartments just around the corner from the castle & the tourist information office, with views of the castle & gorge from the balcony. Excellent value. *B/fast €4.* **$**

✗ **WHERE TO EAT AND DRINK**

✗ **Konoba Vinja** Stacija Pataj 73a; \ 052 623 006; ⏰ 11.00–23.00 Mon–Fri, 18.00–midnight Sat, 12.00–midnight Sun. Hands down the best place to eat in Pazin, with outstanding local pasta dishes including *fuži* with game, Tinjan pork cutlets & other grilled meat dishes & a tasty goat's cheese & olive salad. Friendly staff, a nice covered terrace, & the house wine on my last visit was the gold medal-winning Benvenuti Malvazija. Around 3km southwest of Pazin, just across the other side of the 'ipsilon' (the main road between Pula & Rijeka). **$$$**

✗ **Poli Nina** Trg pod lipom 2a; \ 052 622 022; ⏰ 07.00–22.00 Mon–Sat, 08.00–22.00 Sun. Bistro hidden away off Muntriljska, past Sv Nikola, with a range of dishes including grills & pasta. **$$$**

✗ **Peperone** Franine i Jurine 6; ⏰ 08.00–23.00 Mon–Sat, 15.00–23.00 Sun. Small buffet/bar near the tourist information office with reasonable (though rather less than homemade-tasting) pasta dishes, sandwiches & pizza. **$$**

FESTIVALS

Jules Verne Days (*www.julesvernedays.com*) This festival in mid-June celebrates the connection between the town and Jules Verne's 1888 novel *Mathius Sandorf*, with theatre performances, balloon and helicopter flights, and a treasure hunt for kids.

TradInEtno A well-established annual traditional music festival in June, with performances in the castle as well as in the streets, making it a lively time of year to visit.

SHOPPING

Pazin Market The market is held on the first Tuesday of the month and is probably of little interest to foreign visitors, when the street between the bus station

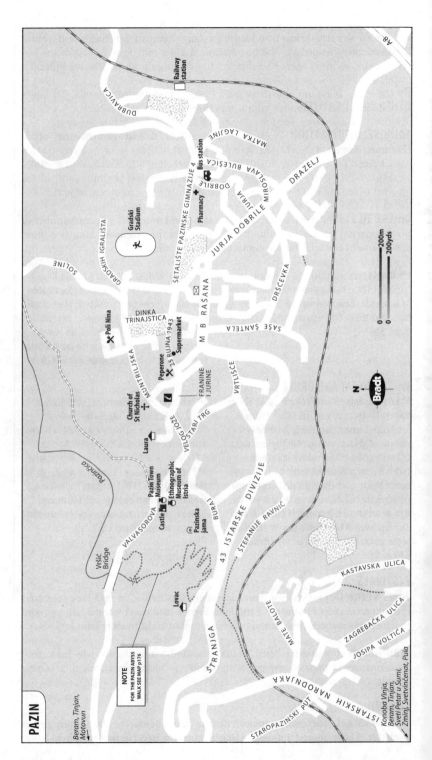

PAZIN

Beram, Tinjan,
Motovun

Railway
station

DUBRAVICA

MATKA LAGINJE

Bus station

DOBRILE

SOLINE

Gradski
Stadium

ŠETALIŠTE PAZINSKE GIMNAZIJE 4

Pharmacy

JURJA DOBRILE MIROSLAVA BULEŠICA

DRAZELJ

GRADSKIH IGRALIŠTA

JURJA DOBRILE

DINKA
TRINAJSTICA

Poli Nina

M B RAŠANA

DRŠČEVKA

Peperone

25 RUJNA 1943
Supermarket

SAŠE ŠANTELA

Church of
St Nicholas

MUNTRILJSKA

FRANINE
I JURINE

VRTLIŠĆE

Laura

VELOŠTARJ TRG

200m
200yds

Bradt

N

Pazinčica

Pazin Town
Museum

VALVASOROVA

Castle

Ethnographic
Museum of
Istria

BURA IVI

Pazinska
jama

43 ISTARSKE DIVIZIJE

STEFANIJE RAVNIĆ

KASTAVSKA ULICA

Vršić
Bridge

Lovac

ZAGREBAČKA ULICA

JOSIPA VOLTIĆA

NOTE
FOR THE PAZIN ABYSS
WALK SEE MAP p176

STRANJGA

MATE BALOTE

ISTARSKIH NARODNJAKA

STAROPAZINSKI PUT

Konoba Vinja,
Beram, Tinjan,
Sveti Petar u Šumi,
Zminj, Svetvincenat, Pula

A8

118

and the town centre turns into a seething mass of stalls selling cheap clothing and all manner of other goods.

Supermarket There's a reasonably sized Diona supermarket on 25 Rujna 1943.

OTHER PRACTICALITIES

✚ **Accident and emergency** Jurja Dobrile 1; ✎ 052 624 643

✆ **Internet** Peperone (see *Where to eat and drink*, on page 117).

✚ **Pharmacy** Šetalište pazinske gimnazije 4; ⏰ 07.00–20.00 Mon–Fri, 07.30–20.00 Sat, 09.00–13.00 Sun

✉ **Post office** M B Rašana 7a; ⏰ 07.00–20.00 Mon–Fri, 07.00–14.00 Sat

WHAT TO SEE AND DO Pazin's dominant piece of architecture is its **castle** (*kaštel*), first mentioned in the 10th century though owing much of its present form to the 16th and 17th centuries. It's a massive and impregnable-looking structure, not least because it sits perched on the edge of a gorge at the top of a 100m cliff, from where the small county of Pazin was governed during the Middle Ages (see *History*, on page 113), while much of the rest of Istria was gobbled up by Venice. The castle now houses the **Pazin Town Museum** (Muzej grada Pazina) and **Istria Ethnographic Museum** (*Etnografski muzej Istre; Istarskog razvoda 1;* ✎ *052 622 220; www.emi.hr;* ⏰ *15 Apr–15 Oct 10.00–18.00 daily; 16 Oct–14 Apr 10.00–15.00 Tue–Thu, 11.00–16.00 Fri, 10.00–16.00 Sat/Sun; entry for both museum collections adults 25kn, children 18kn).* Upstairs you can also see the dungeon from which the hero of Jules Verne's novel *Mathius Sandorf* makes his daring escape into the Pazin abyss (see box on page 120). There is also a good collection of Istrian folk costumes, and a collection of local church bells from the 17th to 19th centuries. As well as the permanent collections there have been some good temporary exhibitions, including in 2012 an excellent series of portraits by German photographer Frank Gaudlitz.

Just around the corner from the tourist information office, the 13th-century **Church of St Nicholas** was rebuilt in the 15th, and 18th centuries, and has an interesting presbytery with star-shaped vaulting, with frescoes dating from 1460, probably the work of an unknown master from Tyrol.

The reason most people visit Pazin is to see the dramatic **gorge** of the Pazinčica River, where it disappears into the **Pazinska jama** or 'Pazin abyss' (*www.pazinska-jama.com*), a cave and sinkhole at the base of a 100m sheer cliff. The cave was popularised in the late 19th century through the writings of Charles Yriarte and in particular the publication of Jules Verne's novel *Mathius Sandorf* (see box on page 120), though much earlier than this it may have provided inspiration for the entrance to Hell in Dante's *Inferno*.

The first serious exploration of the cave was undertaken in 1893 by the pioneering French speleologist **Édouard-Alfred Martel**, who discovered a large underground lake there (subsequently named after him). **Mirko Malez**, founder and president of the Croatian Speleological Association, explored the cave in 1967, and local caving instructor **Drago Opašić** led an expedition into the cave in 1975, in which a second underground lake was discovered, Mitrovo jezero. Despite the popularisation of a connection between the underground course of the Pazinčica and the Limski kanal à la *Mathius Sandorf*, experiments in the first half of the 20th century (including the use of marked eels) showed that it actually drains east into the River Raša.

The Pazinčica Gorge sometimes floods after heavy rain, when the enlarged river is unable to escape underground down into the siphon below Martel's lake fast enough, turning the gorge into a lake – the largest recorded flood being in 1896, when the water rose to just 30m below the castle.

An easy **walking trail** leads down into the gorge from the **Vršić bridge** (you need to get special permission to enter the cave itself, however – contact the tourist information office), and it's also possible to follow the river upstream to **Zarečki krov**, a large waterfall spilling over a rock shelf into a pool (see page 175 for a description of both these walks).

AROUND PAZIN

BERAM Around 3km northwest of Pazin, near the village of **Beram**, is an outstanding cycle of 15th-century **frescoes**, worthy of any amount of detour to see. The frescoes, which date from 1474, decorate the interior of the small **Church of St Mary of the Rocks** (Sv Marija na Škriljinah), 1km northeast of the village itself, and are the work of a local master, Vincent of Kastav. They cover almost the entire wall space in 46 panels, mostly with scenes from the life of St Mary and the life of Christ, including a large (8m long) *Adoration of the Magi*. But it is the extraordinary *Dance of Death*, above the main entrance, which steals the show. Figures representative of an entire cross section of medieval society are arranged in what is more of a solemn procession than a dance, all walking from left to right – a pope, a cardinal and a bishop lead the way, followed by a king and queen, an innkeeper carrying a small cask, a small naked child, a beggar, a knight and a merchant, all interspersed with horn-blowing, scythe-bearing skeletons, and all walking into the arms of death. The frescoes are remarkably well preserved – they were covered up or painted over during the 18th century, and were only discovered beneath a layer of paint and plaster in 1913.

The church is kept locked, so you'll need to contact the local keyholder in Beram, Sonja Šestan (*Beram 38;* ☎ *052 622 903*), who'll come and open it (try to call at least half an hour in advance, preferably more). There's officially no admission fee for visiting the church at the moment, but a small offering of 20kn or similar will probably be appreciated. You can walk to Beram easily enough from Pazin – there's a marked **footpath**, and a small map is available from the Pazin Tourist Information Office (see page 117). In Beram itself, the **Parochial Church of St Martin** has some early 15th-century frescoes hidden behind the main altar.

✗ Where to eat

✗ **Konoba Vela vrata** Beram 41; ☏ 052 622 801; m 091 781 4995; ⊕ summer 12.00–midnight Mon–Sat; winter 16.00–midnight Mon–Sat. Homely tavern opposite St Martin's Church, with dishes including homemade pasta with truffles or game, sausage & pork loin with pickled cabbage. $$

TINJAN ~~East~~ *West* from Pazin on the old road to Baderna and Poreč, the village of Tinjan is these days best known for its excellent *pršut*, considered by many to be the best in Istria and celebrated with a prestigious annual *pršut* festival at the beginning of October. There are good views over the adjacent valley from a broad grassy terrace, and in the old town several houses are marked by carved symbols indicating the trade of their former inhabitants. Note the bell tower of the parish church, with its unusual top. *CRAP.*

✗ Where to eat

✗ **Konoba na kapeli** Milinki 146; ☏ 052 626 318; ⊕ 07.00–midnight daily. Great *konoba* & *kušaona pršuta* – meaning 'a place to taste *pršut*'. There will usually be *pršut* from around 4 different local producers available – best ordered as a platter with local cheeses & other nibbles & savoured with a jug of wine. Just outside Tinjan itself at the junction with the road from Pazin to Baderna & Poreč. $$

SV PETAR U ŠUMI The small village of Sv Petar u Šumi, around halfway between Tinjan and Žminj, grew up around the Benedictine monastery of the same name, rather than the other way round. The **Monastery of Sv Petar u Šumi** (St Peter in the Woods) is first mentioned in 1174, as having already existed for 50 years before

ISTRIAN *PRŠUT*

Though *pršut* (dry-cured ham, similar to Italian prosciutto) is produced widely in Dalmatia, many would argue (the authors included) that Istrian *pršut* is superior.

The village of Tinjan and its surroundings, elevated and exposed to a cool northeasterly wind, are considered to produce the finest Istrian *pršut*, which is still made using traditional methods in this area.

The pig's hindleg is cleaned, lightly salted and left in a wooden press (*kasela*) for about a week, weighted by stones to drain off any blood. It is then rubbed with a mixture of salt, herbs (bay leaves and rosemary) and pepper, before being hung to 'dry' for the winter in the loft or upper storey of a building – and with the arrival of spring and warmer weather, in a cool stone cellar. The entire curing process lasts for between 12 and 18 months, and when the ham has finally matured there can be an enormous difference in taste and colour between hams of different ages and from different producers, even within a small area.

The slightly less muscular fore-leg is also cured in a similar manner, and is known as *špaleta*.

that, and there was probably a monastery here even earlier. In the 15th century the Paulines took over, restoring the monastery and cloister, which is one of the more beautiful in Istria – note the Renaissance columns on the lower level, added at this time, and the earlier Romanesque columns above. Part of the monastery and the adjacent **Church of St Peter and St Paul** were burnt down in the 17th century, and it was during subsequent rebuilding in the early 18th century that the church gained its Baroque façade, and elaborately decorated interior, the work of the painter Leopold Keckheisen and sculptor Pavao Riedl, both of whom were members of the Pauline brethren. The ruined building beside the monastery was probably used for livestock. The Paulines were suspended by order of the Austrian emperor Joseph II in 1783, but returned to Sv Petar u Šumi in 1993.

Legend connects Sv Petar u Šumi with the 11th-century Hungarian king Solomon, who some say spent some years at Sv Petar u Šumi before continuing to Pula, where he ended his life as a monk (see *Chapter 3*, page 62). Others say he was slain on the battlefield near Edirne.

SOUTH TO PULA

ŽMINJ If you're driving south on the old road from Pazin or Sv Petar u Šumi to Svetvinčenat (see below), you'll pass through **Žminj** (Italian Gimino), where it's worth stopping to have a quick look at the massive *kula* or tower, which once would have formed part of a 15th-century castle. Just down the road past two old wells (and a bust of Istrian poet Mate Balota) is the main square and the **Parish Church of St Michael Archangel**, with its Baroque façade. There is a large annual village fair in Žminj on St Bartholomew's Day, at the end of August, known as **Bartulja**.

FEŠTINSKO KRALJEVSTVO Some 8km southeast from Žminj on the road to Barban, in a field near the village of Feštini, is **Feštini Cave** or **Feštinsko kraljevstvo** – literally 'the Feštini Kingdom' (m *091 561 6327;* e *info@sige.hr; www.sige.hr;* ⊕ *Jun–Sep 10.00–18.00 daily; Apr, May & Oct 10.00–18.00 Sat/Sun; entry adults 40kn, children 25kn*), a 67m-long cave slung with stalactites and stalagmites. The cave was apparently only discovered accidentally in the 1930s while a local farmer was digging in the field, and his hoe disappeared into the ground. During the Italian occupation of Istria in World War II the entire adult male population of Feštini was killed, save one survivor who was hiding in the cave.

SVETVINČENAT A few kilometres south of Žminj, the beautiful village of **Svetvinčenat** is best known for its castle, **Kaštel Grimani**, which is one of the largest and best preserved in Istria. Built in the 13th century but owing its present appearance very much to the 16th century and Venetian influence, the castle originally belonged to the Bishops of Poreč, then the Morosini family, and in the 16th century became the property of the **Grimani di San Luca**, a powerful Venetian patrician family (their Palazzo Grimani is a familiar landmark in Venice).

The castle stands on the north side of the remarkably large square or *placa*, at the centre of which is a **well** dating from 1808. On the east side of the square is the early 16th-century **Parish Church of the Annunciation** with its distinctive Renaissance trefoil façade, and there's a **loggia** on its southwest corner. The helpful **tourist information office** (*Svetvinčenat 20;* ✆ *052 560 349;* e *info@tz-svetvincenat. hr; www.tz-svetvincenat.hr;* ⊕ *summer 07.00–15.00 Mon, Wed–Fri, 09.00–17.00 Tue, 11.00–14.00 Sat/Sun*) is on the west side of the square.

A 200m walk southeast of the *placa* will bring you to the small 14th-century **Church of St Catherine** (Crkvica Sv Katerine), the interior of which is decorated with a cycle of frescoes from the early 15th century (the church is kept locked, but someone from the tourist information office should be able to come and open it). The small 12th-century **Church of St Vincent**, in the cemetery on the northeast side of the village, is decorated with three layers of frescoes, the oldest (of which only fragments now remain) date from the late 13th century and show clear Byzantine influence, the others from the late the 14th and early 15th centuries (again, the church will be locked, so ask at the tourist information office first).

 ## Where to stay and eat

⌂ **Apartman Enna** (1 apt, sleeps 4) Svetvinčenat 17; ☏ 052 560 301; m 098 169 1701; e apartman-enna@hi.t-com.hr; www.apartman-enna.hr. Ground-floor apartment in a gorgeous renovated stone house just off the *placa*, with its own terrace & garden. **$$$**

✗ **Pizzeria Grimani** Svetvinčenat 71; ☏ 052 560 395; ⏱ summer 07.00–midnight Tue–Sun; winter 07.00–23.00 Tue–Sun. Well-priced pizzas on the northeast side of the *placa*, with tables outside on the square below the castle walls. **$–$$**

Svetvinčenat has a good number of **cafés** for a place of its size, mostly scattered along the road northwest of the castle. Note the block of stone with an inscription built into the corner of one, with the date 1714 – almost certainly from a nearby church or other building, though no-one's quite sure which.

MOTOVUN

Motovun (Italian Montona), without any doubt the best-known and most photographed of central Istria's hill towns, sits atop a 277m flat-topped hill on one side of the Mirna Valley.

HISTORY Once the site of a prehistoric hill fort, and a Roman settlement from at least the late 2nd century AD, when clay was extracted from the surrounding area for the production of amphorae, Motovun is first mentioned in a historical document from 804, at which time it belonged to the Bishops of Poreč. From the 13th century it came under the sphere of Venice (when the town walls were built), before passing to Austria with the rest of Istria at the beginning of the 19th century, and to Italy after World War I, before becoming a part of Yugoslavia and then the Republic of Croatia.

GETTING THERE AND AWAY Apart from a very limited local **bus** service (departing Pazin 06.45, 13.15 and 15.20, during school term only), the only way to get to Motovun is with your own wheels, either by car or by bicycle. **By car** it's a 15-minute drive to Pazin or Buzet, 30 minutes to Poreč, and one hour to Pula. Note that traffic is highly regulated in Motovun, and you can't take a car all the way up to the top of the hill and the old town (you'll see why when you get there on foot – the streets are tiny – and it makes it a much nicer place to wander around anyway). You can drive to about 250m from the top, where there's a small parking area (15kn per day), from where it's only a short walk up to the main square (if you're staying at Hotel Kaštel they can send someone down to help with your luggage, as long as you let them know in advance). Otherwise, or if the parking area closer to the upper town is full, there's a large parking area at the bottom of the hill. If you're **cycling**, the **Parenzana** (see box on page 128) passes close to Motovun.

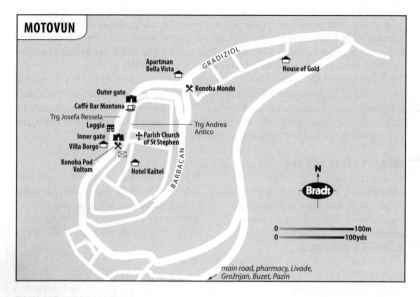

MOTOVUN

- Apartman Bella Vista
- GRADIZIOL
- House of Gold
- Konoba Mondo
- Outer gate
- Caffè Bar Montona
- Trg Josefa Ressela
- Loggia
- Trg Andrea Antico
- Inner gate
- Parish Church of St Stephen
- Villa Borgo
- BARBACAN
- Konoba Pod Voltom
- Hotel Kaštel
- N
- Bradt
- 0 — 100m
- 0 — 100yds
- main road, pharmacy, Livade, Grožnjan, Buzet, Pazin

TOURIST INFORMATION The small tourist information office has local information and accommodation details (*Trg Andrea Antico 1;* ☎ *052 617 480;* e *info@tz-motovun.hr; www.tz-motovun.hr;* ⏲ *Jun–Aug 10.00–17.00 daily, Apr–May & Sept–Oct 10.00–17.00 Sat/Sun*).

WHERE TO STAY, EAT AND DRINK

🏠 **Hotel Kaštel** (3 sgls, 26 dbls, 2 suitesl) Trg Andrea Antico 7; ☎052 681 607; e info@hotel-kastel-motovun.hr; www.hotel-kastel-motovun.hr; ⏲ all year. Lovely boutique hotel occupying a former palace, with the most enviable position in Motovun – right on the square, at the top of the old town. Go for a room with a balcony overlooking the square if you can. There's a wonderful spa with an indoor pool, sauna & massage rooms, & a peaceful, leafy garden. In front of the hotel at one end of the main square is a broad terrace where you can sit & eat dinner or sip coffee in the shade of ancient chestnut trees. Half- & full-board accommodation are only a few euros extra, so is well worth considering. The hotel restaurant **Restaurant Palladio** (⏲ *08.00–22.00 daily*; $$$) is excellent, with plenty of Istrian specialities including homemade pasta & various truffle dishes, *boškarin* beef, & some vegetarian dishes. Highly recommended. $$$$

🏠 **Villa Borgo** (6 dbls, 1 apt) Borgo 4; ☎052 681 708; m 098 434 797; e info@villaborgo.com;

⏲ all year. Nicely renovated place just outside the town's inner gate, by the loggia, with clean rooms, friendly staff & lovely views of the Mirna Valley from its terrace. $$$

✘ **Konoba Mondo** Barbacan 1; ☎052 681 791; ⏲ summer 12.00–15.30 & 18.00–22.00 daily; winter12.00–15.30 & 18.00–22.00 Wed–Mon . Nice little *konoba* with a focus on Istrian specialities & truffle dishes, including wonderful homemade pasta (in particular the giant ravioli stuffed with cheese), beef carpaccio & delicious polenta. $$$

✘ **Konoba Pod Voltom** Trg Josefa Ressela 6; ☎052 681 923; ⏲ summer 12.00–22.00 daily; winter 12.00–22.00 Thu–Sun. Low-key, homely *konoba* hidden beneath the arch of the main town gate. $$$

🍺 **Caffe Bar Montona** Trg Josefa Ressela 2; ⏲ 08.00–01.00 daily. Bar & ice-cream café with an unbeatable view of the Mirna Valley, from tables along this square between the inner & outer town gates.

The tourist information office can supply information on **private accommodation** in Motovun (though you are advised to have booked in advance), otherwise a couple of central places you could try are **House of Gold** (*Gradiziol 46;* \ *052 681 816;* m *098 353 968;* e *zdenkagold@yahoo.com; www.motovunaccommodation.com;* **$$$**) and **Apartman Bella Vista** (*Gradiziol 1;* \ *052 681 724;* e *info@apartmani-motovun.com; www.apartmani-motovun.com;* **$$**).

FESTIVALS The **Motovun Film Festival** (*www.motovunfilmfestival.com*), which runs for five days in July, has rapidly grown into one of Croatia's most important film festivals. Launched in 1999 in response to the ongoing closure of many small and repertory cinemas in Croatia at that time, it tends to focus on low-budget films and World Cinema, with screenings on the main square, and, appropriately enough, in a renovated old cinema which had been closed down.

SHOPPING Motovun has plenty of boutique shops selling truffles, wine, olive oil, art, jewellery and souvenirs, especially along Gradisiol.

OTHER PRACTICALITIES
✚ **Pharmacy** Istarske ljekarne, Kanal 4; ⏰ 13.00–20.00 Mon–Tue, 07.00–14.00 Wed–Fri

✉ **Post office** Mure 2; ⏰ 08.00–17.00 Mon, 08.00–14.30 Tue–Fri

WHAT TO SEE AND DO The main thing to see in Motovun is the town itself – a walled Gothic and Renaissance citadel draped across the top of a flat-topped hill. Walking uphill from the upper car-parking area along Gradisiol, a narrow street lined with boutique souvenir and truffle shops, you pass through the first of the two Gothic town **gate towers**, and onto **Trg Josefa Ressela**, from one side of which there are breathtaking views out over the **Mirna Valley**, and at the far end of which is a **loggia**, first mentioned in 1331. The second **town gate** leads you up under a vaulted ceiling into the citadel and onto the cobbled main square, **Trg Andrea Antico**, which is named after the 16th-century Renaissance music printer, who was born in Motovun. On the far side of the square is the 17th-century **Parish Church of St Stephen**, possibly designed by the great Venetian architect Palladio, with its Baroque façade. The interior has a large *Last Supper* by an unknown Venetian painter. The Romanesque-Gothic **bell tower** dates from the 13th century, and its crenellated top, visible for miles around protruding above the citadel, is one of the more iconic images of central Istria. On the opposite side of the square, the large **town hall** was built in the 13th century, though most of it dates from the Renaissance, and is one of the largest such buildings in Istria. You can **walk** along the 13th-century Venetian walls from the far end of the square. The 18th-century Polesini Palace, now the **Hotel Kaštel**, sits on one side of a terrace shaded by giant chestnut trees.

Some of the best views of Motovun are when approaching from the west, and from near the village of Zamask.

AROUND MOTOVUN

LIVADE There's not much to see in Livade (not to be confused with *livada*, which is the word for meadow), apart from the small **Parenzana Museum** (\ *052 644 150; www.parenzana.net;* ⏰ *summer Mon–Fri by prior arrangement, otherwise ask at Konoba Dorjana across the road*). Truffle aficionados however will want to come here for the **Tuberfest** (white truffle fair) on the first weekend in October (⏰ 11.00–19.00), and for Giancarlo Zigante's restaurant, where the focus is very much on *tartufi*.

IPŠA OLIVE OIL

About 1.5km east from Livade on the backroad to Istraske toplice, a minor road turns north towards Oprtalj, passing above a terraced hillside planted with olive trees, where **Klaudio Ipša** is now widely regarded as producing some of the very finest olive oils anywhere in Croatia. Ipša grows three Istrian varieties of olive – *istarska bjelica*, *bugla* and *črnica* – and the Italian varieties *frantoio* and *leccino*. Olives are hand-picked at optimum ripeness, and cold-pressed within four hours, ensuring maximum freshness and resulting in some wonderfully rich and aromatic extra virgin olive oils, with a slightly piquant taste. In 2005 Ipša's Bjelica and Frantoio olive oils became the first Croatian olive oils to be included in *L'extravergine*, the prestigious Italian guide to the world's best olive oils. They have been included in *L'extravergine* every year since and Ipša's olive oils have also garnered awards from the Slow Food Association and at Vinistra and elsewhere.

You can buy olive oil here and arrange tastings (*Ipši 10;* \052 664 010; m 098 219 538 or 091 206 0538; e klaudio.ipsa@pu.t-com.hr; www.ipsa-maslinovaulja. hr), though not usually during harvest time (second half October), and the Ipša family also offer accommodation in nearby Oprtalj.

✕ Where to eat

✕ **Restaurant Zigante** Livade 7; \052 664 302; www.restaurantzigante.com; ☉ summer 12.00–23.00 daily; winter 11.00–22.00 daily. Opulent & very formal dining experience at the centre of the Zigante empire. $$$$–$$$$$

✕ **Konoba doline** Gradinje 59, Gradinje; \052 664 091; ☉ 12.00–21.00 Wed–Mon. Outstanding *konoba* halfway along the backroad between Livade & Istarske toplice, serving exquisite truffle & homemade pasta dishes in a relaxed, low-key setting. Don't miss the *fuži* with truffles in a cream sauce. $$$

✕ **Konoba Dorjana** Livade 4a; ☉ 11.00–22.00 Thur–Tue. Simple *konoba* with a nice leafy terrace across the road from the Parenzana Museum, with homemade pasta dishes, *maneštra* & other Istrian staples, as well as pizza. $$

OPRTALJ Almost directly opposite Motovun across the Mirna Valley, the village of **Oprtalj** (Italian Portole) receives much less attention – and infinitely fewer visitors – than its more famous neighbour. Perched on a hillside around 7km uphill from Livade, Oprtalj's medieval fortifications have now almost all but disappeared beneath a veneer of brightly painted houses.

At the entrance to the village there is a large Venetian **loggia**, and a lovely **terrace** overlooking the Osoje Valley, which runs southwest to the Mirna, from beneath ancient chestnut trees. There's not a great deal to see within the walls – entering the village through the main **gate** leads you past a medley of renovated and abandoned houses, to the 16th-century **Parish Church of St George** and its square-topped bell tower. Award-winning local beekeeper and **honey** producer **Dario Vežnaver** (*Pčelarstvo Vežnaver;* \052 644 052; m 092 114 2423; www.api-veznaver.eu) has a small shop just inside the main gate (alternatively you can buy honey and other products from the Vežnaver beekeeping farm at Škofi 34, about 5km northeast of Oprtalj).

Just to the south of the terrace and loggia, the small **Church of Sv Rok** has some 16th-century **frescoes** by Antun of Padova (that's not the Padova in Italy, but a village near Butoniga jezero in Istria – and no, that's not called Padova either; it's called Kašćerga); and downhill from the village on the road to Livade is the 15th-century **Church of St Mary**, with frescoes by several different painters including Clerigino, a master from Kopar. Both churches will be locked, so ask at the **tourist information office** if you want to look inside (*Matka Laginje 21;* \ *052 644 077*). Private accommodation can also be found through the tourist information office, and Klaudio Ipša and family (of Ipša Olive Oil; see opposite) have a three-room house and a suite in Oprtalj which can be rented to guests.

Though it is the centre of a large municipality, the village of Oprtalj has only some 100 inhabitants.

✖ Where to eat

✖ **Taverna Histria**   Matka Laginje; \ 052 644 130; ⏱ summer only 08.00–22.00 daily. Nice, low-key *konoba* by the parking area & loggia with tables outside on the terrace beneath the chestnut trees, & dishes including truffles with polenta, plus pizzas. Used to be called Konoba Oprtalj. $$

VIŽINADA   It's worth stopping in Vižinada to look at the large square with its well-preserved Venetian wells and loggia. The Knights Templar established a church here in the 12th century, and Vižinada was also the birthplace of the celebrated 19th-century ballet dancer **Carlotta Grisi**, famous for the title role in *Giselle*. It also lies on the route of the **Parenzana** (see box, page 128).

Just to the northwest of Vižinada (between the villages of Bajkini and Vrbani) are the **Franc Arman Vineyards and Winery** (*Narduči 5;* \ *052 446 226;* m *091 446 2266;* e *info@francarman.hr; www.francarman.hr*), where you can buy wine or arrange a tasting in the old wine cellar or *konoba*. The vineyards have been here since 1850, and Franc and his son Oliver make some very, very drinkable (and award-winning) wines – including a crisp Malvazija and a robust Teran, and an oak-aged Malvazija Classic which can only be described as heavenly.

GROŽNJAN

Grožnjan (Italian Grisignana) is, like Motovun, one of the more popular of the Istrian hill towns, helped no doubt by its relative proximity to the northwest coast. It is a pretty little town, with a well-preserved old medieval centre and fine views over the Mirna Valley. Despite having been left largely deserted after the Italian exodus which followed World War II (see *History*, on page 11), the municipality of Grožnjan today has a higher proportion of people describing Italian as their first language than anywhere else in Istria. Artists in particular were encouraged to move to the largely depopulated town from the late 1960s onwards, and today the self-styled 'Town of Artists' is full of little galleries and boutique shops selling art, handmade jewellery, wine, olive oil, etc. Full being a relative term, of course – Grožnjan, like other Istrian hill towns, is still a fairly sleepy place, and has fewer than 100 inhabitants.

Grožnjan puts on an international **jazz festival** in July, 'Jazz is Back' (*www.jazzisbackbp.com*), with local and international acts which in past years have included the likes of Georgie Fame. The festival was founded by Croatian jazz musician Boško Petrović in 1999, and was voted Europe's best boutique jazz festival in 2008. It also has an art festival in September (**Extempore**), and during the summer is the venue for the Croatian branch of **Jeunesses Musicales International** (*www.jmi.net*), with a summer school for young musicians and various concerts. Grožnjan is around 8km northwest of Motovun, the last section on an unsealed road, or further if you take the sealed road via Buje, and is also on the route of the **Parenzana** (see box, page 128).

THE PARENZANA

The Parenzana was a 123km-long narrow-gauge railway line between Trieste and Poreč, which ran from 1902 to 1935 and connected some 35 stations in Istria, in what is now Italy, Slovenia and Croatia. It was used to carry both passengers and freight – olive oil, flour, vegetables, wine, hides, salt from Piran, lime and stone – navigating the hilly karst landscape between remote villages via a series of tunnels, bridges and viaducts.

In 2002, on the 100th anniversary of its opening, the old Parenzana route was developed into a cycling and hiking route, beginning with sections in Croatia and Slovenia and later the whole line. By far the longest section of the Parenzana is in Croatia (78km, compared with 32km in Slovenia and 13km in Italy), and among the towns and villages it connects between Poreč and the Slovenian border are Buje, Grožnjan, Oprtalj, Motovun, Vižinada and Nova Vas.

Over its history the Parenzana has had several names – to its Austrian builders it was the Parenzaner Bahn, to the Italians it was the Parenzana, in abbreviation it became TPC, and to the local population it was the Istrijanka or Istranka (or sometimes Poreška or Porečanka – after the town of Poreč, known as Parenzo in Italian).

See page 180 for a description of the route between Grožnjan and Livade.

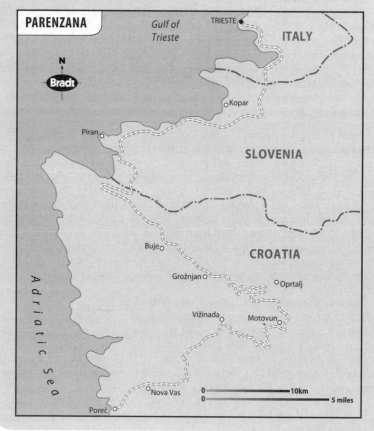

Where to stay, eat and drink

🏠 **Konoba Pintur** (4 dbls) M Gorijana 9; ✆052 776 397; ☉ Mar–Sep 08.00–22.00 Tue–Sun. Small, friendly *konoba* (**$$**) & guesthouse in the centre of town, with tables outside under an old tree. **$$**

🍹 **Kaya Energy Bar** Vincenta iz Kastava 2; ✆052 776 051; ☉ Apr–Dec 09.00–23.00 daily.

Café/bar run by Croatian designer Suzana Colarić, with seating outside on the terrace, & low tables with comfortable wicker chairs in the cool, stone & wood-beamed interior. Note the lamp made from silkworm cocoons at the entrance, & the table bases made from driftwood. Cakes & cheese plates, with an emphasis on local or organic ingredients.

The **tourist information office** (*Gorjana 3;* ✆ *052 776 131; www.tz-groznjan.hr –* look under *Turistička ponuda,* then *Smještaj kod domaćina*) should be able to help with details of **private accommodation**, otherwise a couple of places you could try are **Villa San Vito** (*Trg Kaštela 2;* ✆ *052 776 113;* m *091 528 8253;* e *villa@ san-vito.info; www.san-vito.info;* **$$**) and, about 1km out of town towards Buje, **Casa Margherita** (*Peroj 13a;* m *098 287 433;* e *lorena.oplanic@gmail.com; www. plusing-istra.hr;* **$$**).

BUZET

Perched on a hill and overlooking the truffle-rich Mirna Valley on one side and the forested slopes of the Ćićarija Mountains on the other, Buzet (Italian Pinguente) is, for one of the authors at least, the most rewarding of the Istrian hill towns – with colourful festivals, great hiking and biking opportunities in the surrounding hills and valleys, and a wealth of cultural interest in nearby towns and villages. There's even a good bus service to Rijeka and Zagreb. Nevertheless, Buzet receives much less attention and fewer visitors than Motovun and Grožnjan further west. Often called the 'City of Truffles', there are two big truffle events in its annual calendar, and Istria's favourite local beer, known appropriately enough as Favorit, is brewed here.

HISTORY Like many surrounding hilltop settlements, Buzet was inhabited by Illyrian tribes during the Bronze Age, and was under Rome (Roman Pinquentum) from AD177–476, though unlike many other towns in the region it escaped the devastating plague of the 2nd century AD. It was under Frankish rule from the 8th century, and under the Patriarchs of Aquila until 1497, when it fell to Venice. During this period it became an important regional centre of Venetian power, in particular after becoming the seat of the De Raspo Captaincy (whose coat of arms you'll encounter in the old town) in 1511, when its fortifications were strengthened and several palaces built. After the fall of Venice in 1797 and a brief spell under Napoleon, Buzet passed to Austrian rule until the close of World War I.

GETTING THERE AND AWAY

By train Buzet is on the railway line from Pazin (50 minutes) and Pula (2 hours), and in the summer is connected to Ljubljana (3 hours) – but the **railway station** is around 3.5km northeast and uphill from the bus station (follow the road up through Sveti Martin).

By bus Buzet's **bus station** (*Riječka ulica;* ☉ *06.00–18.30 Mon–Fri, 06.00–11.00 & 16.30–18.30 Sat/Sun*) is a ten–15-minute walk from the old town – from the bus station follow the main road (Riječka ulica) towards the old town, then turn left over the bridge and left up a long flight of steps leading to the main gate, Vela vrata.

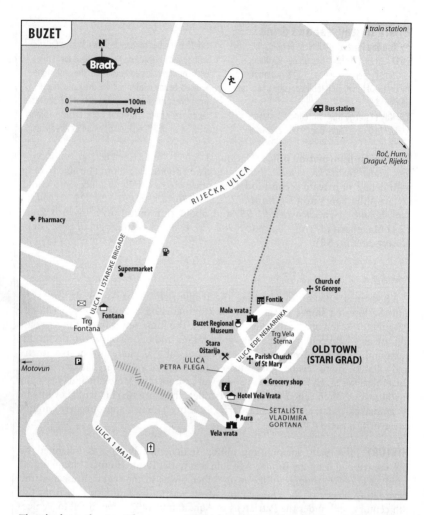

There's also a short cut from opposite the bus station (though it's a steep unsealed road and can be rather dusty, so is highly unsuitable for suitcases) – follow the unsealed road uphill from beside the small supermarket, which brings you to the Mala vrata (small gate) on the northeast side of the old town. There are direct, fast buses to Rijeka (50 minutes) and Zagreb (3½ hours), departing Buzet at 06.10 and 16.40 daily, and two daily services (departing Buzet 15.30 and 17.25) to Pula via Roč, Lupoglav and Pazin on weekdays. There is also a bus service between Pula and Venice, via Pazin, Buzet and Trieste (departs Buzet for Pula 15.30, Pula for Buzet 05.30, Buzet for Trieste 07.05, Trieste for Buzet 14.30; journey time Buzet–Pula 2 hours, Buzet–Trieste 1 hour; daily except Sunday).

By car Buzet is a 50-minute drive from Rijeka, through the Učka tunnel, 50 minutes from Rovinj, and one hour from Pula.

TOURIST INFORMATION Buzet's helpful **tourist information office** (*Šetalište Vladimira Gortana 9;* ☎ *052 662 343;* e *info@istria-buzet.com; www.istria-buzet.com*

or *www.tz-buzet.hr*; ⊕ *Mar–Oct 08.00–15.00 Mon–Fri, 09.00–14.00 Sat; Nov–Feb 08.00–15.00 Mon–Fri*) recently moved to the old town, and is now next door to Hotel Vela Vrata.

WHERE TO STAY AND EAT

Hotel Vela Vrata (18 dbls) Šetalište Vladimira Gortana 7; ☎052 494 750; e booking@velavrata.net; www.velavrata.net; ⊕ all year. Lovely, newly opened boutique hotel in Buzet's old town, with stylish rooms & impeccable service. The hotel has its own restaurant, with tables outside & on the medieval walls themselves, & the food is excellent – from pasta with truffles to tender beef in cranberry sauce, & homemade truffle ice cream. **$$$$**

Hotel Fontana (57 dbls) Trg Fontana 1; ☎052 662 615; e info@hotelfontanabuzet.com; www.hotelfontanabuzet.com; ⊕ all year. The place to go if the Vela Vrata is full, or you are unable to find private accommodation. **$$$**
✕ Stara Oštarija Petra Flega 5; ☎052 694 003; www.stara-ostarija.com.hr; ⊕ 12.00–22.00 Wed–Mon. Excellent restaurant with an emphasis on truffles, from gnocchi with truffles to brown trout with truffles, as well as *fuži* with game & some vegetarian options, & a wonderful view. **$$$**

Camping If you want to get away from it all, there's a nice little campsite up at **Raspadalica** in the foothills of the Ćićarija Mountains (*Kamp Raspadalica*; e *info@raspadalica.com; www.raspadalica.com*), about a 1½-hour hike from Buzet (see route description, page 173), with space for around 30 people (showers but no hot water or electricity, 50kn per person).

FESTIVALS
Istra Open (*www.buzet.tici.hr*) Croatia's top paragliding championship takes off – literally – from Raspadalica, on the cliffs to the northeast of Buzet in July (and there's a further winter event in February).

KIK Fest (*www.poubuzet.hr/fik*) A Festival of Istrian Klapa (*Klapa* is a form of traditional singing in Croatia) is held in Buzet in March.

Subotina Held in Buzet on the second weekend of September, this is one of Istria's most colourful festivals, with people dressed in traditional and period costumes, music, and stalls selling locally made traditional crafts, food and produce – from freshly milled cornflour to *fritule*. On the previous night, to celebrate the opening of the **truffle season**, an enormous **omelette** is prepared in the lower town (on the small square opposite Hotel Fontana, on Ulica Istarske Brigade, in front of one of Zigante's shops) from some 2,000 eggs – 2,013 in 2013, to be precise – and 10kg of truffles. And yes, you get to eat it, too (€4 a portion with a big chunk of bread, which you can wash down with a glass of Favorit or local wine from a stall nearby – how often do you get to eat truffles off a paper plate?).

Weekend of truffles Buzet's premier truffle festival takes place over the first weekend in November.

SHOPPING
Supermarkets There's a large Diona behind the Hotel Fontana (*Trg Fontana 8/2*; ⊕ *07.00–21.00 Mon–Sat, 07.00–12.00 Sun*) and a smaller grocery shop in the old town (*Trg Josipa Fabrijančića 4*; ⊕ *06.30–20.00 Mon–Fri, 07.00–14.00 Sat, 08.00–12.00 Sun*).

Souvenirs There's a nice little shop just inside the entrance to a house on the old town's main square, Trg Vela Šterna, selling handmade jewellery and ceramics, and a branch of **Aura** by the main gate (*Prvi Maj 4;* \ *052 694 250; www.ebuzet.info/ aura*) selling local wines, olive oils, *rakija* and other produce.

OTHER PRACTICALITIES

✚ **Pharmacy** Naselje Gorčica 1; \ 052 662 832; ⊕ 08.00–16.00 Mon–Fri, 09.00–13.00 Sat

✉ **Post office** Trg Fontana 3; ⊕ 07.00–20.00 Mon–Fri, 08.00–12.00 Sat

WHAT TO SEE AND DO Buzet's **old town** (Stari grad) is tiny and it only takes a few minutes to walk from one side to the other. Unlike Motovun's old town, it is accessible by car – though you might prefer to park in the large car park below and walk up the steps into town. From the 16th-century **Vela vrata** (main gate) with its relief sculpture of St George, Buzet's patron saint, turn left past **Hotel Vela Vrata** and the **tourist information office**, with views southwest across the Mirna Valley to the green hills around Vrh from the ramparts on the left. Continue uphill past **Stara Oštarija** restaurant to the 18th-century **Parish Church of St Mary**, with its late 19th-century **bell tower** (though the bell itself is inscribed in Glagolitic with the date 1541). On your left there's a 16th-century **Venetian storehouse** (with one of the many coats of arms you'll see around the old town). Continue past this on Ulica Ede Nemarnika, then turn left to the Regional Museum. Buzet's **Regional Museum** (*Zavičajni muzej; Trg rašporskih kapetana 5;* \ *052 662 792;* e *muzej@poubuzet.hr; www.poubuzet.hr;* ⊕ *09.00–15.00 & 17.00–20.00 Mon–Fri, 09.00–12.00 Sat/Sun; entry 15kn*) is housed in the 17th-century **Bigatto Palace**. Its archaeological collection includes various pieces of Roman stonework and tombstones (including an interesting marble relief with a faun, found in the old town itself), and Iron and Bronze Age objects from nearby caves. There's also a small ethnographic collection and an exhibit of Glagolitic inscriptions, including copies of famous pieces like the Plomin inscription.

From the museum continue to the **Mala vrata** (small gate), completed in 1592, next to which is a stout tower (known as the **Fontik**) which in the 16th century was used by the Venetians as a storehouse for wheat. From here walk up Ulica Mala vrata to reach the main square, **Trg Vela Šterna**, with its 18th-century **wellhead**. At the far (northern) end of the old town is the 17th-century **Church of St George**.

There are several **hiking trails** leading up over the western slopes of the Ćićarija Mountains and Učka – see page 173 for a description of the short walk up to Raspadalica from Buzet's old town – and there are potential **cycle routes** leading in all directions, both road routes and off-road. A visit to the 'pillar of shame' at Salež (see below) via the Bračana Valley is one possibility, or continuing from Salež to Oprtalj (see *Oprtalj*, page 126). Another popular road route is to bike to Roč and Hum, then over to Draguć (see page 134) via Kotle and back to Buzet. **Gral Putovanje** (*Trg Fontana 7/1;* \ *052 662 959;* e *ivana@gral-putovanja.eu; www.gral-putovanja.eu*) is an excellent local agency for hiking, biking, balloon flights and pretty much any other outdoors activity

Truffle hunts and tastings can be arranged with **Karlić tartufi**, in the village of Paladini, near Butoniga jezero (*Paladini 4;* \ *052 667 304;* m *091 575 9196; www. karlictartufi.hr*).

AROUND BUZET

SALEŽ A few kilometres northwest of Buzet and really only accessible by car or bike (with a fair bit of pedalling uphill), the tiny rural settlement of Salež is remarkable for being one of the few places where a so-called **pillar of shame** has survived intact, this one from the 18th century. It's a particularly interesting one, too – shaped as a human figure wearing a fez, and carved from a block of stone not found locally. One of the figure's hands is on his chest, and would once have had shackles attached to it; his other hand is between his legs, covering his groin. Pillars of shame performed a similar function to the stocks – offenders and petty criminals were tied or chained to them, and subjected to public torment and humiliation. Locals call it the *Berlin*.

To get to Salež from Buzet, head towards Motovun then turn right after passing turnings to both Veli Mlun and Mali Mlun, where the road ducks under the aqueduct. Keep an eye out for the ruins of **Kostel (Pietrapilosa) Castle** on a crag on your left, and turn left just before reaching Abramci. Follow the winding road uphill then turn left onto the road to Salež (continuing straight ahead would take you to Zrenj and Oprtalj). The pillar is near the cemetery, which is on the left before the village itself. Whether you are cycling or driving, you can vary your return to Buzet by continuing north from Abramci to the main road (at which point you're less than 5km from the Slovenian border), then turning right and back into Buzet.

ROČ Roč (Italian Rozzo), an ancient settlement with a well-preserved, walled medieval core, lies around 8km southeast of Buzet on the road to Lupoglav and Rijeka. Entering the town through the **main gate** (Vela vrata) you find the first of the town's three churches, **St Roch** (Sv Rok), a Romanesque chapel with frescoes from the 14th and 15th centuries. The **Parish Church of St Bartholomew** (Sv Bartolomej) dates from the 15th century, while the **Church of St Anthony** (Sv Antun) dates from the 12th century and has 14th-century frescoes and a votive cross bearing a Glagolitic inscription from the 12th century. The churches are locked – ask at the tourist information office or parish office on the square (☏ *052 666 462*). Roč was an important centre of **Glagolitic** learning during the medieval period, and it was here that the **first Croatian printed book**, the so-called *Roč Missal*, was prepared in 1483 (that's only around 30 years after the famous Gutenberg Bible). There's a copy of the Gutenberg printing press in the tourist information office, and Roč hosts a Glagolitic script workshop for Croatian schoolchildren in July. Roč also holds an **Accordion Festival** in May.

Getting there and away Buses travelling between Buzet and Rijeka or Zagreb will go past Roč, which is also on the Buzet–Pazin railway line – though the station is around 1km northwest from the village.

Where to stay and eat For **private accommodation** in Roč, try **Apartman Pod Lipom** (*Roč 44;* ☏ *052 666 642;* e *apartman.pod.lipom@gmail.com; www.podlipom. com;* **$**). For somewhere to eat, the homely **Ročka konoba** (*Roč 14;* ☏ *052 666 451;* ⊕ *10.00–22.00 Tue–Sun;* **$$**) serves local Istrian dishes.

GLAGOLITIC ALLEY The 7km of road between Roč and Hum is known as the 'Glagolitic Alley' (Aleja glagoljaša), and is marked at various points by 11 sculptures or monuments relating to the Glagolitic alphabet. The sculptures are the work of Croatian sculptor Želimir Janeš and Croatian philologist Joseph Bratulić, and date from 1977. The series begins with the *Pillar of the Chakavian Parliament* just outside Roč, and finishes with the elaborate door knockers on the town gate at Hum.

HUM The tiny, walled hilltop settlement of Hum – which loudly proclaims itself to be the 'smallest town in the world' – has a grand total of around 20 inhabitants, and consists of little more than a church, a few houses and two streets. The small **Church of St Jerome** has frescoes from the 12th century, along with various bits of Glagolitic 'graffiti' dating from between the 12th and the 15th centuries. The 16th-century altarpiece by Antun of Padova (see *Draguć*, below) which once stood in the church is now in a museum in Poreč. The church is kept locked – ask at the *konoba* for the key.

While in Hum, make a point of sampling **Humska biska**, a local type of *rakija* with white mistletoe and four kinds of grasses (unless of course you're driving, in which case it will put you straight over the limit). Hum holds a *rakija* **festival** at the end of October.

🏠 **Where to stay and eat** For details of **private accommodation** in Hum – there are a couple of rooms and apartments available – *see www.hum.hr* or ask at the *konoba*.

✕ **Humska konoba** ☏ 052 660 005; http://www.hum.hr/humskakonoba; 🕐 15 May–15 Oct 11.00–22.00 daily; 15 Mar–15 May & 15 Oct–15 Nov 11.00–22.00 Tue–Sun; 15 Nov–15 Mar 11.00–22.00 Sat/Sun. Nice little *konoba* with a small terrace serving *fuži* with goulash, pork loin with pickled cabbage & other dishes. This is the only place to eat in Hum & like the town, it's small, so the idea is to time your visit not to coincide with the arrival of a tour bus. $$

KOTLE Turning west at Brnobići on the Roč–Hum road takes you to **Kotle**, where the River Mirna pours over a cascade, and there's a restored **watermill**. Notice how the limestone riverbed has been gouged out into deep hollows (*kotle* means 'cauldrons' in Croatian). There's a *konoba* by the river. A path from Kotle also provides a convenient short cut (either on foot or by bike) to the Buzet–Cerovlje road, which it meets just north of Draguć.

DRAGUĆ A little over halfway from Buzet on the road to Cerovlje, a turn-off to the right (west) leads down to what must be counted one of the most beautiful villages in Istria. Sighted on top of a slight bump in the hillside overlooking Butoniga jezero, it was once an important centre for the cultivation of silkworms, though it's now a quiet settlement with a population of fewer than 100. Draguć is a popular film location and has appeared in Croatian as well as international productions (including *La Femme Muskateer* with Gérard Depardieu and Nastassja Kinski).

On the right before entering the village itself you pass a small cemetery and the 13th-century **Church of St Elijah** – the oldest church in the village – with fragmentary 13th-century frescoes and a Roman stele for an altar. Much more impressive however is the little **Church of St Roch** (Sv Rok), built during the early years of the 16th century as a votive offering to ward off plague, and standing just beyond the far end of the village overlooking a hillside planted with vines. The interior is decorated with an extensive cycle of frescoes, the work of **Antun of Padova**, the same local master who painted the frescoes at Oprtalj (see page 126) and Hum (see above), and are signed by him in both Latin and Glagolitic. Rather confusingly he was actually from the nearby village of Kašćerga – which, as it happens, is visible across the far side of Butoniga jezero from in front of the church – not Padova in Italy. The frescoes were painted in two phases, in 1529 and 1537, and unlike most other medieval frescoes in Istria, were not later covered up with paint. The scenes include an *Adoration of the Magi* and a *Baptism of Christ* and

Temptation into the Wilderness. Both buildings are kept locked. The local keyholder is Zora Paćelat (*Draguć 21;* ☏ *052 665 186*). The medieval **castle** which once stood in Draguć has now almost entirely vanished, though you can see some traces of it supporting one of the walls of the 15th-century **Church of the Cross**.

✖ Where to eat and drink

🖥 **Zora** Draguć 35; ☏ 052 665 105; ☉ summer 10.00–20.00 Tue–Sun. Small, friendly café on the square, where you can get a coffee or jug of wine, as well as local *pršut* & cheese. They also have a couple of **apartments**.

Festivals Draguć holds a *bajs* **festival** at the end of June (the *bajs*, also known as the *gunjac*, is a traditional two-stringed instrument which looks like a cello), with performances in the town square.

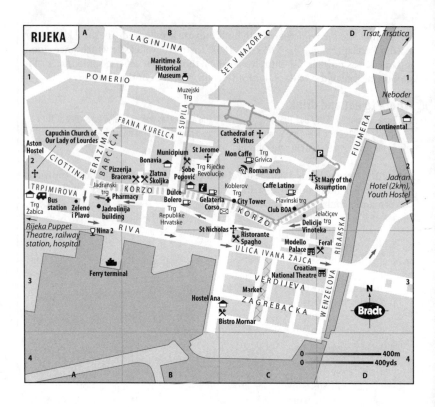

RIJEKA

LAGINJINA

POMERIO

Maritime & Historical Museum

ŠET V NAZORA

Trsat, Trsatica

Muzejski Trg

Neboder

FRANA KURELCA

F SUPILA

Cathedral of St Vitus

Continental

Capuchin Church of Our Lady of Lourdes

Aston Hostel

CIOTTINA

ERAZIMA BARCICA

Municipium

St Jerome

Mon Caffe

Trg Grivica

P

Bonavia

Pizzerija Bracera

Zlatna Školjka

Sobe Popović

Trg Riječke Revolucije

Roman arch

St Mary of the Assumption

Jadran Hotel (2km), Youth Hostel

TRPIMIROVA

Jadranski trg

KORZO

Dulce Bolero

Koblerov Trg

Caffe Latino

Pharmacy

Gelateria Corso

City Tower

Plavinski trg

Club BOA

Trg Žabica

Bus station

Zeleno i Plavo

Jadrolinija building

Trg Republike Hrvatske

KORZO

Jelačićev trg

Delicije

Vinoteka

Rijeka Puppet Theatre, railway station, hospital

Nina 2

RIVA

St Nicholas

Ristorante Spagho

Modello Palace

Feral

RIBARSKA

ULICA IVANA ZAJCA

WENZELOVA

Croatian National Theatre

Ferry terminal

VERDIJEVA

Market

ZAGREBAČKA

N

Hostel Ana

Bistro Mornar

Bradt

0   400m
0   400yds

8

Rijeka

Though located just outside Istria proper at the head of the Kvarner Gulf, Rijeka is a place that many visitors to Istria will pass through, whether they arrive by train, bus or ferry, and it is certainly worthy of a stopover of one or two nights. Croatia's third-largest city with a population of around 128,000 and its busiest port, Rijeka has plenty of grand Secessionist architecture, broad pedestrian streets strewn with cafés, some excellent restaurants, a major pilgrimage site up on the hill at Trsat, and one of the largest, most vibrant carnivals to be found anywhere in Europe.

Like many other towns and cities in the region, Rijeka was once an Illyrian and then a Roman settlement – though unlike much of the rest of the Croatian coast, it has the distinction of never quite having fallen under the rule of Venice. Backed by the great arc of mountains which form the Gorski kotar range, Rijeka has a mild climate, and is a living city all year round, not somewhere which closes up over the winter when the tourists leave. The town centre is divided from the residential area of Sušak by the River Rječina, and gets its name (in both Croatian and Italian) from the word for river, *rijeka* (*fiume* in Italian). Along the coast to the east is the suburb of Pećine, while up on the hill above Rijeka at 138m above sea level is the suburb of Trsat. There are beaches along the coast to the west and southeast of the city.

HISTORY

There was a hill fort at Trsat, the hill behind Rijeka, from at least the 4th century BC, inhabited by the Illyrian Japodes tribe, while the Illyrian Liburni controlled the coast below. Following their defeat of the Illyrians the Romans built a town (Tarsatica), on an area just north of what is now the Korzo, while the hill fort became a Roman signalling station. Tarsatica developed into a walled city, controlled after the departure of the Romans by Ostrogoths, Byzantines, Avars, the medieval Kingdom of Croatia and then Hungary.

A period under the local Frankopans of Krk was followed by Habsburg rule from the 15th to the 18th century, during which it successfully repelled several attacks by Venice (in particular in 1508), and was granted the charter of a free port in 1719. The city thrived – despite much of it being razed by an earthquake in 1750 – receiving heavy Hungarian investment in the 19th century (it was Hungary's only port on the Mediterranean), and gaining rail connections with Budapest and other centres in the Habsburg realm. During this period it was the site of the Austro-Hungarian Naval Academy. Prototypes of a torpedo were tested here in the 1860s, and the world's first torpedo factory, the Robert Whitehead Torpedo Co, was founded in Rijeka in 1875. Rijeka also became the site of the first oil refinery in Europe in 1882.

After World War I the Italian poet Gabriele D'Annunzio marched into town and, despite having no support from Italy, set up his own, short-lived regency here, between 1919 and 1921. Rijeka (Italian Fiume) became part of Mussolini's Italy in 1924, with the border running down the River Rječina, and the eastern suburb of Sušak lying across the border in what was then Yugoslavia. Following the end of World War II Rijeka became part of Yugoslavia, until Croatian independence in 1991.

GETTING THERE AND AWAY

BY TRAIN Rijeka's **railway station** (*Krešimirova 5*) is a five-minute walk west of the bus station. There are four trains a day to Zagreb (4–5 hours), with connections to Budapest and Venice, and two to Ljubljana (3 hours). For trains to Pazin there is a connecting bus service between Rijeka and Lupoglav. For timetables, see www. hznet.hr. There are plenty of city buses going from the centre to the railway station, including #1, #2 and #32.

BY BUS Rijeka is a major transport centre with regular buses from the rest of Croatia, including Zagreb (2½–3 hours; services almost every hour), Pula (90 minutes; at least 14 services daily), Pazin (1 hour; at least six services daily) and Poreč (90 minutes; at least six services daily). Timetables for Croatian buses serving Rijeka can be found at www.akz.hr or www.autobusni-kolodvor.com. International services include Trieste, Ljubljana and Munich.

Rijeka's **bus station** [136 A2] (*Trg Žabica 1;* ✆ *060 302 010*) is a two-minute walk west from the Korzo, or five minutes' walk east of the railway station. It has several small shops and kiosks for emergency, last-minute snack-buying.

BY BOAT Rijeka is Croatia's largest port, and the main headquarters for the state-run ferry company, Jadrolinija (housed in a rather magnificent building on the waterfront; see *What to see and do*, on page 145) – so hardly surprisingly, it is very well served by ferry and catamaran. Jadrolinija has daily catamaran services to Cres and Mali Lošinj (3 hours) and to Rab and Novalja on the island of Pag (2½ hours), and twice-weekly ferries departing on Monday and Friday evenings, which travel down the coast calling at Split (12 hours), Stari grad (on the island of Hvar), Korčula and Dubrovnik (24 hours), where there are connections to Bari in Italy.

The **Jadrolinija office** [136 A2] (*Riječki lukobran bb;* ✆ *051 211 444*) is located on the Riva, just across the road from the ferry terminal.

BY CAR Rijeka is a 90-minute drive from Pula, 40 minutes from Pazin, 2½ hours from Zagreb, 4½ hours from Split and 90 minutes from Trieste.

GETTING AROUND

Rijeka's town centre is fairly compact and can easily be explored on foot, including getting to the bus and train stations and up the hill to Trsat. Local **buses** also ply the centre as well as up to Trsat (#2 and #8) and west to Opatija (#32) and east to Pećine (#1). There are **taxi** stands at the bus station, railway station and on Matije Gupca, and several operators including Cammeo, which as usual offer the best fares (✆ *051 313 313; www.taxi-cammeo.net*), Taxi Rijeka (m *091 500 3355; www.taxirijeka.com*) and Taxi Adria (✆ *051 301 301; www.taxi-adria.com*). **Car-hire** services in Rijeka include Thrifty (✆ *051 325 900; www.thrifty.com*) and Dollar Rental (✆ *051 337 917; www.dollar.com*), both at Riva 22. Note that car-hire offices at Rijeka airport will be on the island of Krk! Rijeka's **TouRISt Bus** offers tours of the city (as well as Trsat and Opatija) in eight languages between June and September. Tickets are valid 48 hours and cost 50kn for adults, 35kn for children (under fours free), which include entry to Trsat Castle.

TOURIST INFORMATION

Rijeka's helpful and friendly **tourist information office** [136 B2] (*Korzo 14;* ✆ *051 335 882;* e *tic@tz-rijeka.hr; www.tz-rijeka.hr;* ⏰ *mid-Sep–mid-Jun 08.00–19.30 Mon–Fri, 08.00–13.30 Sat, closed Sun; mid-Jun–mid-Sep 08.00–20.30 Mon–Sat, 09.00–14.00 Sun, with reduced hours on holidays*) is conveniently located on the Korzo, amidst myriad cafés and ice-cream vendors. Make sure you pick up a copy of the useful city map available here, which includes the centre as well as Trsat and Pećine. There are also two information points (*info punkt*) on the Riva and one at Trsat Castle.

⌂ WHERE TO STAY

Rijeka has several large hotels in the centre and out at Pećine, certainly enough to cater for the moderate number of visitors who stay here; most of them are owned by Jadran (*www.jadran-hoteli.hr*). Several hostels have also opened in the city centre recently, and there's a youth hostel at Pećine. Private rooms in the city centre are fewer than in more heavily touristed areas, though there are several; a good place to start looking for private accommodation is on the Rijeka Tourist Board website (*www.tz-rijeka.hr*).

HOTELS

⌂ **Bonavia** [136 B2] (87 dbls, 20 sgls, 7 suites) Dolac 4; ✆ 051 357 100; e bonavia@bonavia.hr; www.bonavia.hr; ⏰ all year. The 4-star Bonavia is centrally located just off the Korzo & is the most upmarket place to stay in town, with its own wellness centre & highly rated restaurant, & prices to match. **$$$$–$$$$$**

⌂ **Best Western Jadran** (66 dbls, 3 apts) Setaliste XIII divizije 46, Pećine; ✆ 051 216 600; e jadran@jadran-hoteli.hr; www.jadran-hoteli. hr; ⏰ all year. The 4-star Jadran, which opened its doors in 1914, is along the coast at Pećine (a 15min walk into the centre of Rijeka along the coast, or a short ride on the #1 bus), right on the waterfront. Most rooms have sea views & balconies. **$$$$**

⌂ **Continental** [136 D1] (65 rooms, 4 suites) Šetalište Andrije Kačića-Miošića 1; ✆ 051 372 008; e continental@jadran-hoteli.hr; www.jadran-

hoteli.hr; ⏰ all year. My favourite place to stay in Rijeka, renovated in 2008, with plenty of old-world charm & friendly staff (even under pressure with the arrival of a tour bus), a broad terrace shaded by old trees where you can enjoy coffee or drinks & watch the world go by. On the east side of the Rječina & only 5mins' walk from the Korzo, the 3-star Continental was built in 1888 & is the oldest hotel in Rijeka still running. **$$$**

⌂ **Neboder** [136 D1] (54 dbls) Strossmayerova 1; ✆ 051 373 538; e neboder@jadran-hoteli. hr; www.jadran-hoteli.hr; ⏰ all year. While it may not be the most attractive building from the outside, the 14-floor Neboder can certainly claim some of the finest views in Rijeka from its upper rooms. Renovated in 2007, the Neboder has friendly & helpful staff & is just around the corner from the Continental. **$$$**

HOSTELS

⌂ **Aston Hostel** [136 A2] (25 beds) Trg Žabica 5 ✆ 092 138 4210 e hostel.accardi@yahoo.com; www.hostel-aston.com; ⏰ all year. Friendly family-run hostel conveniently located directly

opposite the bus station. Basic facilities but good value for the price **$**

⌂ **Hostel Ana** [136 C3] (18 beds) Riva Boduli 7; m 095 521 2716; e hostelrijeka@live.com; www.

hostel-ana.com/rijeka; ⊕ all year. Budget-priced beds in 3 dorms (one of which can be made up as a double) conveniently located by the Riva. **$**
⌂ **Youth Hostel** (61 beds) Šetalište XIII divizije 23, Pećine; ☏051 406 420; e rijeka@hfhs.hr; www.

hfhs.hr; ⊕ all year. In a lovely 19th-century villa at Pećine, & only around a 15min walk into town (or a short hop on the #1 bus) this must be counted as one of the nicest hostels anywhere in Croatia. **$**

PRIVATE ROOMS

⌂ **Sobe Popović** [136 B2] (2 dbls, 1 trpl) Korzo 22, 3rd floor; m 091 894 8884; e rooms.rijeka@gmail.com; ⊕ all year. You can't really beat these private rooms for location – right on the Korzo,

close to the tourist information office – though you may hear some noise from the street at night. The same owners also offer rooms at Demetrova 6, near the back of the market. **$$**

CAMPING **Camp Oštro Kraljevica** (*Oštro 16, Kraljevica;* ☏ *051 281 218;* e *ostro@jadran-hoteli.hr; www.jadran-hoteli.hr;* ⊕ *Apr–Oct*), around 24km southeast of Rijeka, has 204 pitches and 20 apartments, with pitches priced from 130kn per night for two adults with a tent. **Autocamp Preluk** (*Preluk 1;* ☏*051 623 500;* e *info@autocamp-preluk.com; http://autocamp-preluk.com;* ⊕ *Apr–Oct*), which is 8km west of Rijeka on the #32 bus route, has 100 pitches priced from 127kn for two adults in a tent, though it caters mainly to campervans and motorhomes.

✖ WHERE TO EAT AND DRINK

Rijeka has fewer restaurants than might be expected for a city its size, and most of them are not on the Korzo itself (which instead abounds in cafés and ice–cream shops). However what it might lack in numbers it certainly makes up for in quality, with several restaurants that are excellent.

✖ **Municipium** [136 B2] Trg Riječke revolucije 5; ☏051 213 000; ⊕ 11.00–23.00 Mon–Sat. Upmarket & fairly formal restaurant next to the Dominican monastery. **$$$$**
✖ **Zlatna školjka** [136 B2] Kružna 12a; ☏051 213 782; www.zlatna-skoljka.hr; ⊕ 11.00–23.00 daily. One of the best (& oldest – there's been a tavern here since 1885) restaurants in Rijeka, Zlatna školjka (the Golden Shell) serves a wide range of seafood, including traditional staples as well as inventive numbers such as octopus salad marinated in dark beer & served with wasabi & grilled vegetables, monkfish tempura, or courgette & parmesan flan with scampi sauce. **$$$$**
✖ **Konoba Feral** [136 D3] Matije Gupca 5b; ☏051 212 274; www.konoba-feral.com; ⊕ 08.00–midnight Mon–Sat, 12.00–18.00 Sun. Excellent & very reasonably priced seafood in a low-key, friendly & traditional setting – this is the place to come for succulent grilled squid (*lignje na žaru*), mussels simmered in wine & garlic (*dagnje na buzaru*), seafood stew (*brodet*) & premium fish by the kilo. A local favourite, & not in the slightest bit stuffy. **$$$**

✖ **Pizzerija Bracera** [136 B2] Kružna 12; ☏051 322 498; www.pizzeria-bracera.com.hr; ⊕ 11.00–23.00 daily. Set in an atmospheric passageway off the Korzo, opposite (& under the same ownership as) Zlatna školjka (see above), Bracera turns out excellent pizzas as well as other dishes. The brightly painted interior is decked out with artwork by Croatian painter Vjekoslav Vojo Radojčić, & also sports a traditional local fishing boat (*bracera*, whence its name), & there are tables in the passageway outside. There's also tasty bruschetta, & Pag lamb specialities such as lamb *ispod peka* can be ordered in advance. **$$$**
✖ **Ristorante Spagho** [136 C3] I Zajca 24; ☏051 311 122; ⊕ 09.00–midnight Mon–Sat, 12.00–21.00 Sun. Lovely, stylish little spaghetteria-pizzeria on the corner of I Zajca & I Henckea, with very friendly staff & a good wine list (including several types of Malvazija, & others, by the glass), serving what is without any doubt the best risotto with scampi I have ever tasted. **$$$**
✖ **Trsatica** Šetalište J Rakovca 33; ⊕ 10.00–midnight daily. If you're up in Trsat for the

afternoon or evening then this is the place to come for massive steaks & grills, or a whole hock on the large, breezy terrace with a view. They also have some vegetarian dishes such as stuffed courgettes, & large salads. $$$

✕ **Bistro Mornar** [136 G3] Riva Boduli 5a; ☎051 213 000; ⏰ 08.00–22.00 daily. Well-priced bistro next to Hostel Ana, with set menus for 45kn. $$

CAFÉS What Rijeka may lack in its number of restaurants it certainly makes up for in cafés, of which there are a huge number to choose from both on and off the Korzo, whether it's coffee, ice cream or cakes you're after. A few favourites are listed here, and the terrace in front of the Hotel Continental (see *Where to stay*, on page 139) is another good spot.

⬚ **Caffe Latino** [136 C2] Pavlinski trg 4a; ⏰ 06.30–22.00 Mon–Fri, 07.00–14.00 Sun. My favourite café in Rijeka, on a square hidden away between the Korzo & Ante Starčevica, serving impeccable coffee for 7kn.
⬚ **Dulce Bolero** [136 B2] Krešimirova 60; ⏰ 07.00–22.00 Mon–Sat, 08.00–22.00 Sun. Popular ice-cream café with a wide range of flavours, just off the Korzo.

⬚ **Gelateria Corso** [136 B2] Korzo 20; ⏰ 07.00–23.00 Mon–Sat, 08.00–22.00 Sun. The most popular ice-cream café on the Korzo, with plenty of flavours to choose from.
⬚ **Mon Caffe** [136 C2] Mirka, Burićeva 48; ⏰ 07.00–22.00 Mon–Sat, 08.00–20.00 Sun. Small cake shop & café on the way uphill to Sv Vida, with all cakes priced at 10–12kn.

ENTERTAINMENT AND NIGHTLIFE

☆ **Club BOA** [136 C2] Ante Starčevica 8; m 091 339 9339; http://clubboa.com; ⏰ 06.00–02.00 Mon–Thu, 06.00–05.00 Fri–Sun. Newly opened club-bar just off one end of the Korzo, with live DJs, a lounge bar-style interior & 2 terraces.
☆ **Club Nina 2** [136 A3] Adamićev gat; m 091 531 7879; www.nina2.com; ⏰ till late. Dance club-café-cocktail bar on a boat moored by the Riva.

🎭 **Croatian National Theatre** [136 A2] Uljarska 1; ☎051 355 917; www.hnk-zajc.hr. Theatre, opera & ballet performed in a magnificent late 19th-century building. Performances are often excellent, & ticket prices are much, much lower than in western Europe.
🎭 **Rijeka Puppet Theatre** [136 A2] Blaža Polića 6; ☎051 325 680; www.gkl-rijeka.hr. Great for kids as well as grown-ups.

FESTIVALS

Hartera (*www.hartera.com*) Massive dance-music festival with local and international DJs in July, housed in the disused factory of former cigarette paper manufacturer Hartera (the oldest in Europe).

Fiumanka (International Sailing Regatta) (*www.fiumanka.hr*) Large sailing regatta held in the second week of June.

Fiumare (Kvarner Sea and Maritime Tradition Festival) Second week of June, on and around the Mrtvi kanal (once a centre of commerce in the city), with traditional boats and stands showcasing traditional crafts and local produce.

Revija Lutkarskih Kazališta Rijeka (Rijeka Review of Puppet Theatres) (*www.gkl-rijeka.hr*) First week in September. Rijeka has a long history of puppetry stretching back to the years following World War II, and the work of local and international puppet theatres is showcased in a series of performances at this annual event.

Riječke Ljetne Noći (Rijeka Summer Nights) (*www.rijeckeljetnenoci.com*) June/July, with music, theatre, opera, ballet and other performances throughout the city, from public squares to disused factory buildings to local beaches.

Riječki Karneval (Rijeka International Carnival) (*www.ri-karneval.com.hr*) *The* event on Rijeka's annual calendar (see box, below).

St Vitus Days 15 June sees a series of events centred on Rijeka's patron saint, St Vitus (Sv Vida).

SHOPPING

ZELENO I PLAVO [136 A2] (*Trpimirova 1a;* ✆ *052 322 598;* e *zeleno.i.plavo@ri.t-com.hr; www.zelenoiplavo.hr;* ⏰ *08.00–20.00 Mon–Fri, 08.00–13.00 Sat*) The best place in town to shop for local wine, olive oil, spirits, honey and other products as well as locally made souvenirs.

DELIIICIJE VINOTEKA [136 C2] (*Ante Starčevića 7a;* ⏰ *09.00–21.00 Mon–Sat*) This is another place to shop for local wine and *rakija* as well as international goodies.

RIJEKA CARNIVAL

Held on the last Sunday before Lent (usually February), the Rijeka Carnival (*www.ri-karneval.com.hr*) is now the second largest in Europe after Venice, attracting over 600,000 spectators from Croatia and overseas. Events are spread over several days, culminating in the International Carnival Parade – an enormous event with well over 10,000 participants, which sees a procession of floats and cavorting Croatians in outrageous costumes make their way through the streets of Rijeka. Expect dancing bees, prancing chimney sweeps and all manner of other entertainments, including the increasingly intoxicated, sheepskin-wearing *zvončari* or bell ringers (see box, opposite).

The parade sets off from the corner of the Riva and Riva Boduli, travelling east along Ivana Zajca to the Mrtvi kanal, then turns north and back along the Korzo, before returning to the Riva for ongoing festivities. Most people tend to watch from the Korzo, in which case you need to arrive early enough to get a decent view, but a better, 'insider' tip is to watch the parade from Ivana Zajca, where there are much fewer spectators – you can then cross to the Korzo later to catch some of the participants a second time around. It can take around seven hours between the start of the parade and the last float arriving back on the Korzo, after which the party lasts well into the night.

Don't expect to be able to park in central Rijeka on the day of the parade, and if you're leaving Rijeka by bus or train the same evening, book your seat early in the day as a few thousand other people will also be leaving at the same time, and buses in particular fill up fast.

If you only see one carnival in Croatia, make sure it's this one – and if you're anywhere even remotely near Rijeka at this time of year, you'd be mad to miss it. This is the day (and night) when the city well and truly lets down its hair, and is without question one of the most wildly enjoyable events I've attended anywhere in the world.

ZVONČARI

The *zvončari* or 'bell ringers' – men dressed in sheepskins with elaborate, horned masks and headgear, stylised maces and with huge cowbells tied to their backsides – are among the most striking (and these days, best known) participants of the Rijeka Carnival. You will find references to them all over Rijeka, from tourist souvenirs and trinkets sold on the Korzo to a large mural near the Church of the Assumption. They come from the villages of the Kastav region (the mountainous area inland from Rijeka), and continue an old pagan tradition in which masked, bell-wearing figures would go from house to house in the village before Lent, driving out evil spirits which might have settled there during the preceding winter. There are several groups of *zvončari* from Kastav, including the Halubajski (*www.halubajski-zvoncari. com*). They form part of a wider tradition which includes the *kurenti* of Slovenia, which feature prominently at the Ptuj Carnival. The *zvončari* were inscribed on the UNESCO List of Intangible Cultural Heritage in 2009.

MAIN MARKET (VELIKA TRŽNICA) [136 C3] (⊕ *06.00–14.00 Mon–Sat, 06.00–12.00 Sun*) Rijeka's bustling main market occupies three attractive Art Deco buildings opposite the Modello Palace and near the National Theatre – one for fish, one for fresh and cured meats, one for cheese and dairy produce – with stalls selling vegetables, fruit and flowers spilling out along the streets surrounding these. The buildings date from 1880 and the early 1900s. Often just called the '*plaça*' by locals, it is particularly busy on Friday and Saturday mornings, and is well worth visiting whether you're self-catering or just want a vibrant glimpse of daily life here, with endless temptations to get sidetracked by coffee and freshly made *burek*.

SUPERMARKETS Several supermarket chains have branches in the centre, including a Konzum on Vatroslava Lisinskog by the market, and there's a large Konzum at the Tower Centre.

TOWER CENTRE RIJEKA (*Janka Polića Kamova 81a, Pećine; www.tower-center-rijeka.hr;* ⊕ *13.00–21.00 Mon, 09.00–21.00 Tue–Sat, 10.00–21.00 Sun*) Rijeka's largest shopping complex, outside the centre at Pećine, with around 150 shops on five floors as well as a cinema and an enormous car park.

OTHER PRACTICALITIES

✚ **Accident and emergency** [136 A2] Krešimirova 42; ☎ 051 658 111. Rijeka hospital has another site at Sušak, & there's a children's hospital at Kantrida (*Istarska 43;* ☎ *051 659 111*).
✚ **Pharmacy** [136 A2] Jadranski trg 1; ☎ 051 213 101; ⊕ 24hrs. At the western end of the Korzo & a 2min walk from the bus station.

✉ **Post office** [136 C2] Korzo 13; ⊕ 07.00–20.00 Mon–Fri, 07.00–14.00 Sat, closed Sun. The main post office is conveniently located at one end of the Korzo.

Rijeka   WHAT TO SEE AND DO

8

WHAT TO SEE AND DO

Rijeka has several sites worth visiting, and there's certainly enough to keep you busy for a day or two. Much of what you see of Rijeka today dates from the second half of the 18th century and later: a massive earthquake flattened most of the city's older buildings in 1750.

At the heart of Rijeka's daily life is the **Korzo**, a broad pedestrian artery running from east to west through the city centre, lined with cafés. Partway along the Korzo (between Jadranski trg and Trg Republike Hrvatske) you'll find *The Walker*, a recent (2010) **sculpture** by Ivan Kožarić, one of Croatia's greatest living artists (perhaps most famous for his sculpture of the poet Antun Gustav Matoš sitting on a bench in Zagreb). Other sculptures in the centre include the Croatian avant-garde writer and satirist Janko Polić Kamov leaning nonchalantly on a bridge by the Hotel Continental (he was born just round the corner in the suburb of Sušak in 1886).

The **City Tower** or **Clock Tower** [136 C2] (Gradski Toranj) on the Korzo dates back to the medieval period and marks the site of one of the old city gates, though what you see now is Baroque. Note the imperial coat of arms above the arch, and the relief of the Austrian emperors Leopold and Charles VI.

Rijeka's **old town** occupied the area north of the Korzo, between the Korzo, Muzejski trg and Jelačićev trg, though little evidence of it remains today. The square beyond the City Tower, Trg Ivana Koblera, would once have been the site of the medieval town market. There's a **Roman arch** [136 C2] just off to the left as you walk from the City Tower to the cathedral, which probably gave access to a central compound in the old Roman town. The **Cathedral of St Vitus** [136 C2] (Sv Vida), the patron saint of Rijeka, lies just uphill from the City Tower. It's an unusual design which is more or less unique in Croatia – a large rotunda, modelled on Santa Maria della Salute in Venice. It was built in the late 17th century on the remains of an earlier church (also dedicated to St Vitus) by the local Jesuits. Inside there's a 13th-century wooden crucifix from the earlier church with an interesting cult attached to it. It is said to have bled when a certain ne'er-do-well named Petar Lončarić threw a rock at it, after losing at gambling (and before he was immediately swallowed up by the earth).

West from the cathedral on Žrtava fašizma (note the air-raid shelters on the opposite side, marked *sklonište*, and the massive masonry of the Palace of Justice) is Muzejski trg, which is where you'll find Rijeka's Maritime and Historical Museum and City Museum. The **Maritime and Historical Museum** [136 B1] (quite a mouthful in Croatian, *Pomorski povijesni muzej Hrvatskog primorja Rijeka; Muzejski trg 1;* \ *051 553 667; www.ppmhp.hr;* ⊕ *09.00–20.00 Tue–Fri, 09.00–13.00 Sat/Sun; entry adults 10kn, children 5kn*) has exhibits drawn from Rijeka's extensive maritime tradition, and is housed in the former **Governor's Palace**, which dates from 1892. The Governor's Palace was built by one of the leading Hungarian architects of the time, Alajos Hauszmann, whose other works include the Parliament building in Budapest, though the exterior and grounds these days exude a rather sad air of neglect. Next door is the **City Museum** (*Muzej Grada Rijeke; Muzejski trg 1/1;* \ *051 336 711; www. muzej-rijeka.hr;* ⊕ *10.00–18.00 Mon–Fri, 10.00–13.00 Sat; entry adults 20kn, children 10kn*), which has a variety of exhibits from the city's history, from ethnography to numismatics. There's a lapidarium, and the gardens are filled with old torpedoes (the modern torpedo was invented in Rijeka, and the world's first torpedo factory, the Robert Whitehead Torpedo Co, was founded in Rijeka in 1875).

Two of Rijeka's larger **parks and gardens** are just to the northeast of the Governor's Palace: Mlaka Park and Nikola Host Park, both of which were laid out in the 19th century. For those who want a longer stroll, **Učka Nature Park** along the coast above Lovran has miles of well-marked footpaths (see *Hiking in Istria*, page 171), as does the Gorski kotar region northeast of Rijeka, including Risnjak National Park.

On Trg Riječke revolucije (Revolution Square) you'll find the **Dominican monastery** and **Church of St Jerome** [136 B2], both of which, despite their Baroque appearance, formed part of an Augustinian monastic complex founded in the early 14th century. The church has the (rather faint) remains of frescoes on the vault of one of its chapels. To one side of the square is a stone pillar known as the **Stendarac**. This is where a flag was raised by the emperor Maximilian in memory of the city's loyalty during the (brief) Venetian occupation of 1508. Or rather, this is one of the places it was raised – the Stendarac originally stood in front of the old town hall, and changed its location several times after that. The relief at the top shows St Vitus holding a model of the city of Rijeka, and there are inscriptions from 1509, 1515 and 1766.

Over towards the Mrtvi kanal near Pavlinski trg, is the **Church of St Mary of the Assumption** [136 C2], some of which dates back to the 15th century, though most of what you see now is 18th-century work, when a group of master craftsmen from Ljubljana were brought here to work on the church. The bell tower leans rather precariously, and has the date 1377 inscribed above the doorway. This was the location of the **forum** during Roman times, and mosaics have been uncovered here, as well as evidence of a Roman bath, part of which became a focal point or meeting place for an early Christian cult during the 5th and 6th centuries.

Much of the area south of the Korzo is built on land reclaimed from the sea. The **Croatian National Theatre** (Hrvatsko Narodno Kazalište, or HNK for short) occupies a suitably lavish building near the Mrtvi kanal. There has been a theatre here since the mid 18th century, though this was rebuilt in 1806. The current building dates from 1885 (most of Croatia's National Theatre buildings are of a similar date and style), and was designed by specialised theatre architects Herman Gottlieb Helmer and Ferdinand Fellner of Vienna.

West of the National Theatre across a well-manicured square is the city's **main market** or *tržnica*, occupying three Art Deco halls and, when the market's open, most of the streets surrounding them. On the opposite side of Ivana Zajca are the richly decorated façades of the **Modello Palace** [136 C3] (Palača Modello), built at the same time (and by the same architects) as the National Theatre. The Serbian Orthodox **Church of St Nicholas** [136 C2], around the corner on Ivana Henckea, dates from 1790, and has some beautiful icons on the altar. The church was built by local Serbian families, who controlled much of the trade in Turkish goods brought to Rijeka by the late 18th century. Towards the western end of the Riva is the **Jadrolinija** building – one of the most beautiful in Rijeka – built in 1882, and known as the 'Adria Palace'. Its opulent yellow façades and sheer grandeur are perhaps the finest reflection of the city's pre-eminent maritime history. Just beyond the bus station you'll find the **Capuchin Church of Our Lady of Lourdes** [136 A2], built between 1904 and 1929, with its striking neo-Gothic striped masonry, atop a grandiose double staircase.

TRSAT Up behind the town centre to the northwest is the suburb of **Trsat**, once the site of an Illyrian hill fort, later of Roman defences against barbarian incursions, and Austro-Hungarian defences against the Ottomans.

The 13th-century **castle** here, once a stronghold of the Frankopans, was purchased by Field Marshal Laval Nugent of Austria in 1826, and renovated in its current, Romantic style complete with a small temple (the Nugent family mausoleum) and boisterous-looking bronze dragon. Apparently George Bernard Shaw's aunt was also buried here, though the whereabouts of her and other tombs are now something of a mystery. There are wonderful views of the coast and the city below, and a small café on the breezy terrace where you can unwind.

What brings people up here in their thousands, however, is the nearby **Sanctuary of Our Lady of Trsat**, one of the largest pilgrimage sites in Croatia, which according to popular belief was the site where the wood from the Virgin Mary's house remained between 1291 and 1294, on its journey from Nazareth to Loreto in Italy. Following the departure of these holy relics, a miraculous icon (the Image of Our Lady of Trsat) was given to the population by Pope Urban V in 1367, and the local Frankopans built a small church to house it in (though the icon you see now is a copy). The current church and Franciscan monastery date from the late 17th century. Pope John Paul II joined the pilgrimage to Trsat in July 2003, and a larger-than-life-sized sculpture of him can be found in front of the church, his bronze hand now worn smooth by tens of thousands of passing faithful.

You can walk up to Trsat, following Stube Petra Kružića (also known as 'Trsatske stube'), a long flight of over 500 steps leading uphill from the corner of Titov trg, the route followed by pilgrims – otherwise take bus #2 or #8 from the Riva.

9

The Slovenian Adriatic

Country code +386

Geographical Istria extends into Slovenia, in fact beyond the coastal municipalities into some of the fabulous landscape of the Karst region. The coastal towns of the Slovenian Adriatic – Koper, Izola, Piran and Portorož – are each little gems and a walk, cycle or drive along them reveals a lush and rich panorama of seaside activity. The main town of **Koper** has a rich architectural history and is an important port where luxury cruise liners are known to dock. At the other end of this set of coastal towns, **Portorož** holds natural hot-spring facilities and spas, and the whole coastline has entered another league of sophistication since the Kempinski Palace opened in Portorož in 2008. However for many, Piran is the jewel in the Slovenian Adriatic crown.

Because of the ease and proximity of visiting fairy-tale **Predjama Castle** and the impressive **Postojna Cave**, these are also included in this chapter as day trips.

HISTORY

The history of the Slovenian Adriatic followed a very similar course to the northwest coastal area of the rest of Istria, and was essentially ruled by Venice or its predecessors until the fall of the Serenissima Republic in 1797. At this point the whole of geographical Istria became part of the Holy Roman Empire and became known as the Austrian Littoral (*Küstenland*). With the fall of the Holy Roman Empire, rule of the *Küstenland* passed briefly to the Napoleonic Kingdom of Italy from 1806–1813. The reconstituted Austrian Empire wrested the *Küstenland* back again for just over a century from 1814–1918, and it was during this period that many of the great Schloßhaüser were built in stately-castle style.

By 1918, Trieste had already won autonomy from the *Küstenland*, and after World War I the rest of Istria was also given to Italy in recognition of Italy siding with Great Britain. Fascist Italianisation of the region was vehemently opposed by Slovenes in particular, however, and thus was born the first anti-fascist organisation, Trst Istra Gorizia Reka (TIGR, standing for Trieste, Istria, Gorizia and Rijeka).

When Italy changed sides in World War II, most of Istria went to Yugoslavia. However, the Free Territory of Trieste established under United Nations Security Council Resolution 16 on 10 February 1947 created an internationally administered free city-state around Trieste. In the shape of a bottom-heavy crescent moon around the Gulf of Trieste from Duino in the north to the Mirna River in the south, the area was divided into Zone A (now in Italy) and Zone B. Zone A was administered by British and American forces, whilst Zone B was administered by Yugoslavia. In 1954, the Free Territory was officially dissolved in the London Memorandum, and Italy formally took over the rule of Zone A, with the exception of a few villages on the border with Zone B.

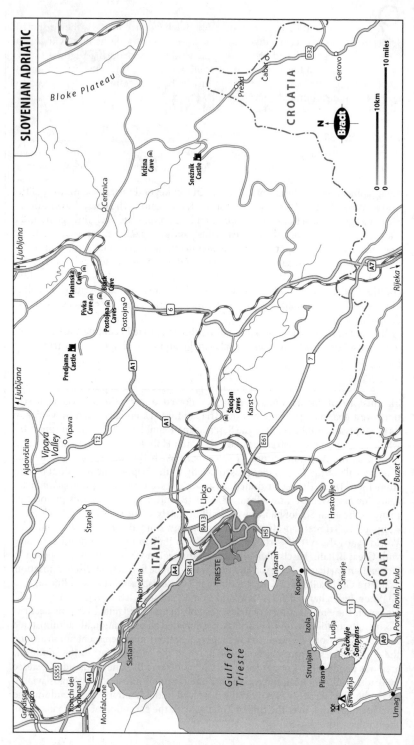

SLOVENIAN ADRIATIC

Bloke Plateau

CROATIA

Cabar
Prezid
Gerovo
D32

Brackt

N

0 ——— 10km
0 ——— 10 miles

Križna Cave

Snežnik Castle

Cerknica

Ljubljana

A7

Rijeka

Planinska Cave
Pivka Cave
Postojna Caves
Black Cave
Postojna

6

Predjama Castle

A1

Vipava
Vipava Valley

Ajdovščina

Ljubljana

12

A1

Škocjan Caves
Karst

E61

7

Štanjel

Lipica

RA13

Buzet

H5

Hrastovlje

ITALY

A4

SR14

Fernetiči

TRIESTE

Ankaran

Smarje

CROATIA

Sistiana

Koper

11

Monfalcone

Izola

Ludja

A9

Poreč, Rovinj, Pula

SSSS

A4

Strunjan

Piran

Sečovlje Saltpans

Gulf of
Trieste

Savudrija

Umag

Gradisca
d'Isonzo

Ronchi dei
Legionari

148

After Slovenia and Croatia both declared independence in 1991, they disputed claims by the other over the division of the border and sea in the Piran Gulf, with Slovenia insisting that it had policed the gulf up to Savudrija during Yugoslav times. This dispute blocked the entry of Croatia into the EU, but since the resignation of Croatia's prime minister Ivo Sanader in July 2009, both countries have agreed to have the dispute arbitrated internationally.

GETTING THERE AND AROUND

From further afield, Koper is the main gateway to the Slovenian Adriatic. From Croatian Istria many will drive in and out of the area via the smaller Sečovlje border crossing connection with Portorož rather than take the main border crossing at Dragonia, especially in the main season, when queues at the border on Saturday changeover day can take hours. This should relax once Croatia enters the EU in 2013. **Trieste airport** is a 40-minute drive from Koper. **Portorož international airport** (*www.portoroz-airport.si*) serves charter flights only. For the best way to make sense of the byzantine complexity of ferries and onward **travel connections** in the region, use www.adriaticferry.com.

AIRPORT TRANSFERS Taxis are expensive in the region, and public buses to the airports are non-existent (except for Trieste airport to Trieste central station on bus #51 (*www.triestetrasporti.it or www.aeroporto.fvg.it*). An economic option is to book a transfer through **Goopti** (*www.goopti.com*), whose online booking system allows them to combine requests and offer usually a minibus service to and from the airport.

BY TRAIN Five trains a day run in each direction between Ljubljana and the end of the railway line in Koper (*Kolodvorska 11;* ✆ *056 395 263; www.slo.zeleznice.si*). The 06.30 train from Ljubljana, which connects with the overnight train from Munich, also has a dedicated bicycle and luggage wagon.

BY BUS Koper bus station (✆ *056 625 100; www.ap-ljubljana.si*) is collocated with the train station. Buses to regional destinations run frequently, with several buses a day to other main towns in Croatian Istria. Sunday buses run less frequently than in the rest of the week.

There is a regular bus service (*www.veolia-transport.si*) that runs the entire length of the coastal road every 15 minutes between between Koper and Portorož via Izola and Piran.

BY BOAT A myriad options are available from **Venice** into the region in the high season, especially at the weekend, for €55 single and €65 return. Most are day-trip tour-boats, so they depart at 08.00 (unless stated otherwise below) and return from Venice at 17.00. The trip takes three hours. The most popular lines are from **Isola**, from where the *Prince of Venice* (*www.kompas.si*) sails to Venice only at weekends, and **Piran**, from where the *Dora* (*www.commodore.hr*) sails to Venice on Saturdays. See also Trieste Lines below.

Trieste Lines (*www.triestelines.it*) runs a daily boat from **Trieste** (09.00) to Piran (09.40), Rovinj (10.50) and Pula (11.50), returning from Pula (17.05) to Rovinj (18.05), Piran (19.25) and Trieste (19.55) in July and August every day except Wednesdays. Ticket prices are graduated, with the longest leg from Trieste to Pula costing €24 single, €40 return.

Boat-taxis between ports (but not internationally) are also popular, and can easily be picked up from the ports.

BY CAR Getting to the Slovenian Adriatic is well served by motorway, but beware that all the towns are pedestrianised, although well served also by frequent bus services and by park and ride. Note that the use of Slovenian motorways requires a toll sticker, which can be bought at most petrol stations and at the border. €15 for a weekly pass is the minimum payment. For more details see www.slovenia. info/?faq=191. For car hire see under *Tourist information*, below.

BY BICYCLE It's perfectly possible to cycle around most of the Slovenian Adriatic, and it's by far the best way to enjoy the coast. To hire bicycles, see under individual towns.

TOURIST INFORMATION

The official tourist information (*www.slovenia.info*) bureaux for Slovenian towns are very helpful, with heaps of free useful brochures and friendly knowledgeable staff. They also have lots of free maps, including for local hiking and biking routes, as well as small general maps. Individual bureaux are listed separately under each town covered in this chapter.

A very useful website specifically for Slovenian Istria is **Info Slovenska Istra** (*www.slovenska-istra.si*). For tour operator services including **car hire**, try **Topline** (*Obala 114, 6320 Portorož;* \ *056 747 161;* e *info@topline.si; www.topline.si*) for tourism services within Slovenia, or **Kompas** (*Pristaniška 17, 6000 Koper;* \ *05 6603 580;* e *kompas.koper@siol.net; www.kompas.si*) for onward travel.

KOPER

The tightly packed old town of Koper is a real gem, with its impressive Praetorian Palace, campanile and loggia dominating the main square Titov trg. Its narrow cobbled streets hide exquisite little shops of Slovenian brands at very reasonable prices, including a chocolate shop, the Salt Museum shop and a handmade shoe shop. This is Slovenia's major port and as a result has a busy dock life only a few steps from the heart of the town.

HISTORY Koper was an island until the 1930s. The ancient Greek name for Koper was Aegida. Then under the Romans it became known by its local name Capraria 'goat island' and the surrounding shallow waters were used to harvest salt. In 1278, Koper joined the Republic of Venice, after which the town walls were slowly demolished and the local saltworks were enlarged. As Koper grew in significance, it became the capital of Venetian Istria, and was known as Caput Histriae, the 'head of Istria'. Today's Italian name, Capodistria, is rooted in this.

Koper's economic standing in the larger Piran Bay was seriously dampened in 1719 when Trieste became a free port of the Holy Roman Empire. During the 19th century, the salines gradually fell into disuse as the price of salt dropped. Under Italian rule after World War I, the area around Koper was drained and reclaimed and Koper ceased to be an island. As a result, the local bay of Škocjan behind Koper became a lagoon and is now an important reserve for marine and wetland wildlife.

In the census of 1900, 92% of Koper was Italian. Today, Slovenes make up over 70% of the town after the majority of the Italian population voluntarily left when

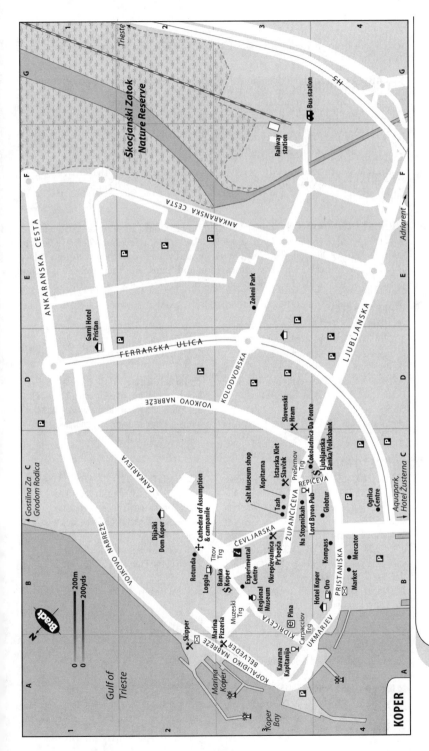

KOPER

Zone B was handed to Yugoslavia in 1954. The Roman Catholic diocese of Koper, which had been merged with that of Trieste in 1828, did not separate again from Trieste until 1977.

GETTING AROUND The old town is pedestrianised. **Buses** #1 and #2 (*www.veolia-transport.si*) leave from the train and bus station around the southeastern quarter of the town and then onward. It's a 20-minute walk from the station to the old town. Several **taxi** companies operate from the station, around the edge of the town, along the coast and to Trieste airport, eg: Taxi Srečko (m *040 386 000; www.taxisrecko.si*); Taxi Ivan (\ *051 602 090;* e *info@taxi-ivan.si; www.taxi-ivan.si*).

Bicycle, boat and waterski hire is available at **Adriarent** [151 F4] (*Ulica XV Maja 10;* *056 632 460;* e *info@renting.si; www.renting.si;* ⊕ *08.00–20.00 daily*). Bicycles rent out at €10 per day and €42 per week.

TOURIST INFORMATION Tourist information [151 B3] (*Titov trg 3;* \ *056 646 403;* e *tic@koper.si; www.koper.si;* ⊕ *summer 09.00–20.00 Mon–Sat, 09.00–13.00 Sun; winter 09.00–17.00 Mon–Sat, closed Sun*) is grandly located in the Praetorian Palace. It is very well stocked with free information and maps, and their website is a good place to find lots of local accommodation, especially self-catering and rural farms.

⌂ WHERE TO STAY

⌂ **Hotel Koper** [151 B4] (65 rooms) Pristaniška 3; \056 100 500; e koper@terme-catez.si; www.terme-catez.si. A very standard 3-star, with all the benefits of a conglomerate including access to Zušterna aquapark 3km along the bay. Unbeatable location though. Front rooms have sea views. **$$$$**

⌂ **Dijaški Dom** [151 C2] (380 beds) Cankarjeva 5; \056 273 250; e dd.koper@guest.arnes.si; www.ddkoper.si. This huge student dorm becomes an international youth hostel in the summer. Single, double & triple rooms; shared washrooms. **$**

⌂ **Hostel Histria** [151 C3] (34 beds in 6- & 8-bed dorms) Ulica pri velikih vratih 17; m 083 824 038; e info@hostel-histria.si; www.hostel-histria.si. Very nice dorms in a renovated stone house above the Lord Byron pub. **$**

✖ WHERE TO EAT AND DRINK

✖ **Istarska Klet Slavček** [151 C3] Županičičeva 39; \056 276 729; ⊕ 07.00–22.00 Mon–Fri. A small local place offering grilled meat & Slovenian stews. **$$$**

✖ **Marina Pizzeria** [151 A3] Kopališko nabrežje 2; \056 271 982; ⊕ 12.00–23.00 Tue–Sun. A wide variety of pizzas as well as other seafood in this busy restaurant above the dock. **$$$**

✖ **Skipper** [151 A2] Kopališko nabrežje 3; \056 261 810; www.skipper-koper.com; ⊕ summer 11.00–22.00 daily; winter 11.00–22.00 Mon–Sat, 11.00–18.00 Sun. In a modern building above the working docks, this is a popular place with the dock staff. Good solid food, & some interesting twists including scampi soup. **$$$**

✖ **Okrepčevalnica Pr'bepča** [151 B3] Čevljarska 36; \056 276 729; ⊕ 09.00–22.00 Mon–Fri. A tiny welcoming place with a big window opening onto the street. Fast-food-style Italian eatery. **$$**

⊑ **Loggia Café** [151 C3] Titov trg 1; \056 732 689; ⊕ 09.00–midnight daily. There is nowhere better than the Loggia to view & enjoy the architectural delights of this Gothic square. Great range of drinks & ice creams, & I ate the scrummiest apple buns here with cream fondant icing.

♀ **Lord Byron Pub** [151 C3] Repičeva 2; \059 159 300; www.lordbyronpub.si; ⊕ 07.00–midnight Mon–Fri, 08.00–midnight Sat, 09.00–midnight Sun. Inside, this looks just like an English pub, except that there's waiter service.

⊑ **Oro Caffe** [151 B4] Pristaniška 5; \059 017 914; e info@torteoro.si; www.torteoro.si; ⊕ 08.00–23.00 daily. What appears like a bog-standard café next to the Hotel Koper does the most amazing array of cakes, including to order (& even gluten, egg or sugar free), & turns into a salsa venue most weekends. Check www.facebook.com/oro.caffe for listings.

SHOPPING Koper is a great place to shop for interesting gifts. Čevljarska and Županičičeva streets hide a myriad little shops mostly sporting very good-quality Slovenian clothes and shoe brands which are sold worldwide. L'Occitane toiletries is about as international as it gets in the old town, and there's even an old-fashioned haberdashery at Čevljarska 43.

Čokoladnica Da Ponte [151 C3] (*Županičičeva 38;* m *041 504 863; www. cokoladnicadaponte.si;* ☉ *09.00–19.00 Mon–Fri, 09.00–13.00 Sat*) Named after the fountain nearby, this is Koper's first chocolate shop. A bewildering array of pralines fill the small shop's counter, and they sell their own brand of teas and coffee beans. The milk chocolate with lavender, and the dark chocolate with salt flower are local specialities.

Piranske Soline [151 C3] (*Županičičeva 40;* ✆ *056 721 330;* ☉ *09.00–17.00 Mon–Fri, 09.00–13.00 Sat*) A branch of the Sečovlje Salt Museum shop. Here you can get candles, body scrubs and lotions, bath salts and soaps, salt grinders, kitchen utensils, recipe books and, of course, salt. Fascinating.

Tash [151 C3] (*Županičičeva 43;* m *040 599 344;* e *info@tash.si; www.tash.si;* ☉ *09.00–17.00 Mon–Fri*) If you want a truly amazing pair of handmade leather shoes, this is the place to come. If you can't afford these in time or money, then Kopitarna Shoes next door does very reasonable Slovenian made shoes.

OTHER PRACTICALITIES

$ Bank [151 B3] Banka Koper, Kidričeva 14; ☉ 08.00–12.00 & 14.00–17.00 Mon–Fri, 08.00–12.00 Sat

🖳 Internet [151 B3] Pina, Kidričeva 43; ✆ 056 278 072; e p.info@pina.si; www.pina. info; ☉ 12.00–22.00 Mon–Fri, 16.00–22.00 Sat/Sun. This funky internet café is part of a multi-media & youth centre, which also prides itself on conducting locally sustainable youth projects.

✚ Pharmacy Kidričeva 2; ✆ 056 110 000; e obalne.lekarne@siol.net; www.obalne-lekarne. si; ☉ 24/7. This is the head branch of a chain of pharmacies along the Slovenian coast, with online ordering available. Well-informed English-speaking staff.

✉ Post office [151 B4] Muzeski trg 3; ☉ 08.00–19.00 Mon–Fri, 08.00–12.00 Sat

WHAT TO SEE AND DO Titov trg [151 B2] is the place to start your look around the historic old town. On the north side is the 15th-century loggia, now a prestigious café downstairs and a small art gallery upstairs, **Galerija Loža** (*www.obalne-galerije. si;* ☉ *15.00–22.00 Tue–Sat, 20.00–22.00 Sun*). On the eastern flank is the 12th-century **Cathedral of the Assumption** [151 B2] containing a Vittore Carpaccio Renaissance painting of 1516, the *Sacra Conservatione*. The cathedral's **campanile** (☉ *09.30–13.30 & 16.00–18.00 daily; entry €2*) holds one of Slovenia's oldest bells dating from 1333. At 36m high, the campanile is another miniature of St Mark's in Venice, and gives the best view of the tightly woven streets of the town, as well as of the working docks and the whole bay of Piran. To the north of the cathedral is the **Rotunda of John the Baptist** [151 B2]. On the southern side of the square is the entrance to the **Praetorian Palace**, which used to be the seat of the Venetian-era mayor and is now the tourist information bureau. The remainder of the palace takes up the entire flank of the western side of the square.

Koper Regional Museum [151 B3] (*Kidričeva 19;* ✆ *056 633 570; www.burger.si;* ☉ *Jun–Aug 08.00–13.00 & 18.00–20.00 Mon–Fri, 08.00–13.00 Sat; Sep–May 08.00–*

15.00 Mon–Fri, 08.00–13.00 Sat; entry €2) The museum is located in Belgramoni Palace on what is now known as Muzeski trg. Among the usual everyday items preserved as a record of life in the past, the museum also holds a copy of the 12th-century painting of the ***Dance of Death***, the original of which lies in Trinity Church in Hrastovlje (there is also an original in Beram; see page 120). Next door to the museum is the **Center eksperimentov** [151 B3] (*Kidričeva 17;* ☏ *056 272 077; www. centereksperimentov.si;* ④ *09.00–13.00 & 16.00–19.00 Mon–Fri, 09.00–13.00 & 15.00–18.00 Sat; entry free*), which those with children might find a lot more fun than the museum. All ages can explore here how machines work, explore gravity, and take part in creativity workshops.

Towards the far end of Kidričeva the churches of St Nicholas and of the Holy Trinity, Totto Palace, and two timber medieval houses at Nos 31 and 33 await renovation. **Carpacciov trg** [151 B3] at the end of the street holds more Venetian buildings, cafés and the nearby Hotel Koper, all looking out on the sea. From here a long **walkway** lined with benches stretches out towards Izola, and eventually becomes a cycle path along the edge of the sea.

ACTIVITIES

Aquapark Zušterna [151 C4] (*Istarska 67;* ☏ *056 100 300;* e *zusterna@terme-catez.si; www.terme-catez.si/en/slovenian-coast/aquapark-zusterna; 3 hrs' entry €11 Mon–Fri, €15 Sat/Sun, 4–14 years 27% off, under 4 years free*) An extensive water park, but with limited restaurant facilities (considering you are not meant to bring your own food in). The **public lido and beach** opposite Zušterna, on the sea-side of the main road, is better value for money (entry €3).

Škocjanski Zatok Nature Reserve (*Bertoški bonifika;* ☏ *056 260 370;* e *skocjanske@skocjanske-zatok.org; www.skocjanski-zatok.org; entry free*) A birdwatcher's paradise as well as for all nature-observers. Walking trails criss-cross the reserve and the Parenzana hike and bike trail (see *Chapter 7*, page 128) skirts part of the edge of it. Guided tours for groups are available during the week (€48 for up to 15 people).

IZOLA

Originally an island, and caught between its larger neighbours of Koper and Piran, Izola has a history of struggling for autonomy and independence. The Roman town and port of Haliaetum was just southwest of the current town from at least 2BC, but the island of Izola itself only saw settlement with the arrival of refugees from Aquileia during the constant conflicts there in the 7th century. Known for harbouring pirates and rebels, in 1253 it declared independence, but by 1267 it joined the Republic of Venice at the same time as Poreč, 16 years before Piran and 20 years before Koper.

Thermal springs were found in Izola in 1820, thus starting its life as a **spa and wellness destination**. The town walls were demolished and used to fill the narrow stretch of sea separating the island from the mainland, which until then had only been connected by a stone bridge. From 1902 to 1935 it was connected to Trieste and Poreč by the Parenzana railway line. Today it thrives as the **arts, film and music capital** of the Slovenian coast.

GETTING AROUND Izola is small enough to walk around. To go further afield **bicycle hire** is available at the Parenzana Railway Museum (see *What to see and do*, page 157) or at Ritoša (*Kajuhova 28;* ☏ *056 415 337;* e *info@ritosa.si; www.ritosa.*

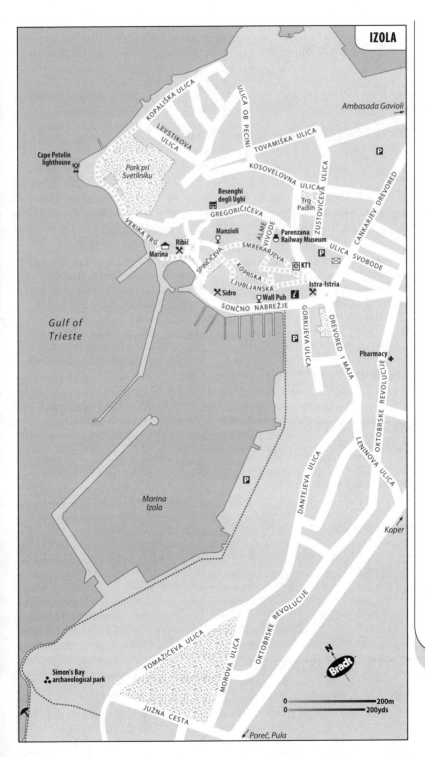

IZOLA

Ambasada Gavioli

Cape Petelin
lighthouse

Park pri
Svetilniku

KOPALIŠKA ULICA

LEVSTIKOVA
ULICA

ULICA OB PEČINI

TOVAMIŠKA ULICA

KOSOVELOVNA ULICA

ZUSTOVIĆEVA ULICA

Trg
Padlih

CANKARJEV DREVORED

Besenghi
degli Ughi

GREGORIČIČEVA

VEKIKA TRG

Marina

Ribič

Manzioli

SMREKARJEVA

ALME VIVODE

Parenzana
Railway Museum

ULICA SVOBODE

ŠPINČIĆEVA

KOPRSKA

LJUBLJANSKA

KT1

Sidro

Wall Pub

Istra-Istria

SONČNO NABREŽJE

Gulf of
Trieste

GORKLJEVA ULICA

DREVORED 1 MAJA

Pharmacy

OKTOBRSKE REVOLUCIJE

DANTEJEVA ULICA

LENINOVA ULICA

Koper

Marina
Izola

Simon's Bay
archaeological park

TOMAŽIČEVA ULICA

MOROVA ULICA

OKTOBRSKE REVOLUCIJE

JUŽNA CESTA

N

Bradt

0   200m
0   200yds

Poreč, Pula

si/services.php; €15/day, €25/w/end, €50/week), who also sell a dizzying array of bicycles and bicycle equipment. Izola's main **bus** stop is outside the main post office on Cankarjev Drevored (✆ *05 6722 525*).

Taxis are also available, at **Taxi Bo-Bo** (m *040 602 602;* e *bobo_izola@gmail.com),* and **Izola Marina** (*Tomžiceva 4a, 6310 Izola;* ✆ *05 6625 400;* e *info@marinaizola. com; www.marinaizola.com*) has 700 berths and 24-hour landing assistance.

TOURIST INFORMATION Izola **Tourist Information Centre** (*Sončno nabrežje 4;* ✆ *05 6401 050;* e *tic.izola@izola.si; www.izola.si;* ⊕ *Jul/Aug 09.00–21.00 Mon–Sat, 09.00–12.00 Sun, Sep–Jun 09.00–18.00 Mon–Fri, 09.00–12.00 Sat*) offers listings of local accommodation as well as all the other tourist attractions in the area, and good local maps.

⌂ WHERE TO STAY

⌂ **Hotel Marina** (52 rooms) Veliki trg 11; ✆056 604 100; e marina@belvedere.si; www. hotelmarina.si. Right next to the centrally located harbour, with views onto the sea, & a small wellness centre, where you can hire the massage pool just for 2. **$$$$**

⌂ **Apartments Mila** (6 apts, with 2–6 beds) Kumajeva 10; m 031 672 494; e info@ apartments-mila.com; www.apartments-mila. com. One street behind the main square & harbour, these new apartments are a welcome addition to accommodation in the town. Clean & bright. **$$$**

⌂ **Hostel Stara Šola Korte** (17 rooms, 2 apts) Korte 74; ✆056 421 114; e info@hostel-starasola.si; www.hostel-starasola.si. As its name in Slovenian says, this is literally an old school. Recently refurbished, it is bright & cheerful with fantastic surroundings, beautiful terrace, grand old stairs, a blue-&-white decorated canteen, & a small library in the old principal's office. The rooms all have single beds or bunks (max 4 in a room) & the apartments come with double beds (& 1 with a jacuzzi). Whilst not by the sea, it is worth going out of your way for. Under 6 years free, 7–14 years 50% discount. **$$**

✗ WHERE TO EAT AND DRINK

✗ **Sidro Inn** Sončno nabrežje 24; ✆056 414 711; ⊕ 08.00–midnight daily, except Thu in winter. With indoor & outdoor seating, the speciality of the house is sea snails with polenta. **$$$$**

✗ **Istra-Istria** Trg republike 1; m 041 345 605; ⊕ 07.00–22.00 Mon–Sat, 08.00–22.00 Sun. A relatively new restaurant in the *konoba-hiža* style, including a fireplace. Seafood of course, but also a pizza oven for really good pizzas, & excellent cakes & coffee too. **$$$**

✗ **Ribič** Velika trg 3; ✆056 418 313; www. ribic.biz; ⊕ 10.00–23.00 daily. Overlooking the harbour (& the car park), this *gostilna* offers a wide range of dishes, both meat & fish. Beware the crab soup with crab-sticks. **$$$**

♀**Manzioli Wine Bar** Manziolijev trg 5; ✆056 162 137; e bruno.zaro@t-2.net. On the ground floor of Manzioli Palace is a relaxed bar, where you can sample local Slovenian wines, including those of the Zaro family who run it. The Zaro family is one of the 2 oldest families in Izola going back to 1348. Their vineyard (*Polje 12a, Pivol;* m *041 738 947*) growing Malvazija, Refošk, & endemic strains Istska Belina, Maločrn and Muškat, is 1km outside Izola & open to visits & wine tastings.

♀**Wall Pub** Sončno nabrežje 12; ✆056 414 273; ⊕ 07.00–01.00 daily. Whether it's for early-morning coffee or a late nightcap, this is still the only watering hole on the harbour. Down-to-earth atmosphere & prices.

ENTERTAINMENT AND NIGHTLIFE

☆ **Ambasada Gavioli** Industrijska cesta 10; m 031 255 706; e fetchthevibe@gmail.com; www.facebook.com/AmbasadaGavioliPage. For many, this nightclub is the highlight of Izola. Besides the attraction of famous DJs from around

the world playing electro house, techno futurism & other modern trends, the fascination of Gavioli is its architecture. Italian architect Gianni Gavioli used themes from Alice's wonderland, Romeo & Juliet's balcony, & Jean Baudelaire's evil flowers. Opened in 1995, for the first 10 years of its life Ambasada Gavioli's musical choice was based in strong ideological grounds following the neuropolitan teachings (that's the practice of communicating with the dead – I had to look it up too) of Chiron Morpheus. Since 2005, the venue has smelled the money & become much more earthly, but the architecture will still blow your mind (& your wallet – entry on some nights is €25).

FESTIVALS Izola Cinema International Film Festival (*www.isolacinema.org*) takes place at the end of May. Showcasing a great range of films, mostly not from western Europe and North America, it's a true exploration of cinema from elsewhere around the world. Many of the festival's films are screened outdoors, including at Manzioli trg, and on the beach at Cape Petelin. Workshops also take place where people can learn some of the secrets of cinematography from the many film directors attending.

OTHER PRACTICALITIES

$ Bank Banka Koper, Drevored I Maja 5; ⊕ 08.30–12.00 & 15.00–17.00 Mon–Fri, 08.30–12.00 Sat

🖲 **Internet** KT1 Cyber Café, Trg Etbina Kristiana 1; ⊕ 12.00–22.00 daily. Popular with gamers.

✚ **Pharmacy** Oktobrske revolucije 11; ☎056 778 250; e lekarna.izola@siol.net; ⊕ 07.30–19.00

Mon–Fri (15 Jun–31 Aug till 20.00 Mon–Fri), 07.30–13.00 Sat, closed Sun. See Koper head branch (*Other practicalities*, page 153) for 24/7 service & contact details.

✉ **Post office** Cankarjev drevored 1; ⊕ 08.00–19.00 Mon–Fri, 08.00–12.00 Sat

WHAT TO SEE AND DO Izola is delightful to walk around. The **park** in the northwest corner, with its minute **lighthouse** (more like a large lamp post really) at Cape Petelin is a favourite destination, also for swimming. The town's winding little backstreets host a multitude of **private galleries and art workshops**. Many are housed in the town's many old palaces. Intent is afoot to turn Koprska and Ljubljanska streets into a **street museum** showcasing the old crafts and trades.

The most revered palace of all Izola is the **Besenghi degli Ughi** (*Gregoričičeva 76*), which is now a music school, from which you can hear high-quality student practising. Completed in 1781, the Besenghi family chose the renowned Milan architect Filippo Dongetti to design it. During its construction, the stone lion – now adorning a corner of the building – was found whilst digging the foundation. The Besenghi family library, containing some 3,000 16th- and 17th-century books and manuscripts, remains intact. The palace is not open to the public.

Parenzana Railway Museum (*Alme Vivode 3;* ☎ *056 417 357;* e *joze.cernelic@ izola.si; www.parenzana.net;* ⊕ *09.00–15.00 Mon–Fri, closed Sat/Sun; entry €2.50, concessions €2*) Aside from telling the history of the Parenzana narrow-gauge railway between Trieste and Poreč (for more details, see *Parenzana*, page 128), the museum holds the private collection of model railways collected by local Izola resident Josip Mihelič. On the ground floor is also a display of model ships, accompanied by technical and artistic drawings, and early black-and-white photos of ships and shipbuilding.

Simon's bay and archaeological park On the next head of land immediately after the harbour is not only one of Izola's best free public beaches, but also the site of a Roman seaside villa, which is now a protected area and free to visit. Recent excavations have revealed a large residence of 3,000m² around a courtyard with a portico to a double-piered harbour. Intricate black-and-white mosaics paved the villa, a copy of one of which is on display, along with outlines of the walls and portico.

The harbour now lies underwater, and with a careful eye can be viewed with a snorkel and mask.

PIRAN

If you've only time to visit one town in the Slovenian Adriatic, it should be the historically and culturally rich Piran. An overnight stay is also well in order. Aside from having some of the best-preserved medieval architecture in all Istria, certain historical events peculiar to Piran have endowed it with some interesting statues and museums.

Piran takes its name from Greek origins from the word *pyr* meaning 'fire', when these were used as ancient 'lighthouses' to warn ships of this angular peninsula. By 1283 it had joined the Republic of Venice, following the local lead of Izola. In 1692 Piran was the birthplace of composer and violinist Guiseppe Tartini, whose statue – erected to celebrate the 200th anniversary of his birth in 1892 – dominates the main square named after him, Tartini Trg. Tartini's house, now a museum, dates from at least 1384. In 1812 the Battle of Pirano took place between the British HMS *Victorious* and the Napoleonic *Rivoli* in the waters just off Piran. It is the only naval battle to take place in what are now Slovenian waters, and more can be read about it in the naval museum at the Gabrielli Palace.

Although never an island, it is surrounded by the sea on three sides and by the considerable remains of its thick town wall on the other. A mere 500m across at the town wall end, tapering gradually to a point less than 1km to the northwest, it is very easy to walk around. Always a completely pedestrianised town, a vehicular service was first introduced to Piran in 1909, when the first trolleybus in the Balkans started in Piran and ran the coastal routes to neighbouring towns. The trolleybus was replaced by an electric tram in 1912 and then by the current bus service in 1953.

GETTING AROUND The closest thing that Piran has to a **bus station** is in fact just a bus stop on the southwest edge of the town and the harbour. It's a ten-minute walk from there to the central square, and only five minutes from there to the park and

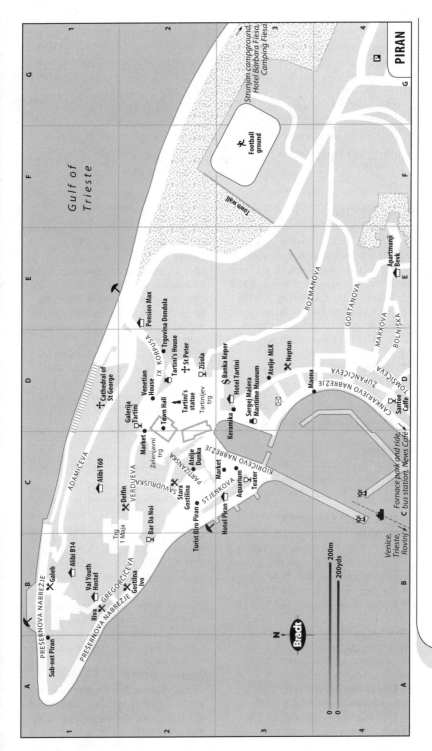

PIRAN

Gulf of
Trieste

Strunjan campground,
Hotel Barbara Fiesa,
Camping Fiesa

Football
ground

Town wall

ROZMANOVA

GORTANOVA

Apartmanji
Bevk

MARXOVA

BOLNIŠKA

TOMŠIČEVA

ŽUPANČIČEVA

ČANKARJEVO NABREŽJE

Santee
Caffe

Maona

D

Neptun

Atelje MLK

Hotel Tartini

Banka Koper

Sergej Mašera
Maritime Museum

Keramika

Žižola

St Peter

Tartini's House

Trgovina Dondola

Pension Max

Tartini's
statue

Tartinijev
trg

Venetian
House

IX KORPUSA

Cathedral of
St George

Town Hall

Galerija
Tartini

Market

Zelenjavni
trg

Atelje
Dunka

Market

Aquarium

Teater

Stara
Gostilna

Delfin

Bar Da Noi

ADAMIČEVA

VERDIJEVA

SAVUDRIJSKA

PARTIZANSKA

STJENKOVA

KIDRIČEVO NABREŽJE

Hotel Piran

Turist Biro Piran

Trg
1 Maja

Alibi T60

Alibi B14

Val Youth
Hostel

Galeb

Gostilna
Ivo

Riva

Sub-net Piran

PREŠERNOVA NABREŽJE

GREGORČIČEVA

PREŠERNOVA NABREŽJE

Fornace park and ride,
bus station, News Café

Venice,
Trieste,
Rovinj

Bradt

N

0   200m
0   200yds

ride further south on the coast at Fornace. A free shuttle bus (a small white bus with a blue-and-white stripe down the side) runs every 15 minutes from near the bottom of the multi-storey car park at Fornace to Tartini trg (show your parking ticket). You can also catch the regular service (plain white bus) between the coastal towns, which also goes into Tartini trg, but this will cost you €1.

Taxi Piran (✆ *05 6730 700;* e *info@bevk.si; www.bevk.si*) can be found near the bus station and the southern end of the harbour, and also between Tartini trg and the harbour.

TOURIST INFORMATION Piran **Tourist Information Office** [159 D2] (*Tartinjev trg 2;* ✆ *056 734 440;* e *ticpi@portoroz.si; www.portoroz.si*) is a sub-branch of that in Portorož.

🏠 WHERE TO STAY

🏠 **Piran** (80 rooms, 27 apts) Stjenkova 1; ✆05 6762 520; e info@hoteli-piran.si; www. hoteli-piran.si. Fantastic sea views, standard 3-star facilities in a 1960s refurbished building, & a small beach across the road in front of the hotel. **$$$$**

🏠 **Tartini** (43 rooms) Tartinjev trg 15; ✆056 711 000; e info@hotel-tartini-piran.si; www. hotel-piran.com. Prime location with standard facilities. Great for people-watching on the main square. **$$$$**

🏠 **Apartmani Bevk** (6 apts) Marxova 13; ✆059 022 111; m 051 623 682; e info@bevk.si; www. bevk.si. Very nice self-catering apartments in 2 renovated buildings not far from each other. Small fitness centre & roof terrace & nicer furnishings in

the 3 apartments on Prežihova. Larger apartments with a roof terrace on Marxova. **$$$**

🏠 **Max** (6 rooms) IX Korpusa 26; ✆05 6733 436; e info@maxpiran.com; www.maxpiran.com. In a beautifully refurbished 1700 building with stone-exposed breakfast room downstairs, this little family-run hotel is hard to beat. A heartfelt breakfast & service is delivered by Max & his staff. Really excellent value. **$$$$$**

🏠 **Val Hostel** (22 rooms) Gregoričičeva 38a; ✆056 732 555; e yhostel.val@siol.net; www. hostel-val.com. Classic hostel with single beds & bunks in rooms (4 beds max) with shared wash facilities on each floor. Washing machine, free Wi-Fi & pet-friendly. **$$**

Camping

🛖 **Fiesa** Fiesa 57b; ✆056 746 230; e autocamp. fiesa@siol.net; www.portoroz.si/en/camping-fiesa; ⏲ 1 May–30 Sep. Just over 1km east of the

old town. Cheap hotel accommodation, & cabins for 4 also available. **$**

✖ WHERE TO EAT AND DRINK

✖ **Gostilna Ivo** [159 B2] Gregoričičeva 31; ✆056 732 233; ⏲ 11.00–23.00 daily. Ivo distinguishes itself from the rest of the seafront restaurants by its simple & consistently good dishes, which, for the same price as other places, are much better value. **$$$$**

✖ **Neptun** [159 D3] Županičičeva 7; ✆056 734 111; ⏲ 11.00–23.00 daily. In the old bus station, this restaurant with fishing nets hanging from the ceiling is very popular with locals, & in part because without sea views & a terrace it is less popular with tourists. Best food in town. **$$$$**

✖ **Riva** [159 B1] Županičičeva 43; ✆056 732 180; e info@riva.si; www.riva.si; ⏲ 11.30–midnight daily. Offering both seafood & grills, including carpaccio of both the turf & surf variety.

Apartments for rent also available. **$$$$**

✖ **Galeb** [159 B1] Pusterla 5; ✆056 733 235; ⏲ 11.00–16.00 & 18.00–midnight daily. Equally popular with locals & tourists on the northern seafront. **$$$**

♀ **Galerija Tartini** [159 D2] Tartinjev trg 3; ⏲ summer 09.00–midnight daily, winter 09.00–18.00 daily. As the name implies, an art gallery & a café in one, from which you can just about observe the whole square.

♀ **Teater** [159 C3] Kidričevo Nabrežje bb; ⏲ 09.00–midnight daily. This place is like it's been lifted straight out of Vienna – high Art-Deco ceilings, tall arched windows, plush chairs & an enviable view of the sea & the dock.

♀ **Žižola** [159 D2] Tartinjev trg 10; ⏱ 09.00–01.00 daily. This tiniest of café/bars looks like it is stuck in time. Often only standing room on popular summer evenings.

OTHER PRACTICALITIES

$ Bank [159 D3] Banka Koper, Tartinjev trg 13; ⏱ 08.30–12.00 & 15.00–17.00 Mon–Fri, 08.30–12.00 Sat

✚ Pharmacy Tartinjev trg 4; ☎ 056 730 150; ⏱ 07.30–19.00 Mon–Fri (15 Jun–31 Aug till 20.00 Mon–Fri), 07.30–13.00 Sat/Sun (see *Portorož*, page 163). See Koper head branch (*Section name*, page 153) for 24/7 service & contact details.

✉ Post office [159 D3] Leninova 1; ⏱ 08.00–19.00 Mon–Fri, 08.00–12.00 Sat

WHAT TO SEE AND DO **Tartini trg** is the central place to head for in Piran. For a tiny town it is uncharacteristically large, and this is because it was in fact an inner harbour until it was filled in to form the current piazza in 1884. Shortly thereafter, **Tartini's statue** [159 D2] was erected there in 1892.

Benečanka [159 D2] At the north end of Tartini Trg is the characteristically deep rustic red Venetian house, with its inscription '*lassa pur dir*' (let them talk). Legend has it that a Venetian merchant had built the house for his local sweetheart, and had the inscription written in defiance of local gossip about their love. On the ground floor is the popular museum shop of the Piran saltpans.

Maritime Museum Sergej Mašera [159 D3] (*Cankarejevo nabrežje 3;* ☎ *056 710 040;* e *muzej@pommuz-pi.si; www2.arnes.si/~kppomm/index.htm;* ⏱ *Sep–Jun 09.00–17.00 Tue–Sun; Jul/Aug 09.00–12.00 & 17.00–21.00 Tue–Sun; entry €3*) The museum houses a variety of local seafaring and coastal-life exhibits in the 19th-century Gabrielli Palace, which was only partially finished and then turned into a museum in 1954. Also run by the Maritime Museum is the **Museum of Salt Making** (see *Sečovlje*, page 164). Look out for the Galeb cutter sail boat, donated in 1994 by the ballet choreographers Pia and Pino Mlaker, in the harbour nearby.

Mestna Hiša [159 D2] The town hall is a relatively new building in Piran dating back only to 1877, when it was built over the site of the old municipal palace with its Venetian loggia. The new town hall is the seat of the mayor and town council and also holds the town archives.

Piran Aquarium [159 C3] (*Kidričevo Nabrežje 4;* ☎ *051 602 554;* ⏱ *Jun–Aug 09.00–22.00 daily; mid–May/Jun & Sep/mid–Oct 09.00–19.00 Tue–Sun, closed Mon; rest of the year 09.00–17.00, closed Mon; entry €2*) A small fish collection.

St George's Cathedral [159 D1] The cathedral dominates the town and Tartini trg from the north. The view from here is definitely worth the trek. Originally built in the 12th century, its current structure dates from its expansion in the early 14th century, and its subsequent Baroque facelift in 1637. The belfry, completed in 1608, sports a magnificent view of the bay, and when the cold northeast *bora* wind blows the skies clear, it's possible to see as far as the Italian Alps and the Dolomites. Inside are two statues of St George, the patron saint of Piran, on his horse (no dragon in sight).

St Peter's Church [159 D2] The church can be found in the piazza. It dates back to 1272 when it stood outside the original 7th-century town walls. As the town expanded, the **town walls** were rebuilt between 1470 and 1534 further out in their current location. Seven town gates are still intact.

Tartini's House [159 D2] (*Kajuhova 12;* ✆ *056 633 570;* ⊕ *Jun–Aug 09.00–12.00 & 18.00–21.00 daily; Sep–May 11.00–12.00 & 17.00–18.00 daily; entry €1*) Tartini's House is on the northeast corner of the square. It is one of the oldest buildings in the town, having been mentioned in town documents dating to 1384. This museum, where Tartini was born, is worth visiting just to see the exquisite frescoes which were uncovered and beautifully restored in the late 1980s. The first-floor memorial room houses some of Tartini's original musical score sheets, one of his many violins, letters from the composer, and his death mask. Other floors, all part of the Italian Community main office, also often hold cultural events and exhibitions.

PORTOROŽ

A miniature riviera (smaller than Opatija's 12km seafront stretch), Portorož is the **spa kingdom** of the Slovenian Adriatic. Thermal waters have been known and used here since Roman times but it was not an area developed during Venetian rule like the other towns along the coast, largely due to the lack of a suitable port. Nonetheless, with the rise of spa tourism during the 19th century, the 'Port of Roses' with its thermal waters was a prime location for development. Its first hotel, the Hotel Palace (now the Kempinski Palace) with its grand façade, was opened in 1910. Since then a slew of large hotels have been built along the coast here such that it is hard to find space to even get into the sea in the high season. Piran's picturesque Venetian-style old town is only 3km along the coastal path.

GETTING AROUND In true health and spa style, just as the doctor prescribes, **walking** is the order of the day. **Bicycle hire** is available through your hotel or from Topline (see *Tourist information*, page 150). Portorož's main **bus** stop is outside the small indoor market opposite the Kempinski Palace. **Taxi Piran** (see *Getting around*, page 160) serves Portorož.

Marina Portorož (*Cesta solinarjev 8;* ✆ *056 761 200;* e *marinaportoroz@marinap.si; www.marinap.si*) is in fact located 1km south at Lucija and is the first purpose-built yacht marina in Slovenia. Built on the old saltpans, it has over 1,000 berths and a full repair service, with the capacity to lift 60 tonnes. The marina also has two restaurants, and a recreational centre with minigolf, table tennis, a variety of other sport pitches, a tennis school with 19 courts, and an outdoor Olympic-size pool.

Confusingly, the street numbering of the esplanade Obala goes 1–27 on the shore side going west to east, and then starts again at the west end of the land side with 28–144. Numbers are not opposite each other, and between the Life Class complex and the Kempinski Palace, numbers 34–44 no longer exist.

TOURIST INFORMATION The **tourist information bureau** (*Obala 16;* ✆ *056 742 220;* e *ticpo@portoroz.si; www.portoroz.si;* ⊕ *summer 09.00–22.00 Mon–Sat, 09.00–13.00 Sun; winter 09.00–16.00 Mon–Sat, closed Sun*) has a very useful website, including information on **church service** times. A friendly tourist agency in Portorož is **Topline** (see page 150).

 WHERE TO STAY AND SPA Private accommodation in Portorož is possible through the tourist agencies, but really people come here to stay at the big spa hotels with full access to the hot springs, and in the hope of catching a glimpse of the rich and famous at the five-stars.

Kempinski Palace (181 rooms) Obala 45; 056 927 070; e reservations.porotroz@kempinski.com; www.kempinski.com/portoroz. A 5-star deluxe Kempinski has standards, & you'll find these here as in any other Kempinski. The only thing that's unique about this Kempinski is its façade, which is exactly that. Originally built in 1910, the building was declared a cultural heritage monument in 1983. As a result, when Istrabenz bought & renovated the building in conjunction with Kempinski, only the façade was kept & the rest was demolished. The Rose Spa is pure luxury & open to outside guests at €25 for a day pass. Massage & treatments extra. **$$$$$**

Life Class Hotels & Spa (791 rooms) Obala 33; 056 925 906; e booking@lifeclass.net; www.lifeclass.net. With 6 hotels to choose from, crammed into the entire complex at Obala 33, you should be able to find a room. The Grand Hotel is 5-star, the remainder (Slovenia, Riviera, Neptune, Mirna and Apollo) are 4-star. A 5-star beach & a 4-star beach across the road are for the exclusive use of guests. Full spa treatments, including Wai Thai, Ayurveda & Thalasso are available, as well as a fitness centre, pilates centre, & an ice-cave in their sauna park, offering 7 different types of sauna & using salt from nearby Sečovlje. Physiotherapy & a host of other treatments can be booked. Outside guests can use the spa facilities & the thermal spring seawater pools (entrance on K Stara St between Obala 33 & the Kempinski) year-round 13.00–21.00. Thermal pool entrance starts at €7 for 2 hrs. **$$$$$**

Marko (48 rooms) Obala 28; 056 174 000; e info@hotel-marko.si; www.hotel-marko.si. A family-run hotel in its own grounds at the western end of the esplanade. Considerably more privacy than the conglomerates. **$$$$**

Forma Viva (11 rooms) Seča 159; m 040 233 093; e info@formaviva-portoroz.si; www.formaviva-portoroz.si. Set in the Forma Viva sculpture park on Seča Peninsula, this pleasant basic pension is considerably cheaper than the upmarket end of Portorož, & quieter too. **$$$**

WHERE TO EAT For a place with such high-end hotels there is a complete lack of high-end restaurants. The rich and famous must go to Croatia for that. Try the following:

Staro Sidro Obala 55; 056 745 074; ⏲ 11.00–23.00 daily. A quiet upper terrace in a leafy setting with sea views is marred by plastic furniture & doubtful music. The food is good, but it's matched with a price tag. **$$$$**

Figarola Obala 14a; 056 742 200; ⏲ 10.00–22.00 daily. Good-standard seaside dishes with lots of outside seating & an AC interior. Popular & reasonably priced. **$$$**

Stara Oljka Obala 20; 056 748 555; www.staraoljka.si; ⏲ 10.00–midnight daily. By far the nicest restaurant in Portorož & far enough down the Obala to be away from the madding crowds. A typical Istrian hiža-style interior with a terrace onto the sea, matched in quality by its food & staff. **$$$**

OTHER PRACTICALITIES

$ **Bank** Banka Koper, Obala 33; ⏲ 08.30–12.00 & 15.00–17.00 Mon–Fri, 08.30–12.00 Sat

Dentist Top Dent, Grand Hotel Metropol, Obala 77; 056 744 310; e top.dent@siol.net; www.topdent.si; ⏲ 09.00–13.00 & 16.00–19.00 Mon–Fri, 09.00–13.00 Sat, Sun by appointment. More expensive than some dentists, in part due to its location, but still excellent prices compared with private treatment costs in the UK or US.

Pharmacy Cesta solinajev 1; 056 778 250; e lekarna.lucija@siol.net; ⏲ 07.30–19.00 Mon–Fri (15 Jun–31 Aug till 20.00 Mon–Fri), 07.30–13.00 Sat, 08.00–12.00 Sun & public holidays (except 1 Jan, 1 May and 25 Dec). See Koper head branch (*Other practicalities*, page 153) for 24/7 service & contact details.

Post office K Stari 1; ⏲ 08.00–19.00 Mon–Fri, 08.00–12.00 Sat

WHAT TO SEE AND DO The coastal path spanning from the saltpans (see *Sečovlje salina*, page 164) and **Forma Viva sculpture park** in the east along the entire coast to Koper is almost 30km, which you can do in three or four hours on a **bicycle** (don't forget to double it to return). A **spa** treatment or massage afterwards (see *Where to stay and spa*, page 162) will be well earned.

The Obala is lined with cafés, bars and pubs, perfect for whiling away the time and relaxing over an ice cream or cake. Many head to Izola for evening cultural events and the fabled Ambasada Gavioli nightclub. Portorož's **open-air auditorium** (*Senčna pot 10;* \ *056 760 373; www.avditorij.si*) holds regular live events too.

The whole coastline is available for a **swim** in the sea, and for **boat charter** try Jonathan Yachting (*Cesta solinarijev 6;* \ *056 778 930;* m *041 719 986;* e *info@ jonathanplus.si; www.jonathanplus.si*) near the marina. **Panoramic flights** are available from Solinair at the airport (\ *056 722 545;* e *info@solinar.si; www.solinair. si*). For information about the sports facilities at Portorož Marina recreational centre, see page 162.

Sečovlje salina and Museum of Salt Making (*Seča 115;* \ *056 710 040;* e *muzej@pommuz-pi.si; www.soline.si;* ⊕ *Apr/May & Sep/Oct 09.00–18.00, Jun– Aug 09.00–20.00 daily; the museum itself closes 13.00–14.00; entry €3.50, concessions for children, students & over 65s*) The Sečovlje saltpans were first noted in court documents from AD804. The *soline*, as they are known in Slovenian, are made up of working saltpans in the northern half (Lera), and a nature park in the now disused saltpans to the south (Fontanigge). The museum, which is a renovated local worker's house, looks remarkably plain, and lies in the south side. Both sides are open to the public – so you can see how salt is harvested in Lera, and see the wide array of halophytes (salt-loving vegetation) and accompanying fauna in Fontanigge.

The area is an ornitholgist's paradise, with over 270 different bird species, including a very high number of wintering birds who migrate from colder climates. Fauna is also abundant, not least because the park harbours four different ecosystems – land, fresh water, brackish water and seawater – in a remarkably small area. It is protected under the Ramsar Convention on Wetlands.

The two sides have different entrances. To enter Lera working area, turn off at the village of Seča. To enter the nature park, you'll need to take the road to Fontanigge which lies in no-man's-land between the Croatian and the Slovenian border posts. Fontanigge and Lera are divided by the Drinica dyke, over which there is no crossing inside the park. The park can be explored on foot or bicycle, but take care on both sides not to disturb the saltpans. This would destroy the purity of the salt harvested in Lera, and disturb the habitat of the many nesting birds in Fontanigge. Sunsets here are spectacular, so I strongly recommend bringing a good camera.

In July and August, a daily boat, the ***Solinarka*** (m *031 653 682;* e *poropat.toni@ siol.net; adults €15, children €10*) sails on Tuesday and Saturday to the saltpans from Strunjan pier at 08.30, Piran at 09.00, Hotel Bernardin at 09.15, Portorož pier at 09.45, and arriving at Lera Soline at 10.15. You have one hour at the saltpans until the boat returns. On Thursdays, the boat leaves Koper at 13.45, Izola at 14.25, Strunjan at 15.00, Piran at 15.45, Bernardin at 16.00, Porotrož at 16.15, and arriving at Lera Soline at 16.45, again with only one hour at the saltpans. If you miss the boat or want longer, then call one of the taxi companies listed on pages 152, 156, and 160.

POSTOJNA

Though it's the nearby Škocjanske jame which has UNESCO World Heritage Site status, it's undoubtedly **Postojnska jama (Postojna Cave)** which you'll hear about more often. One of the most popular tourist attractions anywhere in Slovenia,

Postojna Cave receives over half a million visitors a year – but whatever you've seen or know about the cave, prepare to be genuinely awe-struck when you actually get inside. The other reason to come here is **Predjama Castle**, perched fairy-tale-like within a sheer cliff.

HISTORY Unlike other, smaller caves in the area, in which evidence of human habitation has been discovered dating back some 150,000 years to the Late Stone Age, there is no evidence of prehistoric habitation in Postojnska jama. Perhaps it was simply too large to feel safe, and certainly the constant air movement would have made it a cold dwelling place. Graffiti in Postojnska jama shows that it was visited at least as early as the 13th century, and from the late 18th century this area became the focus for early studies into karst geomorphology and hydrology (see *Geography*, page 4). It was opened to the public in 1819, its first official visitor being Austria's Archduke Ferdinand I (as you sit on the train when entering the cave, spare a thought for the workers whose job it was back in those early days to push visitors around in carriages by hand).

GETTING THERE Numerous agencies in Istria and elsewhere in Croatia, as well as in Ljubljana and towns on the Slovenian Adriatic, run tours and day trips to Postojna Cave and Predjama Castle.

By bus From Postojna there are two buses a day to Poreč and Rovinj (3½ and 4½ hours respectively), two to Rijeka (1 hour 40 minutes), half a dozen to Koper (1 hour 15 minutes) and almost hourly buses to Ljubljana (1 hour). Postojna's bus station (*Titova cesta 2;* \ *057 210 183;* ⊕ *06.00–14.30 Mon–Fri*) is less than five minutes' walk from Titov trg.

By train Postojna's railway station (*Kolodvorske cesta 25;* \ *052 962 100*) is less than ten minutes' walk southeast of Titov trg. There are seven trains daily to Koper (1 hour 20 minutes), two to Ljubljana (1 hour) and two to Rijeka (1 hour 45 minutes).

By car By car, Postojna is a one-hour drive from Ljubljana, one hour from the Slovenian coast, three hours from Poreč and one hour from Rijeka.

GETTING AROUND Postojna Cave is less than 1km northwest of Postojna's town centre along Jamska cesta, so you can easily walk there (less than ten minutes on foot from Titov trg, 15 minutes from the bus station). For a **taxi**, call m 031 777 974. **Predjama Castle** is 9km northwest of Postojna town centre, past Postojna Cave. A return trip by taxi with waiting time shouldn't set you back more than around €20.

TOURIST INFORMATION Kompas Postojna (*Titov trg 2a;* \ *057 211 480;* e *info@ kompas-postojna.si; www.kompas-postojna.si;* ⊕ *Apr–Oct 08.00–19.00 Mon–Fri, 09.00–13.00 Sat; Nov–Mar 08.00–18.00 Mon–Fri*), conveniently located on the main square, has maps, brochures and other information and can book accommodation and arrange tours.

WHERE TO STAY, EAT AND DRINK

🏠 **Hotel Kras** (24 dbls, 3 apts) Tržaška cesta 1; \ 057 002 300; e booking@hotel-kras.si; www. hotel-kras.si. Centrally located though somewhat faceless 4-star. **$$$**

🏠 **Restavracija and Apartmaji Proteus** (2 dbls, 1 quad, 6 apts) Titov trg; \ 052 700 0103; e sales@postojnska-jama.si; www.postojnska-jama.eu. Restavracija Proteus is conveniently located on the main square & serves good, hearty fare such as gnocchi with goulash. It also has one of those rare & most welcome things in Slovenia and Croatia: a self-service salad bar. Above the restaurant (**$$$**) are several smart, newly built rooms & apartments at reasonable prices. **$$$**

SHOPPING If it's souvenirs of Postojna Cave you're after, you'll find a plethora of official shops and kiosks around the entrance to the cave itself, as well as stalls selling local honey, liqueurs and other products. Inside Predjama Castle there's a nice little shop with wine, honey, liqueurs and other delicacies.

OTHER PRACTICALITIES

$ Bank Abanka, Titov trg 1; ⏰ 08.30–12.00 & 14.30–17.00 Mon–Fri. There are several ATMs on & around Titov trg.

➕ Pharmacy Prečna ulica 2; 📞 057 211 700; ⏰ 07.30–19.00 Mon–Fri, 07.30–13.00 Sat

📧 Internet Restavracija Proteus (see page 165) on Titov trg has fast Wi-Fi on the terrace & inside its restaurant.

✉ Post office 1 Maja 2a; ⏰ 08.00–18.00 Mon–Fri, 08.00–12.00 Sat

WHAT TO SEE AND DO On Titov trg you'll find the **Karst Research Institute** (Inštitut za raziskovanje krasa), with a sculpture of an enormous olm (see box, *The human fish*, page 168) at the bottom of the front steps, and behind Restavracija Proteus, the **Parish Church of St Stephen**. However, the main reason most visitors make their way to Postojna is to see the sublimely beautiful Postojna Cave and nearby Predjama Castle.

Postojna Cave (*Postojnska jama; Jamska cesta 30;* 📞 *057 000 100;* e *info@ postojnska-jama.eu; www.postojnska-jama.eu; for opening times & ticket prices, opposite*) Postojna Cave is an amazing place. As you walk through the cave, vast galleries open out, bristling with stalactites and stalagmites of all imaginable shapes and sizes, and ranging in colour from 'pure' milky white limestone to pink and red (the latter due to the presence of iron oxide). Some ceilings are festooned with thin, 'spaghetti' stalactites, while in other places massive columns protrude from floor and ceiling, and elsewhere 'curtain' formations extend down the walls, like some extended sheets of translucent fruit peel.

Postojnska jama was formed more than a million years ago by the underground course of the River Pivka, which disappears underground at the cave entrance and still flows through its lower sections, below the part now open to the public. The river once flowed through the upper parts of the cave, now open to the public – but as it enlarged the cracks, galleries and channels in the limestone rock by mechanical and chemical erosion, its course shifted ever deeper (see box, *Karst*, page 4, for more information on karst).

Postojna Cave is some 11km long (11,235m to be precise), and forms part of a much larger cave system with two other caves: Črna jama (Black Cave) and Pivka jama (Pivka Cave), 3,294m and 794m respectively. Together they add up to a cave system over 20.5km in length, the longest in Slovenia – at least it was thought to be, until, in August 2012, an even longer cave system was discovered beneath a mountain called Tolminski Migovec in Triglav National Park, over 24km in length.

The cave is remarkably accessible, being horizontal rather than vertical, and the whole length of Postojnska jama open to normal visits has no steps at all, just some inclines at different points and an easy, well-maintained path. Visitors are transported from the entrance into the heart of the cave system on small trains, after which the 'standard' walking route is around 1.8km. The cave remains at a constant temperature of around 9°C – so you'll probably want to wear a pullover or fleece, whatever the temperature outside. Črna jama – so called because of the black colouring of the stalagmites and stalactites, which is due to the presence of ash from a massive forest fire in the area several thousand years ago – is even cooler, at around 5°C.

Postojnska jama and Črna jama are linked by an artificial tunnel, dug secretly by the Italians during the 1930s, for strategic military purposes rather than in the name of exploration (Postojna lay on the border between Italy and the Kingdom of Yugoslavia). It is said that the Italians used workers from Sicily rather than northern Italy to dig the tunnel, so that locals would not be able to understand them or find out about the tunnel or exactly where it led. In any case the tunnel was never used by the Italians, and was later bricked up at its halfway point. However, during World War II (when Slovenia was occupied by Germany) the Partisans used the tunnel to enter Postojnska jama from Črna jama, and blow up the fuel depot established by the Germans at the main entrance to the cave (the damage from the huge explosion, combined no doubt with souvenir hunting in the early years of the cave's history, is one of the reasons there aren't many stalactites and stalagmites in the initial galleries on the train route).

Tours last approximately 90 minutes and run every 30 minutes, May/June and September 09.00–17.00, August 09.00–18.00, and approximately every two hours April and October 10.00–16.00, November–March 10.00–15.00. Entry tickets (including tour) cost €22.90 for adults, €13.70 for children. If you're planning to visit Predjama Castle as well, it's cheaper to buy an all-inclusive ticket for both.

Highly recommended is one of the **special tours** of all three caves, starting from Pivka jama, crossing to Črna jama through one of the artificial tunnels, then continuing to Postojna Cave itself through another artificial tunnel. The entrance to Pivka jama is far more atmospheric than the main entrance to Postojna Cave, involving a steep descent down steps from the forest into the cave entrance on foot, followed by a path alongside the underground course of the River Pivka, sometimes roaring, at other times magically silent, as patches of gold and silver algae glitter on the roof of the cave overhead. Note the different-coloured rock indicating the high water level on the cave walls. It's possible to walk out from Postojna Cave rather than take the train, passing through some nice galleries on the way. Other special tours are available, some much more physically challenging and requiring rubber boots and body suits (supplied), with the chance to see olms in the wild – and from 2013 there are plans to offer orienteering sessions in the caves.

Don't forget to visit the **Vivarium Proteus** (adults €8, children €4.80), beside the entrance to Postojna Cave, where you can learn more about the **olm** (see box, *The human fish*, page 168). You can also see graffiti from early visitors, mostly from the 19th century (though there's also some from as early as the 13th century elsewhere, ie: several hundred years before the cave was officially 'discovered').

Predjama Castle
Just over 8km northwest of Postojna Cave, Predjama Castle (ℂ *057 000 100;* e *info@postojnska-jama.eu; www.postojnska-jama.eu;* ⊕ *daily May/ Jun & Sep 09.00–18.00, Aug 09.00–19.00, Apr & Oct 10.00–17.00, Nov–Mar 10.00– 16.00; entry adults €9, children €5.40*) sits massive and impregnable-looking within a 123m-high cave in an overhanging cliff. Built in the 12th or 13th century, it owes much of its present form to the 16th century.

The castle's most famous (or infamous, depending on your point of view) resident was one Erazem, a 15th-century knight. Following a quarrel in which he killed a friend of the Austrian emperor Frederick III, he was besieged in his castle

THE HUMAN FISH

Postojna's most famous resident is the **olm** (*Proteus anguinus*), known in Slovenian as *človeška ribica* (*čovječja ribica* in Croatian), which translates as 'human fish'. One look at the pale, pinkish skin, the embryonic red gills and the tiny, fingered 'hands' and feet will make the comparison seem immediately appropriate. These amphibians can grow to a length of up to 30cm (large enough for locals during medieval times to believe they were baby dragons), and their geographical distribution is limited to the karst caves and subterranean rivers of Slovenia and Croatia, as well as parts of northeast Italy and Bosnia. The animal has become a popular symbol of Postojna, decorating T-shirts and fridge magnets galore, not to mention (in the form of a large sculpture) the wall of the Karst Research Institute in Postojna itself.

Please *do not* use flash to photograph these creatures. Although blind (sight not being a prerequisite for living in pitch blackness), the olm is extremely sensitive to light, and will try to swim away from bright light sources or bury itself under pebbles or small rocks. Excessive exposure to light damages its sensitive skin, which turns a reddish colour as if sunburnt, and can lead to the animal's death.

for a year, taunting his would-be captors by offering them fresh cherries while they sat miserably in the valley below, until he was betrayed (while on the toilet, to be precise) by a servant. He is said to be buried beneath the enormous linden tree by the church, which you pass just before reaching the castle by road.

A secret passage from the castle leads up to the top of the cliff, emerging through a sinkhole. Part of the cave below the castle can also be visited between May and September – at 13km long, it is the third-largest cave system in Slovenia.

Part Three

ACTIVITIES

Hiking in Istria

Istria, like much of Croatia, is covered in an extensive network of hiking trails. The five walks described here can each be done in a day, ranging from one to several hours, and from a simple stroll on the coast to a 1,400m ascent from near sea level. None requires any technical or climbing skills, though a reasonable level of fitness is advisable on the longer routes, and all are on clearly marked paths or tracks. None requires camping equipment. There is of course scope for more walks, including multi-day routes through Učka and Ćićarija (before setting out on one of these routes see the note on fire hazards on page 3).

It has to be said there is a certain allure in being able to hike through beautiful scenery and at the end of your walk find yourself back by the sea or in a medieval hill town, where you can put your feet up with a crisp glass of Malvazija and dine on freshly caught seafood or truffles. Oh, the hardship.

MAPS

The most detailed and accurate hiking maps available for Croatia are produced by **SMAND** (*www.smand.hr*), at a scale of 1:25,000 with 25m contour lines. Hiking trails, huts, springs and other features are all clearly marked. There are sheets being prepared for Učka (15) and Ćićarija (15a), though at the time of writing they were not yet available. SMAND maps are available in the UK through The Map Shop (*www.themapshop.co.uk*), and at bookshops in Croatia (you may have less luck finding them in Istria itself, so try in Rijeka or Zagreb if you're travelling through either of these cities first).

A new series of maps covers the whole of Istria in six large sheets, and these are very accurate, though hard to get. A detailed (1:30,000) map of Učka Nature Park is available from tourist information offices and bookshops in Rijeka, Opatija, Lovran, etc. Some local tourist offices have produced quite detailed maps with cycling or hiking routes marked – the Istria Bike map for Buzet, available from the tourist office in Buzet, covers the terrain for walks east of Buzet. **Pazin Tourist Office** (*www.tz-pazin.hr*) has some route maps and descriptions of walks around Pazin. You're unlikely to need a map for Rt Kamenjak, but there's one available in Premantura, though it doesn't show much detail. There are also military maps covering the whole of Croatia, but these are not usually available commercially.

For information on hiking guidebooks, see *Appendix 2*.

FOOTWEAR AND CLOTHING

Despite the balmy Istrian sunshine, the weather in the mountains can change with very little warning, and you should always carry a waterproof jacket and warm clothing when hiking on Učka and Ćićarija. Hiking in trainers or sandals is not advised in the mountains, particularly on longer routes – you are more likely to sprain your ankle than if you're wearing boots, and sandals are poor protection from snakebite – though for walking along the coast or down Rt Kamenjak, they're ideal.

TRAIL MARKINGS

Hiking trails in Istria, and Croatia as a whole, are almost always extremely well marked with an easily identifiable series of markings (*markacije*), which are maintained or repainted by local hiking clubs. A white dot surrounded by a red circle is what you'll be looking for, or a stripe or arrow (also in red and white) indicating a turn or change in direction, painted on a rock or tree trunk beside the trail. Around Buzet you may sometimes see blue and red trail markings instead, a local peculiarity – in the rest of Croatia blue trail markings would indicate a hydrological feature, but not here. Forestry markings – a series of bars with a number, stencilled or spray-painted onto a tree trunk – have nothing to do with hiking trails and should be ignored.

HUTS AND CAMPING

Although there are only a few mountain huts in Istria, it's worth knowing that mountain huts in Croatia fall into three different types. A *planinarski dom* (often abbreviated PD before the name of the hut) is the most useful, open during the summer or sometimes all year, and often (at least in the main hiking areas and national parks) staffed. There will be beds in dorms with mattresses (though you'll usually need to bring your own sleeping bag); kitchen facilities; toilets; and sometimes, showers. A *planinarska kuća* is similar but is locked, the key being available from a keyholder in a nearby town, so is much less useful. Most of those in Istria are of this type. A *sklonište* is a small, basic, unstaffed shelter, usually open all year.

WATER

Istria is karst country (see box, page 4), and as such most rainwater disappears rapidly into the ground, with streams and even freshwater springs likely to dry up by the middle of the summer. This means that you generally need to carry sufficient drinking water to last for an entire walk (or day, on a multi-stage walk).

1 LOVRAN TO VOJAK (UČKA)

A long but rewarding hike, beginning just above sea level in the small town of Lovran, and climbing to the highest point of Učka, known as Vojak or sometimes Vrh Učka. Almost 1,400m of ascent on clearly marked trails, mostly through forest and sometimes open meadows, are rewarded by spectacular views from the summit, over the Adriatic and the islands of the Kvarner Gulf, and far across the undulating hills of the Istrian interior. Plenty of people drive up to the top of Učka from Rijeka and Opatija, but the path from Lovran is by far the nicest way to approach this mountain, with the road and the huge telecommunications tower just below the summit remaining completely hidden until the final moment. A bus runs between Rijeka and Poklon dom, the mountain hut on the saddle below Vojak, also stopping in Opatija – but it only runs on Sundays (bus #34, departs Opatija at 09.30 and 14.05, departs Poklon dom at 10.30 and 15.45).

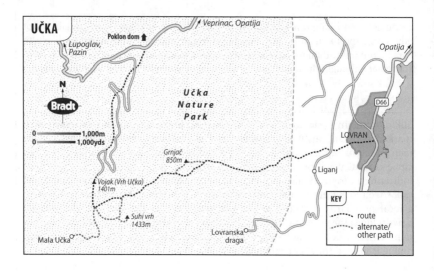

Start/finish points	Lovran (Trg Slobode); see *Chapter 6*, page 105.
Distance	8km
Grade	Medium–hard
Approximate time	4½ hours (ascent only; if you're hiking back down to Lovran allow an additional 2½ hours)
Highest altitude	1,401m
Lowest altitude	5m
Total height climbed	1,400m
Map	Učka park prirode (available at tourist information offices and bookshops in Rijeka, Opatija, Lovran, etc); SMAND Učka (15)
Eating and drinking	Lovran
Best season	Spring, summer or autumn
Water	None between Lovran and Poklon dom (40 minutes from Vojak, and not guaranteed)
Further information	www.pp-ucka.hr

From Lovran's Trg Slobode, walk to the junction and the beginning of the trail markings. Turn right, passing a small votive shrine then following the road around to the left. From here a series of several flights of steep, walled steps lead up past the houses of **Liganj** to a junction, about an hour from Lovran. Keep straight ahead following the signs to Vojak and Grnjac, first on a rocky path and (briefly) a sealed road, then a rocky trail again and a forest track. After crossing a low ridge, the path follows the side of a valley, with wonderful views out over steep pine slopes to the sea from occasional clearings and rock outcrops.

After passing trails to Grnjac, the village of Mala Učka and Lovranska Draga, you reach a series of three clearings with low trees, wild roses and nettles, from where you get a brief glimpse of the red-and-white antenna on Vojak, and pass a small hunting lodge on the left. After the third clearing the path ascends through the trees on a brutally steep set of switchbacks, and passes a trail to **Suhi vrh** ('dry peak'; 1,332m) on the left. If you want some additional exercise (and some super views) you can hike over Suhi vrh as a detour and rejoin the main route later; otherwise keep straight ahead, crossing the forest road twice to emerge on an open saddle (where a path from Suhi vrh meets the main trail from your left), with the imposing limestone bulk of Vojak towering on your right. A final, steep ascent leads to the summit of **Vojak** (1,401m) with its stone lookout tower and spectacular views in all directions.

On a clear day you can clearly see the mountains of Gorski kotar to the northeast, and the islands of Cres, Lošinj and Krk to the southeast, with the Velebit Mountains beyond, and the rolling Istrian interior to the west, dotted with medieval hill towns. Keep an eye out for paragliders to the northwest – the slopes of Ćićarija are one of the best paragliding spots in Croatia.

If you're meeting a car rather than returning on foot, the car park and road are a short distance away, past the huge telecommunications tower. If you're planning to return by bus, you'll need to descend from the car park on a clearly marked path, crossing the road at several points, to the **bus stop** by the old mountain hut, **Poklon dom** (meant to be open at weekends, but often closed). Otherwise, the hike from Vojak back down to **Lovran**, following the same route as the ascent, requires around 2½ hours.

2 RASPADALICA AND KUK

Start/finish points	Buzet (Mala Vrata)
Distance	9km
Grade	Medium
Approximate time	3 hours
Highest altitude	556m
Lowest altitude	210m
Total height climbed	420m
Map	Istria Bike (Buzet)
Eating and drinking	Buzet (see *Chapter 7*, page 129)
Best season	Spring, summer or autumn; the Istria Open Paragliding Championship at Raspadalica takes place during July; winter is also possible for those suitably dressed, when there will be snow on Raspadalica
Water	None after Buzet
Further information	If you want to go with a guide or extend this into a longer walk on Ćićarija, contact Gral-Putovanja (*www.gral-putovanja.eu*)

A short but fairly steep walk from the gates of Buzet's old town, mostly on paths and tracks through forest, to the rocky outcrops of Raspadalica and Kuk, from where you are rewarded with stupendous views back over the old town, the Mirna Valley and Butoniga jezero. The route involves crossing the tracks of the railway line at two points – caution required. Can be extended considerably by continuing from Raspadalica to Gomila (1,029m), one of the many knobbly peaks that make up the Ćićarija Mountains, a route which entails over 600m of additional ascent, making it a very long day from Buzet.

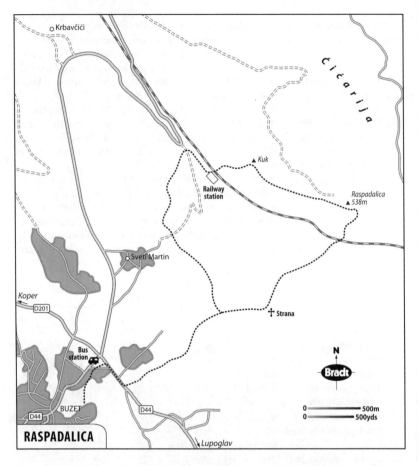

From Mala Vrata in Buzet's old town, follow the unsealed track down to the **bus station**. Turn right on the main road towards Rijeka, then just after the petrol station (there's a sign reading 'Put Raspadalica' on the opposite side of the road, though it's in the wrong place), but before the bridge, turn left onto a faint, unmarked path beside the stream bed. Turn right onto a minor road, where you pick up clear trail markings. Follow the road uphill then take a marked footpath on your left, through typical Istrian forest. On reaching a T-junction turn left, then at a broad track turn right, passing a small **votive shrine**. Walk past the farm and church at **Strana**, until around one hour from the bus station you reach the **railway line**. Cross with care, then continue uphill until emerging from the trees at **Raspadalica** (556m), with superb views.

Raspadalica is the launching point for Croatia's biggest **paragliding championship** in July (*www.buzet.tici.hr*), and there's also a nice **campsite** up here, a world away from the sprawling campervan-filled campsites of the coast (see *Chapter 7*, page 131).

Follow the top of the ridge to **Kuk**, before descending and crossing the **railway line** once more near the railway station, and descending past **Sv Martin** to rejoin the route of ascent near the small shrine mentioned above.

Start/finish points	Pazin Castle
Distance	1.5km
Grade	Easy
Approximate time	45 minutes
Highest altitude	361m
Lowest altitude	230m
Total height climbed	130m
Map	Available from Pazin Tourist Office
Eating and drinking	Pazin (see *Pazin*, page 117)
Best season	Spring, summer or autumn, but not after heavy rain
Fees	Adults 30kn, children 15kn; free Mondays and during winter; ticket office at the Vršić Bridge
Further information	www.pazinska-jama.com

A short, easy walk from Pazin Castle, down into the forested gorge of the 'Pazin Abyss' before ascending again to the terrace restaurant of Hotel Lovac, from where there are superlative views back over the gorge to the castle. The gorge may become flooded after heavy rain, in which case the route will be impassable and should not be attempted. It's possible to enter and explore the cave, but only with a permit and a guide – ask at the tourist information office.

From the entrance to the castle, walk down Valvasorova ulica to the **Vršić Bridge**, and turn left onto the marked footpath down into the gorge. Descend quite steeply to the **Pazinčica**, which you cross on a small footbridge, then ascend on the other side, following a series of broad switchbacks. The entrance to the cave, as well as the cliff down which the hero descends into the gorge in Jules Verne's novel *Mathius Sandorf*, is clearly visible. Entering the cave itself without a permit and guide is strictly prohibited (not to mention potentially dangerous), as is leaving the main path and wandering off along the Pazinčica. It is thought that the gorge may have provided inspiration for the entrance to Hell in *Dante's Inferno* (Dante is known to have visited Pazin). At the end of the path you reach a grassy terrace in front of the **Hotel Lovac**, where you can enjoy a drink, or a meal, while admiring the view back over the gorge, with Učka rising behind the castle in the distance.

Walk back along the road from in front of Hotel Lovac to the Vršić Bridge and Pazin Castle. Alternatively, if you're game, you can cross the gorge back to the castle by flying fox (or 'zip line' as it's usually referred to here), which reduces your journey to six seconds!

4 PAZIN WATERFALLS

An easy walk along the valley of the Pazinčica, where it flows above ground before vanishing into the cliff below Pazin Castle, visiting two large waterfalls and passing the sites of several old mills. The river (and waterfalls) will be less impressive in mid- to late summer, and may even have completely dried up after an extended period of drought such as the one preceding my visit in September 2012. Woodland and riverside paths and unsealed road. This route would also make a nice bike ride, in which case it would be better to ride there and back on the north (right) bank of

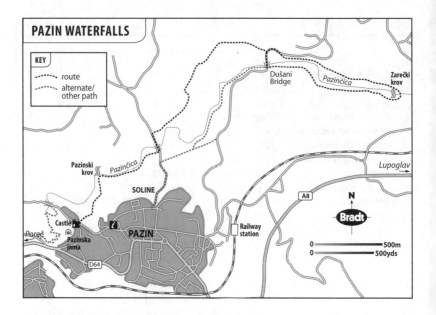

PAZIN WATERFALLS

KEY
······· route
······· alternate/
        other path

Dušani Bridge
Pazinčica
Zarečki krov

Pazinski krov
Pazinčica

Lupoglav

SOLINE

A8

N

Bradt

Poreč
Castle
Pazinska jama
PAZIN

Railway station

D64

0 ———————— 500m
0 ———————— 500yds

Start/finish points	Pazin Tourist Information Office
Distance	7km
Grade	Very easy
Approximate time	1 hour 45 minutes
Highest altitude	361m
Lowest altitude	240m
Total height climbed	130m
Map	Available from Pazin Tourist Office
Eating and drinking	Pazin (see *Chapter 7*, page 117)
Best season	Spring or early summer, when the river is most likely to be full
Further information	www.tz-pazin.hr

the river, rather than returning along its southern side. In any case confirm at the tourist information office how high the river level is; if you can't cross the river near Zarečki krov, just return along the north bank (or follow the south bank from the Dušani Bridge to Zarečki krov).

From the tourist office walk towards the castle, then just before reaching it follow a track down to the right, veer right passing a ruined stone house on your left and walk under the pylons. Turn left on a clear path, which brings you to the river at the first large waterfall, **Pazinski krov**. There were once four watermills here. Follow the path alongside or close to the river then up to the road, and turn left over the bridge, built at the beginning of the 19th century, and nearly washed away by floods in 1993. Turn right after the first house onto an unsealed road, and keep right where this forks. Follow the road round the back of some farm buildings, until arriving at the sealed road at the **Dušani Bridge** (Most Dušani). Follow the road uphill to the left, then turn right onto a rocky terrace overlooking the river valley (where there's a prominent bit of graffiti carved into the rock). Follow this rocky terrace parallel to the river, then about 50 minutes from Pazin you reach a broad, open area of rock and **Zarečki krov**, a large waterfall which spills over a rock shelf into a pool below.

Zarečki krov is a favourite picnic area (which unfortunately means it's not as clean as it might be) and people come here to swim in the pool below the waterfall. There are some climbing routes here as well, including the roof of the cavern beneath the falls.

To return to Pazin, follow a rocky path through woodland on the south (left) bank of the Pazinčica, until reaching the road at Most Dušani again. Though there's a faint and sometimes overgrown path ahead on the other side of the road, you might instead want to just cross the bridge and return to Pazin the way you came. (You would have to leave the path ahead after about 15 minutes anyway – there's a section on private land which is very poorly kept, including two wooden bridges which feel as though they're about to collapse under you – and turn left onto a road which would lead you to **Soline**, from where you would turn left uphill to arrive in Pazin near the stadium.)

5 RT KAMENJAK

Start/finish points	Premantura
Distance	6.5km
Grade	Very easy
Approximate time	2½ hours
Highest altitude	20m
Lowest altitude	0m
Total height climbed	30m
Map	Available from the Javna Ustanova Kamenjak office in Premantura, or Medulin Tourist Office
Eating and drinking	Premantura (see page 66)
Best season	Late spring/early summer (in particular June, when Rt Kamenjak will be awash with wildflowers and butterflies, and the sun won't roast you, as there's very little in the way of shade)
Further information	www.kamenjak.hr

The route, such as there is one, simply involves walking south from the centre of Premantura and following any one of several unsealed roads and tracks down the peninsula to Mala Kolombarica, near its southern tip, and back – and is also popular as a bike ride. There is plenty of scope for exploring the various coves which indent the peninsula's coastline – in which case you'll obviously need to allow more time – or stopping for a swim (though the currents here are very strong, particularly around the southern end of the peninsula, so don't swim out too far, and don't let young kids swim by themselves), and there's a small café/bar at Mala Kolombarica (Safari Bar). Keep an eye out for orchids (of which at least 28 species have been recorded, among the 590-odd plant taxa which have been found on the peninsula), butterflies, and birds such as sparrowhawk, scops owl and a subspecies of the pallid swift. It's worth noting that the black widow spider

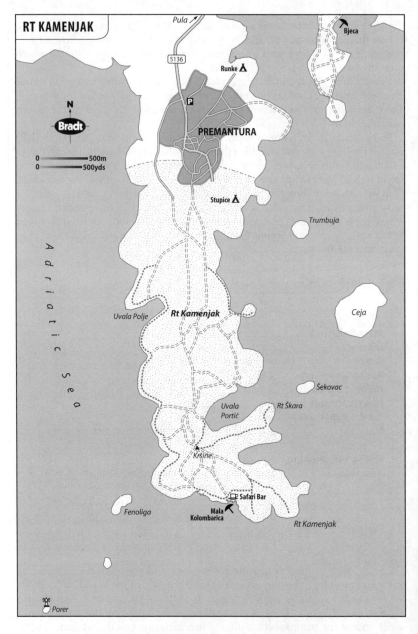

RT KAMENJAK

Pula

5136

Bjeca

Runke ⛺

🅿

PREMANTURA

N

Bradt

0 ————— 500m
0 ————— 500yds

Stupice ⛺

Trumbuja

Adriatic Sea

Uvala Polje

Rt Kamenjak

Ceja

Šekovac

Uvala
Portić

Rt Škara

Krsine

Fenoliga

Safari Bar

Mala
Kolombarica

Rt Kamenjak

Porer

has also been recorded on Kamenjak. Optimists can keep their eyes peeled for the endangered Mediterranean monk seal – the only sighting of which in Croatian waters in the last ten years was off Rt Kamenjak.

Biking in Istria

Istria in spring and autumn is a very popular destination for biking, especially road cycling, but also off-road. During these seasons the temperature is sunny, mostly dry, not too hot, and the roads are blissfully empty. Cyclists frequently visit as organised groups, sometimes by the busload, often as early as February and as late as November.

BIKE RENTAL, SERVICE AND PARTS

Many people bring their own bikes, but they can also be rented in Istria: see individual chapters under *Getting around, By bike*, for where to hire bikes and also where to get them repaired or buy spare parts.

If your bike is due for a service, you would do well to book a session with **Bikepoint** in Poreč (see *Other practicalities*, page 92), where multi-lingual Aldo and his son will give you excellent service at a very reasonable price. You'll need to book ahead in the summer though. Basic bike parts (repair kits, inner tubes, tyres, bells, helmets, etc) are available very cheaply at **Kaufland** in Poreč and at **Pevec** (*www.pevec.hr/prodajni-centri/prodajni-centar-pula-277*) in Pula. Most bicycle rental places will be able to provide you with a local map and suggestions for routes according to your ability.

ROUTES AND MAPS

Istria has a range of well-developed bike routes. Of the many marked routes, both on and off-road, 43 of them can be found online (*www.istria-bike.com*), where maps, GPS files and route cards can be found for each route as well as useful information on local accommodation, service areas and biking competitions and organised days out.

Six bike maps covering Istria at 1:30,000 scale can be purchased in most shops and kiosks. Poreč tourist offices also have a free biking map available showing 14 routes in a 25km² area, and includes basic route cards. The map can be downloaded for free, but few will have printers at home big enough to print an A2-size sheet. Nonetheless, if you would like to have an idea of what it contains to select a route in advance, it can be found at http://www.to-porec.com/sadrzaj/katalog/58748/IB_Porec-Vrsar-Funtana.pdf.

To give you a flavour of the cycling available in Istria we present four routes for you here. These cover the very best of the Parenzana old railway trail and three circular routes. Each of the circular routes starts and finishes in Poreč, but could of course be picked up anywhere along the way. For more on the Parenzana old railway route see *Chapter 7, Parenzana*, page 128.

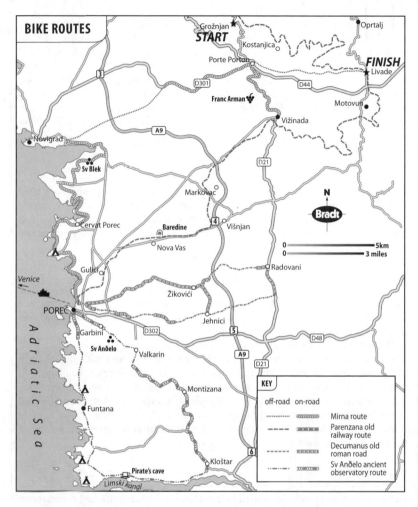

1 GROŽNJAN TO LIVADE ON THE PARENZANA

Distance	20km
Grade	Easy
Approximate time	2 hours
Highest altitude	290m
Lowest altitude	13m
Total height climbed	<10m
Eating and drinking	Grožnjan (see page 127), Livade (see page 125)
Viewpoints	Završje, Antonci and Freski viaducts
Public tour day	Mid-December
Repairs	Bikepoint in Poreč

ROUTE DESCRIPTION This is a wonderful route along one of the most interesting stretches of the Parenzana (see box on page 128), starting near one of the highest points on the entire route and finishing at the small Parenzana Museum in Livade, crossing three viaducts and passing through four tunnels on the way.

Apart from a very short climb near the start, the route is downhill the whole way, following an easy gradient as you cruise across open terraces, through forest and over viaducts, with fantastic views over the Mirna Valley and the air redolent with the scent of pines. This is possibly the most enjoyable bike ride I've ever done. As in the previous route, the Parenzana is very well marked, so route finding is not an issue. Note that you'll need a lamp or headtorch for the longer tunnels, which are not lit.

See www.parenzana.com and www.parenzana.net for more details.

Startpoint Grožnjan (see page 127). From the car park and terrace beside the walls of Grožnjan, head downhill and onto the unsealed road leading towards Motovun. A short climb to the left takes you under a bridge before turning right and cruising blissfully downhill with the wind in your hair. There are splendid views of the Mirna Valley, and back towards Grožnjan, from a raised viewing platform and then from broad terraces near Biloslava. You soon pass under a bridge and reach the first of the tunnels, Kostanjica, 70m long and dim, though not completely dark, at its midpoint. Further along you gain good views of Motovun, with Učka clearly visible in the distance, before the square bell tower and houses of Završje appear above the trees ahead.

After crossing an unsealed road you reach Završje station, most traces of which are now hidden by the less-than-attractive ruined building now standing where the station once was. Olives and other crops were once loaded at Završje, as well as cattle hides for the manufacture of footwear.

Two short tunnels follow: Završje I and II, followed by the Završje Viaduct, 62m in length and 20m high. After this you cross the Antonci Viaduct, 80m long and 25m high; enhanced views can be gained from the bridge (from which a trail leads to Zabrdo) just before it, and there's a rest point and picnic table nearby. This is followed by the Freski viaduct and tunnel, the latter 146m long and pitch black inside – the gravel and rocks can be on the large side in places, and keeping to the side might help reduce the risk of punctures.

Oprtalj station comes next, near the settlement of Grimaldi (the village of Oprtalj itself is a further 3km away up a clear track; see *Chapter 7*, page 126). Nothing of the station remains except a grassy terrace, though it originally had a shed and small warehouse. The Parenzana continues downhill through forest and over the Oprtalj Viaduct, then emerges among open fields and terraces before cruising into Livade to arrive at the Parenzana Museum on the opposite side of the road.

Endpoint The Parenzana Museum (Muzej Parenzana; see *Chapter 7, What to see and do*, page 157) in Livade has a small collection of documents and other objects from the period in which the Parenzana operated, between 1902 and 1935. Near the crossroads and the road south towards Motovun, the buildings of Livade station are some of the better preserved on the entire route of the Parenzana, and date from 1908 – slightly later than most of the other stations on the route. There's a *konoba* to the right between the museum and the crossroads, where you can sit under a quiet, elder-covered terrace and enjoy an ice-cold glass of Favorit.

2 COAST TO THE MIRNA RIVER AND THE PARENZANA

Distance	53km
Grade	Medium
Approximate time	4 hours
Highest altitude	326m
Lowest altitude	7m
Total height climbed	452m
Eating and drinking	Ponte Porton, Vižinada (see page 129)
Viewpoints	Antenal, St Tomo, and Veli Most Viaduct on the alternate longer route
Public tour day	Third weekend in September, and mid-December for the longer Parenzana tour, and a shorter tour of Buje, Tinjan and Motovun
Repairs	Bikepoint in Poreč

ROUTE DESCRIPTION This route is rewarding for combining a variety of what Istria has to offer: some gentle asphalt and tracks partly along the shore and through the once-walled village of Červar Porat; some riverside pathways; a short(ish) section of steep winding uphill (or down in the reverse); and 26km of the old Parenzana railway route (a further 14km for the longer route). Whilst it would be more relaxing to do it in the reverse, until the Parenzana is sufficiently well marked to be easy to find in Poreč, it remains easier to pick it up inland.

Startpoint The old railway station. These old buildings are not marked as the old railway station, but are sufficiently different in style of stone and construction that they give away their 19th-century Italian origins (distinctive on satellite imagery for their grey slate roofs rather than the usual Istrian burnt sienna tiles. Now partially in disuse, partially a bus garage, a plant nursery and a dwelling, these buildings stretch out along the northern edge of the shore. From here keep left at the wide crossroads and follow the old coastal road – which is cut off to main traffic during the summer – past the popular resorts of Pical and Materada to the old walled village of Črvar. Skirting Červar Porat and Autocamp Lanterna, keep on the high road past the old ruins of Sv Blek to join the beautiful coastal road to the mouth of the River Mirna (19km).

From the mouth of the Mirna, below the old lighthouse, head inland on the stone track for the gentle ride along the Mirna until Ponte Porton (14km). Here you can take a longer additional route (see next paragraph) or head south on the asphalt main road, climbing 303m to Vižinada (4km). Stop here for a rewarding lunch after the steep climb. From Vižinada, locate the well-signposted Parenzana route south of the town, which will take you the remaining 26km on a gravel track back to Poreč.

Tip: If you don't fancy the full 14km additional route, I strongly recommend the 3km detour from Vižinada to Veli Most and back, to see this spectacular viaduct of early 19th-century engineering. Don't forget your camera for this one.

Additional route At Ponte Portun, a 14km detour can be taken by keeping to the dirt track 500m north of the River Mirna to Livade. Here you might want to stop at the Parenzana Museum (see *What to see and do*, page 157) or at the most famous **truffle restaurant** in all Istria, Zigante (see box, *Tartufi*, page 38). Heading south from Livade on the asphalt road, you will in fact have picked up the Parenzana rail route. Immediately after crossing the River Mirna again, head southeast (left) to continue on the Parenzana all the way around Motovun, where you might also want to stop for a break (see page 123). The Parenzana snakes its way through the countryside at a relatively level height, passing over Veli Most until it reaches Vižinada, and continues on a straighter route to Poreč.

Endpoint The Parenzana ends rather sadly at the back of Stancija Vrgotin 8, at which point you'll rejoin the asphalt road behind the business park and onto the supermarket road. This will take you down to the main car park in town not far from the old railway station.

3 DECUMANUS MAXIMUS AGRI

Distance	37km (12km asphalt, 22km off-road 4x4 mud)
Grade	Hard
Approximate time	2 hours
Highest altitude	281m
Lowest altitude	16m
Total height climbed	400m
Eating and drinking	Hotel Filipini (see *Where to stay*, page 90), Monte Izzoli (see page 184)
Viewpoints	Monte Izzoli in Vrhjani
Public tour day	None
Repairs	Bikepoint in Poreč

ROUTE DESCRIPTION The Decumanus Maximus Agri was the main east–west Roman road going through the Parentium encampment and leading out to the countryside. It is now a disused 4x4 track consisting of mostly mud, so avoid it after heavy rain unless you're prepared for this. Being mostly under shady trees, the track can retain large puddles even after several days of sun. A circular route combines the southern end of the Staža Sv Maura (Route 142) and part of Zvejždana Staža (Route 131), but the circular route can also be shortened by taking a north–south asphalt road between Bačva and Ženodraga. As the link between the Decumanus in the old town and how it continues towards Vrvari is obscured by new buildings, it is easier to take Route 142 first and then pick up the Maximus Agri at the far end.

Startpoint The roundabout at Konzum supermarket. From here head west past all the supermarkets and continue straight through the two roundabouts past Stancija Portun towards Kosinožići and Žikovići. At Žikovići, a short cut can be taken south towards Pršurići and Jehnići, where you can join the obvious 4x4 track of the Maximus Agri. Although it is not signposted as Route 141, there is a sign for those coming off the Maximus Agri pointing the way to Route 143, the Eufraziana. This short cut shaves some 17km off the longer route.

To continue on the longer route, the asphalt road takes you less than 1km past Žikovići and then becomes off-road track. The route continues over the highway and then to Bačva, where you can pick up Route 143 south to Jehnići, or continue northeast on Route 131, the Zvjezdana Staža, through Radovani towards Vrhjani. Here you can stop at the Monte Izzoli for lunch or dinner. Two kilometres of asphalt road south takes you to the start of the Maximus Agri, heading 17.5km west back to Poreč. For those needing a stop on the way back, the Hotel Filipini offers excellent food in a shady atmosphere less than 1km off the Maximus Agri. The Maximus Agri returns to asphalt at the eastern end of Vrvari. Rather than join the busy main road here, head north past the abandoned old school building and take the back road into Poreč.

Endpoint At the back of the commercial zone behind Lidl supermarket.

4 MALI SV ANGELO OBSERVATORY TO THE LIMSKI KANAL

Distance	46km
Grade	Medium
Approximate time	3 hours
Highest altitude	150m
Lowest altitude	3m
Total height climbed	210m
Eating and drinking	Konoba Gradina (see *South to Limski kanal*, page 99), Bistro Aerodrom (Vrsar; see opposite)
Viewpoints	Mali Sv Andjelo observatory, Montižani
Public tour day	None
Repairs	Bikepoint in Poreč

ROUTE DESCRIPTION This route takes you past a little-known ancient observatory (Mali Sv Andjelo), the tiny winery at Braljići, the monastery village of Kloštar (sadly the monastery is long gone; see box, *Limski kanal*, page 96), and along the dirt track of the tree-shaded clifftop of the Limski kanal to Vrsar airfield. Thereafter the route lies just inland of the coast back up to Poreč.

Startpoint The car park south of Poreč next to the cemetery. Take the asphalt road east to Garbina, after which it turns to gravel. At 1km past the end of the tarmac, just after the woods start, stop and look carefully 50m in from the start of the woods for an obvious opening on the south side of the gravel track for a single-lane path up the hill. This is the path up to Sv Mali Andželo, which is best taken by foot. The gravel track continues to Valkarin and then heads south to join the asphalt road past Starići. At the T-junction turn left up through Dračevac and straight on up to Montižani. (Just before the steep hill up to Montižani is a track on left at an old concrete water bowser hangar. This track leads after 150m to a *boškarin* farm, if you're interested to see these native Istrian cows.)

After the highpoint of Montižani at 150m above sea level the route sails downhill. At the little village of Braljići is a small local winery, where you can drop in to pick up some local wine. On joining the main road, turn left at the T-junction, and keeping south you'll pass the Konoba Gradina, where you can stop for pig roast or fish lunch. At Kloštar turn west and follow the asphalt road into the woods. This joins the dirt track of the signposted Bike Route 171. Take the southern track to keep closest to the cliffside with a glimpse of the gorge through the trees, and to get to the head of the footpath down to the Pirate's Cave and Bar just up from the water. Further on, the track runs along the southern end of Vrsar airfield, where you can also stop for good pizza at Bistro Aerodrom (✆ *052 441 810;* ⊕ *09.00–18.00 daily*).

Continue west along Route 171 and past Kapetanova Stancija to avoid the busy main road into Vrsar (see page 99) in the summer. Between Vrsar and Funtana the bike route runs a few metres in from the main road through the trees, and after Funtana it joins the coast, then over the hill to Zelena Laguna. From here it is the coastal path all the way into Porec, where the traffic is pedestrian, bicycle or electric tourist train.

Endpoint After popping out at Poreč Marina, continue a few metres to the roundabout and turn right. Follow this road uphill for 250m till you get back to the southern car park.

12

Diving in Istria

Like any seaside, the beach and its activities are only half of the picture. Under the water is an entire world, which is teeming with life, screening forgotten stories, and begging our assistance (to survive our excesses). The inherent difficulties of diving (limited air, visibility and warmth) tend to make us more aware of our reliance on the ecosystem we must preserve to survive on this planet. Istria is a good place to explore and learn to respect the relationship between those limits and the freedoms that the sea can offer (weightlessness, omni-directional movement, calm). This is because Adriatic waters are warm enough and calm enough, with little significant tidal difference, to make it a good introduction to diving, yet without it being as oblivious to the limitations that make diving in the tropics seem almost too easy.

Istria's accessibility from western Europe, and particularly for landlocked Austrians and Swiss, makes it a popular destination not only for sunbathing but also for diving. As a result it's well served by diving centres, and even **underwater cultural events**! Its inviting warm Adriatic waters hold a diverse range of wildlife and sites, which have not yet suffered total divers' bleach, especially for the Mediterranean. In addition, Istria has the second-greatest abundance of wrecks for diving (Vis near Split has the most), most dating from World Wars I and II, including two of Croatia's top-three largest **shipwrecks**.

Water temperatures average 21–29°C at the surface in the summer, and 7–10°C in the winter. At 20–30m the water temperature remains a constant 16–19°C from the summer until the end of the diving season in November. Visibility is best in spring, autumn and winter, when summer plankton and spawning algae clouds are completely absent. The range of underwater flora and fauna (including bottlenose dolphins, sea horses and turtles) is immense and unique, as discussed later in this chapter).

This chapter highlights the information you should be aware of if you are considering diving for the first time in Istria. It also lists **eight of the best dive sites** around the peninsula, most of which are accessible to recently qualified open-water certified divers, and a few sites requiring more advanced skills for you to aim towards improving your diving.

PLANNING THE DIVE

DIVE COSTS AND PACKAGES Diving costs with a dive centre range from as little as 50kn for a beach dive to 150kn for a boat dive, and up to 350kn for a wreck dive. A dive guide will be an extra 75kn and an accompanying instructor up to 350kn extra. Many places will do packages, such as a discount for two dives in a day, or up to ten dives in a week, sometimes with limitless shore dives.

All the dive centres offer diving courses at most levels, usually in PADI (Professional Association of Diving Instructors) or with SSI (Scuba Schools International) and sometimes with CMAS (Confédération Mondiale des Activités Subaquatique) or VDST (Verband Deutsche Sport Taucher). BSAC (British Sub-Aqua Club) instruction and certification is not yet available in Istria. Again prices vary, so it is worth comparing websites for up-to-date prices: a Discover Scuba afternoon comes to around 450kn, whilst a PADI Open Water Diver (OWD) course is around 3,500kn. Some centres also offer wreck-diving speciality courses for around 2,000kn.

RULES AND REGULATIONS As with elsewhere around the world, diving in Croatian waters is regulated by several laws. These are overseen by the **Croatian Diving Federation** (Hrvatski Ronilački Savez; *www.diving-hrs.hr*), which grants diving concessions to qualified centres, clubs and individuals. Qualified individuals wanting to dive independently of the dive centres and of local clubs must apply for a concession via the local harbour master (see *Sailing*, page 44, for the contact details for some of the main harbours).

Wreck-salvage laws in Croatia are very strict and very simple: nothing may be removed from a wreck. All battlefield casualty wrecks in Croatian waters are war graves, and thus also deemed cultural monuments. Diving to most Croatian wrecks therefore also requires a special permit, which usually costs €10 and is organised by the local dive centre that has permission to take divers there. Not every dive centre is allowed to go to every wreck.

Wildlife and natural habitat are also protected. It is illegal to even swim in the Limski kanal (diving is permitted at the mouth of the kanal only) and a permit is required to dive around the Brijuni Islands. Those dive centres which have permission and permits to dive the various restricted sites are listed in the following dives in this chapter.

EQUIPMENT All diving centres will have the basic equipment that you find in most dive centres around the world, and in Croatia they tend to be in good condition. Female wet suits are increasingly common, but female BCDs (buoyancy control devices) are rare, as are BCDs with integrated weight systems. Even in the summer, diving is usually done in a 5mm full wet suit, with boots and strap fins. Only some centres have Nitrox.

For those bringing their own equipment, note that it is difficult to get your equipment serviced in Istria. Most dive centres will not do this, especially in the height of the summer, and at the time of writing there is nowhere to buy dive gear in Istria proper (as opposed to snorkelling gear which is ubiquitous). This arrangement is likely to change once Croatia is in the European Union. Several dive shops are within an hour's drive.

🤿 **Oceanik** Polje 21, 6310 Izola, Slovenia; 📞+386 56 401 100; m Mojca: +386 40 367 377, David +386 41 854 118; e info@oceanik-trgovina. si; www.oceanik-trgovina.si; ⏱ 12.00–17.00 Mon–Fri. Nice little shop with a bit of everything on the east outside of Izola opposite the sea. Sadly their website is only in Slovenian.
🤿 **Pop** Valmade 58, 52100 Pula, Croatia; 📞+385 52 214 185; e pop@cressi-sub.hr; www.cressi-sub.

hr; ⏱ 10.00–17.00 Mon–Fri. Distributor for Cressi, but does not service gear. Also has a small shop on Ciscuttijeva 9 around the back of Pula's old town. Pop's English website is often several months out of date behind the Croatian version.
🤿 **Ronilački Konzalting** Šetalište XIII, divizija 28, 51000 Rijeka, Croatia; 📞+385 51 432 600; e divecon@divecon.hr; www.divecon.hr; ⏱ 10.00–17.00 Mon–Sat. Distributor for

The Adriatic is a rich, fascinating and unique body of seawater. It is unique largely because no more than 4% of the water-flow of the northern Adriatic around the Istrian Peninsula escapes into the southern Adriatic (beyond Dubrovnik). Over 75% of the Adriatic's water-flow, which is anticlockwise, recycles around at Split. On its way around, the water-flow picks up more polluted waters from the eastern Adriatic coast and organic matter from the main Mediterranean basin and mineralises it through a system of combination with the clean karst-rock waters from Croatian rivers.

As a result of all this, the Adriatic is home to over 70% of all the fish species to be found in the whole Mediterranean, and over 30 of these are found only in the eastern Adriatic due to the karst rock formations of the region and their abundance of fresh spring water. Seven species of fish found in the Adriatic are endemic (ie: found nowhere else in the world). Sadly, however, overfishing in the last 50 years threatens the extinction of 64 fish species found in the Adriatic (see the table on pages 6–7 to learn about which ones not to buy for dinner).

COMMON SIGHTINGS Crabs, moray eels, goby, cleaner shrimp, and lobsters are very common. Others include:

Alcyonacea – soft corals, particularly **gorgonian sea fans** and sea whips, are common in waters with higher nutrient value (and therefore lower visibility) where they filter-feed off plankton as well as through some photosynthesis in a symbiotic relationship with algae. A large gorgonian colony can be over 1m high and wide, but only some 10cm thick. They will be oriented across the current to maximise access to food. Those unable to photosynthesise are more brightly coloured.

Chromis chromis – juvenile **damselfish** are deep lightning blue in colour and only 2–3cm in length. Shoals of 20 or 30 are common at 3–4m. Adults are dark brown or black.

Conger conger – the European conger eel, like the moray eel family, is found in cracks and crevices. European congers are grey, whilst moray species tend to be more colourful. Neither species is poisonous or dangerous unless provoked (although, if eaten, the flesh of morays eaten can be poisonous if the moray itself has eaten something else poisonous). The European conger can grow up to 3m in length (morays up to 4m).

Hermodice carunculata – **bearded fireworms** grow up to 15cm long and, if touched, are **poisonous**, causing sharp irritation where bristles enter the skin, and dizziness and nausea in severe cases. Bristles are sometimes successfully extracted using sticking plaster, and the irritation can be relieved by applying neat alcohol or white spirit.

Nudibranchia – these amazing tiny **shell-less molluscs**, often only 1cm long, are abundant for those with the patience to see them. A torch helps in order to highlight their colours in lower visibility. *Flabellina affinis* (fuchsia pink) and *Janolus christatus* (electric blue) are especially common.

PROTECTED FLORA AND FAUNA

Aphanius fasciatus – the Mediterranean **killifish**, also known as the south European toothcarp, is a locally protected species, which is more abundant elsewhere in the Mediterranean. It is becoming rare in Croatia due to the destruction of its preferred lagoon habitat.

Asteroides callycularis – orange **stony coral** are best seen on a night dive when their colours show up brightly in a torch's rays and when these primitive animals feed on the likes of tiny brine shrimp.

Caretta caretta – the **loggerhead turtle** is an extremely rare sight along the built-up and shallow shores of the northern Adriatic, but the clean waters of the eastern Adriatic are their preferred choice.

Gerardia savaglia – sometimes better known as 'black' **tree-coral**, this fast-growing branchy primitive animal is beige-yellow when alive and leaves behind a brown-black skeleton. Found below 15m depth and as low as 120m, it is has been a popular souvenir leading to its destruction.

Hippocampus ramulosus – the long-snouted **sea horse**, like all sea horses, is a protected species. They are particularly vulnerable because of their commercial value in traditional Chinese medicine (to counter weak constitution in children, adult male impotence, and bed-wetting!), and for aquariums, for which over 25 million are caught wild every year. Slow moving because of their tiny fins, they are very shy and tend to hide in sea grass, which they cling to with their tails to prevent being swept off by sea currents. Sea horses have been seen at Lanterna dive site near Novigrad, and Karbula near Poreč. They can grow up to 15cm in length.

Ophidiaster ophidianus – the long-armed **purple starfish** grows to 15–40cm in length. Usually found below depths of 5m, they can sometimes appear red or orange

Pinna nobilis – this is the largest **bivalve mollusc** in the Mediterranean, and can grow up to 1m in height. Great care should be taken not to touch it.

Posidonia oceanica – **Neptune grass** is endemic to the Mediterranean and only grows in very clean waters. It is thus of course on the decline. It tends to grow in meadows on sandy beds and can grow up to 1.5m in height. Lesser Neptune grass (*Cymodocea nodosa*) is also protected but can be found outside the Mediterranean.

Tethya aurantiacum – the **sea orange** sponge, which looks exactly like an orange. I love this quote by Barnes, Fox and Ruppert (2004) 'some are known to be able to move at speeds of between 1mm and 4mm per day'.

For a full list of protected sea flora and fauna, see www.aquarium.hr/eng/species-list. The aquariums at Rovinj and Pula jointly run a **turtle rescue centre**, excellent information on which can be found at www.aquarium.hr/eng/marine-turtle-rescue-centre, including what to do if you find a stranded turtle.

Diving in Istria   PLANNING THE DIVE

12

Scubapro & Subgear, & can service these brands. 3km southeast of Rijeka centre on the seashore. Their website is only in Croatian.

☞ **Sepadiver** Via Colombara di Vignano 6, 34015 Muggia (TS), Italy; ☏ +39 40 232573; e info@sepadiver.com; www.sepadiver.com; ⏰ 09.00–12.30 & 14.30–18.30 Tue–Sat year-around, and additionally on Mon (same hours) May–Aug. A good range of equipment mostly stocking Apex-Aqualung, Mares & Scubapro, as well as some of their own equipment such as semi-dry suits. Their website does not show all the items in the shop, so it is worth going over personally.

SAFETY Diving safely is the responsibility of every diver. In general, if you've not dived for three years or more, most dive centres will want you to do a refamiliarisation dive or scuba tune-up with an instructor (for around €80). If you've not been diving over the winter, or for a year or so, then your first dive of the season should always be a check dive, especially if you have your own equipment, to ensure that you and your equipment work as you expect them to. Check dives are usually done from the shore in front of the dive centre, as these are the cheapest, and it is easy to go back to the centre if something's not working. Istria's hyperbaric chamber is in Pula (*Polyclinic for Hyperbaric Oxygen Medicine Oxy Kochova 1/a;* ☏ *052 215 663* m *24hr emergency number (Dr Mario Franolić) 098 219 225;* e *polilkinika@oxy.hr; www. oxy.hr*).

WRECK DIVING With over 25 wrecks, Istria is a great place to explore the fascination of wreck diving. Most sites are within 90–100 minutes' boat ride from a dive centre, and over half lie within Croatia's stated recreational dive limit (40m). That said, diving at 20m+ in Croatia is not like diving in the clear blue waters of the tropics or off Egypt, Malta or some of the Pacific islands. Planning the dive and diving the plan is essential in waters that can have low visibility, even when you are outside of the wreck. Navigational and decompression skills are a must, as is a Nitrox qualification if you want to stay down long enough to make the descent worthwhile.

As a result of the higher skillset required to dive wrecks, most centres will require that you are qualified to at least CMAS 2* level (equivalent to PADI rescue diver, SSI Advanced Open Water Diver (AOWD) +40 dives, or taken the BSAC Dive Leader course even if you have not qualified with all the dives). Dives on some of the simpler, shallower wrecks, such as the HMS *Coriolanus*, might allow PADI AOWD divers once they've dived with a centre a few times and shown their competency. Some centres will also require that you show a current (within the last year) fit-to-dive medical certificate. If you have not brought one from your usual doctor, then sometimes these can be obtained through a private doctor in Istria. Your dive centre will be able to tell you where if there are any indications that you need one.

EVENTS

The big diving event of the year is the **Bjelilav Underwater Film and Photo Festival** (*www.bijelilav.org*), which first took place in 2010. The exhibition of winning films and photos takes place on the middle or last weekend of September in Rovinj town, Crveni Otok (Red Island) and in the surrounding waters (some exhibits being literally underwater).

Puffer dive centre has its **Eko Akcija** day at the beginning of June to clean up around Crveni Otok. Diving numbers are limited to 50, diving costs for the clean-up on the Saturday are free, with several other dives offered throughout the weekend for 50% of the normal price, including to the famous *Baron Gautsch* wreck. Accommodation on the island is also available at rock-bottom prices. For more, see www.rovinj-diving.hr.

Equipment test days are available in three dive centres (for contact details see next): Valdaliso around Easter; Sv Marina at the end of May; and Indie in September. These test days give you the opportunity to test the centre's new equipment for free. If you are considering branching out to get your own equipment, this is a good way to test some of what the manufacturers have to offer before buying.

DIVING CENTRES

There are over 25 diving centres in Istria alone. The ones listed here are chosen for their spread along the peninsula's coast and for their access to some of the best dive sites in Istria. Most dive centres are open from May to September unless otherwise listed. Key staff at the centres all speak English (as well as Croatian, German and Italian). Diving centres in the northwest tend to offer only PADI courses; those around Rovinj offer SSI courses; whilst those on the east coast offer a mix of CMAS, PADI and VDST (Verband Deutsche Sport Taucher) courses. Going anticlockwise from northwest to northeast:

SUBAQUATIC (*Stella Maris Campsite, 52470 Umag;* \ *052 710 981;* m *092 261 6168;* e *subaquatic.umag@gmail.com; www.subaquatic.org*) The northernmost of all the dive centres, and good for accessing the wrecks of the *Gilda* and HMS *Coriolanus*. Provides PADI courses. A popular centre due to its location and thus not cheap, with the exception of the scuba review session, which is usually held with a number of divers needing review.

ZEUS-FABER (*Sportski centar Valeta, Lanterna 52465 Tar-Vabriga;* \ *052 405 045;* m *098 951 2986;* e *info@zeus-faber.com; www.zeus-faber.com*) Run by brothers Dalibor and Nikola Šolar since 2004 in response to the overspill from Umag. Located at the mouth of the beautiful River Mirna and near the 19th-century lighthouse on Cape Tooth (Rt Zub) in view of Novigrad's old town, it offers some great locations for beginners and hopes of seeing sea horses and the fabled *Zeus faber* (John Dory) itself. Offers PADI courses.

DIVING CENTRE POREČ (*Brulo bb (parking at Hotel Diamant), 52440 Poreč;* \ *052 433 606;* m *(Olwyn) 091 452 9071, (Miloš) 091 452 9070;* e *info@divingcenter-porec.com; www.divingcenter-porec.com;* ⊕ *Apr–Nov*) Olwyn (from Newcastle, England) and her husband Miloš pride themselves on providing fun and safe dives, catering particularly for the beginner end of the market during the high season. As a result, the centre's PADI courses are very reasonably priced, and its shore and boat dives are the cheapest in Istria. Perfect English, Croatian and Dutch are spoken at the centre, as well as German and Italian. The house shore dive is a real gem at night, with regular sightings of octopus, plaice, red mullet and feeding *Pinna nobilis*. Labyrinth is another truly excellent dive of theirs. It's a ten-minute walk from the parking at Hotel Diamant to the dive centre (head left down the path by the tennis courts along the back of the hotel grounds). Off-season it's possible to drive to the dive centre. See advert on page 198.

STARFISH (*Autocamp Porto Sole, 52450 Vrsar;* \ *052 442 119;* m *(Lydia) 098 335 506, (Christoph) 098 334 816;* e *info@starfish.hr; www.starfish.hr*) Starfish's bright yellow 15m boat takes up to 25 divers, and includes an overhead awning for shade and a toilet.

It is the only dive centre north of the Limski kanal that is licensed to take divers to the *Baron Gautsch* and *Hans Schmidt*; it also offers seven other wreck dives. A double wreck dive (bring your own lunch and water for the boat) costs around 600kn. To get to Starfish, take the northern entrance into Vrsar and straight on to Koversada. Some 50m before Koversada, turn right towards Autocamp Porto Sole. You can drive up to the dive centre, but will need to leave your car in the camp car park. Provides Nitrox, PADI, TDI/SDI and DSAT courses. See advert on page 198.

VALDALISO (*Valdaliso Campsite, Monsena bb, 52210 Rovinj;* ✎ *052 815 992;* m *(Stojan) 098 212 360, (Suzy) 099 733 8227;* e *valdaliso@diving-rovinj.com; www. diving-rovinj.com;* ⊕ *15 Apr–15 Oct)* This centre concentrates on the more serious end of diving, with a wide range of wreck dives every morning. A medical certificate needs to be shown to dive the wrecks, and this can be obtained from a diving doctor in Rovinj (ask at the dive centre for details). It offers an unbeatable weekly rate for diving equipment. See the dive centre in advance for a car-parking pass into the campsite. Conveniently located only 500m beyond Blu restaurant (see *Where to eat*, page 77) for a nice meal on the beach afterwards. Offers Nitrox, and SSI courses.

PUFFER (*Hotel Istra, Otok Sv Andrija, Crveni Otok, 52210 Rovinj;* ✎ *052 802 540;* e *info@rovinj-diving.hr; www.rovinj-diving.hr)* Filip Višić of Puffer organises the Bijelilav Underwater Film and Photo Festival, and is keen on preserving our seas. Puffer's 12m boat is equipped with all the usual safety equipment, an upper sun deck and a toilet. It concentrates on the beginner end of the market, but wreck dives, including the *Baron Gautsch*, are available for more advanced divers. To get to the centre, take the Crveni Otok boat which leaves from Rovinj harbour once an hour on the half-hour, and then walk a short way beyond the Hotel Istra to the watersports centre. Offers SSI courses.

PUNTIŽELA (*Autocamp Puntižela, 52100 Pula;* ✎ *(15 Apr–15 Oct) 052 517 474,* *(16 Oct–14 Apr) +49 9188 305 415;* m *098 903 3003;* e *info@relaxt-abgetaucht.de; www.relaxt-abgetaucht.de)* This is the only dive centre with access to the Rt Peneda dive site at the Brijuni Islands. Almost all the centre's dives are within a ten–20-minute boat ride away, and so the centre often succeeds in providing up to four dives in a day (including a night dive). Offers Nitrox, and SSI and CMAS courses.

ORCA (*Hotel Histria, Verudela bb, 52100 Pula;* m *098 409 850;* e *info@orcadiving. hr; www.orcadiving.hr)* With easy access from the Hotel Histria car park (a three-minute walk), this dive centre concentrates on diving rather than courses. It has a large number of varied excellent sites, including drift dives, and wreck dives including of course the *Baron Gautsch*, a U-81 German submarine, and the *Maria* wooden 'pirate' ship. Offers only the PADI Open Water Diver course for €670 (seven days).

INDIE (*Autocamp Indie, Banjole, 52203 Medulin;* ✎ *052 573 658;* m *(Sandra) 098 698 622, (Robert) 098 344 396;* e *divingindie@divingindie.com; www.divingindie.com;* ⊕ *all year)* This is one of the biggest dive centres in Istria, with three boats and able to handle up to 55 divers. Offers double wreck dive trips with lunch on their boat (or bring your own lunch). Offers Nitrox, trimix; also PADI, CMAS, SSI courses.

SV MARINA (*Autokamp Marina, 52220 Labin;* ✎ *052 879 052;* m *091 187 9074,* *(Valter) 091 474 7481;* e *info@scubacenter.de; www.scubacenter.de;* ⊕ *Apr–Oct)*

This place is out of the way but worth the drive if you want your dive to feel a bit less like the latest fad in outdoor sports. Great wall diving available on the mouth of the deep Raša Bay. Offers Nitrox, and teaches PADI and CMAS/VDST courses.

MARINE SPORT (*Aleja Slatina bb, 51417 Mošćenička Draga;* m *(Robert) 091 515 7212, (Darko) 091 293 2440;* e *info2@marinesport.hr; www.marinesport.hr;* ☺ *Easter–Nov*) On the east coast of the peninsula, this dive centre has access to some fantastic wall and drift diving. Offers Nitrox, and teaches PADI courses.

1 HMS *CORIOLANUS*

Description	45m British Royal Navy minesweeper sunk in 1945
Depth	15–28m
Location	West of Novigrad: 45°19'239"N, 13°23'406"E
Difficulty	CMAS 2*, AOWD
Visibility	Low in summer, better in winter
Dive centres	Diving Centre Poreč, Starfish

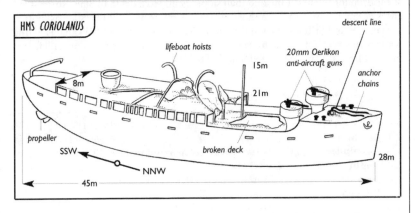

Interestingly, German guidebooks on this wreck site describe the *Coriolanus* as a radio-monitoring ship, whilst British and Croatian descriptions of it state it was a minesweeper, and some hint that it was a 'spy' ship. Clearly a trip to the British National Archives is in order to get to the bottom of this story. Nonetheless, it was sunk on 5 May 1945 when it hit a floating mine, which had been laid as part of the German defence line.

Although visibility is low to moderate during the main dive season, on a good day, the top of the wreck can be seen from the surface. In 2012 the wreck was largely uncluttered by fishing nets and it's possible to dive the entire outside of the *Coriolanus* in a 25-minute bottom time, so it is quite a good introduction to wreck diving.

Overall, the wreck is in relatively good condition, save for the mine explosion hole in its starboard side, and its missing mast and bridge, which were possibly mined after it was sunk so that it would not snag sea traffic. Two mounts with 20mm Oerlikon guns are aft, and one is on the stern of the upper deck. It also carried a 12lb anti-aircraft gun. It is thickly encrusted with shells and coral and the roof of its mid deck has caved in. Entry into the wreck is not recommended for sport diving.

2 KOVERSADA WALL

Description	Wall with small caves at the edge of protected waters
Depth	3–30m
Location	North side of the mouth of the Limski kanal
Difficulty	Easy
Visibility	Moderate
Dive centres	Diving Centre Poreč, Starfish, Valdaliso

The Limski kanal itself is out of bounds for swimmers and divers and is home to the much-sought-after Limski oysters. Being so close to protected waters, Koversada wall, which lies just below the nudist camp of the same name, is rich with yellow and white Gorgonian sea whips, various sponges and moss animals (*bryozoa*). Fish include most of those you'll have for lunch, including John Dory, octopus, and scorpionfish. At shallower depths, sea horses have also been seen.

This dive is a good introduction to deep and multi-level diving. The wall is a sheer drop for the first 13m, and then slopes gently to a depth of 30m. Three small caves at 8m, 6m and 5m hide those creatures preferring less light, such as lobster, conger eels and brittle stars. On the south side of the mouth to the kanal is **Saline wall and a wreck** (of a small tourist boat), which are equally rich in flora and fauna, but require a little more navigational skill to dive.

3 BARON GAUTSCH

Description	Luxury passenger steamship sunk in 1914
Depth	28–39m
Location	West of Brijuni, 44°56'4"N, 13°34'7"E
Difficulty	CMAS 2*, AOWD
Visibility	Low in summer, better in winter
Dive centres	Puffer, Starfish, Valdaliso

Built in Scotland's Dundee shipyard Gourlay Brothers & Co, this Austro-Hungarian passenger steamship was launched in 1908 and became the pride of the Austro-Hungarian shipping fleet Austrian Lloyd (today's Italia Marittima) based in Trieste. It sailed the Trieste–Kotor route (in Montenegro), and was leased by the Austro-Hungarian navy in World War I to transport military personnel to Kotor. On a return trip on 13 August 1914, laden with civilian passengers and refugees, the ship hit a mine and sank west of the Brijuni Islands.

Accusations were levelled against the crew for mismanagement (including lifejackets locked away to prevent third-class passengers using them to sleep on), and Austrian Lloyd was sued in the Viennese courts by dependents. Riots in Vienna in 1925 torched the courthouse records of the case, and later in 1939 the offices of the defending lawyer Dr Shapiro, who was Jewish, were ransacked in pogroms. As a result the only remaining official record of the event lies in Rovinj's city archives.

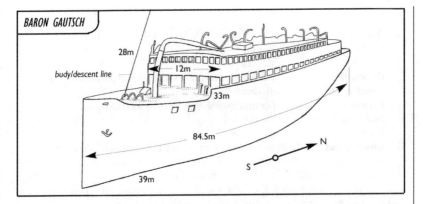

The wreck is a war grave, and has been looted extensively in previous years. After almost 100 years, the wreck today is quite decayed but the overall structure retains its shape. The wreck is marked by a buoy and, as visibility can be low, descent and decompression is by the buoy line. This can get busy in the summer. A double wreck dive trip to this and to the nearby torpedo boat *Guiseppe Dezza* is offered by Starfish Dive Centre.

Further information on the *Baron Gautsch* can be found at www.adventuredives. com/barong.htm.

4 BANJOLE SPILJA CAVE

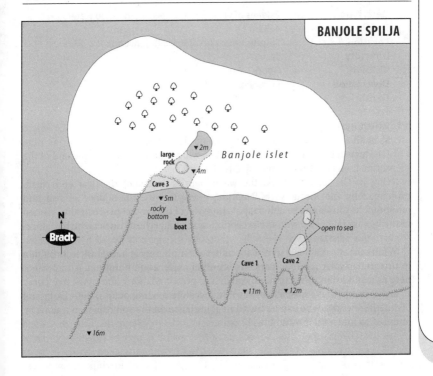

Description	Cave dive with a fallen roof, emerging into sunlight
Depth	5–30m
Location	West of Rovinj
Difficulty	OWD, lamp recommended
Visibility	Moderate to good
Dive centres	Diving Centre Poreč, Starfish, Valdaliso

This dive is around and beneath a small islet, where three tunnel formations can be dived. The entrance of the shallowest and largest lies at 6m, and emerges after 30m into a crater in the centre of the islet where you can surface into sunlight. This effect lights up the bottom of the seabed below and gives an obvious area to dive towards, making it an excellent introduction to diving with overhead cover.

On exiting the first tunnel, and keeping the islet on your left, head down to 13m where a second tunnel opens onto two galleries with small openings to the sea overhead. A little further along the islet is a third short tunnel. The islet reef continues westward, where at 30m larger shoals of fish can be found and the occasional John Dory. The caves themselves are home to various sponges and sometimes bright red-orange scorpionfish or lurking conger eels.

5 RT PENEDA, BRIJUNI NATIONAL PARK

Description	A series of walls and tunnels in protected waters
Depth	4–35m
Location	Southernmost tip of Veliki Brijuni Otok
Difficulty	Easy
Visibility	Good
Dive centre	Puntižela

It is worth making the extra trip to dive at this site, as it is the only place where diving is allowed around the Brijuni Islands. Rt Peneda has one of Istria's nine 19th-century lighthouses (see box, page 16), which can be viewed at the end of the 15-minute boat ride from Puntižela Dive Centre.

Being in the national park, the water here is spectacularly clear and clean, evidenced by the meadows of Neptune grass and the abundance of fish and nudibranch. You should be able to spot almost all of the protected species mentioned in the box on page 189, with the exception of the loggerhead turtle, which requires a much more distant dive.

Whilst the site is a real paradise for underwater photographers, flash is forbidden in this underwater national park. As on other reefs, good buoyancy is important here to avoid killing the coral, especially the protected stony and black tree coral. A night dive here is especially rewarding revealing feeding octopi, John Dory and bearded fireworks, who can be found in abundance on the soft coral – but don't be tempted to touch their poisonous bristles.

6 FRAŠKERIĆ ISLAND

Description	System of four tunnels with light shafts
Depth	3–26m
Location	Northern side of Otok Fraškerić
Difficulty	Easy
Visibility	Moderate to good in the summer
Dive centre	Puntižela, Orca

This is a good site for beginners wishing to expand their experience with easy wide tunnels lit periodically by overhead sun shafts. The various tunnels lie between 3m and 18m and the reef itself contains numerous other small pocket caves. For many, this is one of the best dives available is Istria, especially for those interested in marine photography. The interplay of light shafts with easy-access caves hosts a wide variety of photographic subject matter in the clearer waters of the more southerly half of Istria.

The site frequently sees catshark and electric rays as well as John Dory and lobster, John Dory, scorpion fish, conger eels, octopi, crabs and lobsters.

7 NIKOLAI'S CAVERN

Description	A small diveable cave along a cliff wall in very clear water
Depth	24–40m
Location	A few minutes south of Marina Autocamp
Difficulty	Medium
Visibility	Good
Dive centre	Sv Marina

Most of the east coast of Istria is characterised by a steep drop-off, which is the continuation of the Učka Mountains towering above it. There are several excellent dives along this coast, one of the best being this high-ceilinged cave, 6m in diameter and 8m in length at 24m depth. The rough sandy floor makes it easy to navigate and the walls are bright with coral and sponges. Outside the cave, however, has even more to offer, with red Gorgonia sea whips and large deep-red hand corals and all the fish species that these attract. The drop-off south of the cave's entrance almost gives the impression of being in the tropics, if it wasn't for the slightly colder water.

Rocky Dome, a little further south, is another similar dive site. North of these dives is the shipwreck **Vis**, a Yugoslavian cargo ship, which hit a mine on 13 February 1946. She lies at 38–60m and is only for technical divers.

Across the strait at Rt Pecanj on Cres Island is the January 1914 wreck of the Italian cargo steamship *Lina*. She lies at 20–55m and is thus a possibility for advanced open water divers.

8 BRSEČ PINNACLE

Description	A spit of sand and a small bay teeming with fish
Depth	7–45m
Location	Below Brseč village
Difficulty	Easy
Visibility	Good
Dive centre	Marine Sport

This spit of sand jutting out below Brseč village shelters a small steep bay in which numerous fish gather and feed from the slight current coming around the spit. Known also as John Dory Bay, the young of this fabled fish are often seen here in the spring. In the summer the bay is known for sea horse sightings. South of the spit are a couple of car wrecks at 25m. North of the spit is a 30m-long wall, rich with anemones and sponges, with a shallow cave at the end. Below the wall is a series of small cliffs reaching down to 45m, in which hand corals, conger eels and lobsters can be seen.

Accessible by both boat and shore, a shore dive offers the opportunity to spend time among the anemones of the bay and their many electric-blue partner cleaner-shrimp (*Periclimenes longicarpus*).

The place to eat after the dive is at Restoran Johnson (see *What to see and do*, page 104) at Mošćenička Draga, or at Hotel Draga di Lovrana (see *Lungomare to Lovran*, on page 105) above Medveja.

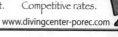

Appendix 1

LANGUAGE

INTRODUCTION Croatian is a phonetic language – that is, every letter in a word is pronounced, and the pronunciation of any given letter is always the same, making it far more consistent in this sense than English or French. There are, however, a few things which the uninitiated may find difficult or confusing at first, such as consonant clusters, with tongue-twisters like *vrt* (meaning 'garden') or *trg* (meaning 'square') common enough. Also, unlike English (but like most other languages including French and Italian), nouns in Croatian have genders (ie: masculine, feminine and neuter), as well as cases (which will be familiar to anyone who has studied a language such as German or Russian, for example).

PRONUNCIATION A number of Croatian letters are not found in the English alphabet, and some familiar letters are pronounced differently in Croatian – in particular j (pronounced like an English 'y') and c (pronounced 'ts'). See the list below.

a	pronounced as the 'a' in father
b	pronounced as the 'b' in bread
c	pronounced as the 'ts' in cats
č	pronounced as the 'ch' in church
ć	very similar to č, but slightly softer, as the 'tj' sound in picture
d	pronounced as the 'd' in dog
đ	pronounced as the 'j' in jam
dž	very similar to the above
e	pronounced as the 'e' in egg
f	pronounced as the 'f' in feel
g	pronounced hard, as the 'g' in give
h	pronounced as the 'h' in hot
i	pronounced as the 'i' in ill
j	pronounced as the 'y' in yes
k	pronounced as the 'k' in king
l	pronounced as the 'l' in loud
lj	pronounced as the 'lli' in million
m	pronounced as the 'm' in mother
n	pronounced as the 'n' in now
nj	pronounced as the 'ni' in onion
o	pronounced as the 'o' in hot
p	pronounced as the 'p' in press
r	rolled slightly
s	pronounced as the 's' in snake

š	pronounced as the 'sh' in sugar
t	pronounced as the 't' in tea
u	pronounced as the 'oo' in pool
v	pronounced as the 'v' in very
ž	pronounced as the 's' in pleasure

There is no q, w, x or y in the Croatian alphabet.

GREETINGS AND GENERAL PHRASES

Hello/Good day (formal)	*Dobar dan*
Hi! (informal)	*Ćao!* (pronounced as *ciao* in Italian), *Bog!* or *Bok!*
Goodbye	*Do viđenja*
Bye! (informal)	*Ćao!* (pronounced as *ciao* in Italian), *Adio!* or *Bog!* or *Bok!*
Good morning	*Dobro jutro*
Good evening	*Dobra večer*
Good night	*Laku noć*
Have a good trip	*Sretan put*
Yes	*Da*
No	*Ne*
Please	*Molim*
Thank you	*Hvala*
You're welcome	*Nema na čemu*
I beg your pardon?	*Molim?*
Sorry!	*Oprostite!*
Excuse me (when about to request something)	*Oprostite*
Here you are! (when offering something)	*Izvolite!*
Cheers! (as a toast)	*Živjeli!*
Do you speak English?	*Govorite li engleski?*
I don't speak Croatian	*Ja ne znam hrvatski*
I don't understand	*Ne razumijem*
How are you? (formal)	*Kako ste?*
Fine, thank you	*Dobro, hvala*
Pleased to meet you	*Drago mi je*
Where are you from?	*Odakle ste?*
I'm English	*Ja sam Englez*
I'm from …	*Ja sam iz …*
Mr	*Gospodin*
Mrs	*Gospođa*

NUMERALS

0	*nula*	9	*devet*
1	*jedan*	10	*deset*
2	*dva*	11	*jedanaest*
3	*tri*	12	*dvanaest*
4	*četiri*	13	*trinaest*
5	*pet*	14	*četrnaest*
6	*šest*	20	*dvadeset*
7	*sedam*	21	*dvadeset jedan*
8	*osam*	22	*dvadeset dva*

23	dvadeset tri	100	sto
30	trideset	110	sto deset
40	četrdeset	120	sto dvadeset
50	pedeset	125	sto dvadeset pet
60	šezdeset	200	dvijesto
70	sedamdeset	300	tristo
80	osamdeset	1,000	tisuća
90	devedeset	million	milijarda

TIME, DAYS OF THE WEEK AND MONTHS

minute	minuta	week	tjedan
hour	sat	month	mjesec
day	dan	year	godina

What time is it?	Koliko je sati?
09.25	devet i dvadeset pet sati
09.30	devet i pol
14.00	dva sata (or četrnaest sati)
At 10.15	u deset i petnaest

Sunday	nedjelja	Thursday	četvrtak
Monday	ponedjeljak	Friday	petak
Tuesday	utorak	Saturday	subota
Wednesday	srijeda		

January	siječanj	July	srpanj
February	veljača	August	kolovoz
March	ožujak	September	rujan
April	travanj	October	listopad
May	svibanj	November	studeni
June	lipanj	December	prosinac

spring	proljeće	yesterday	jučer
summer	ljeto	day	dan
autumn	jesen	night	noć
winter	zima	afternoon	popodne
today	danas	in the morning	ujutro
tomorrow	sutra	in the evening	navečer

GENERAL VOCABULARY

after	poslije	from	iz
and	i	green	zeleni
beautiful	krasan	here	ovdje/tu
before	prije	hot	vruće
black	crni	how?	kako?
blue	plavi	in	u
cold	hladno	large	veliki
difficult	teško	later	kasnije
easy	lako	left	lijevo
far	daleko	much/many	puno/mnogo
fast	brzo	near	blizu

now	*sada*	to	*u* or sometimes *na*
of	*od*	under	*ispod*
on	*na*	very	*jako*
or	*ili*	what?	*što?*
red	*crveni*	when?	*kad?*
right	*desno*	where?	*gdje?*
slow	*polako*	white	*bijeli*
small	*mali*	who?	*tko?*
that	*ono/to*	with	*s/sa*
there	*tamo*	without	*bez*
this	*ovo*		

ACCOMMODATION

apartment	*apartman*	reservation	*rezervacija*
bathroom	*kupaonica*	room	*sobe*
bed	*krevet*	double room	*dvokrevetna sobe*
bed and breakfast	*noćenje i doručak*	single room	*jednokrevetna sobe*
half board	*polupansion*	swimming pool	*bazen*
hotel	*hotel*		

BANKS, MONEY, POST AND INTERNET

ATM	*bankomat*	money	*novac*
bank	*banka*	small change	*sitno*
exchange office	*mjenjačnica*	post office	*pošta*
exchange rate	*tečaj*	Wi-Fi	*wi-fi*
internet	*internet*		

CULTURAL SIGHTS

Baroque	*barok*	loggia	*lođa*
bell tower	*zvonik*	mill	*mlin*
bridge	*most*	monastery	*samostan*
castle	*dvorac, kaštel*	monument	*spomenik*
cathedral	*katedrala*	museum	*muzej*
cemetery	*groblje*	painting	*slika*
chapel	*kapelica*	palace	*palača*
church	*crkva*	Roman	*rimski*
citadel/old town	*stari grad*	Romanesque	*romanički*
city walls	*zidine*	sculpture/statue	*skulptura*
cloister	*klaustar*	square	*trg*
exhibition	*izložba*	street	*ulica*
frescoes	*freske*	town/city	*grad*
gallery	*galerija*	Venetian	*venecijanski*
garden	*vrt*	village	*selo*
gate	*vrata*	wall	*zid*
Glagolitic	*glagoljica*		

TRANSPORT

aeroplane	*avion*	bus	*bus*
airport	*zračna luka/aerodrom*	bus station	*autobusni kolodvor*
aisle	*prolaz*	bus stop	*stajalište*
arrivals	*dolazak*	bicycle	*bicikl*

boat	brod	petrol	benzin
by train	vlakom	petrol station	benzinska stanica
car	auto	platform	peron
catamaran	katamaran	seat	sedalo
departures	odlazak	return ticket	povratna karta
direct	direktni	single ticket	u jednom smjeru
driver	vozač	station	kolodvor
driving licence	vozačka dozvola	taxi	taksi
ferry	trajekt	ticket	karta
luggage	prtljaga	ticket office	prodaja karta or
main (railway)	glavni (željeznički)		blagajna
station	kolodvor	train	vlak
motorbike	motor	window	prozor
on foot	pješice		

One ticket to …, please	Jednu kartu do …, molim
What time does the train to … leave?	U koliko sati ide vlak za … ?
Which number?	Koji broj?
Which platform?	Koji peron?

SHOPPING

bakery	pekarnica	market	tržnica or placa
bookshop	knjižara	open	otvoreno
chemist	apoteka or ljekarna	price	cijena
closed	zatvoren	shop	dućan, trgovina

I'm just looking, thanks	Samo gledam, hvala
Please could I have …	Molim vas …
Do you have … ?	Imate li … ?
How much does it cost?	Koliko košta?
Can I help you?	Mogu li pomoći?
There is/there are …/is there?/are there … ?	Ima …/ima … ?
There isn't/there aren't …	Nema …

EATING OUT

bar	bar	table	stol
café	kafić	terrace	terasa
menu	jelovnik	wine list	vinska karta
outside	van		
restaurant	restoran/konoba/		
	gostionica		

I've already ordered, thank you	Već sam naručio, hvala
Can I order, please?	Mogu li naručiti?
Can I have the bill, please?	Molim vas račun?

FOOD

breakfast	doručak	entrée	predjelo
lunch	ručak	main course	glavno jelo
dinner	večera	dessert	desert

AI

baked	*pečeno*	pasta	*tjestenina*
boiled	*kuhano*	polenta	*palenta*
bread	*kruh*	rice	*riža*
cheese	*sir*	risotto	*rižot*
cheese with truffles	*sir s tartufima*	black (cuttlefish)	*crni rižot*
goat's cheese	*kozji sir*	risotto	
eggs	*jaja*	sauce	*umak/saft*
food	*jelo*	soup	*juha*
fried/deep fried	*prženo/pohano*	vegan	*vegan*
grilled	*na žaru*	vegetarian	*vegetarianac* (m),
homemade	*domaće*		*vegetarianka* (f)
organic	*ekološko*		

Meat (*meso*)

bacon	*špek*	pancetta	*panceta*
beef	*govedina*	pork	*svinjetina*
chicken	*piletina*	prosciutto	*pršut*
cured meat	*suho meso*	sausages	*kobasice*
game	*divljač*	veal	*teletina*
ham	*šunka*	venison	*srnetina*
lamb	*janjetina*	wild boar	*vepar*

Fish (*riba*) and shellfish (*školjke*)

crab	*rak*	oysters	*kamenice*
cuttlefish	*sipa*	prawns	*kozice*
gilthead bream	*orada*	salmon	*losos*
John Dory	*kovač*	sardines	*srdele*
lobster	*jastog*	scampi	*škampi*
mackerel	*lokarda* or *skuša*	sea bass	*brancin*
monkfish	*grdobina*	squid	*lignje*
mussels	*dagnje*	trout	*pastrva*
octopus	*hobotnica*	tuna	*tuna*

Fruit (*voće*) and vegetables (*povrće*)

apple	*jabuka*	potato	*krumpir*
bay leaves	*lovor*	French fries	*pomfrit*
blueberries	*borovnice*	rock melon	*dinja*
cabbage	*kupus*	salad	*salata*
corn	*kukuruz*	mixed salad	*mješana salata*
courgette	*tikvica*	seasonal salad	*sezonska salata*
cucumber	*krastavac*	sour cherry	*višnja*
fig	*smokva*	strawberry	*jagoda*
grapes	*grožđe*	Swiss chard	*blitva*
lettuce, green salad	*zelena salata*	tomato	*pomidoro, rajčica*
olives	*masline*	truffles	*tartufi*
orange	*naranča*	black truffles	*crni tartufi*
pear	*kruška*	white truffles	*bijeli tartufi*
plum	*šljiva*	walnut	*orah*
poppy seeds	*mak*	water melon	*lubenica*

Cake (*kolač*) and dessert (*desert*)

chocolate	*čokolada*	(apple) pie	*pita (od jabuka)*
ice cream	*sladoled*	strudel	*štrudla*
pancakes	*palačinke*		

DRINK

beer	*pivo*	mineral water	*mineralna* or
bottled	*flaširano*	(carbonated)	*gazirana*
draught	*točeno pivo*	mineral water (still)	*obično voda* or
cocktail	*koktel*		*negazirana*
coffee	*kava*	tea	*čaj*
cappuccino	*kapučino*	herb tea	*voćni čaj*
coffee with milk	*kava s mlijekom*	tea with lemon	*čaj s limunom*
espresso	*espresso* or *obična kava*	tea with milk	*čaj s mlijekom*
fruit juice	*voćni sok*	water	*voda*
apple juice	*sok od jabuka*	wine	*vino*
orange juice	*sok od naranče*	red wine	*crno vino*
milk	*mlijeko*	white wine	*bijelo vino*

LANDSCAPE

beach	*plaža*	peninsula	*poluotok*
cave	*špilja* or *pećina*	river	*rijeka*
coast	*obala*	rock	*kamen*
drystone wall	*suhozid*	sandy	*pješčan*
forest	*šuma*	sea	*more*
hill	*brdo*	sinkhole	*jama*
island	*otok*	spring	*izvor*
lake	*jezero*	stony	*šljunčan*
meadow	*livada*	summit	*vrh*
mountain	*planina*	valley	*dolina*
path	*staza*	waterfall	*slap*

WEATHER (*VRIJEME*)

cloudy	*oblačno*	sun	*sunce*
dark	*mrak*	sunny	*sunčano*
rain	*kiša*	wind	*vjetar*

PLANTS (*BILJKE*) AND ANIMALS (*ŽIVOTINJE*)

bear	*medvjed*	grass	*trava*
beech	*bukva*	horse	*konj*
bird	*ptica*	lavender	*lavanda*
buzzard	*škanjac*	oak	*hrast*
cat	*mačka*	pig	*svinja*
chestnut	*kesten*	pine	*bor*
cow	*krava*	pine marten	*kuna*
deer	*jelen*	polenta	*palenta*
dog	*pas*	rabbit	*zec*
eagle	*orao*	sheep	*ovca*
fish	*riba*	snake	*zmija*
flower	*cvijet*	tree	*drvo*
goat	*koza*	wild boar	*divlja svinja*

EMERGENCIES

ambulance	*hitna pomoć*	hospital	*bolnica*
Be careful!	*Pazi!*	Please call a doctor!	*Molim vas pozovite*
Danger!	*Opasnost!*		*doktora!*
doctor	*doktor/liječnik*	sick/ill	*bolestan*
Help!	*U pomoć!*		

Appendix 2

MARINAS AND SAILING CLUBS

MARINAS The **Adriatic Croatia International Club (ACI)** (*www.aci-club.hr*) is a network of 21 marinas across Croatia. The club works to improve cleanliness and maintenance standards in all of its marinas, several of which have been awarded a European Blue Flag – indicating they have received an eco-award for safety and sea cleanliness.

ACI Marina Opatija (Blue Flag) (*PO Box 60, 51414 Ičiči;* ✆ *051 704 004;* e *m.opatija@ aci-club.hr; http://www.aci-club.hr/hr-hr/marinas/kvarner/aci-marina-opatija*) About 2km south of Opatija in Icici, the ACI Marina Opatija has 302 berths and another 35 places in drydock. All berths have water and electricity. Facilities include a reception desk, exchange office, restaurant, café, toilets and showers, laundry service, grocery store, nautical gear store, repair shop, a 15-tonne crane, slipway and parking. Fuel is available 2km to the north in Opatija.

ACI Marina Pomer (*Pomer bb, 52100 Pomer Pula;* ✆ *052 573 162;* e *m.pomer@aci-club.hr; www.aci-club.hr/hr-hr/marinas/istria/aci-marina-pomer*) Pomer has been recently expanded to include nearly 300 berths and another 30 in drydock – all with water and electricity. It is open year-round and has a reception desk offering currency exchange, Wi-Fi, shower and toilet facilities, a restaurant, grocery store, laundry facilities, repair shop including a ten-tonne crane, and parking. Fuel is available in Pješčana uvala, which is about five nautical miles north and west.

ACI Marina Pula (*Riva 1, 52100 Pula;* ✆ *052 219 142;* e *m.pula@aci-club.hr; www.aci-club.hr/hr-hr/marinas/istria/aci-marina-pula*) The marina has 200 berths although it does not offer any in drydock. The water berths all have water and electricity. The marina is open year-round and has a reception, parking, fuel station, an exchange office, a new bistro Torta that opened in 2012, and a repair shop with a ten-tonne crane. Pula itself has a wide range of shopping and tourist services.

ACI Marina Rovinj (*Vladimira Nazora bb, 52210 Rovinj;* ✆ *052 813 133;* e *m.rovinj@aci-club.hr; www.aci-club.hr/hr-hr/marinas/istria/aci-marina-rovinj*) The marina has 386 berths and 40 boat places on land. Berths have water and power supply. There is also a reception, exchange office, restaurant, toilets and showers, repair shop, ten-tonne crane, parking, grocery store, nautical gear store, and a fuel station nearby.

ACI Marina Umag (Blue Flag) (*52470 Umag;* ✆ *052 741 066;* e *m.umag@aci-club.hr; www.aci-club.hr/hr-hr/marinas/istria/aci-marina-umag*) Alongside the Adriatic Hotel, Umag's ACI Marina is open year-round and has 490 berths plus another 90 in drydock.

All berths have water and electricity. On site is a reception and exchange office, as well as a grocery store, 50-tonne crane, parking, a repair shop, a fuel station nearby, a restaurant, toilets and showers, and a laundry service.

Marina Admiral (*Hotel Admiral; Maršala Tita 139, 51410 Opatija;* ✆ *051 497 170;* e *marina-admiral@ri.tel.hr; www.liburnia.hr/admiral*) Located at the Hotel Admiral, the marina has 160 berths and 40 more in drydock. Each has electricity and water. It is open year-round. Opatija itself has a full range of tourist services (see page 102).

Marina Funtana (*Ribarska 11, 52452 Funtana;* ✆ *052 428 500;* e *funtana@montraker. hr; www.montraker.hr*) Funtana's marina is open year-round and has 180 berths and 50 more at drydock. All have electricity and water. The deepest is 4.5m. The marina has a reception desk, toilets and showers, a café, parking, laundry, ATM, and a repair shop including a crane. In town there are multiple grocery stores, an outpatient clinic, post office, cafés, engine repair, and diving services.

Marina Parentium (*Trg Slobode 2a, 52440 Poreč;* ✆ *052 452 210;* e *marina.parentium@ lagunaporec.com; www.lagunaporec.com/marinas/marina-parentium*) The Marina lies within the Zelena Laguna resort, approximately 6km from Poreč. It has 184 berths and a maximum depth of 5m. All have electricity and water. The marina also has a repair shop with an electrical engineer, a plastics expert, and a joiner, among others and a ten-tonne crane to hoist the boat. The reception desk is open in the summer 07.00–21.00 while the marina is open year-round. There is a restaurant, a grocery store, and toilet facilities on site while nearby there is a hotel, a post office, cafés, some limited shopping and an ATM.

Marina Vrsar (*Obala M Tita 1a, 52450 Vrsar;* ✆ *052 441 052;* e *vrsar@montraker.hr; www.montraker.hr*) Open year-round, the marina has 220 berths and can accept yachts up to 50m long in the deepest ones (14m). The marina has water and electricity at all moorings, video security, fuelling station, ATM, restaurant, showers, parking, 30-tonne crane, repair, shopping, Wi-Fi, laundry service, with diving outfitters, a nautical gear store and nightclubs among other facilities in the vicinity.

Tehnomont Marina Veruda (Blue Flag) (*Cesta prekomorskih brigada 12, 52100 Pula;* ✆ *052 224 034;* e *marina-veruda@pu.tel.hr; www.marina-veruda.hr*) Tehnomont is one of the largest marinas in Istria. Its 18 piers have 630 berths with another 250 in drydock and it operates year-round. It has two cranes: one of ten tonnes and the other of 30 tonnes. There is video surveillance. The marina can take mega-yachts so long as they don't require more than 4m of depth. In addition Tehnomont has full service repair and maintenance services, two restaurants, multiple shower and toilet locations, laundry services, a grocery store, an equipment shop, ATMs, parking and a fuel station.

SAILING CLUBS
Jedrilicarski Savez Istarskih Zupanije (JSIZ) (*F Barbalića 2, 52100 Pula;* ✆ *052 210 436; www.jsiz.org*) The association that manages all the *jedriicarski klub (JK)* yacht clubs in Istria – based in Pula. It also keeps track of races and regattas, rankings and results.

JK Alernativa (*B Borisia 2, 52452 Funtana;* ✆ *052 445 188;* e *mladen.grgeta@pu.t-com. hr; no web address*)

JK Brioni (*Titova Riva 7, 52212 Fazana;* m *098 500 222;* e *jk.brioni@gmail.com; no web address*)

JK Fiandara 1975 (*Kravlji Rt bb, 52470 Umag;* ☎ *052 741 333;* e *info@fiandara1975.hr; www.finadara1975.hr*)

JK Histria (*Sv Marija na Krasu 31, 52470 Umag;* ☎ *052 732 359;* e *jkhistria@histria.hr; www.histria.hr*)

JK Horizont Poreč (*Nikole Tesle 16, 52440 Poreč;* m *098 188 558;* e *jk.horizont@gmail. com; www.jk-horizont.hr*)

JK Maestral (*Obala Vladimira Nazora bb, 52210 Rovinj;* ☎ *052 813 437;* e *jk.maestral. rovinj@pu.t-com.hr; www.maestral-rovinj.hr*)

JK Poreč (*Molindrio 13; 52440 Poreč,* ☎ *052 432 560,* e *boris@bomar.com; no web address*)

JK Vega (*Valsaline 31; 52100 Pula,* ☎ *052 391 168;* e *ted.weidlich@pu.t-com.hr; www. vega.hr*)

PSRD Delfin (*Kandelerova 25, 52100 Pula;* ☎ *052 217 635;* e *psrd.delfin.pula@pu.t-com. hr; www.delfin-pula.hr*) A sporting and fishing society.

Appendix 3

FURTHER INFORMATION
BOOKS
Guidebooks
Abraham, Rudolf *Walking in Croatia* 2nd edition; Cicerone, 2010
Abraham, Rudolf *Croatia: Island Walks* Cicerone, 2013
Cuddon, J A *The Companion Guide to Jugoslavia* 3rd revised edition; Collins, 1986
Čujić, Boris *Croatia: Climbing Guide* 4th edition; Astroida, 2009
Letcher, Piers *Croatia: The Bradt Travel Guide* 5th edition; Bradt, 2013
McKelvie, Robin and Jenny *Slovenia: The Bradt Travel Guide* 2nd edition; Bradt, 2008

History
Alberi, Dario *Istria: Storia, Arte, Cultura* Lint, 1997. At 1999 pages, this is the most comprehensive book you'll get on Istria, even by Croatian standards, but it is currently only available in Italian.
Bracewell, Catherine Wendy *The Uskoks of Senj: Piracy, Banditry and Holy War in the Sixteenth-Century Adriatic* Cornell Univesity Press, 1992. Not about Istria, but this is the definitive account of the Uskoks, who after being disbanded were outlawed to Žumberak and Ćićarija.
Curta, Florin *Southeastern Europe in the Middle Ages 500–1250* Cambridge University Press, 2006
Glenny, Misha *The Fall of Yugoslavia* Penguin, 1992
Goldstein, Ivo *Croatia: A History* C Hurst & Co, 1999
Mesić, Stipe *The Demise of Yugoslavia: A Political Memoir* Central European University Press, 2004. Personal memoir by Croatia's former president, who was also the final President of the former Yugoslavia before its demise.
Obolenski, Dimitri *The Byzantine Commonwealth: Eastern Europe, 500–1453* Weidenfeld & Nicolson, 1971
Silber, Laura and Little, Allan *The Death of Yugoslavia* Penguin and BBC Books, 1995. Probably the best account of the disintegration of the former Yugoslavia.
Singleton, Fred *A Short History of the Yugoslav Peoples* Cambridge University Press, 1985
Tanner, Marcus *Croatia: A Nation Forged in War* Yale University Press, 1997
Wilkes, John *The Illyrians* Blackwell, 1992. The definitive text on the history of the Illyrians.

Art and architecture
Beckwith, John *Early Christian and Byzantine Art* Yale University Press, 1970
Fučić, Branko *Vincent iz Kastva* Kršćanska Sadašnjost, 1992. Account of the Beram frescoes and the medieval painter responsible for them (Croatian/German/Italian text).
Mlakar, Stefan *The Amphitheatre in Pula* Archaeological Museum of Istria, 1984

Natural history

Arnold, E Nicolas and Ovenden, Denys W *Reptiles and Amphibians of Europe* Princeton Field Guides, 2002. Worth getting the Princeton rather than the Collins edition as it's paperback and therefore more pocketable.

Gorman, Gerard *Central and Eastern European Wildlife* Bradt, 2008

Polunin, Oleg *Flowers of Greece and the Balkans: A Field Guide* Oxford University Press, 1980

Polunin, Oleg *The Concise Flowers of Europe* Oxford University Press, 1972

Svensson, Lars, Grant, Peter J, Mullarney, Killian and Zetterström, Dan *Birds of Europe* Princeton University Press, 1999. Worth getting the Princeton rather than the Collins edition as it's paperback.

Tolman, Tom and Lewington, Richard *Collins Butterfly Guide* Collins, 2009

Language

Hawkesworth, Celia (with Jović, Ivana) *Colloquial Croatian: The Complete Course for Beginners* Routledge, 2005

Norris, David *Teach Yourself Croatian* Teach Yourself, 2003

Travel literature

West, Rebecca *Black Lamb and Grey Falcon: A Journey Through Yugoslavia* Macmillan, 1942. Still a must read for anyone interested in southeast Europe.

Fiction

Verne, Jules *Mathius Sandorf* Le Temps, 1885. Now available for free download at http://archive.org/details/mathiassandorfp00verngoog. This is the epic journey of Count Sandorf, who fights for freedom, ends up in Pazin prison, and escapes via the Limski kanal and Rovinj. A page-turner.

WEBSITES
Tourism

Istrian Tourist Board www.istra.hr
Croatian National Tourist Board www.croatia.hr
Slovenian National Tourist Board www.slovenia.info
Buzet Tourist Board www.tz-buzet.hr
Motovun Tourist Board www.tz-motovun.hr
Central Istrian Tourist Board www.tz-pazin.hr
Pula Tourist Board www.pulainfo.hr
Poreč Tourist Board www.to-porec.com
Rijeka Tourist Board www.tz-rijeka.hr
Rovinj Tourist Board www.tzgrovinj.hr
Histrica www.histrica.com
Visit Croatia www.visit-croatia.co.uk

Transport

Bus timetables www.autobusni-kolodvor.com and if arriving from Zagreb www.akz.hr
Taxi Cammeo www.taxi-cammeo.net
Commodore Cruises www.commodore-cruises.hr
Goopti www.goopti.com
HAK (Croatian Automobile Club) www.hak.hr
Jadrolinija www.jadrolinija.hr
Train timetables www.hznet.hr

Train timetables (Slovenia) www.slo-zeleznice.si
Trieste Lines www.triestelines.it
Venezia Lines www.venezialines.com

Government departments
Croatian Bureau of Statistics www.dzs.hr
Ministry of Foreign Affairs www.mvp.hr

Weather
Croatian Meteorological and Hydrological Service http://meteo.hr

Outdoors
ACI Club www.aci-club.hr
Bike Istria www.istria-bike.com
Croatian Diving Association www.diving-hrs.hr
Croatian Mountaineering Association (Hrvatski planinarski savez) www.hps.hr
Parenzana www.parenzana.net
SMAND (hiking maps) www.smand.hr

Accommodation
Croatian Camping Union www.camping.hr
Croatian Youth Hostel Association www.hfhs.hr
Direct Croatia www.apartmanija.hr
Lighthouses of Croatia www.lighthouses-croatia.com

Food and culture
Gourmet Istria www.istria-gourmet.com
Istrapedia www.istrapedia.hr
Manjada http://manjada.org
MDC (Muzejski dokumentacijski centar) www.mdc.hr
Milka Šćulac Sennett www.milkasculacsennett.com
Smrikve www.smrikve.com

Media
Glas Istre www.glasistre.hr
HRT (Hrvatska radiotelevizija) www.hrt.hr
TV Istra www.tvistra.hr

National parks, nature parks and reserves
Brijuni Islands National Park www.brijuni.hr
Učka Nature Park www.pp-ucka.hr
Pazinska jama www.pazinska-jama.com
Postojnska jama www.postojnska-jama.eu
Rt Kamenjak www.kamenjak.hr

Environment
DZZP (State Institute for Nature Protection) www.dzzp.hr
Natura Histrica www.natura-histrica.hr
Zelena Istra www.zelena-istra.hr

Index

Page numbers in **bold** indicate major entries; those in *italics* indicate maps.

INDEX OF ADVERTISERS